MASTERS OF L

Masters of Light

CONVERSATIONS WITH CONTEMPORARY CINEMATOGRAPHERS

Dennis Schaefer
and
Larry Salvato

With a New Preface by the Authors
New Foreword by John Bailey

UNIVERSITY OF CALIFORNIA PRESS
Berkeley   Los Angeles   London

University of California Press, one of the most distinguished
university presses in the United States, enriches lives around the
world by advancing scholarship in the humanities, social sciences,
and natural sciences. Its activities are supported by the UC Press
Foundation and by philanthropic contributions from individuals
and institutions. For more information, visit www.ucpress.edu.

University of California Press
Berkeley and Los Angeles, California

University of California Press, Ltd.
London, England

ISBN 978-0-520-27466-2

The Library of Congress has catalogued an earlier edition as follows:

Schaefer, Dennis.
    Masters of light.

    Includes index.
    1. Cinematographers—Interviews. I. Salvato, Larry.
II. Title.
TR849.A1S33   1985   778.5′3′0922   84-2512
ISBN 978-0-520-05336-6

Manufactured in the United States of America

22   21   20   19
10 9 8 7 6 5 4 3 2

Contents

	Foreword	vii
	Preface	xvii
	Introduction	1
1.	Nestor Almendros	5
2.	John Alonzo	23
3.	John Bailey	47
4.	Bill Butler	74
5.	Michael Chapman	99
6.	Bill Fraker	127
7.	Conrad Hall	152
8.	Laszlo Kovacs	175
9.	Owen Roizman	194
10.	Vittorio Storaro	219
11.	Mario Tosi	233
12.	Haskell Wexler	247
13.	Billy Williams	267
14.	Gordon Willis	284
15.	Vilmos Zsigmond	311
	Glossary	339
	Index	345

Foreword

Near the end of his interview in *Masters of Light,* the Hungarian cinematographer Vilmos Zsigmond responds to a question about how difficult it was for him and his friend Laszlo Kovacs to break into the mainstream of Hollywood studio movies in the 1970s. "I always tell them [students] that it will take ten years," he begins. "Very few people find themselves becoming a cameraman after finishing USC or UCLA. Very seldom will you become a cameraman in less than ten years."[1]

Masters of Light was published in 1984. What Zsigmond affirmed then was accurate. He and Kovacs had come up through low-budget, nonunion filmmaking, shooting action and thriller films for the B and drive-in markets. When the studio system fractured into a kind of chaos with the "youth quake" of the 1960s, young cinematographers such as John Alonzo and Mario Tosi were well positioned to walk into a moribund structure. They were also influenced by the aesthetic and technical revolution of the European New Wave, whose influence was then breaking on American shores. Several of those young European cinematographers, such as Nestor Almendros and Vittorio Storaro, benefited from this shake-up in the American industry and began parallel careers in the American mainstream: Almendros with the directors Robert Benton, Monte Hellman, and Terence Malick; Storaro with Francis Coppola and Warren Beatty. Two other American-born cinematographers, Conrad Hall and William Fraker, gained prominence by coming up through the union ranks. There is a famous photo of Hall, Fraker, Bobby Byrne, and Jordan Cronenweth as the union camera crew on Richard Brooks's western *The Professionals.* Haskell Wexler, ever the rebel, clawed his way in through low-budget films in the late 1950s, garnering his first Oscar for *Who's Afraid of Virginia Woolf,* a movie whose documentary style and harsh lighting of the stars Elizabeth Taylor and Richard Burton inflamed the conservative old guard. Wexler and Hall closed ranks from their differing origins in forming a successful company for TV commercials. Gordon Willis also began his career shooting commercials and documentaries, but he, too, spent many years as an assistant cameraman. For my own part, I began working on nonunion and NABET (National Association of Broadcast Employees and Technicians) features as a camera assistant. Even after getting into the union in May 1969, I fell prey to a strict seniority structure in which I was allowed to work on a feature film only after members of greater seniority had been employed. My first studio feature as a camera assistant was Monte Hellman's 1971 *Two-Lane Blacktop,* now a cult classic of the era but widely reviled at the time of release for its long takes and frequently deadpan acting.

Although the Hollywood studios were in major transition in the late 1960s, the union locals of the IATSE still wielded considerable power. Perhaps the most powerful of them was Local 659, the camera guild for Hollywood and the western region. IATSE Local 644, for New York and much of the East Coast, was only slightly less rigid. It was virtually impossible to build a feature career as a cinematographer outside this structure. One way or another, all American cameramen had to come to terms with the unions. This is part of the unstated subtext that Zsigmond alludes to in his interview.

This apprentice/journeyman/master guild system has held sway in the American studios from the 1930s to today. But an alternative way now exists—one that could not have been foreseen by the fifteen cinematographers who were interviewed for Dennis Schaefer and Larry Salvato's book. This new approach is what Francis Coppola and others have called the "democratization" of filmmaking. In certain respects, the breakdown of an entrenched motion picture hierarchy had begun with the post–World War II Italian Neorealist films and their offspring, the French New Wave. A recent exhibition at the Academy of Motion Picture Arts and Sciences (AMPAS) of behind-the-scenes photographs of classic French films of the 1960s such as *Jules and Jim* and *Breathless* by the set photographer Raymond Cauchetier shows how the compact crews of the time exploited the new lightweight equipment, fast emulsions, and direct sound technology of cinema verité to create more naturalistic films: a revolution in French cinema, reacting against what François Truffaut sarcastically dubbed the "Tradition of Quality." One of the most amusing of Cauchetier's photos is of the cinematographer Raoul Coutard handholding an Éclair CM3 for a dolly shot of the actor Jean-Paul Belmondo. The director Jean-Luc Godard is pulling the wheelchair dolly.

This "democratization" of cinema is a product of several factors that were not yet operative when *Masters of Light* was published; it gives the interviews a kind of historic glaze, not unlike that of an earlier book of interviews by Leonard Maltin. In 1971, the then twenty-year-old critic published *Behind the Camera,* with an insightful introductory essay, as well as interviews with five established cinematographers. Conrad Hall was one of them, as well as Lucien Ballard, both men having photographed iconic "new westerns" in the 1960s. The other three were, even then, legendary cameramen: Hal Mohr (who was president of the camera local when I joined in 1969), Hal Rosson (who was noted for his luminous black-and-white imagery and his two-year marriage to Jean Harlow), and Arthur C. Miller (who won the first of his three cinematography Oscars for *How Green Was My Valley* in 1941, edging out the more flamboyant work of Gregg Toland in *Citizen Kane*). Like many of his generation, Miller was a workhorse, photographing as many as a half dozen films a year, an IMDb total of 145 titles.

Zsigmond speaks of the role of the film schools at USC and UCLA. Certainly, many of my generation of cinematographers were film-school brats. My friend the cinematographer Caleb Deschanel and I were at USC Cinema at the same time. But nearly twenty years before us, so was Conrad Hall. The difference between our film-school years and today is that USC and UCLA, along with NYU and a few other schools, were then the whole enchilada. Some universities offered a survey of film history, often tied to a "novels into film" course within the English Department, but few colleges offered cinema as a major. Even fewer had full-fledged film production facilities, such as equipment and stages. Today, there are hundreds of schools with richly endowed film and TV departments. "Cinema" has also become an academic discipline, fodder for legions of "critical studies" doctoral theses. Cozy tie-ins between many film schools and the studios have become commonplace; USC Cinema is widely regarded as a recruiting arm of Hollywood. When I began searching for an entry-level job straight out of USC, I was advised, above all, not to speak of having attended film school. There was plenty of residual old guard resentment about these upstarts with their fancy foreign-film predilections.

Today, it is almost unimaginable that a director or cinematographer would not have attended film school. The films they make there are widely seen by studio executives and talent agents. Screenings of student films to the industry, as well as their presence in the film-festival circuit, assures broad-based visibility, if not ready distribution. Many of these student films are extremely well crafted, often employing professional actors, and are aimed squarely and unabashedly at landing studio development deals. Student thesis projects shot as feature-length films are not unusual.

This democratization of cinema is not only a product of the film schools but also of recent digital video technology, a sea change that the 1984 interviewees could not have anticipated. Small, affordable digital cameras (even with full high-definition—HD—resolution) are rapidly replacing the 35 mm film cameras that have been a century-old standard for image capture. A fellow cinematographer (a peer, recently retired) quipped that even film school is becoming optional. It does help to establish future working relationships, he insists, and it may be crucial as a venue to have your work seen by prospective employers. "But today," he jokes, "anyone can call himself or herself a cinematographer. All you need is two thousand dollars to buy a Canon 5D and another fifteen dollars to print up 'director of photography' business cards." Young film-school graduates who face incredible competition for even these entry-level positions may not concur. If a new edition of *Masters of Light* were written today, one seeking out the most cutting-edge image creators at the cusp of mainstream Hollywood careers, it would likely present a roster of background and experience very different from that in the present volume. I meet young cinematographers (and thankfully, an ever-increasing number of women among them) who are not members of a union and who exhibit little enthusiasm to join one. The union training regimen is simply not in their game plan. Just as the number of film-school graduates resembles a population bomb, the rate of technological change in equipment and new distribution platforms keeps accelerating. Last year's must-have digital video camera becomes this year's hand-me-down. Last year's viral video becomes curiously quaint. Last year's film-school wunderkind is this year's has-been. It takes only one box-office dud to end a career before the dust even settles.

This reverse pyramid of technical and human obsolescence presents several conundrums. Just how much time can the young cinematographer expect to expend in glossing the intricacies of new cameras and of their interfaces with multiple postproduction platforms? If your idea of filmmaking is only equipment based, then you are likely to be a very happy duck. But if you are interested in how to use the equipment to create compelling images in the service of a dramatic narrative, you may be slogging uphill even as the studios race to the bottom. There is no question that the increasing sophistication of digital cameras and their quest to equal the resolution and dynamic range of film is succeeding. Most of the cinematographers profiled in *Masters of Light* did not enter into the digital realm. Haskell Wexler *did,* and early on. He recently has made a video documentary about the week-long May 2011 conference of international cinematographers hosted by the American Society of Cinematographers (ASC). I, too, am making the transition. Vilmos Zsigmond continues to work in film, as does Vittorio Storaro, who also continues teaching cinematography in L'Aquila, Italy, between movie assignments.

The conundrum of digital video filmmaking lies partly in the simultaneous complexity of the cameras themselves and the apparent ease of actually creating images. In his interview, Gordon Willis talks about the efficacy, even necessity, of testing motion-picture film when you are at a learning stage—or even when you are an experienced cinematographer using a new Kodak film emulsion. (Much space is devoted in the book to the characteristics of high-speed film emulsions and how they influence lighting styles.) Willis documents the exposure curve of film emulsions, and the characteristics of over- and underexposure in half-stop increments, then waiting to see the projected dailies a day later to evaluate the response. Learning the characteristics of emulsions is ground-level knowledge in the era of 35 mm film that is the focus of the book. But such knowledge may be all but irrelevant in digital video. A high-resolution reference monitor that very closely shows what the camera tapes, drives, or cards record can seem to be all that any young cinematographer needs to guide him or her in learning about lighting and exposure. What you see on the monitor is what you get. Even grizzled, film-based cinematographers who have embraced the world of digital cinema tell me that they no longer sleep fitfully after a challenging day of edgy lighting, or do not get up early to see dailies at the lab before the next day's call time. It is tempting to surrender to what seems a foolproof technology.

I admit to not always looking at dailies when shooting on HD video. What surprises can there be? What latent anxiety lurks? Such ease of image creation can make one lazy: lazy, if you think of the era of film materials as the norm. But what is the norm before us in digital video? Film, 35 mm and 16 mm film, is rapidly disappearing, much to the chagrin of art-house screens, film societies, film archives, and indie and experimental filmmakers. One of the latter is Tacita Dean, who, in an expansive film installation at the Tate Modern's Turbine Hall, recently pleaded for the necessity of maintaining film as a viable creative medium—one inherently different from video.

That is a case that I also made in an article I wrote for the Arts and Leisure section of the *New York Times* in February 2001. More than a decade ago, when I was finishing my first digital video feature, *The Anniversary Party,* it was clear that a confrontation between film and digital video was looming. My article was titled "Film or Digital? Don't Fight. Coexist." The directors Alan Cumming and Jennifer Jason Leigh had decided with me to shoot on video with a Sony ENG camera at PAL resolution. At that time, the only HD camera readily available was the Sony 900, and getting it was beyond our budget means. Today, a decade later, many producers insist (wrongly) that 35 mm film is beyond their means. It is why I am shooting my third consecutive low-budget movie with the Arri Alexa. It is difficult to make a case for the primacy of film when conventional wisdom asserts that video is cheaper, ignoring, of course, the hugely expensive storage resources demanded by the captured zeros and ones when the camera is left running constantly between takes, a common indulgence by many of today's directors.

The title of this book hints at the primacy of lighting for the cinematographer. And it is true that most cinematographers interviewed referenced lighting more than composition, editorial coverage, continuity, or camera movement. In the classical-era English system, the director of photography was called the lighting cameraman; the camera operator was called the operating cameraman. David Watkin and Geoffrey Unsworth are notable examples of the former. Despite the changing technology of lighting equipment, just as with the cameras themselves, certain verities remain. It is this focus on art and craft rather than on changing technology that gives *Masters of Light* its ongoing relevance. Lighting units may appear and disappear from year to year, but the creative wrestling of these mechanical lumen beasts, the shaping and molding of their output in the service of compelling, emotive image making, is timeless and constant. When Gordon Willis speaks about his trials with the Hollywood old guard when he employed uncompromising top light and below-standard Kelvin temperatures in *The Godfather,* he is arguing for an aesthetic and a style that is grounded in character and drama, just as his looming shadows in *All the President's Men* were not a technical conceit but were rooted in the mystery of the Deep Throat plotline. The same is true of Conrad Hall when he talks in his interview about his attraction to "despair" as a driving metaphor in *Fat City,* even, I would add, in much of his seminal work. Hall was attracted to the dark side of human behavior, to the Outsider figure. I wrote about this in a posthumous tribute article in the May 2003 issue of *American Cinematographer* magazine devoted to him. The biting overexposed key and rim light in many of the close-ups in Hall's films dramatizes the character's alienation and despair, just as much as the top-lit, dead, lost eyes in Willis's *Godfather* portraits.

Much is made today about how digital video requires so little light. It is true that the sensors of the Alexa and the Sony F65 have an exposure index of 800—but that is only slightly faster than that of existing Kodak and Fuji film stocks. There is no situation that I have yet encountered shooting with digital video, that I could not also have done on film. (John Alonzo used to brag about how he force processed new film negatives to an EI of 1600, a full stop above today's video sensors.) The falloff into darkness or the burnout into pure white overexposure may be different in film and video, a product of what overexposure, especially, does to the two different recording materials. Depending on your perspective or on a given situation, you may prefer one medium to the other. But the aesthetic consequences of exposure decisions based on lighting are inherent in the choices that any cinematographer makes. It is this balancing act that lies at the heart of much that is discussed in *Masters of Light,* issues irrespective of any existing or evolving technology, issues faced by Storaro as well as by earlier artists such as George Barnes, Karl Struss, Gregg Toland, and George Folsey. This lies at the heart of the book and makes it still compelling reading, not only for cinematographers but also for anyone interested in the creation of movie images.

There is much discussion of how new technology in the 1960s, 1970s, and early 1980s influenced the look of motion pictures. Zsigmond talks about "flashing" the negative to cut contrast or to introduce a base fog level into a film such as *McCabe and Mrs. Miller.* That aesthetic rationale is still fascinating, even if Zsigmond can accomplish much the same effect today on the DaVinci Resolve in the digital intermediate suite—and with none of the potential pitfalls that handling film negatives in pre- or postexposure devices entails. Gordon Willis, again, talks about the homemade rig for top lighting actors, a wood, paper, and rope device that could be rigged on a practical location's ceiling—a rig known disparagingly among the conservative Hollywood cinematographers as a "coffin box."

I was camera operator on a TV series at the old Hollywood/Burbank studios when Willis was photographing *All the President's Men.* A traditional way of lighting a large set, such as the offices of the *Washington Post,* would be to construct the ceiling with removable bleached muslin, wood-framed sections, lighting the exposed, open sections from the "green beds" framing the set perimeter. Willis chose, with production designer George Jenkins, to construct a hard-ceilinged set with real fluorescent fixtures. Fluorescents were anathema to Hollywood cinematographers of the time. Not only did the implanted ballasts hum and buzz to an ungodly level but also the uneven chromatic spectrum played havoc with human skin tone. Willis had the ballasts removed and placed outside the stage. I remember walking by several times on the way to the commissary, seeing and hearing the stacked ranks of ballasts around the stage perimeter. Favorite gossip among conservative on-lot TV cameramen was to jeer at this impostor from New York City to whom they had recently denied an Oscar nomination for *The Godfather.* One day, I was allowed access to the tightly secured stage; I stood in wonder at the seemingly infinite set that was cached onto the stage, barely allowing space for the required fire lane. It was only a decade later that fluorescent technology with isolated ballasts and color correct tubes became available. Once again, technology rose to the service of creative vision. Frieder Hochheim was the gaffer on the 1987 film of Charles Bukowski's novel *Barfly,* photographed by the ever-innovative Robby Müller. The practical location of the bar was so constricted that there was nowhere to hide normal studio lighting units. Today's ubiquitous KinoFlo line of fluorescents was born for this film; Hochheim has become one of the industry's leading innovators of lighting equipment. The newest incarnation of adapting industrial lighting technology to movies is LEDs, at first as block like "bricks," but now as the lumen source for traditional Fresnel lensed lamps. So, technology is always in rapid cycles of creation and obsolescence. What remains is the creative vision and insight into problem solving that is the true mainstay of the working cinematographer. It is this spirit that lies at the heart of the interviews in *Masters of Light.*

The most important thing that you can glean from these interviews is an understanding of how the inherent planning and discipline required of the cinematographer in the film/photochemical era helped shape the way he approached his work. The constant exploring, evaluating, and adjusting that was demanded by the workflow of celluloid spilled over into a broader consideration of the dynamics of camera and lighting style. The ritual of "dailies" projected on a large screen was a kind of laboratory for director, cinematographer, editor, and production designer to critique the evolving dynamics of the movie in a collaborative way. A kind of previsualization was necessary for the next day's preparation, based on the previous evening's "dailies." This technique fostered a macro view of the cinematographer's role as visual storyteller, engaged in translating character and story into supportive and emotive images. This discipline may still be exercised in the digital era, but it is no longer so universal. The creation of each image in digital video can be more improvised: the screen of the reference monitor becomes a kind of canvas on which the cinematographer paints—seeing the immediate result of each "brushstroke." This can be exciting in a way. Imagine Jackson Pollock "in the flow" of one of his drip paintings. But this immersive approach to cinematography can also be limiting; the "action" itself may become the motivating force. It is tempting to sidestep the more rigorous task of executing a layered preparation— mere play trumping a carefully wrought plan.

Of the fifteen cinematographers interviewed in the book, none is a woman. It is a situation that would be unlikely in any compilation today, as women are rapidly achieving prominence in the field. Of those interviewed in *Masters of Light,* five are deceased: Nestor Almendros, John Alonzo, Bill Fraker, Conrad Hall, and Laszlo Kovacs. Mario Tosi, the same age I am, has been inactive since the early 1980s. Owen Roizman, retired since the mid-1990s, is a past president of the ASC and is very active in the organization. Like me, he photographed three features for the director Larry Kasdan. Roizman had a recent exhibition at AMPAS of his portraits of cinematographers. Bill Butler is now ninety-plus. His most recent credit is from 2009. Billy Williams retired a decade ago and now teaches. Michael

Chapman is a recent recipient of the ASC's Lifetime Achievement Award; he was Gordon Willis's operator in the early 1970s. His last credit as cinematographer was about five years ago. Vittorio Storaro, who was one of my great mentors, along with Nestor Almendros and Willy Kurant, has recently done a number of films about painters (a further distillation of his ongoing theme of bio films). He and the director Carlos Saura are planning a film about Pablo Picasso and the creation of the large painting *Guernica,* his memorial to the Spanish town bombed by the Luftwaffe during the Spanish Civil War. Gordon Willis, also retired, lives outside Manhattan, as revered by the current generation of cinematographers as he was at the time of his interview. He and the late Bruce Surtees share the moniker "Prince of Darkness." Haskell Wexler continues to produce a stream of activist documentaries and is also a vital member of the ASC. Vilmos Zsigmond has moved from the Hollywood Hills to Northern California; he continues to work unabatedly. In the past decade, he has made three films with Woody Allen, and another with his longtime collaborator Brian de Palma. He recently filmed a thriller in Canada and has also worked in his country of origin, Hungary. Last, my own update. I have always been somewhat chagrined that I was included in the esteemed group selected by Schaefer and Salvato. I was the new kid on the block, somehow slipping onto the team. Yet, I am the one to make the transition to the digital era of feature films in a substantial way. My first encounter with digital video cameras was in the aforementioned *Anniversary Party* in the summer of 2000. I have photographed in several digital video formats including a feature film in NTSC with Werner Herzog, *Incident at Loch Ness,* made with my two still-hearty Panasonic DVX100s. At the time of writing this foreword, June 2012, I am prepping my third digital video feature film this year. I call it "my Alexa hat trick."

The question one must ask, the question any young and emerging cinematographer, writer, director, editor, or production designer must ask, is "What now?" Although filmmaking technology has been in constant, sometimes confusing and erratic, flux since the Lumière Brothers introduced their Cinematograph in 1895, the primacy of storytelling and character have remained constant elements, as has the capture medium of film. Now, the very nature of movies is changing. Recent camera and editing technology is altering the century-old tradition of how feature films are shot, edited, and exhibited. A younger audience raised on the fluid dynamics of information and visual media possible in the laptop, smart phone, tablet age finds traditional media, even traditional filmmaking, wanting.

I find myself straddling two worlds. On the one hand, I treasure the continuity of the era of the great cinematographers such as those profiled in this book, artists who exposed images one day and saw the results the next, practicing a kind of flying by the seat of their pants, albeit very well tailored pants. I feel a visceral connection to the pioneers and masters of celluloid such as Billy Bitzer, Karl Freund, William Daniels, James Wong Howe, Boris Kaufman, and Phil Lathrop. I have known all of the cinematographers interviewed in *Masters of Light,* and even worked as camera assistant or operator with a half dozen of them. I see several more regularly at the ASC and other industry events.

On the other hand, I love the ease and portability of the newest HD cameras and look forward to "filming" with the Sony F65, which I have tested. And Panavision will soon introduce its own follow-up to the Genesis. In digital video, the current "game-changer" camera itself keeps changing. I look forward to the exciting but uncertain future of cinematography, even as I cringe at its devolving status in the digital age. The hoary cliché that "the past is prologue" is, nevertheless, appropriate as our art form faces the future. Yes, I do long for the next time I can return to 35 mm film in the anamorphic aspect ratio. I have made dozens of movies in that format. Anamorphic aspect ratio and film are, for me, still the gold standard for image creation.

John Bailey, ASC
June 2012

1. When the book was initially published (in 1984), there were no women in the professional union. That situation is changing dramatically, but we have chosen to retain the term *cameraman,* using it as a gender-neutral synonym for *cinematographer.*

Preface

Almost thirty years have passed since *Masters of Light,* a series of interviews with more than a dozen cinematographers, was first published. At the time, we hoped that the interviews would be interesting, important, and relevant to aspiring cameramen as well as everyday filmgoers and movie buffs.[1] What we did not anticipate was that the book would become a classic, remaining in print all these years, to be read by an entire generation of students, aspiring cameramen, and professional cinematographers throughout the world.

In the initial review of the book in *The New Republic,* the film critic Stanley Kauffmann commented that the work of the cameramen presented in the book probably represented the high-water mark of cinematography as we know it.

Coincidentally, many years later, in December 2011, the director Christopher Nolan gathered together many of the most important filmmakers in America at the Directors Guild, ostensibly for a screening of the first six minutes of his new film, *The Dark Knight Rises.* Once the directors were assembled, however, he made a plea for saving 35 mm film. *The Dark Knight Rises* was shot on celluloid, he explained, and he wants to continue to shoot on 35 mm film, the dominant format of the movies for more than a century.

But the digital age is encroaching on film and traditional cinematography: in 2012, the majority of theaters are showing films in the digital format. By 2015, it is expected that only 17 percent of theaters will be projecting celluloid, and thus 35 mm film, for all intents and purposes, will be dead.

That evening, Nolan encouraged filmmakers to assert their right to choose the format for their films. If enough directors strongly make their wishes known, he believes, film will have a better chance of surviving in this pervasively digital age. To boil it down to its essence: 35 mm is the gold standard of filmmaking; nothing else looks quite like it.

So perhaps, looking back on it now with the perspective of time, the late twentieth-century period covered by *Masters of Light* was actually, as Kauffmann presciently suggested, the golden age of cinematography. Many of the films discussed in the book are now considered classics, and many of the cameramen featured in the book are considered some of the best and brightest who ever stood behind a camera. For many years, their work represented the high point for the electrochemical process known as 35 mm motion picture film cinematography.

At present, only three of the cinematographers interviewed here are still making films; many have retired or passed on. In this reissue, we refrained from making any changes to the original text; some of it is now dated or even archaic and probably becoming more passé as days go by. But these interviews are like snapshots in time, capturing what it was like to be a cinematographer during that period. The challenge of being both an artist and a craftsman in that time are discussed in detail, as well as how those problems were resolved with insight and creativity. If, in the twenty-second century, someone wants to know how movies were made back "in the dark ages," the cinematographers profiled here paint a portrait of their work in their own words.

We do not remember who said something to the effect that we will long remember those who have gone before us. Our addendum to that truism would be that anyone who gets behind a camera today is standing on the shoulders of the giants in this book. We feel both honored and privileged to have documented the lives and times of these cameramen, and we will always feel a special bond with them and their work. They are truly "masters of light."

> Larry Salvato
> Dennis Schaefer
> July 2012

---

1. As mentioned in the foreword, when the book was initially published there were no women in the professional union. That situation is changing dramatically, but we have chosen to retain the term *cameraman*, using it as a gender-neutral synonym for *cinematographer.*

Introduction

The aim of this book is to explore the everyday working world of the feature motion picture cinematographer in his own words. As these conversations indicate, the cinematographer's workday is a demanding one. He does not just direct the operation of the camera at the proper time and punch out at the end of the day. When he is working on a film, the creative cinematographer eats, breathes and lives cinematography twenty-four hours a day.

"Cinematography," says Mario Tosi, "is more than just making pretty pictures." A successful cinematographer (also known as director of photography) is just as familiar with the history of the visual arts as he is with the light sensitivity of film emulsion or the electrical intricacies of rigging a huge sound stage for a big production number. He takes orders from the director but he is also his collaborator and confidant; he must help and support the director in getting exactly what he wants even when the director is not fully able to articulate it himself. He must deal on a daily basis with art, set, property and costume departments of the production to assure that their contributions are consistent with the overall tone and style of the film. In addition, he is the personnel manager and chief motivational force of the film production crew. Their response to his direction can determine whether the film stays on schedule and on budget; more importantly, it determines the quality of what finally ends up on the screen. The assistant cameraman, electricians, gaffers, grips and gofers (see Glossary for explanation of these terms) look to him for leadership and direction. He hires, fires, cajoles, counsels, and amidst all this, he creates. Outside of the director, he is normally the single most important force on the set. He must maintain firm control of all aspects of the shooting process in order to meet time and budget restrictions. When something does go wrong—and an average production weathers at least a dozen major crises a week—the cinematographer's high profile makes him an easy target for criticism—fair or unfair. Consequently, a director of photography is paid very well for his work—a job that, at times, has little to do with capturing an image on film. The consummate cinematographer is able to meld all the required technical and supervisory skills together so that he is an efficient line manager and a superb technician as well as a visual artist.

In the past decade the cinematographer's star has burned ever more brightly. Upon entering the Hollywood mainstream, young directors like Coppola, Scorsese and Spielberg wanted a unique look for their films. They succeeded in finding a number of open-minded cameramen not necessarily restricted by conventional traditions and techniques. It was this collaborative sense of youthful exuberance and inventiveness that helped produce varying but always interesting visual landscapes on the screen. Those cinematographers who met the challenge of doing something different contributed to the higher visibility of their profession within the film industry as well as among the larger moviegoing audience. Since one of the most readily apparent features of a film is its visual quality, it is easy for alert present-day filmgoers to distinguish the contributions made by the director of photography. This too has no doubt helped elevate his status at the popular level. The contemporary cinematographer has proven himself to deserve more than a mere technical credit by quietly drawing attention to his visual creativity.

This was not always the case, however. In the early formative years of motion pictures, such tinkerers and inventors as Lumière and Edison had to be cameramen because no one else could quite make this invention do what they wanted it to do. When the inventors moved on to other pursuits, the fate of motion pictures was left to businessmen who promoted the "light shows" and the artists like Georges Méliès and Edwin S. Porter who actually produced, directed and shot the films. Later on, when motion pictures began to tell more involved dramatic stories, the responsibilities of director and cameraman were separated, with the director becoming more concerned with the direction and the acting. G. W. "Billy" Bitzer, for example, worked with D. W. Griffith and was one of the first cameramen to specialize solely in the mechanical and technical aspects of filmmaking. Even the most conscientious cameraman of that day had his hands full just hand-cranking the camera and generally keeping all the equipment under control while trying to capture a focused image. When sound was added it was hailed as a great advance. The camera, by this time, had become quite bulky and it was made even more unwieldy by the additional equipment necessary to deaden the camera noise. In fact, in the thirties, many cameramen, working within the restraints of sound-recording needs, were resented by directors and producers forced to bow to the technical requirements of the camera set-up rather than the dramatic elements of the particular scene. In other words, it became commonplace for a cameraman to dictate to a director what shot he could or could not do. Some directors became frustrated in this working environment and consequently they sought out more daring, skillful and innovative cameramen for their films. But even this solution was not altogether workable since, in those days, most cameramen were under exclusive contract to an individual studio. If you were directing a film at MGM, the chief studio cameraman or one of his right-hand men would shoot your film. If you had a project at Warners, their resident director of photography would handle the technical chores for you. A cameraman might move from one studio to another but, for the most part, his style didn't move with him. He was expected to conform to the style of that particular studio as fostered by its camera department. The implication of this studio philosophy is that cameramen were quite interchangeable and that it really made no difference who shot your film; it would all look the same anyhow!

The innovators who stepped out and broke the rules got away with it in that closed system because the results they achieved were visually unique. They were groundbreakers at a time when most of Hollywood wanted to put cameramen in straightjackets. The adventurous cinematographer, Gregg Toland, when asked why he wanted to work with Orson Welles in *Citizen Kane*, remarked something to the effect that it was because novice film director Welles wouldn't know what he couldn't do. Therefore he wouldn't be restricted by hidebound, hoary Hollywood traditions. The artistic cinematographer always keeps an open mind and he more than appreciates a director who does likewise.

The studio contract system dominated the industry until the middle fifties, making it difficult for a young cameraman to break into Hollywood feature productions. The traditional way to become a director of photography was to start at the bottom, loading film magazines and slowly working your way up the ladder, a process that could take ten to fifteen years. This conservative system began to crack with the advent of television. Suddenly many new cameramen were needed to meet the often hectic production demands of this burgeoning medium. Impatient would-be cameramen jumped into the gap, hoping to establish their credentials. As a result, many new and relatively inexperienced cameramen were accepted into the union ranks and, in time, some were able to cross over into film production as well. Television commercials also provided another training ground. It's safe to say that if it were not for the advent of television and commercials, an entire generation of intelligent and innovative cinematographers would not have had the opportunity to enter the industry and thus would not now be working in feature films.

In the sixties, independent non-union productions also served as a training ground, in much the same way, for cameramen who were having a hard time cracking the Hollywood establishment. They eventually won recognition with their innovative low-budget work and they became an important factor in moving big studio productions out of sound stages and into real locations.

During the same period, Hollywood cameramen began to be influenced by European cinematographers, especially those associated with the French New Wave, who often went to visual extremes to prove that they were not tied to the Hollywood conventions of brightly lit, high-key, sound-stage-bound films. Their effect on mainstream Hollywood production was subtle to be sure, but many of the younger cinematographers took these new visual freedoms to heart and bits and pieces of this influence started to surface in their work.

All these various factors helped to propel cinematography into a new era of inventiveness and creativity. With the fading of the studio contract system and the rise in independent production, the cinematographer now exercises his judgment in the choice of film projects. He does not come into a film with a preconceived style; rather he and the director work out the visual look of the film together, often months in advance of shooting.

The auteur theory, the notion that the director should be considered responsible for everything in a film, is now in decline; filmmaking has come to be viewed as a cooperative and collaborative effort by a team of artists, technicians and crafts-people. The cinematographer is thus being recognized along with writers, pro-ducers and performers as a major participant in the filmmaking process, not only artistically and technically, but also in terms of salary, credit and even public rec-ognition. It's in this spirit that we present this volume of interviews. We propose to illustrate, in the contemporary cinematographer's own words, exactly what it is he does, why he does it and what effects it has on the filmmaking process. As a by-product, we hope to help give recognition to the art of cinematography and to some of the individuals who have sought to extend its artistic parameters, providing the filmgoer with a much richer visual experience.

This is not a "how to" book, although many technical details are discussed in the course of these conversations; there are a number of cinematography manuals and handbooks already available. This is a "why" book. In our interviews we were above all concerned with what an individual cinematographer's perspective is and the reasons he has adopted it. We were concerned with a specific personal point of view, a way of looking at things. In fact, we were interested in fifteen different ways of looking at things: each cinematographer's *mise-en scène*, if you will. Al-though they use the same equipment and go about the process in approximately the same way, they come up with fifteen different results—sometimes strikingly dif-ferent, sometimes subtly different.

In preparing this book, we interviewed many more cinematographers than we were able to include here. We feel, however, that the book covers a comprehensive range of backgrounds, perspectives and styles.

The artistic achievements of the cameramen we talked with are, individually and collectively, extremely impressive. During our conversations, we also came to appreciate their original and innovative ways of approaching their work, and we were often intrigued by their complex personalities. We are grateful to them all for generously making their time available to us, and through the book that follows readers have the opportunity to sit in on what amounts to a professional course in the basics and the nuances of the cinematographer's art.

1

Nestor Almendros

"I start from realism. My way of lighting and seeing is realistic. I don't use imagination, I use research. Basically, I show things as they are, with no distortion."

Nestor Almendros visibly flinches whenever anyone asks how he likes being a Hollywood cameraman now. He has to point out that he's never shot a film in Hollywood. *Days of Heaven* was shot in Canada, *Going South* in Mexico, *Kramer vs. Kramer* and *Still of the Night* in New York City and *The Blue Lagoon* in Fiji. But that's not really surprising since, in his twenty-year career as a director of photography, he has shot film in almost all corners of the world. And while he has never shot a film in Hollywood, he is one of the leading cinematographers in the American film industry: of the five major American films he's done, three have been nominated for the Oscar in cinematography. And, in 1978, he won for his exquisite naturalistic photography on *Days of Heaven.*

Almendros's cinematic roots are unusually deep. Born in Spain and raised in Cuba, he wholeheartedly embraced the cinema as a student; he and his friends were always making short 8mm and 16mm films. They realized, however, that they had to leave Cuba in order to broaden their knowledge of filmmaking. Almendros came to New York City where he studied at City College and met experimental filmmakers Hans Richter, Maya Deren and the Mekas brothers. He returned to Cuba after the fall of the Batista dictatorship and was hired to make propaganda documentaries, which he quickly became bored with, although he considers it was a good training ground for him and it had an influence on his style. But France beckoned: the New Wave was at high tide. In Paris he fell almost by accident into a job shooting for Eric Rohmer. The result of that initial collaboration is that he photographed six of Rohmer's "Moral Tales." François Truffaut has used him for eight films while he has worked with Barbet Schroeder on six major films plus assorted documentaries. Even if Almendros had never begun to shoot "American" films, his world reputation would have been assured. An urbane and witty conversationalist, he is a cosmopolitan man of the world and even an author of a book on cinematography. Inundated with job offers after his Oscar win, Almendros would prefer a more leisurely work pace of shooting only two features a year. But now with the demands of both French and American filmmakers for his services, that may not be possible. As in a classic demand-supply relationship, the supply is limited because the quality that Almendros puts on the screen is often hard to come by.

1964	*Paris Vu Par* (shared credit)	1976	*The Marquis of O*
1966	*La Collectionneuse*		*Days of Heaven**
1967	*The Wild Racers*	1977	*The Man Who Loved Women*
1969	*More*		*Madame Rosa*
	My Night at Maude's		*Beaubourg*
	The Wild Child		*Koko, The Talking Gorilla*
	The Gunrunners		*Goin' South*
1970	*Bed and Board*		*The Green Room*
	Claire's Knee	1978	*Perceval*
1971	*Two English Girls*		*Love on the Run*
	The Valley		*Kramer vs. Kramer†*
	Sing Sing	1979	*The Blue Lagoon†*
1972	*Chloe in the Afternoon*	1980	*The Last Metro*
1973	*Gentleman Tramp*	1981	*Still of the Night*
1974	*Idi Amin Dada*	1982	*Sophie's Choice†*
	Cockfighter [*Born to Kill*]	1983	*The Texas Project*
1975	*The Story of Adele H.*		
	Maîtresse		

*Academy Award for best achievement in cinematography.
†Academy Award Nomination for best achievement in cinematography.

We read an article that you wrote for Film Culture *when you were a young cameraman; you were impressed with the neorealist cinematography of G. R. Aldo. We wonder how that's affected your work?*

Enormously. I really owe a lot to Aldo. I think he really was an exceptional case. Aldo was even before Raoul Coutard in using indirect lighting, using soft lighting. And I think that's because he came to motion pictures from still photography. He came to the cinema not through the usual way of the period, which was to be a loader, an assistant, a focus puller, a camera operator, and after all that, many years later becoming a director of photography. He came straight from still and theatrical photography and only because Visconti imposed on him. That's why his lighting was so unconventional for the period. He had not come down the same path.

But he really was a source of inspiration. Other films of the period like *Open City* and *Shoeshine* made by other cinematographers had an interesting look *not* because the director of photography wanted it that way; it was due to lack of money. They looked interesting in spite of them. I'm sure that if they had given those cinematographers more money and technical support they would have done something very professional and slick. But Aldo knew he was doing something different. Visually, *La Terra Trema* is a very modern movie and *Umberto D* is too, as well as *Senso*. Aldo photographed them.

It would seem that the cameraman who shot Open City *was a cameraman that had been working in a studio situation and then suddenly he had to make do with what he had. Whereas with Aldo, it was different; he knew what he wanted. How does that affect you today? Do you have any basic philosophies about filmmaking?*

I always hear Americans say "philosophy"; it's such a big word.

I meant where you start from or your point of departure.

I start from realism. My way of lighting and seeing is realistic; I don't use imagination. I use research. I go to a location and see where the light falls normally and I just try to catch it as it is or reinforce it if it is insufficient; that's on a natural set. On an artificial set, I suppose that there is a sun outside the house and then I see how the light would come through the windows and I reconstruct it. The source of the light should always be justified. And when it's night, my light simply comes from the lampshades or any natural source light that you see in the frame. That is my method. I haven't invented that, of course. They used to do that before my time, but they used to use hard lights with fresnel lenses. Hard lights only exist in the theatrical world; if you were filming a play or a nightclub, it would be justified. But in normal situations, very seldom do people have spotlights in their houses. When there should be sunlight, then there's nothing better yet to imitate real sunlight than arc lights, which unfortunately, in many small productions, you cannot afford. I used arc lights outside the prison in *Goin' South* to imitate the sunlight falling inside through the windows.

How did you first meet Eric Rohmer and start working on his films?

After I decided to leave Cuba, I chose to come to France because I very much liked the New Wave movies. For three years, I relied on my former profession, teaching language, and I survived. Then by chance, I met Rohmer. To make a long story short, I just happened to be on the set while he was shooting *Paris Vu Par*. Well, the cameraman left because he quarreled with Rohmer and they couldn't get anyone, so I said, "I am a cameraman." And they just tried me and they liked the rushes afterwards. It's like the story of the chorus girl who replaces the star in the show who has twisted her ankle. Something like that.

Barbet Schroeder was producing the film?

Yes, and Rohmer was directing. I did some of the other sketches as well.

You shot two or three of the sketches for that film then?

Officially, I shot two episodes but I did camerawork and retakes on all the others. It was in 16mm, and hand-held; it was in that period in which we thought 16mm was going to be the thing. I had a lot of 16mm experience in Cuba plus my underground experience in New York. Later we abandoned 16mm because we realized that we had confused the issue; we had thought that it was a question of millimeters.

What about the first feature that you shot with Rohmer, La Collectionneuse*? Barbet Schroeder, who produced the film, said that he had a vivid memory of the*

shooting and that both you and he were influenced later by the style of that film.
Can you explain that?

That film is very important to me. When people ask me what is my favorite movie that I did, I always say *La Collectionneuse*. On that movie, there was already everything that I did later, in an embryo way, you know. But everything was there already. It's a movie that I can't forget. My first was also my best. It's a landmark for me as well as Schroeder and Rohmer.

It was intended to be done in 16mm; that was when we were giving up fighting for 16mm. We decided to make the film in 35mm but shoot it as if it were 16mm. Because what gives 16mm the look that we like in the movies—it wasn't the millimeters, it was the way you made them. And of course, those things always go together; the fact that you had a small budget, you had so few lights, forced you to use natural sets and natural light. If you do all those things and just change one— go to 35mm—then you still keep this look and acquire some technical qualities which will make the film more interesting for the audience. So we shot the film in 35mm but we hardly had a crew. Barbet Schroeder was the producer and also, at the same time, a sort of gaffer, grip, superintendent; everything really. I was also loading the camera and doing some of the focusing myself. We did it like we would do a 16mm underground movie, only we were doing it in 35mm. We used the technique of not lighting; we waited for the right light. Like we are sitting in this room here; I like this light here the way it is now so why change it if I had to film it? And with this technique, we saw that the results were not only as interesting as in 16mm but even better because they were not degraded by the inferior quality of 16mm. Also the sensitivity and latitude of the film was greater so we could actually go further.

Use less lights?

We used less lights than we used in 16mm; we practically needed none. And we also realized that most technicians had been bullshitting, you know, and inventing uses for enormous amounts of light to justify their importance, to justify their salaries and to make themselves look like someone who knows a secret, when there is technically very little to know.

That's the New Wave?

Yeah, but the first New Wave movies—I think that's where Rohmer was great— they were not that conscious about those things. They were still a little naive, they were undergoing a transition. But I believe we went a further step, thanks to Rohmer.

In general, from the New Wave directors that you've worked with, what do you find their attitude to be toward the camera work? How do they deal with it? Do they put a lot of emphasis on that?

They do give a great deal of importance to the camerawork. But, at the same time, they don't like it to overwhelm the movie, like it used to be. Because, in the past, the cameraman was like a dictator, you know. There was so much time for preparing the shot and so there practically was no time for the actors to rehearse or the moviemakers to make the movie. There was all the business of putting the lights up and it was a big ritual. I think we work faster now than they used to. And that comes also from the reduction of the shooting time in Europe.

But even with all the business of working faster, the directors still wanted good cinematography?

Oh sure, they certainly care a lot about it. The fact that they don't have an army of technicians any more doesn't mean that they don't care about the photography. On the contrary, they dislike that glossy look, that artificial look that films have, especially old French films. The Americans never went that far; the French films of the fifties especially were unbearable in that regard. They were so artificial; actors could hardly move because they had a light on their eyes that was hitting them in a certain manner and the actors had to be there still on that spot and so they had to be acting as if they were mummies because they could not move. Instead of the lighting being for the actors, it was the actors existing for the lighting.

You've done a number of pictures with Truffaut; could you describe what your working relationship is with him; what kind of input you have to him and vice versa; what emphasis he places on the camera.

To begin with, Truffaut is one of the nicest persons to work with. He's a man who believes, like Jean Renoir, that a good atmosphere during the shooting will be good for the film too. On the set, there's no hysteria, there's no screaming; everybody on the crew are like family. We are working together to make a movie. Everything goes very smoothly and it's a work of cooperation. He's a man who, amazingly for his enormous talent, listens to people who work with him. You would tell him something and he would take it into consideration; he might reject it but it's not just the attitude of "I'm a genius and I don't need any kind of help." He listens to the people who work with him, whether it's a set designer, assistant director or actor or even a grip. And he will use things that people bring to the movie and use them so the film looks like Truffaut nevertheless. That's one of his great talents.

The camera, for Truffaut, is much more mobile that it is with Rohmer. Rohmer likes for the characters to move in the frame as in *The Marquis of O* where they come close to the camera and they go back, back, back to the end of a corridor. And the camera just stays there and they go in and out of the frame. Truffaut, on the other hand, usually follows the actors; he's always in a sort of medium shot position; that's his favorite distance. He goes more often to close-ups in certain movies, especially on contemporary subjects. So he moves the camera but it's hardly noticeable because it's following the action so closely that it's justified and it's almost invisible. In this sense, I think he has learned a lot from the American cinema of the thirties. He admires very much Leo McCarey, Capra and all those people that have this almost invisible camera. That's for light comedies. But when it comes to drama, then he would have camerawork that is more underlying, where the camera is almost like a character in the film.

As in The Story of Adele H?

Yes, or in *The Green Room* in which the camera does actually describe things and underline them. Big dolly shots, big camera movements come from the geography of the place (location) instead of in the editing. He is the master of the "plan-séquence." That's a French expression. It does not really indicate a master shot because a master shot implies you're going to do close-ups and insert them on that master. His conception of a shot is such that it's just the way it's going to be and there's no other way to fill in any close-ups. The camera will go from one character to another or will move to another room, all without a cut. He tries not to edit. If he can keep it all in one shot, he's very happy.

What sort of problems does that style of shooting present to you?

Well it does present some problems and some advantages. One of the problems is focus, for instance. When the camera is moving all the time, it is quite difficult for the focus puller; he has to keep following and keep the correct distance. Also it presents a problem for the camera operator, which is me, because in Europe I do operate the camera. At every moment in every camera movement, there has to be a composition that looks good. So it's like making a thousand compositions in a very short period of time. On the other hand, you have an advantage in that you have no problem about matching. When you're editing and you're going from one shot to another, you have to make sure that the eyelines are right, that the lighting is the same for every shot of the sequence. When you do a "plan-séquence," it takes a long time to prepare; you might do one a day, but you save time in the long run too.

The shot may make up several minutes of the finished film.

Well, in the editing of the film, there is less work to do because the whole thing is preedited. So you work the whole day and you only do one shot, but you save all the time in the editing later.

Monte Hellman whom you worked with on Cockfighter *said that you were fast; that it was one of the first things that came to his mind about you.*

Good, I'm glad he said that. I don't boast about being good but I boast about being fast.

He said, "Of course he's good; you've seen his films, but the thing you don't know is that he's also very, very fast."

The reason being that I light very little. For a cameraman, most of the time is lost in lighting. Well, very often I go to a place and I realize that it is very nicely lit as it is. So what we do is we choreograph the actors in relationship to the existing situation and it's easier that way. I think that by spending too much time in lighting, you end up being *mannerist*. And that's something I learned from a short experience that I had with Roger Corman. Right after I made *La Collectionneuse*, we made a film in Europe that was produced and codirected by Corman; Daniel Haller was the other director. It was called *The Wild Racers*. It was an insignificant movie. But the importance of that experience was we learned to work very fast. It's a twofold area; we realized that because you are faster, you are not necessarily worse in cinema; and because you take a long time to prepare something, it's not necessarily going to be better. With every shot you take time somehow; some shots you take longer than with others. But, on the whole, you just have to go ahead and shoot and follow your intuition. Sometimes if you think too much you sort of lose the intuition and the natural flow.

But still you get the wonderful compositions; how do you achieve such quality and still work with such economy? It does seem like a contradiction.

If it is so, I guess it also has to do with the fact that I come from reportage, from newsreels, documentaries, and television and that was my training ground. If you would measure the amount of film that I shot in my career, the ones that people know are just the part visible of the iceberg. I shot an enormous quantity of film in Cuba for television and newsreels; also for school television in France. That's a lot of footage; that keeps you in training.

So it's your training as a documentary cameraman that gives you that intuition?

Also, every situation that you face in a new movie, you have faced it before. It's not new to you. And that's the reason why I could make five feature films last year. Whereas the year that I made *La Collectionneuse*, that was the only film I made and it left me exhausted. It's because you learn to work faster and, I hope, better.

What about now that you're working in Hollywood?

I haven't worked in Hollywood. *Days of Heaven* was shot in Canada. *Goin' South* was shot in Mexico. *Kramer vs. Kramer* was in New York. But I know what you mean by Hollywood.

So you shot none of that in a studio?

Well *Days of Heaven* was totally on location but they built sets on location. On *Goin' South*, we used the sets of the western town that John Wayne had built in Durango. It doesn't make too much difference whether you shoot in a studio or a natural set if the sets are reconstructed. The only difference is that you can go from the outside to the inside on a natural set, which is, by the way, one of the things that Truffaut likes. And you can't do that in a studio. Truffaut likes to always link the exterior with the interior. You often have people going from the outside into a house in one shot like in *The Wild Child*. So that people can really see the connection between the interior and exterior. It also makes the people participate in the film. It's not like the films made in the fifties, where you would have an exterior shot really on location and when people crossed the doorway, suddenly you were on a studio set and it was very obvious.

So you've really never made a film in the studio environment?

At times I have, like *Madame Rosa*. The apartment scenes were shot entirely in a studio in Paris. Now I haven't shot in a Hollywood studio but I've seen films being made in Hollywood and it's not too different from our way of doing things. Only in Hollywood, you have more hours, more gaffers, more grips, more coffee and more doughnuts.

Do you have a preference for studio over location work?

Yes, I think when we were younger we fought the wrong battle for 16mm as much as we fought the wrong battle for natural sets. I am more eclectic now. There are situations where natural sets are excellent; in other situations they are useless. For instance, in *Madame Rosa*, about two-thirds of the film took place in that apartment; in *Kramer vs. Kramer*, two-thirds of the film also took place in an apartment. There's no doubt that you can control the lighting better by being on a set, especially when you have long scenes. If the scenes are very short, if they are vignettes, like in *La Collectionneuse*, I agree it's good to have natural light because it falls very nicely and you just cut to another scene. But when you are shooting a very long scene (with natural light) the light is falling a certain way like it's falling in this room now; but in an hour from now, the light will be falling differently. So paradoxically, a natural set will sometimes give a non-realistic feeling to the audience because the lighting will change from shot to shot. There will be no continuity. You want to get a smooth continuity and there's nothing better than a studio for that, especially for those long scenes. *My Night at Maude's* was also shot partially in the studio. Maude's apartment was a set and there's no doubt that it helped the actors to be relaxed. When the actors have to perform long sequences and a great deal of dialogue, if they are disturbed by traffic in a street or a helicopter passing over and you have to call "cut" every minute because the take is no good for sound, then the performers get in a bad mood; all the stopping and starting is disturbing them. When you are in the studio, you control your work; you are comfortable and the actors perform perfectly.

What film do you use in Europe; do you use Kodak?

We use Kodak Vincennes as opposed to Kodak Rochester; Vincennes is the town in France where they make it.

Is it the same film, the same emulsion?

Kodak says it is but we know it isn't. It's a little softer I think. In theory it's exactly the same but something is slightly different.

I thought possibly you used Agfa or some other European stock.

No, I haven't used Agfa; I'd like to make some tests with it. I've seen the Fuji film. In fact, it's unfortunate that Kodak practically has a monopoly in this area. Because it's like a painter had to have only one palette; it would be interesting to use other things. The problem is that the other things might not be as good.

How do the labs differ?

The labs are better here. For one thing, they are cleaner, much cleaner. And that's very important; what always infuriates me is white spots on the film done in French labs because of all the dust. The air extractors are not good enough; the transportation of the film from one room to another is not carefully done. People in the labs are underpaid, of course, so they don't work as well. Also the opticals are badly done in Europe. Whenever there is a dissolve, it's not very good. But in America, they are very well done. When I see the work that was done by the lab on *Days of Heaven*, it just absolutely amazes me; I can't believe it. What the MGM lab did was incredible and I'm very pleased with it.

You've done a number of documentaries with Barbet Schroeder. What can you say about the shooting of Idi Amin Dada?

I could say we came to a point which is interesting as journalism and cinema. Taking into account that it was journalism, you had to be unobtrusive; the smaller the crew is, the better. We knew that Idi Amin was very temperamental and that he was not going to be bothered. So we just had to be as invisible as we could. We knew what we were shooting was so exciting that there was no place for aesthetics.

We had to do photography that was more intelligent than beautiful, more functional than aesthetic. We did very little lighting because we had a very small kit for lighting and we lit everything ourselves without electricians. We hand-held the camera very often. That time, we were using 16mm; I think that's where it should be used, for that kind of thing and not for fiction. But for that kind of movie, we could have never done the film in 35mm. It would have been impossible.

One scene where you went into the meeting with his aides—I can't believe he allowed you to film that.

Well, he was actually quite proud of showing that. He told us we could shoot for five minutes only. But then, when the five minutes passed, he didn't acknowledge it, so we just remained there and he never said anything about it. So we just kept shooting. And he actually got very excited about that sequence and he was probably very proud of it. The only problem I had there, from the point of view of lighting, is that their newsreel people were also shooting and they were throwing their light intermittently all over the place. I had set all my lights in advance and suddenly my light reading would change completely and that was a big problem for me because it suddenly got overexposed or underexposed.

The footage we shot was of course very much longer than the film itself because Idi Amin repeated himself a lot; he said the same things for about three hours. We shot all the ministers in the meeting to use as cutaways. But I wasn't very well located, so that the one minister who was killed 15 days later was precisely the one I had not gotten a shot of alone. I just got him in a panning shot. Then we learned that 15 days later he was found dead on the banks of the Nile. When Amin was talking to him in the meeting, he was telling this man how he had not done his job well. Little did we know what was to happen later. But Amin wasn't actually looking at him. He was talking to the air so we had no way to know which man he was admonishing. Well, we found out about this man's death back in Paris when we were looking at the rushes. So we had the laboratory freeze the frame on this man. Now when the film came out, Amin wasn't happy. So he tried to exercise censorship by taking hostages. He put the French residents of Uganda in prison. It's the first time that this kind of censorship has been perpetrated in the history of the cinema. So that by this taking of hostages Barbet was forced to cut the freeze frame and the phrase about his murder from the film.

Goin' South was only Jack Nicholson's second film as a director. Was he anxious about taking on that role again?

He's a total director. He was very excited, not nervous but very excited and very pleased and happy to have the chance to direct. He really enjoys directing as much as acting. He enjoys acting a lot too; you can tell, he's got such fantastic energy and enthusiasm and he communicates this to the whole crew. Everybody follows him as a real leader.

Did he depend heavily on you for the visual look and style of the film?

He doesn't depend on anybody; he has his own ideas. But he relied on me a lot; he listened to me a lot and he was happy to have my viewpoint on things and it really worked wonderfully well. It was a fantastic experience.

Was the mine shaft sequence in Goin' South *lit totally with those lanterns?*

Yes, basically. There was a little help with some soft light. But just a little because I wanted to give the impression that those lights were actually petrol lanterns and that the mine was very dark. So you had to guess more than see, which also made some of the crew unhappy because they built that mine set and they were questioning whey they should build such a good set if it was not going to be seen.

But I was lucky enough that Jack Nicholson agreed with me; that it was not necessary to see it; that you could show a beam here and a little stone there and guess about the rest. And that would be much more realistic than knowing exactly how the mine was laid out.

And, in that scene, Nicholson was wonderful because he was carrying the lantern and he understood very quickly how the lantern had to be at eye level so that the faces would be seen. Also by waving and shaking the lantern, you would see patterns of light. So he actually did it, he was lighting for me. He was acting but, at the same time, he was a gaffer. It was wonderful. And I asked him if he would mind doing that, explaining to him how it would look better. I asked him if it hampered or handicapped his acting and he said, "Quite the opposite, it helps me due to the fact that I'm thinking of something else so I can act better." It's really an ideal thing for a director of photography to have an actor like that.

Some of the scenes were very dark, at least by American standards; I'm thinking of an early sequence in the jail where all the faces are very dark. Was that intentional?

Yes, definitely. I like arc lights very much and we used arc lights there to imitate sunlight coming into the jail. Now I don't like arc lights outside to compensate, you know, when they use it on exteriors. That I hate; I never do that. But I wanted to use arcs in that scene and Nicholson like the idea of the jail being very sordid and very dark. And then the faces sort of emerge from the darkness and come into this stream of light. He staged the action for that as you could see. So, in that scene, Nicholson himself was almost backlit, almost invisible and only those who came to visit him in jail would be seen. It was an exciting scene to do actually. In fact you've mentioned the two scenes that I prefer in the movie, from my point of view and the point of view of my work: the mine and the prison.

What was your aesthetic approach to the timing of Goin' South?

I did the timing but unfortunately I did not do the final timing because I had to start another movie. I'm not that happy about the final release print of *Goin' South.*

On that film, we agreed that we would like the photography to have a very warm feeling. So instead of having the 85 filter on the camera, which is the normal one, we used an 85B filter, which is slightly warmer. The location in Durango didn't really look like as much of a desert as we wanted it to be, so by using the 85B we made it look more dry. So the plants, instead of being totally green, looked slightly more yellowish and orangish. The first print that the lab did on its own appalled both Nicholson and me because they had color-corrected and subtracted that. We had to tell them to put the warm colors back in.

About those scenes in the desert, did you use any fill light or white cards?

No, the desert is also very easy to shoot because the light bounces off things naturally. It's only when you have lots of green, the green of nature, that it becomes difficult because green absorbs the light and then there is no bounce or fill light.

Another scene I had great trouble with was the sequence with the gallows because we were having some very stormy days. Sometimes it would be sunny and five minutes later it would be cloudy. So matching shots was really a nightmare. I don't know if you noticed it but some shots really don't match at all. It was a very long scene, shot over a whole week, and we could not stop production just because it didn't match. What we did to get around that was shoot very tight on the action so you don't see that it's so cloudy outside: by doing that you can hide the fact that the weather conditions have changed. You get by, although it's not perfect.

Of course, Nicholson cared more about the performances and the story rather than the lighting in that sequence. Because of that, we didn't stop shooting; and he probably was right about that for what it was.

What about the experience of working with Terrence Malick?

Days of Heaven was a fantastic experience also. He's an artist from head to toe. Every little molecule in him is an artist. For a director of photography to work with him, it is the treat of your life. Because he's very much oriented to photography, more than any other director that I've ever met. And he knows more about photography than any other director I've named. He could have actually filmed this movie and done it very well. He knows about light and mood. He knows that a light can be almost like an actor; that it will give a scene a feeling that is as strong as a good actor. He gives great importance to it.

We shot a lot of film; we shot under very exceptional lighting conditions. We very often shot in what he called "the magic hour." We would prepare and wait the whole day, then we would shoot at the time after the sun set. We had about twenty minutes there before it got dark. We would just shoot frantically to make use of this beautiful light.

You would have to open the lens up further and further as the light began to go?

Yes. We started with the normal lenses and we would change to the fast Super-panavision lenses which open up to $f1.1$. Well, first we went to a $f1.4$ lens, then there was one lens, a 50mm, that opened up to $f1.1$, so we would rush to get the 50mm and put it on as the light went; then we would pull the 85 filter off to get another stop and then as a last resort we pushed the film. So we expanded this 20 minutes to 25 minutes of shooting time. Of course, we were quite determined to match everything. And it gave a quality that I don't think has ever been seen in movies. Because you don't know where the light comes from; it's a strange type of light. The quality of the skin tones is very extraordinary. I allow myself to boast about it because I credit that to Terry; I just helped him in achieving what he wanted.

How did Terry Malick communicate to you how he wanted Days of Heaven *to look? How did he explain it to you?*

He was very clear about it; he talked to me by phone because I was in Europe making a film when he contacted me. And we prepared the film by phone. I read the script and took some notes and we talked a lot by phone about the look of the movie. Then when I got to Los Angeles and later to Alberta, we talked more at length. But he insisted from the very beginning that he wanted to shoot some scenes of the film in this "magic hour." He wanted to know if the film stock was capable of doing it and I said, "Absolutely, I've done it before." We did some tests in the area (Lethbridge, Alberta) before we started shooting. We did tests that involved pushing the film and shooting after sunset. We found the tests very convincing; it looked good so we went ahead.

But that was his main concern: to use that type of light in color, which hasn't been done too much. In black and white, of course, Orson Welles used that type of light in the first part of *Touch of Evil* and there have been other black-and-white movies that utilized it.

We also talked about the colors of the set and the clothes. We didn't want too many colors; we leaned heavily on browns and period colors, colors that were not bright because historically they were not bright in that time. Patricia Norris got old clothes and old textiles, so that the clothes wouldn't have that synthetic quality that they now have.

So it sounds like Terry Malick knew very specifically what he wanted?

At the same time, nothing was that rigidly planned. We would find things on location also; there were many things that would just happen. As we were doing the film, we would be finding things. There was lots of improvisation in the shooting, in the acting and all respects.

For instance, there would not be a call sheet that went into great detail as to what we were to shoot that day. Our schedule was dictated by the weather, the conditions and the way we were feeling. This made some people on the crew, which was basically a Hollywood crew, unhappy.

Who determined which sequences were to be shot in the "magic hour" and which ones were not?

Well, it had to do with the logic of it. For instance the scene in which Richard Gere has a fight with a worker who asks him if his sister is keeping him warm; well that scene takes place at lunch time in the fields so obviously it could not be the "magic hour." So there's a logic to it. And also we shot at the "magic hour" when actually, in the movie, it was supposed to be dawn or dusk. But that's a known fact—that farmers wake up very early to do their work. So we shot in the "magic hour" for both sunset and dawn sequences. It made sense, it wasn't gratuitous. And some scenes, like the scenes by the river with Brooke Adams, they had to be shot at the "magic hour" because it was supposed to be after work. So it was all justified by the logic of the script.

Did you use any filters or put anything in front of the lens?

No, not at all. We didn't use any filters or any diffusion; we wanted the image to be very sharp and crisp. We didn't use any fog filters either. We sometimes took out the 85 filter in order to gain one stop in exposure, a supplementary stop. In doing that, of course, the image becomes bluish. In some situations, like when Richard

Gere and Linda Manz are roasting a chicken in front of the fire, it worked very well and we left it as it was without color correction. It all became very blue, you remember? And the only thing that has color is the fire and the sparks of fire. But in other scenes, we had the lab correcting the color so it wouldn't be so blue and so it would match with the rest of the film.

How did you go about shooting those night exteriors, especially the scene where they have the celebration around the campfire?

For that scene, we used a new technique, at least as far as I know. We used propane bottles with burners to simulate the light of the fire. I mean, normally when you shoot a scene that's supposed to be firelight, you have a spotlight and you wave and shake pieces of clothes or plastic or something in front of it to imitate the flickering of flames. But that always looks very phony and ridiculous. So since my technique has always been realism, I thought why not go to the real thing and use real fire? So we had the bottles of propane with the burners and we put them as close as we could to the faces of the people, but out of range of the camera. We lit it exactly as we would light it with electric light only we used a flame instead. And that light had the real flickering, the real movement and also the color temperature because it's very warm and has its own kind of reddish quality that you don't get in electrical light. You know the scene when the fiddler is playing and all the people are dancing? All that is lit with propane.

And of course that made the gaffers, the grips and the prop men unhappy. No one knew whose job it was to handle the propane. The electrician would say, "That's not electricity so why should I be lighting with that; it doesn't belong to me." The prop man would say, "Why should I be handling these bottles? This is lighting." Nobody wanted to take care of it. It was confusing.

Concerning that night sequence with the grasshoppers and the fire, did you enhance that light? It looked perfectly natural.

The fire was shot actually as it was. It was real fire. No enhancing, no nothing. In fact, if you light fire, you spoil it. Because if you overlight a scene where there is fire, then the fire doesn't give the proper effect. We did some tests, of course, and we saw that it looked better that way; that it looked better without any kind of "enhancement." Then when we had scenes of people's faces looking at the fire, we would use the flame of propane bottles in order to control the effect.

What about that great sequence right before the burning with all the lanterns and commotion?

That was in the script actually; Terry had the idea of people carrying lanterns. The problem is that when people carry lanterns in film, they usually light nothing. Because the lanterns are just props, you see. But we wanted the lanterns to really light the scene. So what we had were some battery belts with electricity hooked up to the lanterns which had warm color bulbs in them so that it would give the color temperature of a flame; not white light. What was important was that the people were carrying lanterns that actually did give light; it doesn't matter whether it was a real flame or electricity. What we wanted was that those lanterns would actually lead and that they would be believeable.

So we had some smokey color on the lanterns and so on; there was a prop man who did some research on it and we did some tests. Later on I used that technique again in *Goin' South* on the mine scene. If you have real lanterns with real petrol, they really give so little light that it doesn't read; the film doesn't register.

But that was the extent of your lighting in that sequence?

No, I had some fill light, too. We had some machines making smoke and I used some back light in order to make the smoke appear quite strongly; otherwise the smoke wouldn't have been visible. I had some front light also, but very little. I used the front light in a way that the lanterns that the people were carrying would actually do the lighting job.

What percentage of the film would you say is shot with natural or practical light?

Almost all of it. There was very little lighting. Only the scenes at the end where the jealous husband goes up and finds her in the room; there we had a couple of lamps with lampshades in the room but we did some lighting there also. But the lighting was always justified because it was coming from the direction of the actual light. Also when you had views of the house from the outside at night, of course that was artificial light in the windows. We needed it stronger than it was in reality, but not by much; it was very close to the truth.

When we had day scenes in the house, it normally was window light actually lighting the scene. We had done some tests; some with artificial lighting and some without and Terry liked it better without the lighting and I did too. So the window light would be the light that was doing the job.

And you would prefer to use the natural light anyhow?

Well, it's always been my thing. I did a lot of that in *The Marquis of O* but this movie gave me a chance to do it again, even more so. Rohmer, you see, doesn't like high contrast; he doesn't like black backgrounds, he wants you to see things. So with Rohmer, although I had the window light doing the job, I had to put some fill light up so that the backgrounds could be seen. On the other hand, Malick liked to leave things the way they were, which, of course, made me very happy.

That would also be responsible for the skin tones; they had a sort of soft, glowing quality to them.

Yes. At the same time, the scenes had to be staged with the consideration that the depth of field was very small. And that's where a director like Malick is very important for that kind of movie. The lens is wide open so that the actors would be in focus at one point and then go totally out of focus at another point in the same scene. But Malick was very much aware of this; he would stage the scene so that both of the actors would be in the same focal plane.

In Days of Heaven *the colors are very saturated; what causes that effect? What were you doing to give it that saturated look; is it because of "the magic hour"?*

I suppose so and also because we had to push the film.

How much?

One stop only. Also things vary from lab to lab. That film was developed in a provincial lab in Vancouver called Alpha Cine and they did a very good job. So it gave a different quality to the film. Otherwise, both *Days of Heaven* and *Goin'*

South were shot with the same camera and the same lenses; so was *Kramer vs. Kramer*, and the results are different there also. It has to do with the light of the place and the quality of the landscape. Canada is not the same as Durango, Mexico, you see.

On Kramer vs. Kramer, *can you comment about your aesthetic or photographic approach to the film?*

It's a contemporary movie and it takes place in an Upper East Side apartment, upper-middle class; also there are scenes that take place in skyscrapers with long views of New York. We use restaurants and courthouses as locations too. It's very banal, it has to do with things of today. So, in that way, the film looks more like *Bed and Board* or *Chloe in the Afternoon*, which are the other two contemporary movies I've made. It looks a little like *The Man Who Loved Women* too.

Normally when you make a film about a contemporary subject, people think you should not care too much about the visual side of it. Normally they are done more quickly and more carelessly. There is no set designer, no costumer; you just shoot things as they are. But, in this film, fortunately we have done things with time and research. Robert Benton wanted to come from Piero della Francesca, amazingly enough for a contemporary subject; but that was the painter we studied to begin this movie. We looked at a lot of frescoes and books.

As the film went on, I found that the objects in the film have no connection with Piero della Francesca; we had the colors and we tried to match the colors on the walls and clothes, etc. But, little by little, in the middle of the movie, I began to get interested in David Hockney. Then, just the other day, I was very happy to find out that David Hockney admires Piero della Francesca a lot and he actually considers himself a follower of his. So I was not that far off. I've been searching through David Hockney lately because he uses contemporary things like chairs, cactus in a pot, lampshades and windows; things that look like things that are in this movie. That's my source of inspiration now.

But it's done very carefully. I have time to do it and I'm never rushed.

By the way, just as a point of reference, the painters we studied for *Goin' South* were Maxwell Parrish and Maynard Dixon. In *Days of Heaven* we used the photography of the period as is indicated in the credits. In *Claire's Knee*, we used Gauguin; in *Adele H.* we used Victorian painting.

So you communicate a great deal through reference to the other visual arts?

Yes, I think using painting is very important because it gives a reference to the director, the set designer, the costume designer, etc. In *The Marquis of O*, for instance, we used German romantic painting. Sometimes you have movie references. For *The Wild Child*, our inspiration was Griffith and black-and-white movies of the past.

It's always very useful to have a reference to give a style to the movie; otherwise the film would just go into so many directions.

What about contemporary American cinematographers? Whose work do you look at; whose work do you admire?

I think we've seen a great renewal in America in the last twenty years [in cinematography]. A tremendous renewal because they had come to a dead end. I admire very much Gordon Willis, of course; he's a great artist. I admire Chapman (Michael), a very good disciple of Willis. Here on the West Coast, there's Haskell Wexler, who worked a bit on *Days of Heaven* after I left because I had committed to do a film with Truffaut. Since I was committed to it before, it was Haskell who shot about two weeks of filming after I left. It worked out fabulously. Then of course, the Hungarians are very good too; Laszlo Kovaks and Vilmos Zsigmond are really fantastic. Adam Hollender is also a great cameraman; Alonzo is very good too. Also Butler is very good too and Conrad Hall. There are a lot of great cameramen here.

Can you comment on the way American directors work as opposed to their European counterparts?

The Americans use much more film; they use thousands of feet of film and get much more coverage. They cover everything from every possible angle; they do many more takes of a scene. There are many more scenes that are never used. In Europe—and when I say "in Europe," my experience is very limited, I am always faithful to the directors I work with and that is Truffaut, Rohmer and Barbet Schroeder—anyway, they don't shoot too much film. They don't do much coverage. It only takes Rohmer eight days to edit his films. Eight days! All Rohmer does is, since there is no coverage at all, splice one sequence after another and so the film is almost done. So that the rough cut and the final cut are very similar. All they do is cut a little here and a little there. So that you can say the film is really all there in the rough cut. So when I say eight days, I mean eight days for the rough cut.

Whereas here, with *Days of Heaven*, it has been about three different movies; they edited it one way, then they reedited it again another way and then they cut scenes and added still other scenes. It's totally different here. On *Goin' South*, Jack Nicholson had three editors working simultaneously on the film. One would be editing the gunfight, one would be editing the love scene and one would be editing something else, all at the same time. We don't do it that way and so our films are perhaps more personal and more individual. Which doesn't mean that Malick or Nicholson or Monte Hellman aren't individuals, they are. I admire them for their ability to do their own thing in spite of all the obstacles. It's amazing. When you think of the past and the enormous pressure of the producers and studios and when you see that every John Ford picture had a signature, had a style, it's just amazing. How did they do it?

What about the actors and actresses here? Do you think part of the reason for shooting a lot is on their account?

The American actors are much more energetic than the Europeans. They go through many hardships. In *Days of Heaven*, Richard Gere fell 15 times on an icy river for 15 takes without much protection; I really admire that. He did it himself and he never protested it at any time. Nicholson does the same thing too.

American directors shoot too much, I think. I don't think it's necessary, at least not to that extreme. Sometimes producers want them to do it because if you don't shoot enough they think they will not have a good film.

But then again, the cheapest thing you have to work with is film; that's your smallest expense on a film.

But then, on the other hand, you have a tremendous amount of film. And it takes more time for editing; you have too many choices, you have too many angles. With many of the films that I've seen in America, I have the impression that they're always cutting for no reason; it's just because they have another shot of it. The films have the tendency to all look alike because they all go through the same method of shooting. It comes out as if it were made by computers. A computer could actually make a movie; it could see how many camera positions you can have for the scene; ask the computer and it will tell you.

Then by having all these choices, the editors also chop up the film too much. You have to have a close-up here and an insert there, a long shot here, an establishing shot there and it becomes too mechanical. It becomes just a mechanism and it has no personality, the film has no style. I believe in limitations and discipline.

Possibly the Truffauts and the Rohmers are more secure in their visions; they know exactly how they want it?

I believe the director should know in advance and not afterwards on the editing table. He should edit his film in his head already. In Hollywood, that's the way it used to be a long time ago. But of course all these things are theories; and some people with other theories might get a good film. Good films get made in every possible way and sometimes under great pressure.

We understand that the last film you made with Rohmer, Perceval, *was quite different from your previous work. In what way?*

The film was totally made in the studio and Rohmer did not want a realistic look at all. So that's totally breaking with my tradition. And, I must say, at the beginning, I was totally lost. In the first two weeks, I had to do many retakes because it was really very bad and I didn't know where I was going. I had to relearn everything again; because Rohmer wanted a look that was not realistic, not naturalistic. He wanted it purposely to look artificial. Having been a realist all my life, it was really quite hard. On the sound stage, we had a whole cyclorama with castles made of plywood, trees made with plastic, painted grass and backgrounds. It had to be reconstructed light. And also Rohmer did not want something that would have direction of light because he was getting his inspiration from the miniatures of the Middle Ages; and the miniatures had no shadows, they only had color and form; there was no direction of light and no perspective. So we had to have light but, at the same time, with no direction and it couldn't be flat either. So I used arc light and it was really hard.

Also, you know, people have not been working in the studios lately, especially in Europe, so studio lighting has almost become some kind of lost art. It's a secret that was buried with the people who used to do it; it hasn't been passed on. Of course, they were working in black-and-white and we are working in color, so even if you research the old books, it doesn't totally work the same.

So it was very exciting and anguishing too because I was afraid of really goofing it.

It was a big challenge?

Yes, that's right. Unfortunately the film hasn't been a big commercial success in America.

Would you say that it was your most difficult film?

Yes, I would say that this is the most difficult film I've made. Because even my first film, *La Collectioneuse*, like all first films, was very difficult but still there were points of reference. But *Perceval*, it was total invention.

2

John Alonzo

*"There's no such thing as just flipping right into be-
coming a cameraman. For me it was the quality of
what I could do plus being there at the right time and
being tenacious about it."*

As much as anyone can be, John Alonzo is a student of film. As he grew up in
Mexico and later Dallas, Texas, movies were his source of entertainment; he sometimes saw two or three films a day. Although, at the time, he wasn't viewing films
for the sake of cinematography, they certainly played a large part in forming cinematic ideas and concepts that he would later develop in his work.

He first came to Los Angeles to host a children's show on local television which
featured Señor Turtle, a character he had created for a show in Dallas. Señor Turtle
found the going considerably tougher in Los Angeles. When the show was can-
celled after a short run, Señor Turtle retired and Alonzo turned to acting. In between acting jobs, he earned a few extra dollars by doing publicity photos of other
actors. Soon acting was taking a back seat to photography; Alonzo began to devote
a great deal of his time to studying the cinematographer's role. Among his favorite
classic Hollywood cameramen were Walter Strenge, Floyd Crosby, Winton Hoch
and James Wong Howe.

It was, in fact, the late Howe, or "The Chinaman" as Alonzo affectionately
refers to him, who gave him his big break. Howe was shooting *Seconds* for John
Frankenheimer and Hollywood production was in such an upswing that Howe was
having trouble keeping a camera operator on the film. Alonzo, who had been
shooting documentaries for David L. Wolper, was sent down to the set to help out,
even though he didn't have a union card. Both Howe and Frankenheimer were so
impressed with his talent and enthusiasm that they went to bat for him in getting
him into the union.

After that, Alonzo's rise into the top echelon of American cinematographers
was relatively rapid, culminating in his Academy Award nomination for his superb
work on *Chinatown* in 1974. With such a calling card, he has been able to pick and
choose from the many projects offered to him every year. Recently, he has taken up
directing too, making his theatrical debut with *FM*, followed by several movies of
the week for television. He has no plans, however, to abandon cinematography in
favor of direction; in fact, on his television films he has skillfully handled both
directing and cinematography chores.

23

As Actor:
1960   *The Magnificent Seven*
1964   *Invitation to a Gunfighter*

As Director of Photography:
1969   *Bloody Mama*
1971   *Vanishing Point*
        Harold and Maude
        Get to Know Your Rabbit
1972   *Sounder*
        Lady Sings the Blues
1973   *Wattstax*
        Pete 'n' Tillie
1974   *Conrack*
        Chinatown †
1975   *The Fortune*
        Once Is Not Enough
        Farewell, My Lovely
1976   *I Will, I Will . . . for Now*
        The Bad News Bears
        Black Sunday

1977   *Casey's Shadow*
        Which Way Is Up?
1978   *The Cheap Detective*
        Norma Rae
1979   *Tom Horn*
1980   *Back Roads*
1981   *Zorro, the Gay Blade*
        The Kid from Nowhere (TV)
1982   *Blue Thunder*
        Crosscreek
1983   *Scarface*
1984   *Runaway*

As Director and
Director of Photgraphy (TV)
1978   *Champions: A Love Story*
1979   *Portrait of a Stripper*
1980   *Belle Starr*
        Blinded by the Light

As Director (theatrical)
1977   *FM*

† Academy Award Nomination for best achievement in cinematography.

I'd like to talk about some of the technical aspects of cinematography.

Fine. I'm not bored with technology. We're in a marvelous period to be cinematographers, because of the new technology that keeps coming out. We look a thousand percent better to a producer than someone like Jimmy Wong Howe did. Yet they didn't know what he went through. I mean, that man was running around with a 165-pound camera and here we run around with a 45-pound camera that you can manipulate and move around. Technology to me is not a boring subject. Anything you want to know I'll tell you, if I can.

Harold and Maude: the film had a sort of dreamy, somber look to it, and I'm wondering how that look was arrived at, and finally how you achieved it?

Well, Hal Ashby really was the instigator of that, as most directors usually are. They instigate what kind of a look they want. I wish that I could do that picture now, with what I know now. And also with the certain reputation that I have now, I could have been even braver than when I did that picture; because that was only the third film that I'd ever shot. And when I met Hal Ashby, I was very impressed with him because he'd done a picture called *The Landlord* that I liked very much. Haskell Wexler got me the job. He recommended me to Hal. So there I was in the position of really wanting to be gutsy and do something dramatically different. By the same token, I didn't want to ruin my friend's recommendation. And I must say Hal was very patient with me, and so I went a little bit but not as far as I would have liked to go. All Hal told me was that all the sequences with Harold in his home should have a certain sort of sterility; sort of clear, clean, pure, no diffusion. The angles were to be more symmetrical; sort of meat and potatoes. And every time we ended up with Maude, it would have a slight craziness to it, just a little kookiness, a little tip (of the camera) up, a little tip down, a little diffusion. Also in the answer print, every time it was Harold and Maude, or Maude, it was a slightly warmer, toastier, softer look. And Harold and his mother and by himself, it was a slightly colder world, maybe a more realistic world to him. I wasn't as brave then; I wish I could do that again.

Around that time you had, or I guess gained a reputation for working rather quickly and with great mobility. I think that's one of the reasons why you went on Sounder. *The producers thought that you could save some money.*

Yes, that was a very inexpensive film. Yes, I do work very fast. I don't think any picture I've shot has ever gone over schedule. But a lot of it is, to give the devil his due, not really so much how fast the cameraman is as what kind of communication and rapport he's got with the director. If that director is not communicative enough, then you find a lot of very fast cameramen are slowed way down. Now, the quality I have for working fast may be because I came from the world of documentaries. In documentaries I did everything myself. We functioned rather quickly, we had to get in and out, not for economic reasons but for expediency. So the first picture I did was *Bloody Mama* with Roger Corman, who is a fast person himself. Well, we just communicated very easily. He would say, "Are you ready?" I'd say, "Yes, I'm ready." Even if I wasn't ready, I would design something that would work. I was thinking two steps ahead of him. So not knowing any better, I just continued to work that way. Plus, I have tried to keep the same crew all the way through, who help me tremendously. They almost read my mind and they know how we work and how we function.

Now *Sounder* was what I consider my breakthrough into the big time as far as directors go. Marty Ritt was the first big, established director I ever worked with.

On *Sounder* Marty said to me, "It must have a lyrical quality," so you find that most good art is really terribly simple. The basis of good composition and good painting is simplicity itself. And Marty is such a good stager; he stages things so pretty. And I taught him a couple of things that I brought in from my world, and he taught me a great deal about directing. And he did that very fast, and very economically. The picture ended up costing only $860,000. So we did it fast but we had six or seven weeks; it wasn't like a movie of the week in 18 days.

He had this wonderful joke he performed for us all the time. He had his little trailer that he would park somewhere out of the picture and he'd say, "How long will it take you?" I'd say, "I don't know." He'd say, "Well, just call me when you're ready." And we'd watch him and just before he'd get to the trailer, we'd say, "Marty, we're ready." And he'd turn around and look and say, "You'd better be ready." We'd never let him get to his trailer.

If you had to analyze it, where do cameramen go wrong when they become slow? I mean, what quality do you have, what makes you fast, what things did you nurture to give you that speed?

Well, my theory, and really it's just a theory has to do with the fact that in documentaries you make instant decisions because your subject doesn't stand still for you. So you make decisions while you're looking through the finder. What is it you're going to stay with? And there's a certain bravura, I suppose, in letting the camera roll on someone and knowing that, if you stay on him, that's better than to pan over here where something more exciting is going on because out of that you might just end up with nothing. So it's that kind of training, plus the time limits that you have in documentaries. But when I brought that to features, I think that I unconsciously applied it.

Now, the other part of my theory is what might happen to some cameramen—and I don't know specifically if it applies to all of them—is that you do get to a certain point where you start working on pictures of great magnitude or some very important film, and people go around patting you on the back and saying, "Jesus, you're great, this guy is terrific. He is fast." You might start asking yourself "why?" And that will slow you down, you see. It happens. You reach a point when you say, "Wait a minute, why am I so good, what is it about me?" So, as a cameraman, you get there, you look at a set, you start to think about it, you start chewing on it too much and then, all of a sudden, you're taking too much time. I think that's what happens. I went through that to a degree, right after I did *Chinatown*.

On Vanishing Point, *you had a film crew traveling over a lot of space and you're filming a story that keeps moving, that's episodic. What are some of the problems that the cameraman has to face when shooting a film like that?*

The logistics, of course, were tough: the cameras, the heat and the dust. We'd take some great chances; we did some stunts with one or two cameras and never waited to see if the lab would say it was okay. We just went on to the next location. We were very lucky; we didn't lose a single frame, never lost any negative. For necessity's sake it was a very small crew; the entourage for the picture was bigger than the crew. I only had two grips and two electricians and myself and a couple of assistants and that was it.

What sort of problems did you have in the desert with the dust?

The cameras can get thrown into worse positions than they used to. An example would be in *Vanishing Point*, using the Arriflex so much. And to put it in the front of a car and shock the shit out of it. Well, that camera was designed as the gun camera for the Messerschmidt so that was a pretty secure camera, and we used it constantly, because it was a rugged piece of equipment. We were lucky it was just a straight Arri with no sync pulse at all, just a motor. We did have a sync camera, we shot an Arriflex sync camera. I made damned sure that I personally inspected those cameras within an inch of their lives. I went through all of them and it sounds silly to do that but you should do that. Under those circumstances, if I hadn't done it, I might have suddenly discovered in the middle of the desert that some strange refraction created a fog and ruined my film.

This is in the way of tests, going through and checking the camera?

That's one thing that a lot of filmmakers don't want to do. It's so boring to do that, but it's something that should be done.

The preparation and the boring aspects of checking scratches on film, checking the light-tightness of the magazine, and the lenses matching, that the motor's functioning, letting it run back long periods of time with dummy rolls—it pays off, psychologically it pays off. Maybe the guy that rents you the camera says it's perfect. Don't take his word for it, make sure it's perfect yourself.

On such mobile locations as those in Vanishing Point, *is it difficult with lighting? It seems like you're always on the run; do you use one light more, one type more than another?*

The lighting was very, very tough on *Vanishing Point* because sometimes you had to fight the exposure while he was driving the car. It was $f2.8$ inside and outside it was $f16$. When you have someone driving a car and, let's say for the sake of argument, the exposure reads $f2.8$ on his face and behind and through the windows, the background reads $f16$. Well, you're better off under-exposing him a full stop, maybe two stops to $f3.5$, $f4.5$, because when you print it, it looks more natural to have him darker than the car and the background will not look as hot.

Now, if you have the advantage of adding a light to it, and if the exterior is $f16$, and you can bring his exposure up to $f5.6$ and light him, then expose it down to $f8$, another stop, another stop and a half. Again you get a sure sense of reality and you'll never see the light. You don't know where the light's hitting; you only see it in his eyes. Also, when you have reflections on the windshield of a car, never expose it the way the light says to read it on the face, always over-expose it. Because over-exposure cuts through reflection on glass. You over-expose it and then print it down. In other words, if you used a spot-meter, the reflection would literally cover up the actor's face. Set somebody behind a steering wheel and take different exposures and then try it and see what will happen. It's the fastest way to learn a lesson that I learned the hard way. But it's an advantage because again it's expediency. You don't have to say, "Oh, I've got to pump him up with light." In the old days they used to. Some cameramen still do; they'll pump up the driver so much, like in *Adam-12*, or they'll cover the whole thing to get rid of reflections, which is not real.

You did Sounder *and* Lady Sings the Blues, *where the majority of the actors are black. Black obviously reflects differently than white; that's a fact of life. Do you have any special theories or special ways that you went about lighting them?*

Well, I had a theory. I found it's not a matter of how much light you put on black people, it's how little light you put on white people. In other words, you don't have to burn up Bill Cosby just to see him. Leave him alone, but don't put as much light on the white person. Expose for the black person and the white person will not be over-exposed. I just used that rule of thumb. There is an interesting facet of photographing black people as there is photographing a lot of us that have darker pigment in the skin. Diana Ross, for instance, had a sort of chocolate kind of quality to her skin, whereas Cicely Tyson had a slight bluish quality to her skin. So for Cicely I would use a warmer light; instead of a blue, daylight fill light it would be a regular tungsten warm light, and it would give her a little warmth to her skin. With Diana Ross having this little warm quality against Billy Dee Williams, her eye light always was a little colder blue to bring her back within the range of Billy Dee. You find that's true about all black people in the sense that they reflect a certain cast. And the film being very sensitive to blue, it is the one color that you really don't want to introduce into their faces. I found that just playing around with the light and accentuating the best features of a person as you would do with a white person, is just really the way to attack the problem of lighting black people. And the other theory is not to put as much light on them as you might think.

Sounder and Lady Sings the Blues *were both period pieces. One was an urban period piece and the other a rural period piece. I'm wondering what went into your lighting of both those films to enhance the periodness of them.*

Well, *Sounder* was an exterior picture and I tried to give the interiors a sort of available-light quality. In other words light comes in through a window, that's what the inside should look like. That's the way it is. And also with the night interiors, we tried to give them a certain available-light quality and let the bugs float around the lamps and all of that. The only difficult thing about *Sounder* was the beginning; the coon chase. And I called Jimmy Wong Howe on that. That's how the picture starts at night, chasing the coon. Where does light come from? And I called Jimmy (he was very sick at the time) and I said, "You know Marty better than I and I'm about to give him an idea but I don't want it to blow up in my face." And he said, "What's your idea?" And I said, "My idea is that we shouldn't shoot it day-for-night just in order to see. The audiences nowadays are too hip and they know exactly what's going on. Why not shoot it at night and light it, but instead of lighting it from a high angle, light it from very low angles; just straight shots, light through the trees. Make it graphic, a graphic look, because it is the beginning of the picture and you want to set up a certain pace to it."

He agreed with me: "Tell Marty I said so and if he gives you any trouble, you tell him that's the way it should be done." He was a feisty old man; I loved him. So I approached Marty and he said, "Well, I don't know what you're talking about. Try it, see how it turns out." Chasing and following the lantern very close through the forest, through the trees was very interesting. Instead of really trying to track through the forest with that thing, I sat on a Lazy Susan with a hand-held Arri following the thing very close and asked Paul Winfield and the little boy to run around me; and every once in a while to go around one tree, come back around the tree and back and forth like that, changing sides. And I did a 360° spin and they ran around 360°. Well, when you cut that shot in you can't tell it's going around; it looks like it's going right straight through the forest. And that was it. Also I had lights hidden behind trunks shooting right at them and sometimes right at the lens, but you wouldn't see the source of the light, you'd just see a flare of lighting. And it added a certain excitement to the whole thing. All those shadows, if you notice, are going straight across, they're not down. The purist would say, "Well, that's not source light, that's the cameraman's light." But you must think in terms of the material that applies.

Day interiors were done as naturally as possible. I did use reflectors way out in the distance and shot them through windows so that they would burn up as they went through. But, if you notice, it was really real. I made sure that you were never really aware of a key light on an actor in *Sounder*. Even if it was outdoors and you had to use an arc for some reason or other, I would use it but the lens had to be stopped down so much that it really had very little effect except in the eyes. So you didn't have a lit quality, if that's possible.

So essentially what you did was just try to light it as naturally as possible and any period quality would be picked up from the sets?

From the subject, right? From the behavior and the artwork. See, it's a good point for all cameramen to take in. It really applies not just to period pictures, it can apply to everything. I've seen Gordon Willis do it very well, I've seen Owen Roizman do it. What happens is that they take a situation in a room and they look at it the way it really looks and all they do is intensify up to exposure, and then stop it down a little bit more so that intensification doesn't show. And that's the best trick I could advise anybody about doing the naturalistic type of photography. It's like Rembrandt lighting.

*I can remember scenes in.*The Godfather *where Willis did that.*

Even the silhouette scenes, he had lights on those people. Because of the chemistry and the mathematics of the negative, you must have some light, otherwise it's kind of greyish mud. He had light on them but he still stopped it down so you didn't see the light on them and they still were silhouettes. That's the best rule to follow, if you want the so-called available-light, natural look.

Now, compared to Sounder, Lady Sings the Blues *was much different. I guess that gave you more room to . . .*

That was more show-biz and you could do more lighting effects. And I went in for color there, a lot of color. Some of the nightclubs had canvas ceilings so instead of lighting the ceilings from underneath, I shot lights through the canvas and put dots of light on the canvas. I tried to create an atmosphere that even the camera may not have seen, but it was an atmosphere for Diana Ross. For example we'd have a window on the set which the camera never saw. But I would put little twinkly lights out there and traffic lights going through so when she looked out the window she could see something. And a lot of times it's good for a cameraman to do that, and to help the director in that respect. Because sometimes you have actors that really must function in an atmosphere that is not a movie set. Which is another reason I very seldom take walls out in the set—I feel that if I keep the walls in, it keeps the actors in. It makes them think that they're really in the atmosphere where they belong. And *Lady Sings the Blues* gave me an excuse to be more bizarre; I threw light in whether there was a reason for it or not, if I liked it. In other words, I never had an excuse. You saw a very cold, dry look when she was shooting herself up in the white bathroom; a tricky exposure. That applies again for shooting a black object in a white room, a dark object in a white room. Again, you don't take the walls into consideration. Expose for that face of the black person and then you can always print it up or print it down. And also soft light in a white room is much better than hard light. Hard light will bounce the white right back at you. We had smoke effects on that film which I hadn't done before, and colored smoke wherever possible. For the period cars and exteriors I had a light fog filter to give it a little period-ness. In the beginning of the picture I used too much fog, I think.

You fogged the cars to make it not look like they just rolled off the assembly line.

That's right. I also used nets. When I shot her face I used nets, like hair nets, to put in front of the lens for that purpose. To just take it out of the realm of reality and more into the period piece. When she was very, very young I had fog filters and nets to give it a kind of way-back-when quality. And the colors were simple; it was not overly colorful. It didn't get colorful really until she walked into the nightclub. Then she saw her new world, which was the nightclub she wanted to sing in.

It seems that you're one of the few cameramen who give credit to the set de-signer and the art director and the wardrobe people.

You have the set decorator, the wardrobe designer and also the wardrobe person. They break down scripts just like I break down scripts to shoot. Theirs is probably more complicated in the initial stages. And then they're at the mercy of the camerman. They really are. And I hate it. I respect fellow artists and I hate it when you don't utilize what they've gone to a great deal of trouble to do. In *Harold and Maude* the art director gave Maude's place a boxcar full of detail. They knew that the camera sometimes would never pick up some of the stuff but they were creating an atmosphere, and I was always conscious and aware of that. But when you work with people like Harry Horner, Richard Sylbert and Dean Tavalouris, they had that attitude to begin with. They always figured that they couldn't go to a cameraman and say, "Get your ass over here and look at what I'm doing." It really is incumbent upon the cameraman to approach the production designer, and not the other way around, because he is going to be the responsible party for putting that image up there. A very good thing to talk about would be Dean Tavalouris and I on *Farewell, My Lovely.* Dean had just finished doing the *Godfathers.* I had just finished doing *Chinatown.* And here we are doing a period picture again, very similar to what we'd been doing. So we had the task of avoiding copying ourselves, and we also had to work very closely together because I was trying very hard not to make it look like *Chinatown* and it was very near to the same period; and he was going to try not to art direct it similar to the *Godfathers* that he'd done. So we were very trepidacious about that. I attacked it first of all by shooting with Fuji film. And that was different. I used a net for the whole thing which I hadn't done before. I used more color than we had done in *Chinatown*, with far more reds, blue lights and green lights. And he had a wonderful, wonderful idea of the sheen and polish on the wood that he hadn't really done as much on the *Godfathers.* And the sort of abstract way that he furnished rooms was great.

You have previously said that Chinatown *was your masterpiece. This is the film where all the elements came together, where everything coalesced.*

Up to that point in my career, yes, it was the culmination of a lot of experience put to use and it did offer the opportunity to try things I had never tried to photograph.

Could you elaborate on that? What things were involved there that didn't come together on pictures before?

I think I said this before; it particularly had to do with Polanski and the way he handled the whole thing. He brought everybody up to a level of competence: the prop man, the production designer, the wardrobe designer, all the heads of departments involved in the movie. He sort of psyched us up to such a degree that we were all putting out top, top efficiency. It gave him a great deal of security to know that when I was going to walk on the set it was going to be perfect. It was a concept that we all had in mind. In other words, none of the little irritations were there like "I forgot to do this or I forgot to do that; there wasn't enough money to do this." It was immaculately produced. To everybody involved, that gave us a sense of freedom to really go into the aesthetics or into that realm of trying to create something better in compositions, lighting, and camera moves. We did them with absolute security that everybody else's job had been finished and was complete and we could be brave and try different things. And Roman would put me to the task many times, not necessarily how difficult it was to light it but rather to light it in a fashion so that it carried a visual look that was even throughout the whole piece.

Polanski didn't want any diffusion and I guess that caused some problems. Will you talk about that?

Well, the first cameraman hired was Stanley Cortez. And Roman hired Stanley because he had shot *The Magnificent Ambersons*. They had a big artistic difference, the two of them. Cortez did not want to photograph Faye Dunaway without diffusion and without the proper lighting, and Roman didn't want that. He wanted to put on film a sort of natural but somber kind of look. And Dick Sylbert had his act together; those sets were brilliant. He had them all designed perfectly. And he had indulged the cameraman, given him places to put giant lights and all of that. It was just a big difference of opinion and so they fired Cortez. And I was called in immediately, like overnight. I read the script on Thursday night; I met with Bob Evans and the producers and I met Roman Polanski on the set on Friday morning to shoot one scene: the barbershop scene. And we had a little dialogue and shot that little scene and quit. Then we went to Bob Evans's house to look at all of Roman Polanski's films. The three of us sat there and looked at films; I asked him questions, he asked me questions, and he wanted to make sure that my head was going to be where his was. And I said, "I have no objections to shooting it without diffusion." I said, I do have a theory and I tried to point it out to him and he went along with it. I said, "In the anamorphic aspect ratio, there's a workhorse lens called the 40mm lens. The reason I like that lens for shooting and the reason I like to shoot Panavision anamorphic (the anamorphic ratio is 2.35 to 1) is because it is probably the best representation of true human perception." You and I see—you can check me out on this—we see a great deal with peripheral vision, but our brain can really only compute about 15-20° this way and about 40° this way. No matter what distance you're at, the angle remains the same. That's what the brain can really conceive. And also, our brain can see that perspective. That perspective is *this* room is *this* size.

The best way for a cameraman to check that out is put a zoom lens on a camera, a 25mm to 250mm lens, or any zoom lens that has that range, look through the lens with one eye at somebody's face and look at the person's face with the eye that's not looking through the lens and then match those images. The left eye sees one size; now keep zooming the lens until the lens gets approximately the same size. And you're looking at somewhere between a 37 and a 47mm lens. So now this is what I'm saying about the anamorphic process. I said to Roman, "To me the 40mm lens is the best reproduction of what the human being perceives as correct perspective. Really, it's like a 43-44mm, sometimes a 45 depending on the set." And I said, "If we shoot the whole picture, as much as possible, with a 40mm lens, we'll have really a reproduction of the sets the way they are." Dick Sylbert immediately said, "I know that. If I could get a cameraman to shoot everything with a 40mm, I'd be very happy."

And as far as diffusion was concerned, I was perfectly willing as long as he was willing, you see. You do have that situation sometimes, where you have a producer or a director say, "I want her to look ravishing. I don't care what you do." But up front we understood that we were going to try to photograph raw beauty and Faye Dunaway is not difficult to photograph without any diffusion. Plus Roman had another thing which I thought was very interesting. He liked putting the camera very close to the performers, right on top of them. Now that's an intimidating thing to any actress who is so beautiful. Well, it added to her performance, I really believe, it made her nervous. Because here is this camera; here I am on top of her with a camera. So my task was to angle the camera in such a position where I got the least amount of distortion. And Roman never questioned me on that. I would try to line up the camera dead center to her eyes so at least her close-ups did not distort. We even shot some with the 40mm lens which is really dangerous.

And you tried to put the camera where?

At an angle. In other words, where the film plane is parallel to the plane of the face. If you move the camera one way, you distort the chin; if you move it another way, you may distort the forehead or the nose. So you have to find just the right height and watch it very closely.

In Repulsion *he used that to great effect especially toward the end of the film.*

There was reason in everything that Roman did. I, of course, had a ball with it, because it was giving me a chance to do a certain kind of lighting. We put ceilings on all the sets. We sprayed them, we put lights through them. We used black-and-white drops outside instead of color drops. So it looked like the city was washed out; there was no color outside through the windows. And Roman showed me about perspective again. He said, "That backing back there is out of whack. Tip it this way so when we look through the lens it'll straighten up or tip it this way to back it up." I mean, the man's brilliant as far as his technology is concerned. So I learned a great deal from him and I taught him a great deal about composition within that aspect ratio of 2.35 to 1. You don't have to fill the edges of the screen.

You do it with lighting if you want to fill the edges, or let the edges go. And then it looks more like an old-fashioned view camera when you look through the viewfinder. The edges are dark but there's the center. It's a D. W. Griffith kind of bright center and dark toward the edges. So he liked that, it appealed to him. Another thing to consider for a cameraman is that there is something to be said when you use symmetry, composition. A close-up of you, for instance, using a 40mm lens and with the window moldings back there; if you're shooting slightly down, those window moldings will climb a little bit this way. If you're slightly up, they will do something else. So it's always best to try to shoot straight on; keep that symmetry going wherever possible. And if you notice, a lot of artists, when they paint something, will sometimes bend a tree so that it's parallel to the frame that they paint it to. And I used that unconsciously in *Harold and Maude* and in almost all those pictures because I've studied art. Since you have a "hard matte" to work with on the screen, if there's a wall or building to the edge of the screen, I make sure that the gap is not like this or like that, but it's perfectly parallel. In other words, the edges of your information are parallel to the edges of the screen. It's a subconscious thing, and I think that people will like it. They won't know why; but wherever possible you do that and try to straighten it out.

There are certain directors that always shoot at eye level. Bresson's films are always right at eye level.

It's effective. Also just because one person is standing and one person is sitting, you don't have to shoot the person sitting down from the point of view of the person standing up. It's quite legitimate to drop down here and let that person look at the top of the screen. It's legitimate to be parallel up here and let that person look down the screen. It works. Only when you want to do a Kubrickesque type of situation where you want that distortion. I did a lot of that in *The Cheap Detective*. I copied all the great old films and copied shots and so on. But that's an important thing studying composition for the 2.35 to 1 format; for the spherical format it's a little more square, it's a little different. And there you're locked into using the wider angle lenses. *Farewell My Lovely* was shot with the wider angle lenses and in spherical as opposed to anamorphic.

It seemed from reading your American Cinematographer *article that you like to use a lot of lights; you don't have any problem with lights, using as many lights as you need or want. With some other cameramen, it seems their attitude from the beginning is the least amount of lights as possible. Would you say that's true?*

Not really, in reality I like to use very few lights. I mean, that's one of the problem things. On *Chinatown* they had a 40-foot van full of lights that I never used; I just got rid of it. The budget savings were enormous. They had lights strung up all along the catwalks and I got rid of them; I don't need them. In the morgue scene with Jack Nicholson, all I had was one chicken coop coming straight down and a light on the camera, so that wherever he went you would never see the shadow. That, to me, is no light at all.

A "chicken coop?" What is that?

A "chicken coop" is a very old type of lighting fixture. It's a giant sort of box with these great big bulbs that are painted silver on the bottom. The wattages of the bulbs are enormous and they're screwed up into the coop which is painted white so it reflects and gives you a soft top light. Then there is a piece of chicken wire across the bottom to protect the actors from the danger of breaking glass. It's a device that's been around for years. So we used a chicken coop and we put a black skirt around it so it just became a soft pool of light from the top. And the only front light I used was a light mounted on the camera itself. The shadow from that light went directly behind the actor and you'd never see it.

But I don't like to use a lot of light, depending on the picture. On *The Fortune*, we used a tremendous amount of different lighting. I was using a great deal of light in the background as opposed to on the actors themselves. I was sort of painting with light, really changing the aspects of the little bungalows and so on. I used a lot more individual, small units and so the amount of light was greater. I don't like to use a lot of light because it has an effect on the actors when they have a tremendous amount of light on them. You lose a certain amount of reality. You'd be amazed at the difference in a performance when an actor has to go to a regular lamp and one lamp lights the whole scene. They get the feeling that they're really where they're supposed to be. It's psychological plus it also has a very interesting look. Gordon Willis proved that.

But it's wrong to think that because you've got a lot of paint you're going to get a good painting. You can have a wonderful painting with just one color. I mean, children can show you that in a child's drawing. They'll stick to particular colors and it looks wonderful. Picasso loved to do that. On *Lady Sings the Blues* I had a lot more lighting. On *Black Sunday*, for the effects that I had to have on the sound stages because of the front-screen and rear-screen projection, I had a tremendous amount of lighting. But that was to bring up a key. And I totally disagree with the philosophy of the old cameramen that you take a giant 10K and then put a Christmas tree in front of it. What do you prove? Just that you're very clever at using one light to do the job of five or six other lights? I'd rather just key the person with one light there, put another light over here, you know, and then a little backlighting wherever possible.

Do you believe that source light is a sacred commandment? Or is it like painting?

No, it's like painting. Rembrandt never gave you a source light really. If you look at his work very closely he's got a lot of stuff coming from different directions and you don't know why. It's not important. Jimmy Wong Howe is the one that told me that. He said, "Source lighting is only for the American Society of Cinematographers conventions." He said, "You do it any way you want to. Do what looks the best." Source lighting is totally impossible in some situations. For example, a dark bedroom at night with no light on; where's the light coming from? Certainly not by moonlight. And if you really tried to reproduce the moonlight effect through a window it looks like daylight. So what do we do in movies? We put a blue filter on it and say, "Hey, it's moonlight." It should be done to the taste of the cameraman, the way he thinks. There's no such thing as a rule or a commandment about that.

We understand that Norma Rae *was shot 99% hand-held. What sort of lighting problems did you encounter?*

Tougher ones because the camera wandered around everywhere. And being in practical locations, we couldn't necessarily hang lighting units from up above. In the factory, it was all fluorescent lighting so again, we mounted a light on the camera. I had a very clever gaffer who could adjust the dimmer on it if an actor got too close. In the houses and other places where we had to go hand-held, Marty and I would talk about it and he would give me a corner to work in and I could light from that direction. Or I would light through the windows if it was daylight and just let them burn up. Now when I was shooting an actor directly against a window, I would neutralize or neutral density the window to balance it out. But most of the time, when the actor was away from the window, I'd take the neutral density out and let the light coming through the window be the key light and use white cards to balance it. It presents a lot of problems because with a hand-held camera, you never know where it's going to be. It's also tough on the sound man because he doesn't know where the headroom is all the time with the boom. So the sound man had to use radio microphones all the time just to cover himself.

If you had to give advice to a young student or cameraman about the lab, what kind of advice would you give?

I'd say learn everything you can about the lab because laboratories are not unlike a lot of the highly technical people that you meet sometimes in life. They can razzle-dazzle you with technological mumbo-jumbo, you know, especially if they don't know who you are. And a lot of times it's done just to impress themselves, but a lot of times it's done just to sort of get rid of you. "The lab will fix it," is a common cliché. There's no such thing. They can, to a degree, help you but any filmmaker, cameraman, director or producer, should really know the goings-on in a laboratory; how it functions and why it works the way it works and what your limitations are. Even if it's just a simple thing that you know that they have a printer scale of 0–50 lights and the preferential exposure is a 25 light. Then if you just know that much, when the man says you printed at 26, 27, 29, you know what he's talking about and you should know that those three lights refer to the cyan, magenta and yellow colors. If you know just that much already, the lab can't bullshit you. You should also know the inner workings of their back-end of the picture, back-end of production. Why they have to make the CRI [color reversal internegative] in a certain way. What's a CRI? And why can they only give you so many release prints? Because as a cameraman, if you're going to give them a very delicate negative to work with because that's what you want, you must tell them; most of the time they say don't do that because we may not be able to give you a release print. You will be able to come back and say, "Yes, you will. All you have to do is make me the best CRI in the world, make three of them if necessary. I don't care how many you have to make but protect my original and don't touch it." If you didn't do that they would talk you into shooting the picture differently just to accommodate them. That's happened to me many times even at this stage of my career now where the MGM lab tried to tell me how to shoot *Casey's Shadow*. And

I said, "No, you're wrong. I'll expose it the way I want to expose it because I know it can be done." Also on *The Cheap Detective* it was the same way. The bottom line is the MGM lab lost *The Cheap Detective* because they couldn't come through.

We've heard other people say that there is no substitute for a strong director. That the director's strength filters down to everybody and it makes everyone feel secure.

Sure. I totally concur. The director is the leader of the thing, supposedly the man in charge. Although the cinematographers are more and more becoming the titular heads of the crew. They are in a sense the right arm of the director. They supply the spit to get the crew to do what the director wants. The director doesn't have to be strong technically; he doesn't have to know if he wants a particular 75mm lens here. He can just say, "I want a shot this size here." Now he relies on your competence and knowledge to know what lens to use for that shot. But he polices the creativity of everybody; unless he does that people are left floundering. You know, all of a sudden you have inconsistencies, from hair dressing to wardrobe. The director really has to be very strong in communicating exactly what he wants and in being faithful to what he has said and not wavering because the minute he wavers everybody sort of feels that lean, and it's not good. It's not good when a cameraman suddenly gets a reputation of being the guy who really helped to direct a picture. I've heard that about some cameramen. Or the guy who was really in charge was the cameraman and the director sort of followed him around. That's not the way the system is designed.

That's what people have said. People we've talked to that have been in situations similar to that have said that invariably their camera work suffered because if they had to pull the director along they didn't have time to do what they wanted to do and should have been doing in the first place.

And it's not fair; it's not fair to the cameraman. Because you have a situation where you like the project and the director says, "Help me out." Sometimes they say that, "Help me out, I don't know what to do here." Well, your concentration goes now into his realm of creativity and yours has to suffer somewhat. I don't like to be put into that position. That's probably why I'm more selective now as to who I would work for. Marty Ritt is my mentor, my hero; if I can get on a Marty Ritt picture every time, I'll be very happy.

Talking about Martin Ritt, is there any special spark of creativity when you have worked with a director a few times? Is there some kind of electricity or is it you just work together really well, that allows you to produce such good work?

Marty is the only experience I can give you as I have worked for him more than anybody else. I've done six pictures with him. What happens is, I can't really describe it. It is a chemistry situation. It's just something that functions. I have a tremendous love for the man and his talent. He has a tremendous amount of respect for anybody that knows what they're doing, and that already opens the door for anybody to be creative. And I can't tell you what it is; all I know is that if he called me to do a picture tomorrow and I have another picture going, I'll drop the other picture and go with him. Because I know that under his auspices and guidance, I will have total freedom to just go as far as I want to photographically. Plus he also, in his own way, teaches me a great deal about directing, which I want to learn about. He teaches me a great deal about the discipline of filmmaking and I find myself making sure that when I compose a shot it isn't a self-indulgent thing; it isn't a cameraman's shot but it's something that's appropriate to the story and he brings that out in you. I think maybe that's what happens with a lot of other relationships like that. The director and cameraman are almost equal in stature but yet each one knows his position. I don't know what else to tell you about that. It's not easy to be articulate about it.

It's a tough thing but there's a lot of people out there who want to break into the industry. Can you say what's the best way, or the way that worked for you?

Everybody's gotten in differently. For me, it was a matter of being there at the right time and being tenacious about it. That should apply to everybody who wants to get into the industry. There's no such thing as just flipping right into becoming a cameraman. And this really sounds boring, like an old cameraman talking, but if someone had told me in 1969, "You got to shoot *Black Sunday*," I would not have been prepared. I would not have known how to do that. So that somehow God gave me the thing to do at the right time. *Bloody Mama* showed me I could do that kind of picture and *Vanishing Point* was still within the realm of reality for me. By the time I went to *Get to Know Your Rabbit*, I had two pictures under my belt; enough to control people, enough to know how to work stage lighting. *Sounder* was very tough. *Lady Sings the Blues* was tougher, and so that by the time I got to *Black Sunday* my control of the technology was totally secure.

I was in the union retroactive to 1964, but actually did not become a union Group 1 until 1966. And in three years time, by 1969, I was shooting a picture, and that's very fast. And I've not been out of work since. But a lot of that has to do with the quality of what I can do, and a lot of it has to do with being tenacious enough to study and to learn. Because I didn't go to school, but I don't say that you shouldn't go to school. If you go to school, you get a lot of that out of your way. But if you want to get in, go to work, if you can, for a documentary house or go to work for a commercial house, public television but whatever you do, don't stop shooting. Keep shooting and teaching yourself, go out and do it even if it's just a still camera you're using, develop your own stuff, look at it. That taught me a lot. I learned a lot. Get books like, hopefully, this one. It will provoke questions. I give a lot of cinematographers' manuals to people, not because they're necessarily the Bible but they will provoke questions. Why use a neutral density filter? Why? Why an 85B as opposed to 85A or 85C? The book doesn't tell you, but if you look at it and you see this guy is using a 23A and a 20 something 5 red and blue filters to shoot day for night in black and white—why? And it gets the saliva going and gets all of these fundamentals into a nice secure place so you can say, "I know it." Now someone says I want to shoot this kind of picture and you've got the technology out of the way and you can get into the artistic realm.

That goes back to what you were saying about being able to look at a situation and make decisions. You're secure because you've been there. And therefore you know what you're doing and you do it. So, like you said, I guess that takes time.

I think that's what kids nowadays can do; shoot film, borrow cameras, do whatever they can but keep shooting. If you can get a fairly decent film together, there are enough people in this town who will look at it and that's a way to get into it. Then if you have the fortitude to stay in a loading room, if you have to be in a loading room—be in a loading room. Whatever way you can get in because there is a tremendous need for new cameramen in the industry. The old ones are not being accepted by the new directors, you know. The new guys, the kids coming out of UCLA and USC that are directors, they don't want to hear from an old cameraman. They want a Zsigmond, they want a Kovacs, and if there's a better one coming up, they want him. They want Michael Chapman or they want one of these new guys who are coming up. Fujimoto, they want him now, because he's done something. Also because he relates closer to them; maybe they are on the same level intellectually. I intimidate certain new directors, you know, and so does Gordon Willis and people like that. You get a new guy who calls you up and says, "Do you mind shooting this for me?" Well you can hear in their voices; they automatically assume that I'll say, "No" or "Here's the way you do it, kid." I don't do that. I have worked with first-time directors and I don't think a single one will tell you that I have ever ramrodded him in any way whatsoever. I may have coaxed them to do better, but that's the reason they would go for newer people and there's a need for those people.

You can go to work for commercial houses that have a union/non-union situation. You go to work for their non-union situation. You must make a pest of yourself. Otherwise you ain't going to get anywhere, they aren't going to come to you, and that's always the advice I give. The union is not that difficult. First of all, it's not a hiring hall. They don't get you the job, so don't make them a bad guy right off the bat. Use them.

What about documentary work? What did that, in a nutshell, basically teach you that would come in really handy later on in features?

What I learned primarily from documentaries was coverage. In documentaries, a lot of times, you are forced to cut the material yourself, but when you have a situation, an event happening and you are documenting it, obviously you can't be at both places at once with one camera, so you must make the decision of how to cover it kind of like a master shot. When the event is over with, somehow find some other element that is the cutaway from when you were out of focus or whatever and if you learn that, it applies to features, even better. If you really know that, you can make a feature run much faster. You can say to the director, "Here's a place you can cut." The most important thing you learn is how to think on your feet. Which is really the basis of what a good cameraman is: to be able to think on your feet. The one thing it does not teach you, because you're by yourself and you don't have a director, is how to handle people. But that you can evolve in projects when you work with other people doing your own films. You can learn how that cameraderie has to be established by going on sets. The egos in this industry are so horrendous that you really should study how not to behave, you know what I mean?

On your first feature, Bloody Mama, *how did it feel that first day and you were finally the DP, you were to run the crew. How did you prepare for it?*

I didn't know anybody in the crew. Roger Corman was a major producer and he was directing. I got my crew just from the recommendations of the American International people. And so when somebody would say to me, "Well how many 10Ks do you want?" I really didn't know. So I kept my cool as much as possible and tried to visualize from what I had seen at Fox, the behavior of the cameramen, and what I had done in documentaries; out of that came a behavior where I made, thank God, the right decisions. So I talked to Roger; he said, "I want a very raw, cold look. I don't want anything glamorous." And also I went to the lab. At that time the lab had nothing to do with me because I was nobody and they said, "Well, do some tests and we'll develop them for you." Well, I didn't have the facility to shoot tests and I didn't get a chance to test anything. So I really went very unprepared, and the crew I got was not the world's greatest. They were the ones who wouldn't cross the line; the electricians wouldn't help the grips, etc. But because I came from documentaries I was physically doing work myself and that was against the rules too. But Roger kind of liked that. He liked the fact that I climbed up a ladder and set a light and did this and that. Eventually I charmed the crew into kind of joining me a little bit and they liked the idea. So maybe what I was doing was whistling when I was afraid, you know what I mean. Because there's no such thing as not being able to do it, unless you're totally ignorant about it. I can't tell you that I was cocky and confident. You know I was scared that I would make a mistake and waste people's money. But the nice thing about Roger was that he didn't focus on it. He saw the dailies. I expected something like, "This is not right and that is not right," and all that. He looked at them and said, "Okay, John. Very good. Thank you." So I said, "Okay, if that's the attitude, I'll just keep on doing what I'm doing."

I suppose if you had a more insecure director, it could be very easy to blame things on you.

Or a new director who needed a lot of help. I would not have been able to give him as much help, at that point. It was a good experience for me. As I say, it was something that I could handle, at that time. The technology that I knew was just enough to handle that picture. Of course, you had damn good actors who were in control. And I did a lot of hand-held in it because I was an expert and was very secure at that. Roger loved it. He never really worked with anybody who did a good hand-held job; so I did it, again violating the rules of the union because the operator that I had couldn't do it as well as I could do it.

As you advanced in budgets with each picture, did it present any problems to you in the sense that you're working on a $600,000 picture and the next picture is suddenly $1½ million? Or were they all at increments that you could handle?

Let me tell you this. I've never been aware of the budget from the point of view that I say, "Well, I've got enough money, I can do this." I try to do everything as economically as possible. Because I know that appeals first to the production manager and producer. They love it. The cameraman says, "Well, forget the 10Ks, we can do it with two 5Ks, it's cheaper." Well, I never have to get into that point with them because I'm always very cost-conscious. If I have the money and it does not have a bearing as to what equipment I'm going to use, I tell them what I need, you know. Then they tell me, "You can't afford it." Then I say, "Okay, we'll go in this direction." On *Black Sunday* I had to have 35 arcs and they said, "John!?!" But I said, "There is no other way of doing it." I said, "Check me out, check out the technology. You know there's no other way of doing it." And they said, "Okay." So there's no problem. And because of that attitude, I think that's one of the reasons I probably get along well with production people. With *Norma Rae* I did not take a generator. I took four electricians and four grips. It's a 5-million-dollar picture; I could have taken more. I could have taken more lights to cover myself and to make sure that if I needed something I had it. But I knew that I didn't need it, you see. I always make sure the production manager, the director and the producer are aware of that because as long as they know that about me, they know that I'm not bullshitting them when I suddenly say to them I need $55,000 today for lighting. They'll say, "Okay, you've got it." There's never a question about that. And my crew has been taught to do the same thing. Never over-order. Don't do what they call "protect the cameraman" bullshit. Just order what you think is necessary. Because one of these days you're going to run into a nice young Francis Ford Coppola who's got a little movie he wants to make and wants to make it for a nickel and, if you don't know how to do it, you know, you're just fooling yourself. You're going back in reverse. I've seen Billy Fraker shoot very tiny, cheap movies and very big movies and so have I, and the budgets have always been a point. The only thing I'll fight for in a budget is the crew's salary. Because I work with such small crews, I want them to be paid for it.

This may not be a fair question, but is the cameraman who shot Vanishing Point *the same cameraman who shot* Norma Rae?

I think so. I know a lot more now. I know a hell of a lot more now. I wish I knew as much when I shot *Vanishing Point*. It would have been a lot better. Whenever you have a quality that is good, you try to maintain that good quality all the time; sometimes it means cutting into yourself a little bit, cutting into your own ego. To knock your ego down, to go back to your roots to what you were really good at. The bravery of hand-holding the camera not because you want to show you can do it but because that's the way to do it at that moment; not doing it because I'm Mr. Big and I have to show off. The guts to say, "I'm sorry, Marty, it's going to take five hours for the shot." In *Vanishing Point*, I was able to say that because I didn't know any better, but now I know not to say that to certain people because it will scare the shit out of them. But the bravery, the guts to say, "That's it; no more or no less, that's the best shot and that's what we should do." The guts to say to Marty, "It's 2:00 in the afternoon, the light is totally wrong." When I did *Vanishing Point* I didn't know any better and I thought you could say that but I found out later that you couldn't do that; you could get into a lot of trouble by saying that to a director or producer. With Marty, because of our relationship, I'm able to do that because we were going for quality. But the no-generator idea took a lot of guts. To do a major picture like *Norma Rae* with very little light and no generator was not a grandstand move on my part, it was just an impulse I had. I knew it could be done and it disciplined me to do the lighting in a certain way. I wouldn't have the convenience of big lights. I thought that would give a picture quality no one else has done recently.

How did the advances in lenses and film speeds change the way you do things? I mean, over the past ten years, they just keep getting better and better.

Oh, dramatically. When Panavision designed the so-called PSR camera, which was much lighter than the Mitchell, right away they designed a smaller dolly and it wasn't necessary to have the giant dolly. They came out with speed lenses and it was a big rage for a while to shoot with them. And then almost immediately came the Panaflex, the little tiny camera, and the speed lenses. The laboratories, TVC in New York and Deluxe and Technicolor here in Los Angeles, all were into experimenting and have accomplished a great deal in development of film, to the point where you can force a picture two stops. *The Cheap Detective* was forced two stops all the time. *Black Sunday* was forced one stop all the time and sometimes two. On *Norma Rae*, all the interiors were at a process of 600 ASA and done by Deluxe. Instead of doing it by time and temperature, they do it chemically, similar to the TVC process but much better quality. It's terrific quality. Now in the beginning, when all these advances came up, faster film, faster lenses, we would go out and shoot available light at $f1.1$ or $f1.2$, and we'd say, "Oh, it's terrific." Of course, a lot of things were out of focus because there was no depth of field. Now I've been working more on pictures where I don't necessarily use less light. I keep the same amount of light but I stop the lens down more. I mean, you see it in *The Cheap Detective* and it's a very subtle thing. But because I forced it two stops, most of my average shooting in interiors was $f4.5-f5.6$, which gave the anamorphic lenses more depth of field than people are used to seeing. Things were in focus.

If you shot it normally, you'd have so much light in there to get a $f5.6$ that you'd burn up the actors. If you forced it, it was grainy. And also the Panaflex in *Chinatown* proved to be invaluable. You can put the Panaflex in a bathroom without taking the walls out and shoot scenes in there. I mean, it's not only a dramatic advantage to the director but it's also a physical advantage for the cameraman. So in the last ten years there have been radical changes.

All of this is challenging the filmmakers. Fortunately for us, the filmmakers are new people, like Francis Ford Coppola, people that are up with that technology. It's very difficult for directors that come from the old school to get used to it. Marty Ritt, with whom I've done six pictures, has kept up with the times. I mean, he loved it. *Norma Rae* we shot 99% hand-held. There's maybe four shots that are not hand-held in that picture. Now there's a director from the so-called old school who has got the guts to do it. I'm not saying that others are not around, they just haven't had the opportunity. Maybe they haven't had any of us to work with.

What has been your experience with the new higher-speed Kodak film stock 5293?

I shot all of *Scarface* with 5293; all of *Crosscreek* was with 5293. I've had very good experience with it. The interesting experience with 5293 was doing *Crosscreek*; we were shooting in mostly daylight situations and using a high-speed film outdoors. Normally you don't need high-speed film for that. But we were able to use it very effectively in the swamps under the trees where it's very dark. The 5247 stock would not have been enough in that situation unless we had a lot of light. Shooting in the swamps, you see daylight way in the distance but mostly it's shadow inside. 5293 picked up good detail in the shadows and did not let the distant sunlight overexpose too much. It was very valuable to me. We were able to use it in the wee hours of the day or in the morning; we just kept changing the ratings for the appropriate exposure. Of course, we stayed with the same film stock at night. I knew what the film could do at night and that was no problem. The question was basically if it could hold up as well and be equal to the quality of 5247 on day exteriors. And I found that it was.

I also understand that the 5294 stock is now out; this stock is supposed to be a refined version of 5293.

I have used it. It's probably a little bit finer-grained stock. I find that the latitude is very good; if forgives you for over- and underexposing a bit. It doesn't make an enemy out of you if you make a small mistake. I think that with the 5294, Eastman is legitimately saying that it should be rated at an exposure index of 400. That would be a good mean exposure for it but you can, as I have done, go up to 2000 indoors and at night. And you can rate it down to 125.

You wouldn't be shooting exclusively with 5294 now necessarily?

Oh sure, there's no reason to use 5247 anymore.

You mean this is a better film in all respects?

Yes, if you look at *Crosscreek* and *Scarface*, they don't look any different than if they had been shot with 5247. Where I rated 5293 rather high at 2000 ASA, it looks like 5247 pushed one stop. But that's not objectionable. I would use it overall because I think it's great. The nice thing that Eastman has done is now they have come out with a compatible print stock so that it's able to pick up the subtle nuances of the 5293. The only case where I might not use the new film stock is if I was doing a picture with a tremendous amount of opticals, with layer upon layer of negative going to be laid on top of each other. Then I might go with 5247 because of its finer grain. I think 5247 is still a very fine piece of material but why start out using it on a film and then find you can't shoot with it because you run into some dark sequences?

Have you had any experience with lightflex?

I haven't tried lightflex yet. I've done my own version of lightflex, which is what Ozzie Morris did on *Oliver Twist* and those movies back then. What you do is put a controlled amount of light on a net in front of the lens to give a certain washed look to the print. I did a little bit of that on *Backroads* and *The Cheap Detective*. But now they have lightflex which is an actual unit that goes on the matte box and it has absolute control over the amount of light that you can expose to it. It's a very effective way of getting a certain look. But I haven't had the occasion to do a picture that called for that type of thing.

Will it replace flashing? Do people still flash film?

I think a few people still do. But it would replace flashing; I would prefer it over flashing because I would have absolute control. I could look right through the matte box and know exactly how much light I'm putting on the film. I'm curious to see what 5294 would look like if you flashed it. I know I will probably experiment with it on the next picture I do.

You've also had some experience with the Panacam.

I used the Panacam a great deal to do some of the video sequences for *Blue Thunder*. I'm very impressed with the camera especially because it uses all the Panavision lenses. It's very much like a motion picture camera except that it's recording on video. A lot of the video cameramen are very happy with the idea that the video designers have now made a camera that's more comparable to the movie camera.

The idea is that the quality of video will improve as more motion picture cameramen cross over and do video with this type of camera?

That's the hope. I just did an MTV thing for a rock group. But they wanted it done on film because they wanted a "film look." Some of the things on MTV are very creative and almost all of them are done on video. It would be interesting to see some of them done on film because the opticals would be much better. There is a quality that the lighting cameraman for cinematography brings to his work that the electronic cameraman doesn't because he's restricted by the electronics. But now people like myself and others I know are doing some video things. We don't know the rules; we don't know any better so we light it as if we're shooting film. Then we get together with the engineers and see how we can overcome the problems. And most of them are quite open and cooperative about it.

The technology should not control the art. The art should control the technology. The technology should be for servicing the art and not vice versa. TV and video has a tendency to control the aesthetics because of all the electronic technology it deals with. I know it doesn't have to be that way because otherwise we wouldn't have *Masterpiece Theatre* and those things that have been so beautifully done in England with the electronic system. I know that it can be done here. In the future, I can see a lot of episodic television being done with the Panacam on video because the quality will be just as good if not better. It would help bring the cinematographer's techniques into the video realm and episodic TV would look ten times as good. It wouldn't be so flatly lit and so boring to look at.

Have you seen the reel on the Skycam?

Yes, the Skycam is a Garrett Brown invention that Panavision is developing a lightweight camera for. It was just marvelous to see the things that this camera can do; it looked like it was literally suspended in air. It's a very ingenious design of poles very high up that suspend the camera. It's gyroscopically and radio controlled and it does everything but make martinis. I see a great value to it; you could use it in sequences where you couldn't lay a dolly track. For instance, in a battle scene or something with a great many people, where you want the camera to travel around at people's eye levels and then move all the way up and see the entire overview.

Do you think it's quite a bit of trouble to set up?

No, it'll go through the same growing pains that the Steadicam and the Panaglide went through. In the beginning, everybody overuses them like crazy;

now they are starting to use them properly. The Skycam is going to have the same problem. It's going to be used like crazy until some good, intelligent directors use it appropriately. For example, the Steadicam was used very appropriately in *The Shining* but it was not necessary in many other films I've seen. The visual is such an important aspect of our business that when a new piece of equipment comes out, it has a tendency to be overused. But it has to go through those growing pains otherwise you never discover what its limitations are.

I think the same thing with the 5294 stock. Cameramen are a little more conservative about the film because they get used to one thing and they don't want to change. But as they start to discover the value of 5294 and how versatile it is, you'll see more and more people using it and eventually pushing the film to its limits. I went to 2000 ASA on it and I think that's about the limit on it. I did do some tests at 4000, 6000 and 10000 ASA and got an image, believe it or not!

Didn't you use the 5293 stock on Blue Thunder?

Yes, but we didn't have enough for the whole picture. We used it for some of the night sequences with Roy Scheider on Hollywood Boulevard, we used it for the scenes inside his apartment and we used it for some of the process photography in the helicopter where we'd get a lot of depth of field. I rated it 1700 ASA and got an $f5.6$ stop which gave me more depth of field. We wanted to use it for all the night photography but we couldn't get it.

That was your first experience with the 5293; how did you feel about it at that stage?

I loved it. I did some very extensive tests on it. At that time Eastman was a little hesitant for this film to be used in a major motion picture because they really weren't sure of the kind of animal they had created. And it would have been very risky had it been a failure. But I felt very confident, once I tested it, that it would be good.

The end of the picture, with all the slow-motion night photography of the train crashing into the helicopter, was a once-in-a-lifetime shot. There was no gambling there. I had to shoot high-speed cameras with very little light and I had to rate the film at around 1600–2000 ASA. And we got a very good image out of it. If we had not been able to shoot that scene with 5293, we would have had a full day's rigging of lighting just to get the lights bright enough for an exposure at 76 or 96 frames a second. We would have to have had an awful lot of light for that. So it was a godsend to have 5293 for that purpose.

It's been a long long time since cameramen carried any weight whatsoever. And I think that gives rise to everything in this book because it's a subtle change that people haven't caught up with yet.

Well, cameramen, at one time, had a great deal of power in the studios. People like Leon Shamroy. When they were under contract with the studios, they had a tremendous amount of power. But it wasn't directed in the right direction, I don't think. Because in those days a director went to Fox and he had a film to shoot. He didn't ask for the cameraman, the studio said, "Leon'll shoot that one for you." And that was it. And the director was the slave of the cameraman because of the technology and the enormous time that it would take to do pictures like that. I mean, I remember when I was at Fox for about six months as an assistant. I remember walking on sets with Leon Shamroy and the director literally changing the shot for the convenience of the mechanics. In other words, Leon would say, "You can't do it that way! Put him over there! Move him over there, it's much easier to light from here." And that was totally against Francis Ford Coppola's philosophy, against any of the younger guys today. They revolted, and I don't blame them. The mechanics should adjust to the artistic, to the aesthetics, not the other way around. That is a rule, as far as I'm concerned. There should be no such thing as the cameraman saying to the director, "You'll have to change your staging because I can't shoot it through a hot window." You should have the knowledge to say, "Okay." And if you've got a reflection problem, solve it. If the director is asking for a total impossibility, you must be articulate enough to say why it is. But not say, "Put it over there." You say, "Where would you like to do it? I can't do it here; can you find another spot to do it in?" That's the way to approach directors. So now you're finding a resurgence in the power, so-called "power of cameramen," because you are dealing with newer directors and younger directors and people that are interested in not just the artistic but also the mechanics. And you find that most of us really trying to satisfy that ego are getting more into the director's rice bowl, so we can understand where he's coming from. And as a result, we've become a more viable instrument for the director, so they give us a little more credit. And you find directors really wanting Vilmos Zsigmond or Lazslo Kovacs to shoot their picture and they are going to bat for them. So that's okay with me, because it's really back where it should be. As you know, the first directors were cameramen. Now it's leaning more in that direction. There's a great collaboration. There's no ego problem either. Roman Polanski and I had no ego problems. I didn't have any ego problems with Mike Nichols. And Marty Ritt and I certainly don't have ego problems. We respect each other's ability, that's all there is to it. In the old days there used to be that sort of thing but for a valid reason. The director didn't get along with the cameraman because he was at his mercy.

He wielded the power and would tell him "No," and that would be that. That's interesting because it becomes apparent to us that there were subtle changes that took place in Hollywood maybe ten years ago that are just now starting to have an effect to the point where people can say, "Well, you know, it's really changed." Now you're really starting to see things done differently and this is one aspect of it.

Well, you'll find the 15–20 of us that work all the time. We are hired and we attend rehearsals. We're there to watch where the head is going. That was unheard of. That had never been done; where a cameraman was hired in advance enough and asked to be present at rehearsals, just to be on the sound stage where they were walking through the scenes. And most of us now are dealing with art directors and wardrobe designers. I walked in to see Edith Head on *Pete and Tillie*. I went with Marty Ritt to see Edith Head about the wardrobe for Carol Burnett. She was very funny. She said, "I haven't seen a cameraman in my office in 15 years."

How do you choose your film projects?

By the quality of the script. That's sometimes more important than the director.

I feel that if the script is there, then the next thing is I meet the director. He interviews me and I'm interviewing him at the same time.

Do you plan to go into directing exclusively now? Will you still work behind the camera? What's your approach in that area?

No, not exclusive. I've done CBS Movies of the Week; I want to do some more of those. I would like to do some features as a director. I don't want to stop shooting; I like it too much and I'd be very frustrated if all I did was directing. Because it is frustrating to a degree, especially the post-production aspect of it. But as long as Marty Ritt's alive, I'll probably sit around and wait for him to shoot some more movies. Now I can limit myself as to who I work for. I have enough offers to direct so that I don't have to worry about where my next job is coming from. I like directing very much; I like shooting and directing even better.

On this Movie of the Week, you wore both caps; you directed it and you shot it too. Was your attention divided? How did it work out?

I found it to be very easy. I used my regular crew and they know what I want as a cameraman. So I can give them the set-up and I can go away to work with my actors; then they call me when they're ready. I come back in, watch my actors go through it, maybe change the lighting a little bit and then we start shooting. I've found it easy to do that. My concentration was 90% towards my actors and 10% towards my cinematography which just fell into place. It wasn't difficult at all. It might be difficult with a strange crew. In certain projects it might be difficult also. I might get into a very heavy dramatic piece where I really should have a cameraman do it so I can deal more with the script and the actors. But I'm not going to give up cinematography.

3

John Bailey

"Cameramen don't necessarily determine the look of a picture as much as the cameraman and director together. It's a dialogue. For me, the most successful experiences are with a director who already has some kind of vision."

Due to union seniority rules in Hollywood, most cinematographers are just beginning to hit their stride and explore their potential around the age of forty-five. John Bailey, in his mid-thirties, is making his mark ten years early. After seven features in the last five years, he has rapidly gained a reputation as a cinematographer with fresh insight, invention and the ability to carry it off on the screen. Another Hollywood overnight success? Not when you hear about Bailey's fifteen years of hustling.

An alumnus of the University of Southern California Graduate School of Cinema, Bailey attended at the same time as George Lucas, John Milius and Randall Kleiser. And while these fellow students were directing films within a few years of leaving the academic halls, Bailey was still struggling to get his union card. In his two years at USC, he shot dozens of student films and later he worked on low-budget productions, always gaining valuable filmmaking experience in the process. After getting his union card, he was an assistant cameraman for five years and then moved up to camera operator on films such as *Three Women*, *Welcome to L.A.*, *The Late Show* and *Days of Heaven:* the traditional Hollywood version of working your way up through the ranks, though for Bailey the process was somewhat accelerated. He paid his dues to become a director of photography, always trying to align himself with cameramen, directors and projects that he felt would be the most beneficial to him in terms of personal growth. He prepared for his DP role by watching, working and learning from every cameraman he ever worked with and now it's paying off. He is not a slave to any particular style or mode of shooting; stylistically, *Ordinary People* and *American Gigolo* are worlds apart. Bailey is adamant about giving every film its own unique personality, trying to let the visual style reveal and reinforce the ideas inherent in the material. In the ranks of Hollywood cinematography, Bailey is a relative youngster, but that's exciting because he has the imagination, capacity and time to take his visual concepts to the limit in the years ahead.

1978	*Boulevard Nights*	1982	*Without a Trace*
1979	*American Gigolo*		*That Championship Season*
1980	*Ordinary People*	1983	*The Big Chill*
	Continental Divide		*Racing with the Moon*
	Honky Tonk Freeway		*The Pope of Greenwich Village*
1981	*Cat People*	1984	*Mishima*

Boulevard Nights *was your first film as director of photography?*

Yes and it's a film I'm very fond of. It came out at the same time as *The Warriors*. There was a lot of turmoil about gang pictures and violence. *The Warriors* made all the money and the rest of the films took the heat. *Boulevard Nights* was totally misunderstood. It wasn't an exploitation film. It wasn't as much about violence as about the relationship between two brothers who happened to live in the barrio. I found it very intriguing because, as a personal experience, it was like making a film in a foreign country. We employed a lot of local people; many of the secondary characters in the picture were gang kids. We had people who wouldn't show up because they'd been busted. It was a sociological experience as much as a filmmaking one. I'm very close to it; it was a nice film for me to have done at that point.

What was it like your first day as director of photography?

I felt very confident because Michael Pressman and I had prepared everything carefully. We had been to the locations. We had worked out a shot list. We knew exactly what we wanted. It was a day exterior so I didn't have any lighting to worry about but we did do a couple of very nice dolly shots. So it went very smoothly for me.

No anxieties, no apprehensions?

Oh I had a certain amount of anxiety; I do when I start every picture. But it was evolutionary for me. When I did my first show as an assistant, I was probably more nervous than my first day as a director of photography. The first day of my first show as an operator, I remember being very nervous too. It takes about three pictures before you really start to feel confident and comfortable. And sometimes not even then. The first day of *Cat People* was tense for me because it was a very difficult day on a small set. Certain famous concert musicians, for instance, say that every time they're standing in the wings waiting to go on stage, they don't know whether they're going to overcome the nausea to be able to go out and do it. That's true for anybody who's been putting their ass on the line, where you have to go out and perform. If you're just punching a time clock, then it's a different story.

How did you originally become interested in cinematography?

I guess it goes back to when I was in college and first started seeing foreign films.

This was the early sixties. I started seeing Bergman and a lot of the early French New Wave films, the early Truffaut, Chabrol and Godard. It was a kind of filmmaking unlike anything I'd ever seen. And I realized the excitement was in the imagery more than in what was being said, especially with the Nouvelle Vague filmmakers. I knew I wanted to get involved in film. I finally decided to join the graduate program at USC, which was just starting up. They had their undergraduate program for many years but the graduate program was new. It was a very heady two years. Since it was a new program, they didn't have a notion of how it should be structured, what the academic requirements were, etc. It was very freewheeling and very exciting. Basically what I got out of it was the opportunity to look at hundreds and hundreds of films. We'd run Museum of Modern Art prints of twenties German expressionist films over and over again, all night long. We did things like that. I was at USC at the same time as George Lucas, John Milius, Hal Barwood, Matthew Robbins, Randall Kleiser, Walter Murch, Willard Huyck. After they got out of film school, they really started working in the mainstream of the industry and doing their own films. I was still struggling to get into the union as an assistant.

Did you go into the program with the idea of a career in cinematography or did you just want to be in film in general?

The whole notion of image making and how the image process fit into the narrative line of filmmaking really interested me. And just in the course of looking at all these films—turning the sound off and just watching the shots, running them back and forth—I decided to take a cinematography course. The teacher, Gene Peterson, was a very dynamic and energetic guy who really turned me on to cinematography. He's not by any means a theatrical cinematographer; his background is in documentaries. But he was so positively certain that films were made by cameramen that he kind of convinced me. That's when I decided that regardless of what I wanted to do later on, I had to have a firm grounding in what the camera was, how it worked and what its power was. For the two years at USC, I concentrated on shooting student films. When I got out I started working as an assistant at whatever odd jobs I could. It became more and more of a commitment and an obsession. Once I got into the union, I felt at least I was in the ballpark and had a uniform. I might be a batboy but someday I'd be a pitcher. It was just a question of putting in the time. I became aware very quickly that there were a lot of directors of photography that didn't have the kind of obsession or even the interest that I and some of my friends had. So I felt there wasn't that much competition; that there were a lot of people hanging on. I decided to try to single out the cameramen, directors and projects that I felt could be the most beneficial for me in terms of personal growth.

What determines a good composition or a good frame to your eye? Is it symmetry, lighting, color, focus? What are the determinants?

I think for any given shot there are a number of elements that, at different times, may have greater or lesser value. If the shot is totally abstract, it's basically the color. You have to decide what color will recede and what color will assert itself and how you balance them. When you're dealing with monochrome, it may be just the question of the light. You decide whether you want a very strong back light or cross

light, etc. So there's really no formula for it. The first thing I look at when I set up a
shot is the composition; that's what I analyze first. The important considerations
are color, the focal length of the lens, movement, structural balance and focus.
Those are the principal elements and I run through them unconsciously every time
I pick a shot. I spent four years as an operator and, because of that background,
composition is very, very important to me. I don't think there are too many American cameramen who have real concern with composition; a lot of the foreign cameramen do. If you came out of non-union productions, where you basically operated and lit everything yourself, the last thing you were able to consider was how to
compose a shot, especially if you were on short schedules. You were so busy
lighting and setting the thing up that composition became sort of an afterthought.
Because I had absolutely nothing to consider for four years except to study fifteen
different ways to compose any given shot, it became very crucial to me.

But operating was a good preparation for moving up to director of photography?

Yes, it was. Also I was able to dispassionately analyze the styles of different
cinematographers. And there are a lot of cinematographers that have either come
up through non-union productions or commercials where they have essentially
been their own boss from the beginning. They haven't had the luxury that I've had.
I was just this morning discussing the same thing about directors. Unless a director
has theatrical background from the stage, he hasn't had the opportunity to watch
other directors work. He doesn't know much about directing films except what he's
learned himself. And the same applies to cinematographers who have essentially
had no one else to study, except for monitoring their own work. I've had the privi-
lege of working with a lot of cameramen that I thought were very good and I
learned a lot from them. So, in that way, it was excellent preparation.

*What cameramen or photographers have had an effect on the way you look at
things?*

Gordon Willis, more than anybody. I don't speak for everybody my age, but for
me he is the preeminent American cinematographer. I think he's single-handedly
responsible for the respect and acknowledgement that cinematographers now
have. He has consistently aligned himself with brilliant directors and material. A
lot of other very good cameramen have not had that instinct for picking the right
directors and the right scripts to attach themselves to. Gordon has. Even those of
his films that have maybe been flops, have been interesting films. Photographically,
I like his lighting very much; he's very courageous. He's obsessed with control of
composition to the extent now that I think he's almost become a still photographer.
He doesn't move the camera anywhere near the amount he used to and when he
does move it, it's very deliberate. As soon as you start to move the camera, you lose
control over the lighting and you lose control over composition. It's just inherent;
there's no way you can prevent that from happening. For me, it's a tradeoff and it's a
fair tradeoff because I love the excitement of moving the camera. So what I lose in
control in the other areas, I gain just by the energy and the momentum of being able
to move the camera. Movement makes your job very challenging. If you've got a
dolly or a crane shot moving from one corner of the room to the other and you're

panning around two hundred and seventy degrees, you have to figure out how the hell you can light the damn thing, especially if you're on a practical location. You get into some very involved ways of hiding lights. You're forced to find new ways of lighting scenes all the time; ways that you might not have initially chosen but which can turn out to be very interesting. I respond to that a lot and consequently I like working with production designers who think of their stage sets as practical locations. I know designers like very much to build sets that have hard ceilings; I like the feeling of a hard-ceiling set too. We had a lot of them in *American Gigolo*. The designer, Nando Scarfiotti, builds a lot of his sets that way. It creates certain problems for me but it also makes me more responsive. It's challenging. Nando was the designer on *Cat People* too and we had a lot of hard-ceiling sets again. A lot of the sets were two-story so the bottom floor has to have a hard ceiling and even the second floor of some of the sets had hard ceilings. We shot a lot of low angles with wide lenses so we saw ceilings a lot.

But back to the question about other cameramen, I like Vilmos Zsigmond's work very much. I like Nestor Almendros's work obviously. Of the French, I like Pierre Lhome a lot. I love the pictures of Jean Boffety who's done most of Claude Sautet's films and a lot of Robert Enrico's films during the sixties. I'm a big fan of Geoffrey Unsworth. There's an Italian cameraman, Luigi Kuweiller, who did Elio Petri's films. I think that probably more European cameramen than American cameramen have influenced me. When I was looking at the Nouvelle Vague films in the early sixties that was the kind of photography that made an impression on me. It was photography that was either in the streets or on real locations and it had a very natural look. When the European cinematographers started using color, they were using a very soft color that was unknown in the Hollywood mainstream at the time. I think the English and French cinematographers in the middle to late sixties had a tremendous effect on what happened to color photography in Hollywood in the seventies. When most productions started going to color, most of the cinematographers who were shooting them were the old guard who were black-and-white cameramen or else they were the high-key color musical type. When color prevailed, they continued to light in the same way: with hard light, a lot of heavy hair light, no top light and real strong fill light on exteriors. I didn't like that look at the time. I liked the Godard look that Raoul Coutard was doing. Also Henri Decae and the early Truffaut films. I was quite young then and I thought that was real. I thought the glossy, slick Hollywood look wasn't real at all. I've sort of come around now; I look at that type of classic Hollywood film now with a great deal of admiration and respect. But it's still not really my style although I've begun to integrate some of it. The cameramen who were the younger ones at that time when the European look really started to penetrate here—people like Laszlo Kovacs, Vilmos Zsigmond and John Alonzo—were very much in sympathy and accord with what the European cameramen were doing.

How would you define your function as a cinematographer? What is it that you do?

I work for the director. That's my primary line of communication and my primary responsibility. That's something I feel I learned from Nestor Almendros. He is, for me, a paragon of the cinematographer who is totally committed to understanding, sharing and evolving a sense of style with the director. He's not there to uniquely bring the film in on schedule and satisfy the studio. I think preproduction time is extremely important and I just won't walk into a film two weeks before the start of shooting and have a couple of vague meetings with the director. I like to see a lot of films with the director and talk about style, to go through the script sequence by sequence and, in the case of Schrader, shot by shot, essentially storyboarding what we want to do. It may all change once we get on the set and we see that the scene lays out quite differently.

But you like to lay the foundation beforehand?

I like working on that basis; I like that kind of preparation with the director. The director is really the key to whether the film works or not and if the director's vision isn't realized somehow, the film really doesn't have any chance at all. So that's where my responsibility is.

So you're basically implementing the director's vision?

Yes. Again, I've been fortunate enough to work with directors that I think have a vision. I don't know how I would deal with a director that I didn't think had one. My one experience with a director that you would not immediately consider a visual filmmaker was Robert Redford. Up until that time he'd been considered only an actor even though he had a tremendous amount of influence and control over all the films that his company did. He really is a filmmaker although most people didn't recognize it. When I was doing *Ordinary People*, I would get asked, "You're working with an actor; what kind of vision does he have?" Well, he had an incredible vision about what he thought *Ordinary People* should be, not necessarily specifically in terms of shots, but in terms of the tones and textures of the film. He had very clear ideas; he'd spent a lot of time evolving and considering it. He'd bought the book when it was in galleys and had labored over the screenplay with Alvin Sargent for several years. So he had lived with it.

Generally, how much creative freedom do you have in setting the visual look and style of a film?

I think probably quite a bit. I consider it a dialogue with the director. I think a director would be interested in hiring me not because he wanted a specific look. Most of the films I've done have had very different looks. *American Gigolo* was very different from *Ordinary People* and I shot them back to back. So if I get a call from a director to do a film, it's because he may have a certain stylistic approach he wants but usually he's very open to developing that with me. Sometimes I haven't any strong notion of what I want to do until late into preproduction. On *Cat People*, Schrader and I didn't really know what kind of style we wanted except we wanted it to be different from *American Gigolo*. So we started looking at films. As it turned out, a lot of the films we looked at were twenties German expressionist films. They had a stylized sense of irreality. Even the exteriors tended to look like interiors. We started to focus in on that. We also looked at Cocteau and Franju for a sense of film poetry. The German cinema of the twenties had a very hard edge to it. Cocteau and

Franju have certain stylistic tangents with the Germans but by virtue of that poetic French sensibility, there's a softness there. We tried to integrate the two, to take elements of both. I find that looking at films with the director is the thing that I key off of.

It's really a good reference point for you?

Yes. For instance, one of the key films for me is *The Conformist*. Oh, we were talking about cinematographers and I didn't mention Storaro. Gordon Willis and Vittorio Storaro are really the two that are my idols. I've seen *The Conformist* probably twenty-five times. Schrader and I saw it five or six times while we were preparing *American Gigolo*. For me, it's a real treasure chest; it's almost a textbook on filmmaking. So *American Gigolo* very deliberately had a lot of stylistic characteristics of *The Conformist*. We were also looking at Welles. We looked at *The Trial* several times since it was wide angle and forced perspective. The film that we looked at a lot when we were preparing *American Gigolo* was *Touch of Evil*. And one afternoon I watched *The Conformist* and *Touch of Evil* back to back. I realized that Bertolucci's sense of movement, that particular kind of crane movement that he has that totally surprises you and takes your breath away, comes from Welles. There's an awful lot of Welles in Bertolucci and it's not immediately apparent because, other than that, they are very different in tone and texture. The poetry of their filmmaking is almost antithetical. Yet the way they move the camera is very similar. If I recall correctly, in Bertolucci's *Before The Revolution*, he quite literally stole a lot from Welles. Filmmakers do watch films a lot.

Do you generally like to work with a director who goes off with the actors, leaving the technical details to you or would you rather work with a director who wants some input and interplay back and forth?

I know there are several cinematographers who like that sense of total control; the director works with the actors and he tells the cinematographer the basic kind of coverage he wants and the cinematographer sets it up. I could do that; it's intriguing in a way. But the irony is that even though you have total freedom, you really don't have any freedom at all because the only freedom you have is within the context of what the director is going to do with the actors. A director who only works with the actors is not going to come up with very inspired blocking. The blocking is what you key off of for your sense of camera movement and the kind of visual dynamics you have inside of a scene. I'm much more intrigued with working with a director who thinks of blocking the scene with the camera and the actors. There's a dance and an interplay that goes on. Sometimes it might seem that it would be frustrating to have a director say, "I want this kind of shot." But, in fact, that isn't what happens. Usually that's an initial idea and then by talking about it something quite different may evolve. That happens to Schrader and me a lot. It's something that neither one of us initially imagined but which hopefully becomes something even better. Really exciting directors see actors as elements inside the film, though the most important ones. Everything else is secondary to performance and the screenplay. But even a director like John Schlesinger, who is very actor oriented, is also incredibly visually oriented. He has very specific ideas about how he wants a shot. On *Honky Tonk Freeway* we had several very big shots which were costly in terms of production. If something happened, if the actors didn't hit the mark, if they didn't do it right so we got the composition, if the light hit an actor in a way other than we had already decided, Schlesinger would sometimes call "Cut," or we would do another take. He was most uncompromising in getting all the elements to come together. Performance of course was paramount but it had to be in concert with composition, camera movement and lighting. A sense of detail about all those elements and being able to juggle them is what makes a director a filmmaker and an artist.

Generally though, you've always worked with someone who's visually oriented. You haven't made the choice to work with somebody who's not visually oriented.

Only Redford. I told him the first time we met, I had a need to do that film that was probably as strong as his. I read the novel when it first came out and was obsessed with it. I was an operator at the time. Redford's then producer, Walter Coblenz, was an old friend of mine. He had been the assistant director on *Two Lane Blacktop*, on which I was assistant cameraman. Walter and I had stayed in contact during all those intervening years. He subsequently left Redford's Wildwood Productions to go off on his own but he plugged me in to Redford. I told Redford, "I've got to photograph this film."

What happened there? Thinking of the cameramen Redford had worked with before, he could have asked Roizman, Willis, Hall or any other number of people. But instead he hired you.

I never asked him why. One thing is I don't think he wanted a cameraman that was a star. He didn't want someone who would be an element that he would have to deal with that would distract him from the total control he wanted with the actors. Yet he wanted somebody that he felt could deliver. He's a very, very articulate and intelligent man. He's specific in what he focuses on. I think he also wanted somebody that he could have that kind of dialogue with who was a little flexible. Also the absolute conviction I had to do the film may have influenced him. He saw the first Karen Arthur film I did, *Legacy*, which was shot in 16mm and dealt with a woman whose story was very similar to Mary Tyler Moore's in *Ordinary People*. *Legacy* follows her life one day in summer when her husband's away on business and her kids are at camp. She breaks down and goes crazy at the end of the day. The woman is compulsively ordered, clean and disciplined very much like Beth in *Ordinary People*. Redford plugged into the feeling that photography somehow enhanced and expressed something about that woman. *Legacy* was shot in 16mm so it was a square frame; it was very severely designed and it was a cleanly realized film. That was basically the way I saw *Ordinary People* looking: clean, severe and having very direct imagery. We talked about *Legacy* quite a bit.

In preproduction, what kind of conversations did you have about the visual style of the film, of how you wanted to mount the film?

Well, we looked at *The Conformist*.

Again!

Yes, I ask every director I work with to look at *The Conformist*; even if we decide
it's flamboyant and totally wrong for us, there's such energy there and it's such a
springboard for discussion, that it's always fruitful. Redford found that stylistically
it was just too rich for him. He was most closely tuned into the character of Beth. In
preproduction he understood that character more clearly than any of the others. So
we talked a lot about her, about how the house should be perfect and have no flaws
in it but yet it should look askew somehow. He was always calling up images about
how you would see something on a table. Everything was right about that table but
the positioning of some object on that table was just slightly wrong. He felt that
finding things in the house that were just slightly out of context or in conflict would
help give a sense of tension to what was going on. I think it wasn't as closely
realized as either he or I wanted.

*What experience, unrelated to filmmaking, do you feel has helped you in your
career as a filmmaker? I notice that you have quite a great interest in art.*

I've collected Indian art for many years. Art is very important to me and I spend
a lot of time looking at it. American Indian art is very abstract. It deals with all the
materials of earth. I learned about American Indian art before I learned about
European art. I don't know that it has any direct influence on me; I just love having
it around me. I also collect still photography; I've been doing that for about six
years. I got involved in collecting still photography because I started buying Edward Curtis's American Indian imagery. And it just seemed that since I was involved in photography, it was natural that I started studying it. When I was in film
school, I spent virtually no time at all looking at photography. It's only in the last
five years that I've really methodically collected and studied photography. That's
had a very strong influence on my work because most of it has happened since I've
become a director of photography.

In what way?

Most of the photographs I have are black-and-white. There's a control still photographers have over the image that cinematographers can't have. So by virtue of
looking at the design elements in the still photography I really admire, I get ideas
and try to think of ways I can take some of those elements and apply them in a
cinematic context. For instance—and we're not talking about fine art photography
here—in *American Gigolo*, because Richard Gere's wardrobe was Armani, I
started looking at a lot of the Italian fashion magazines. I noticed a real strong
sense of what used to be called Hollywood hard light being used in the fashion ads.
This was at a time when our fashion photography was still very soft and pastel. I
started seeing a lot of photography that had hard shadows on the wall; the sort of
thing that has become very popular in the last two years. I was very intrigued with
that as a style for the film. Schrader and I looked at a lot of vintage fashion photography and decided to use hard light in *American Gigolo*. We used the shadows on
the wall as a compositional element; we made them elements in the frame, balancing Gere's shadow against his image. Scarfiotti, the designer, deliberately gave
Gere's apartment that grey, monotone look so that we could use the walls to create

shadows and light forms. Everytime you see the apartment it has a different look in terms of the kind of light that's being projected on the walls. The wall itself almost becomes a canvas.

The interesting thing visually about American Gigolo *is that it doesn't look like Los Angeles. At least it doesn't look like the Los Angeles we see in television series or even other movies. It looks interesting and sensual in* American Gigolo. *You captured a certain quality of time and place that really hasn't been seen a lot.*

We knew that the interiors were going to be very stylized and have a very specific look; we wanted strong compositions and strong lighting. We felt we just couldn't go out on the streets and make do with what was there. If we did, it would just make the film schizophrenic. So we spent a lot of time scouting locations. We modified some locations. We shot certain things at a specific time of day. We tried to shoot at the magic hour. When we didn't have any of that going for us, we tried to find disturbing compositions of rather boring places. For example, there's an establishing shot of Sotheby Parke Bernet which is a very boring building. But I tried to find a composition that was not normally the way you would frame it. In fact, that whole scene inside the building, with the camera moving from one wall to another, was staged in a way so that it was constantly disorienting. The last shot of that sequence is outside in back of the building but we shot it in the magic hour because I knew that the blue light would look very good against the green lawn. The house in Palm Springs was another very deliberate choice. Paul wanted to have a white facade against the mountains; that way we had the dark blue sky, the black outline of the mountains and the white facade of the house. It was strictly a matter of two-dimensional planes. Again, Gere driving up to that house was a very abstract shot. Also the beach house was picked not necessarily for the strip of beach that it was on but rather because of what was under the house. That row of houses was all on pylons and it had just such a bizarre sense—houses hanging right above the sea. In a sense, it was a landscape of the mind, being under that house and walking along there. The end of the sequence plays with Richard and Nina against some of the posts. The tag shot is of them leaning up against a couple of the supporting pillars of the last house and beyond you see a little cove and a boat. It's just like it's the end of the world. It's at a point where Gere is in total despair; he feels that the world is closing in on him and there's nowhere for him to go. And yet the shot has an incredible kind of sensual density to it though it's a very despairing moment in the film. Paul and I were constantly intrigued with that kind of juxtaposition.

On day exteriors, you somehow have to impose your will on the environment. You have to work with what is given. How do you do that?

A lot of times you're lucky enough to have a director and producer who share that kind of concern. They will want to shoot certain scenes under specific light conditions, such as Schrader wanting to shoot at magic hour. Redford wanted to shoot at a certain time of the year in the Midwest; when the leaves were falling, when the skies were leaden and overcast and you have that almost English light. So that makes it very easy when you schedule those things. But that doesn't happen a lot. Beyond that, for me it's a question of finding compositions and movement.

There's not too much you can do to control sunlight. Some cameramen who don't like hard sunlight will stretch huge parachutes or silks up to filter and soften the light. But that doesn't fundamentally change anything; you can't affect the colors or anything. It's still there. I like harsh sunlight; when it's very clear and sharp, I like it a lot. There's a lot of it in *Honky Tonk Freeway* because everybody is on their way to Florida to find the sun. I made the most of using the hard sunlight. On *Continental Divide*, we wanted the mountain sequences in Colorado to be very sunny, bright and saturated. We were lucky that we got it; there was little overcast while we were there. The Chicago scenes we wanted to be almost claustrophobically sullen. It was starting to get pretty late in autumn and the skies were leaden and dark. We shot a lot around the Loop. So that the sunlight, when it did come, never much reached us. It was like shooting in the canyons of New York. All day long we had this grey, unappetizing light. I liked that because that's the way I wanted Chicago to look in contrast to the mountains.

What are the first things you do when you begin to light a set or location? What are the things that get your immediate attention?

The first thing I look for is a light source, assuming that it's a scene that warrants source lighting. Or even if it isn't, I have to have an imaginary source even if there's no logic to it. I have to find someplace where I could imagine, either on real or surreal terms, there would be illumination. If you're on location, that's usually easy because nature speaks to you very clearly. That's one reason I like to shoot on practical locations. If we were to shoot in this house, I could probably shoot most of the day with existing light and maybe a little fill. It's a look that's hard to duplicate on a sound stage.

That natural light look?

Yes. The look you get from a real house or store is hard to duplicate. When I'm on stage, I will try to duplicate it. In *Ordinary People*, there's a story point that the meeting that Conrad has with Dr. Berger takes place between four and five o'clock. The time that the story spans is approximately early October until February and that's basically when the days are getting to be their shortest. One hour of time in the late afternoon goes through a great change of light quality. So each one of those meetings is set up to have a very different light. We started off with an afternoon scene in an overcast light; the second meeting had just pieces of sunlight; the third was a very stylized sunset; the fourth was magic hour with some blue light outside; in the fifth there was full night with an outside neon sign flashing. The last meeting takes place in the middle of the night and I basically wanted to feel that there was nothing on in the room except the overhead light that Berger turned on as he opened the door. I wanted it to have that gritty, grimy feel that you have in the middle of the night with just a single light on. The light source wasn't in the picture because it was high overhead. It was a coop light like Gordon Willis uses. It was very intense for the center of the room where they sat most of the time. It fell off as you got closer to the walls. I didn't use any other light so the farther they got away from the light, the darker they got. When Conrad retreated into the corner, he got very dark and gritty looking. Then when they were under it, the light was very hot on top of their heads. So that's the kind of thing it was in terms of deciding how to light a set; it was all of a piece.

A lot of times on practical locations I'll run into fluorescents. Rather than turn them off and try to control the light, I'll usually use the existing fluorescents and supplement them with our own. I love fluorescents. There's a unique look they have that just can't be duplicated any other way. The newspaper office in *Continental Divide* was all done with fluorescents. Fluorescents have traditionally been a bane to cameramen and most cameramen just hate them. But Gordon Willis used fluorescents for the *Washington Post* sequences in *All the President's Men*. That was a stage set and he could have installed any kind of lighting he wanted but he chose to put in hundreds of fluorescent units and place the ballasts along the outside stage wall. He didn't correct for them in the camera; it was all done in the lab as far as I know. I used to correct fluorescents with filters. Now I don't. I just let the lab make the correction and they turn out looking quite good. But the fact that you have assaulted the negative—and that's the only way you can describe it—with that green light that fluorescents have when they're uncorrected, there's a residual texture that is very much the way institutional lighting is today. It's part of an emotional attitude we have about office buildings. To do it any other way just doesn't work for me; I like that fluorescent look.

Do you pay any attention to lighting ratios and color temperatures? All the cinematography books written for students emphasize them.

That's a tyrannical old-guard way of looking at photography. While that was pretty much in vogue when I was studying cinematography, it's been pretty well thrown out now. Color has become such an important dramatic accent that cinematographers deliberately violate balanced color now. But no, I don't pay much attention to color temperature at all. In fact, I use a lot of gels to alter it. As far as lighting ratios are concerned, I used to do that. I used to light very strictly by ratios because I wanted consistency. I didn't want one close-up to have a four-to-one ratio and another one a six-to-one ratio and then have to intercut them. Now I just fill by eye. I've had that much more experience. Most cinematographers do fill by eye.

What has been your experience with the higher speed Kodak film stock 5293?

The first time I used it was on *Without a Trace* and I've used it to some extent on every picture since then. I used it a lot on *The Big Chill;* almost all the interiors are photographed with 5293. Then, at the time I was doing *The Big Chill*, I was answer-printing several other films and I became very critical of contrast and grain problems, especially going through the dupe with 5293. I guess I should have expected it with the higher-speed film but everybody seemed to be so enthusiastic about it when it came out. Plus it looked so good in daily form that nobody anticipated having problems. But we were having so many problems with print stocks that it diverted us from the real problem of 5293. I came to terms with it head on when I was doing *Racing with the Moon*. It was a period film. I didn't like the dailies I was getting the first week and I decided to shoot certain scenes using 5247. I saw a marked improvement because I was using the new modified 84 print stock. So I used very little 5293 on *Racing with the Moon*. Looking back on it now, I think the

5247 stock is far superior; it's got more latitude, it's less contrasty, it has much less grain and it holds up better through the intermediate dupe. I'm trying to avoid using 5293 but that's a moot point now because it's been discontinued and replaced with 5294, which is supposed to be a little bit faster. Now I'm using some 5294 for the first time on *The Pope of Greenwich Village* but I'm not particularly enthusiastic about it. I'm only using it for night exteriors. I'm going to continue to use 5247 as much as I can.

So right now you feel that 5294 has limited applications.

It's axiomatic that the faster the film, the grainier and contrastier it's going to be. I use it on night exteriors; most of your frame is black anyway so you don't notice the grain. But I rate 5247 at 200 ASA and most of the time that's enough for me. In any place where I have a controlled light situation, I don't need any faster film than that. I don't like to stop down very deeply anyway because I use nets and if I stop down beyond $f3.2$ or $f4$, the pattern of the net starts to show with the wider lenses. So I have very little reason to stop down to $f5.6$ or $f6.3$, which I would be forced to do if I were using a faster film.

Is there a noticeable difference between scenes shot on 5247 and 5293?

Yes, especially in *The Big Chill*. If you started looking at the answer print with a critical eye, you'd be able to tell right away which scenes were 5247 and which were 5293. It's very apparent, especially when one comes right after the other and they are both interior scenes. But there's such a lag period involved here. You shoot with a new stock and you don't have a chance to really confront the end result until you answer-print it a year later. By then you've shot another couple of films.

Have you had any experience with lightflex?

No, I haven't used it because it basically does something to the film that I normally don't want to do. Essentially, it flashes the film. A very primitive type of light flashing system that flashed white or colored lights on a piece of glass in front of the lens was used by Freddie Young on a picture called *The Deadly Affair* in the mid-sixties. Then an English cameraman later perfected the system and initially used it to introduce an overall color haze in certain scenes of *Young Winston*. According to the color of light you flashed through the gels, you could change the color from scene to scene.

Is this a process that is going to replace flashing?

I think flashing has lost some of its mystique, partly because it requires extra handling of the negative in lab and that's dangerous. Most of the time people use flashing in a situation which they could control if they just used a little more fill light. For example, sometimes on a night exterior, I'll get a big 12 foot by 12 foot silk and put a 10K through it maybe 75–100 feet behind the camera. Now that's introducing real light into the scene and it's not affecting the black sky. But when you flash, you affect everything on your negative including all your blacks. I don't like that. I like blacks to be very rich. There is one situation where I might use it and that would be one where I had extensive day exteriors with hard sunlight and I wanted them to be less contrasty but I couldn't use any fill light. For instance, if I were doing a scene in a jungle where I had to go in with a very small equipment package and I couldn't fill the scene, I would probably use something like lightflex.

What about the Panacam? Have you used it?

Only in demonstrations. I think it's marvelous. What I like about it is that it's designed for cinematographers; it was made for people who don't have a highly technical electronic background and who approach their work as photographers. It's very much like a Panaflex. It takes Panavision film lenses, filters and matte box. You essentially have the feel of using a motion picture camera not an electronic camera as such.

It brings the two worlds together?

I think it does. It's a major breakthrough in terms of breaking down the rather artificial barriers between film and video because the two areas are going to get closer and closer as technology improves.

The feeling is that the quality of video will increase as more film cameramen become involved in video because they will bring more of a film look, in lighting, to a video production.

That's definitely happening. You look at English video and they're lit, photographed and framed with almost a film sense because they've had film technicians working in both areas. Here, it's only recently that video has been exposed to film technicians and artists. I think a lot of cinematographers are interested in working in videotape.

Have you heard anything about the Skycam, a new piece of equipment invented by Garrett Brown, who previously perfected the Steadicam?

I've seen a demonstration tape. The Skycam is a camera that hangs down on a rod from a series of pulleys or rollers and these run along wires. The wires are supported at three or four different points. Through a remote controlled system of these wires, this camera moves in all the axes that you can think of. Hovering above the ground, it can go up and down. It can move along any north-south, east-west axis or anything in between. It can pan and tilt. It's essentially free hanging. It's operated through a video monitor where you control the focus and the iris. This thing can go from ground level to however high you have the wires; so it can do anything a helicopter can without rotor wash. It can start right on a close-up of somebody, pull back up in the air, move around them, drop down behind them, etc. It's really extraordinary and I think it's going to be used a lot.

Is it any more trouble than, say, laying dolly tracks?

I think initially it might be because these poles and wires have to be rigged. But it gives you total freedom of movement with the camera; you can make moves that have never been done before.

How closely do you monitor what the lab does?

Very, very closely. Whenever I'm in town, I usually go in to the lab in the morning before the shooting call and see a high-speed projection of the dailies. I do that almost every day. When on location, I have daily phone conversations with the lab. I like working with Technicolor lab because so far my contact with them has been very, very good. The labs are technically pretty much the same; it's then a question of the feedback and service. When on location, you're very vulnerable. You phone in and ask about the dailies. If you've got somebody that's halfway intelligent at the other end who knows what you want, you know where you stand.

What kind of advice would you give to a student in dealing with the lab?

I think the most important thing is to get a tour of a lab to understand what happens mechanically to the film and how different the parameters of control are from a custom still lab. You have to realize that the responsibility is in your hands not in the lab's. What the lab delivers is a standard-issue item. In terms of daily one-light prints, anything that you want to have on the film, you have to build into it. Any effect you want, you've got to do at the time you're shooting. It's a very simple realization but it's one that doesn't happen until quite late in the game with a lot of cinematographers. You've really got to be responsible for controlling the elements that you put in there. The more you understand how a lab works, the better off you're going to be. It's like any business; if you talk to people by their first name, you're going to get better service than if you're arrogant.

A lot of times when a film is being answer-printed, the cinematographer is on another film. I've been very insistent about answer-printing every film I've shot. It's very important. If your dailies don't have pretty much the look that you want the finished film to have, it's very hard to get it in the answer-printing, even if you are there. By then the director and the editor have become used to what it looks like and they become very resistant to changing it.

Gordon Willis's philosophy, at one time, was give the lab something in a narrow range so the lab will have less opportunity to screw it up.

I try not to work on the edge and give them a thin negative that they can't print up. I try to work with very strong printing lights so that there's good density in the negative. If I want it to be dark, it's dark not because I haven't got any negative left but because I'm printing on a printer light high enough to dig into it. If I do run into any problems I'll be able to print it up. So you have to play it both ways. I try to give a director as balanced a look as I can in the dailies because I think it's important that he be able to evaluate whether the film is working or not. If you're trying to study a sequence from a dramatic standpoint and you've got one shot that's a stop hotter than the shot after it or one shot is green and the next is blue, then it's very hard to concentrate on the dramatic values.

How much do you use filtration?

Very little—basically if I've got a lighting condition that I can't control the way I want to. If I want a softer look on an exterior and it's a very hard light and I can't silk it or tent it in, then I'll use a low-contrast filter or a light fog filter. I don't really like to use either of them because I feel they soften the image in a way that's not a controlled softness. Filtering is sort of a compromise. In terms of color filters for interiors, I prefer to do it on the set lights because you can be more selective. In other words, if you put a coral filter in front of the lens, the whole frame is going to have that degree of saturation. If you do it on specific lights and you leave one or two lights with a clean, white reference, it makes the part of the frame that's colored more dramatic. When you're dealing with exteriors of course, and you want an overall color look but you can't shoot it at the time of day you want or under the light conditions you want, then you've got to use something. That's about the only time I really use color filters.

I use nets a lot; I have a series of them. I shoot a sharp negative and when I want softness I try to build it into the lighting. I don't use diffusion filters because they tend to break up that sharpness. It makes the image muddy. But very light nets, especially for close-ups, can soften an actress's or actor's face. It's not to flatter them so much but rather it's so that you aren't distracted by certain physical problems that make-up can't cover. Also if you use diffusion with one of the actors in the scene, you have to do it with all of them, maybe varying the degree. In *Ordinary People*, whenever I used a net on Mary Tyler Moore, I used one on Donald Sutherland too. In fact, most of *Ordinary People* was shot with a net, even the exteriors. I normally don't use nets on exteriors because when you stop the lens down as far as you do outside you tend to see them, especially on a panning shot against the sky. But we were shooting under very diffused light and I was shooting exteriors sometimes at the same stop as the interiors. The nets were helpful because it gave the film a very uniform look.

Is there a different approach to lighting a black person as opposed to a white person? I'm thinking of Bill Duke in American Gigolo.

There's a scene where Duke and Gere are on the steps at the back of the nightclub and it's lit with blue light. I probably had two and a half times the amount of light on Bill Duke that I had on Richard. Some black people happen to take a lot more light, some don't. Duke did. It was difficult doing two-shots. I find that's a case where meters go out the window. On *Cat People*, I worked with Annette O'Toole, who has red hair and is very fair-skinned. She sometimes took half the light that I expected. I'd get her lit at what I considered key and she jumped out from everybody else. So you have somebody like Duke at one extreme and O'Toole at another. Finally you just have to look through the finder and evaluate it by eye.

Have faster film, faster lenses and other technological advances changed the way you do things? It has for some of the veteran cameramen, but you're much younger than they are.

Probably not for me so much. Already when I did *Boulevard Nights*, Panavision had their Ultraspeed lenses and I shot a lot of things on the streets of East Los Angeles where the key lights were practical lights such as store front windows and neons. I used fill light that essentially balanced that. A good deal of that film was shot wide open with Ultraspeed lenses. Now I use the Ultraspeeds and stop down to where I might with more normal lenses. I shot a lot of *Boulevard Nights* at $f1.4$, $f1.6$; never more than $f2$ for the night exteriors. Consequently it has a very real look. When you're out on the street at night like that and you've got five or six different light sources coming in, you can use them and get an incredibly rich look. But as soon as you turn on one theatrical light, you overpower it all. Then you're back to lighting for movies again.

Do you prefer working on a sound stage or a location?
I like both.

Is one more difficult or challenging to you than the other? Are there any distinctions to be made there?

No. Some practical locations can be enormously painful, others are easy. It seems most of the recent films I've done have had significantly more stage than location work. *Cat People* was almost all stage because it's very surreal. It's a designed film and you only get that kind of control on the stage. Except for two days, *Boulevard Nights* was all on practical locations. *Honky Tonk Freeway* was a mixture of both. I think films are coming back to the sound stage more and more, for example, *One from the Heart* and *Pennies from Heaven*. They're almost prophetic of how films are going to go back to a very designed, controlled look with a sense of filmic reality rather than naturalistic reality. Just out of sheer perversity at this point, I think I'd like to do my next film totally on the streets.

How do you maintain consistency from set-up to set-up?

If you're on a sound stage, it's very easy. I try to work at the same f-stop all the way through a scene. It's easier for communication. The gaffer knows, unless I tell him otherwise, that he's working key to a certain level. And we set everything else by eye. The balance is determined by the amount of fill light. That gets to be a subjective rather than a mathematical thing. When I first started I would set fill light by the light meter but the dailies that came back wouldn't always look consistent. So I began to realize that there are a number of factors that affect the apparent consistency of the fill light such as where the actors move in the room, what's behind them and how much of the key light is actually hitting them. There are just a number of factors like that you have to evaluate as the shot moves. So I found that I very quickly got rid of the mathematical aspect of it and I tried to train my eye. It was more difficult in the beginning but now I find that most of the time I come pretty close. It's something that's very hard to hit right on because there are so many variables from day to day.

Your films are real consistent. You are able to maintain a certain look from beginning to end.

I have the assistant keep a shot-to-shot log book which gives the f-stop, the filtration, whether there were any nets, the focal length of the lens, etc. A lot of times you can't complete a sequence on a given day. Maybe you have to come back and finish it three weeks later but you want everything to match. The only way to really remember that clearly is to keep a log book. Also you may have shot and wrapped the picture and then three months later the director decides he wants to pick up some extra shots or an additional sequence. If you don't have those notes, it's very hard to match.

With the majority of the cameramen using the same film, the same equipment and the same printing stock, do you think that leads to more of a homogenized look? Isn't it getting harder and harder to make something look "different?"

There are parallels in painting or still photography. You have Cartier-Bresson, André Kertesz and Gary Winogrand—three very different kind of still photographers, all of whom use basically the same kind of camera, an old non-reflex Leica.

It really has very little to do with the equipment. Unless you're in a situation where the kind of camera you're using only allows you to use two or three lenses. That can make a difference. But ninety-nine percent of the films are shot with Panavision equipment and you can have any range of lens you want. So it really has nothing to do with the equipment. Cameramen don't necessarily determine the look of a picture as much as the cameraman and the director together. It's a dialogue. For me, the most successful experiences are with a director who already has some kind of vision.

The younger cameramen have not been locked into the old apprenticeship/journeyman system where you learn to do something this way and you repeat it because that's the way it's been done for thirty years. So many of the younger cameramen, under forty-five or so, have come in from other areas as opposed to that system. They each have a unique way of looking at things. If anything, I think it's easier for cameramen to shoot in different styles. Back in the old days and even up until the middle sixties, sometimes it was very hard to tell who the cameraman was that shot the picture. The films of many of the cameramen were almost interchangeable. It's not just the cameramen either because the directors all tended to work in the same way too. As idiosyncratic as cameramen are becoming in their styles now, the directors have also developed very personal styles.

What kind of relationship do you have with your crew? What should a cameraman do to nurture a good relationship with his crew?

I think respect is really the key. I try to hire the best people I can find, not just technically but in terms of personality and cooperation. So much of the job has to do with administration, communication and personality. When people live in such close contact for a long time, it's important that they get along because they're spending more time with each other than they are with their families. I want to let them do their jobs and not step on their toes. The more freedom you give the individual crew member, the harder he'll work and the more committed he'll be to the film. I really believe it's a collaborative medium.

So you're not too autocratic?

I try not to be. But just as the director has a strong conviction about the dramatic and narrative values, the cinematographer has to have the same conviction about the overall photographic values and, to a greater or lesser extent, all the designed visual values. The production designer or the visual consultant is not usually on the set that much. As with Nando on the films we've done, I become his eyes and ears on the set. So I tend to be very strong when we want something a certain way that we have discussed. But I try to assimilate everybody's point of view because you never know where tremendously wonderful ideas come from. I don't believe in the autocratic approach though I believe very much in the *auteur* concept of filmmaking.

I would think that everybody in your crew would have a basic idea of what you want and they try to stay within that realm without going off the deep end.

Sometimes exactly what you need is an off-the-wall idea. Because even if it's not an idea you want to consider, it may force you to think in a slightly altered mode. It might bend your own perception to come up with something even better. Most of the time now, I'll ask the operator, "What do you think? How would you like to frame this?" and basically look at his idea before I show him what I want. I used to always show the operator the composition I wanted and then ask him whether he liked it or saw something different. Now I try to ask him first because it puts him in a position of being a contributor rather than doing it the way I want it. Sometimes I get some terrific surprises.

How important is photographic style in determining the success of a picture?

That's really hard to say. In the case of *Honky Tonk Freeway*, almost none at all. The design of the film was terrific; Nando did a fabulous job of catching a certain gone-crazy pop Americana. I'm happy with my work in it. The critics, however, have trounced the film. I think it's one of those films that five years from now somebody may look back on it and say, "Why did that film take such a beating; it's kind of interesting."

I don't know; I think maybe the technical credits don't really matter that much, except in a case like *American Gigolo*, where so much of the style was the content. I think that if the photographic style, the design, the music and the wardrobe had not been all complementary, the film would have really suffered. In *Ordinary People*, I think it enhanced the film a lot but I still think it would have been as powerful a film as it was without it. Take another film that I think had the same kind of impact on people, *The Great Santini*. In terms of the technical level of execution, *The Great Santini* is a much simpler film. But a lot of people were very moved by it and had the same kind of dramatic experience. I think that's basically why people go to movies. It's a typically Hollywood conceit that we think the packaging of the film is so important. If the sound is muddy and incomprehensible and the photography out of focus then you'll have a problem. For instance, as much as I like John Cassavetes's films, the lack of technical values, especially in his earlier films, made it very difficult for an audience to put up with what was going on.

Along the same lines, how do you think the average audience perceives the cinematography of a film?

I don't think they pay much attention to it. What they notice are pretty exteriors, you know, postcard photography like sunsets, mountains and oceanscapes. A lot of the response I get on *Continental Divide* is about how beautiful the mountains were. The part of the film I'm most satisfied with is the claustrophobic segments in downtown Chicago around the Loop at night. Cinematographers and the general audience are looking at very different things when they talk about photography.

You've worked with an interesting range of directors with diverse backgrounds. What talents and abilities do you regard as essential in a director and in your working with him?

A strong narrative sense is the most important. The director is the custodian of the story the same way the actor is the custodian of his character. An actor can't be expected to go beyond his own character and understand the whole weave or the whole pattern of the film. A cinematographer can't be expected to. Even the writer, who is hardly ever around, is fairly insulated from the day-to-day goings on. It's really the director who has to understand the unfolding of the story. Most people go to the movies to see a good story. That's the most important thing. Schlesinger is a very good storyteller. Despite the inherent difficulties with the script of *Honky Tonk Freeway*, there's a very intricate weaving of the characters, especially as they all come together in the scene in the fish restaurant. Schlesinger knows how to do that and all his films have that same kind of quality. Redford had a tremendous ability to focus in on the details of unraveling the story. So much of the strength of *Ordinary People* comes from very specific detailed behavior. And Redford has an incredibly incisive eye for gesture and nuance. That's part of the whole success of that film. That non-verbal storytelling is a part of storytelling too. A lot of the really wonderful moments in *Ordinary People* go beyond the dialogue, as good as it is, into little quirky things, especially with Tim Hutton's character.

A director's awareness of photography, design and even editing is really secondary, assuming that he gets proper coverage. A good editor and a good cinematographer will be sure he gets that.

What films are you the most happy with and why?

As films or as photography?

Both, as a total piece and as to your work.

As a total piece, I guess *Ordinary People* is the most satisfying for me and not simply because it won so many Academy Awards. It represents the kind of film I want to make. It's humanitarian filmmaking. For me, *Ordinary People* was the strongest synthesis of all the filmmaking elements. I was so pleased with what Redford and I were able to do photographically, within the context of not distracting from what the story was about.

Stylistically I'm very, very happy with *American Gigolo* because it was the first piece I did where I felt I had enough freedom to do almost arbitrary things. Things that would not be distracting but would flow into the whole feeling of the film. I'm very happy with *Honky Tonk Freeway*. Structurally, it was the most complex film I've ever worked on. It was really like fitting together the parts of a puzzle. Every day it was fascinating to me to watch how Schlesinger was going to pull it off. It was a very ambitious undertaking. I am amazed, given the density and complexity of the film logisticially and character wise, just how much of it did come together.

Honky Tonk Freeway *looked like it had an incredible amount of logistics involved.*

Just moving the equipment from one place in the country to another was difficult. There were a tremendous number of car mount scenes and they are infuriating because it's so hard to get the camera exactly where you want it. It's hard to shoot from one vehicle to another and to coordinate the movement of the vehicles. It's very difficult to shoot moving cars at night and not make the lighting look artificial. We had a couple of involved rain sequences at night which were difficult. It's hard to create the illusion of rain and depth with moving cars on the freeway. After you have the lighting roughed in then you have to light the rain as a separate element. It's the first complex rain sequence I've ever done. Schlesinger was totally uncompromising. He's used to creating depth in his pictures; usually as far back as you can see in the frame, there's something happening. That's the way he wants it and rightly so. It was a real challenge for me to work in depth the way he wanted.

On Honky Tonk Freeway *was there a lot of second-unit work? I've always wondered on a logistical film like that how much work you do and how much does the second unit pick up?*

There was more second unit work on that film than anything I've ever done.

In your experience, what kind of work is relegated to the second unit?

Almost anything that does not involve dialogue and principal actors could be considered second-unit work. Certainly stunts could be considered second-unit although the crash that ends the film was all done as first-unit. Also explosions, inserts and basically non-people kind of things are second-unit. Any time you're dealing with one of the principal characters, even if they're not speaking, I consider to be first-unit work.

Do you have any control over how the second unit turns out its footage?

Absolutely. I try to have the second-unit people see dailies with me as much as possible so that they understand where their footage fits in and what style I'm going with. I have a close dialogue with them regarding lenses, filtration and angles. If it involves lighting, a lot of times I will send the best boy or one of the prinicipal electricians from the first unit to supervise the lighting of the second unit.

Harsh sunlight dominates the scenes in Honky Tonk Freeway. *You were really going for that look.*

That was the whole point. There was a sequence where all the vehicles crossed the bridge into Florida; it was a series of helicopter shots where they all come together. We wanted a very sharp-edged light, almost etched. The bridge that we picked was essentially an unfinished bridge. There were no side railings, no lines painted, no detailing of it at all. It was just this band of concrete over the water. It was the white concrete, the dark water and this tremendous pure blue sky; it was a very primary look that we were going for. It contrasted with the other locations.

You probably shot most of the scenes during the heat of the day, between ten and two?

We sure did. A lot of times, cameramen will want early morning and late afternoon light. I wanted midday light. I wanted it straight down, hard and hot.

Did you have any problem with harsh shadows? That kind of light tends to look ugly if you don't know how to deal with it.

We had tremendous problems. I used a tremendous amount of fill light. I used arcs like I've never used arcs before. I like to go very soft with arcs, like through tracing paper. But there were times that I had to put them right behind the camera, pump them in and burn the actors up. I hated to do it.

But there's no other way.

There's no other way. If the background isn't important, you can open up and expose for the highlight a little bit and burn out the background. But John and I wanted a very clean, dense background. John understood what it took to accomplish that. A lesser director would have given me a lot of problems with that. But

John knew how it had to be. I'm always very apologetic to the actors when I do that because some of them have very sensitive eyes. It's not like the old days when if you wanted to be an actor, you learned to put up with it or otherwise your career was shelved. Today, actors tend to be very intolerant of the technical problems sometimes. But I find that if you explain the problem to them in advance, most of them are more cooperative.

How do you choose your projects now? You're in between films and you're reading a lot of scripts. What are the determinants?

First of all, it's the script. The more experience I get the more I see that a problematic or mediocre script in the hands of a brilliant director is still going to have problems. A brilliant script in the hands of an okay director can still be a very good film. I'm coming to have more and more respect for what that script is and whether it can be successfully wrought or not. And if it isn't, what chances it has of being pulled together before you start shooting. Sometimes I'll read a script that I'm very attracted to but it seems to have problems so I have to take a calculated guess whether those problems will be straightened out before we start shooting. Because the other thing I'm absolutely convinced of is that a script that is not whipped into shape by the time you start shooting is never going to be right. The problems of shooting are so overwhelming and so all-consuming that script problems never get worked out while you're making the movie. So ideally, I try to find a script that is already all there; a script that works. Then if the director is somebody that I feel also understands the material and is someone who I can respect and get along with, it's a very easy decision to make. It's also very easy to dismiss bad scripts that are going to be done by bad directors or directors that I consider to be problematic.

What makes a cameraman worth what he's paid?

Well, a cameraman takes a lot of heat. The cameraman is really the focus of most of what happens when you're on the set shooting. The director can insulate himself with the actors; in fact a lot of times, the director is expected to be above it all and somewhat aloof. There are a lot of directors who insulate themselves from the technical problems of filmmaking. But the cameraman is there on the set. He's got to keep his crew happy. He's got to effectively coordinate all the shot-to-shot elements of getting the work done with every department. He's got to be in touch with the production elements—the assistant director, the production manager—in terms of what's happening tomorrow and the day after. He's got a tremendous responsibility to the producer and the studio to make the film consistent on a day-to-day basis and deliver it with the kind of professional gloss that's expected. Today there're so many first-time directors coming from all different areas and they really don't understand the elements of filmmaking. Finally, it's the director of photography who is expected to carry the ball.

So what you're saying is that the director of photography really has an incredible responsibility all the way around.

Absolutely. I think it's important to detail why the cameramen get the kind of money they do. If things are not working, he's the first guy to get axed. In other words, if the picture is in trouble, they're going to fire the cameraman before they fire the director. You know, the way to scare the shit out of a director is to fire the cameraman. It serves as a warning to the director. That happens a lot.

There's the other side of the coin too. You have the director who has a very strong sense of how he wants the film to look. Maybe it's a fantasy that he's somehow got into his head and isn't based on any real technical expertise on how film is exposed. However, the director has this notion and the director of photography may or may not be able to deliver that. It's a tremendous responsibility. There's a real kind of amorphousness to it. A lot of times the director will say, "I kind of want it to look like this." What does that mean? But still you have to deliver it. All the departments, from set decoration to wardrobe, come to dailies to see if their stuff is photographed in a way that's satisfactory to them. So it all focuses back down on the cameraman. He's the guy that gets the praise or the heat.

You operated for several years. Do you feel that there's a lot of unconscious material expressed in the photographing of a picture? For example, you may not logically be able to explain why you choose to shoot a scene at a certain angle, but you just instinctively feel it's right.

Yes, in a way. But because I spent those years as an operator where I had to study the frame so much of the time and consider the fifteen different ways any given shot could be framed, I became very deliberate and very analytical about making those choices. When I was an assistant cameraman, I was very analytical about where the focus should be and when it should jump from one place to another. That all accumulated as baggage when I became a director of photography. So I don't find a very high level of unconsciousness for me. Now it may be very intuitive for a lot of other people. But in so far as I have the time to reflect, I do try to consider as many options and elements as I can. I feel that I'm very deliberate; I don't arbitrarily put a 35 mm lens on the camera. To me there's a big difference between a 29mm, a 35mm and a 40mm lens. There's a very strong difference in what they can do. Especially when you stop to consider that if you have the room in a set, the difference between using a 29mm and 35mm lens is just the difference between moving forward or backward two steps. You get the same field size. If you're on a dolly, where you can easily move the camera up and down, you can spend a couple of minutes deciding exactly how high or how low you want to put the camera. There are just all these variables. I have an unconscious checklist I go through; that part of it, in a sense, is unconscious and intuitive. I run through a ritual almost of elements I consider every time I do a shot. I do it much more so in setting the camera position and choosing the lens rather than the lighting. Once you have established what the source of the light is, you basically spend the rest of the shots in that sequence making it consistent. So you follow almost a predetermined guide that you've established at the beginning. You're filling in the blanks. The mechanical setting up each shot photographically is very, very deliberate.

Where it doesn't become deliberate is when a cameraman and a director decide to slap on a zoom lens and then shoot ninety percent of a picture with it. What you tend to do is that wherever the camera roughly happens to be, you leave it right there, zooming in or out for your frame. So by not considering the focal length of the lens, you don't consider whether the camera should be three inches further left or right or six inches higher or lower. I find that by using fixed focal length lenses I'm forced to deal much more methodically with every element of selection.

How have you found working with Paul Schrader, the nominal leader of New Wave Hollywood, if there is such a thing?

By directing, Paul has had to confront some of his demons. Paul is an introverted person and directing is not an introverted experience. So I've seen a tremendous evolution in Paul from *American Gigolo* to *Cat People*. Paul has been growing outward and facing the world around him a lot more. That might be one of the reasons he decided to direct. Writing is a very solitary experience obviously. I have a good relationship with Paul; we get along terrifically. We love the same filmmakers: Bresson, Franju, Renoir. Paul's grasp of film history and film aesthetics is more profound than anybody I've ever worked with. It's nice for me to be able to deal with that directly and not have to worry whether or not I should mention to this director that this scene is similar to a sequence in *Beauty and the Beast* or *A Man Escaped*. Paul and I can talk about that. As a matter of fact, we look at a lot of films before we start production. Preparing for a film with Schrader is almost like going to film school.

Do you yourself have any aspirations to direct?

I've got myself committed slightly in that direction. A year ago I denied it even while I was trying to work to make it happen. I've optioned a novella. It's not something that I'm just entertaining; I'm actively working on it.

What is attracting you to directing as opposed to what you're doing now? What more is there for you in it?

It's the total experience of making a film, of making a statement. It's dealing with my own perception of the world and the way we live in it. And finally, a cameraman can't make any direct comment about that. I mean, he can through his choice of images but you really make your statements through characterization. It's not that I have an overwhelming urge to make the jump just for the sake of doing it. It's that there are very specific stories I want to deal with. I love photography and I don't expect to ever give it up. If I'm fortunate enough to direct a film, I might find it a totally disillusioning experience. But I want to try it once. And if I'm successful, I would still want to continue shooting. I can imagine that there are a tremendous number of films I would be attracted to as a cinematographer but that I would never want to direct. For instance, I would love to do another picture that had the scope of *Honky Tonk Freeway*; but as a director I don't think I would want to do something with that scale. I'm very interested in more intimate relationships. So it's the ability to have the best of both. Also by virtue of having a craft, I can go out, get a job and work. It's not just a question of supporting yourself but rather the satisfaction you have of working day by day. A cameraman goes out every day and does his job. A director today has become a writer, producer, editor and everything else. So much of his energy is taken with putting all the elements together and getting ready to shoot that the actual shooting of the film is only a small part of it. For a director to take a project from infancy to maturation may require several years. I don't know if I can take that because I like production. I don't know if I have the temperament to deal with all the other things you have to deal with to get the project done. I know directors who would love to be able to do two pictures a year but instead are able to do one picture every two or three years.

Could you give me a thumbnail, one-paragraph sketch of your artistic and aesthetic approach to each one of your films? What were you trying to do photographically?

Boulevard Nights for me was primarily an exercise in nighttime street photography. Most of the film takes place along and around Whittier Boulevard in East Los Angeles. Those cars have a very magical feel; I wanted them to kind of dance, to come alive and sparkle. The scenes with the gangs I wanted to have a much funkier look. So within the element of nighttime street photography, I wanted to deal with the textural difference between the gangs, who were the have-nots, and the car club people, who were the haves. And that's exactly the dichotomy manifested in the relationship of the two brothers. Chuco was a gang kid and he walked most places while his brother Raymond, who used to be a gang kid, had this incredibly manicured car. It was part of the dramatic chasm between them, part of what kept them from really being able to communicate and understand each other.

American Gigolo was basically an exercise in high-tech chic. Not high tech in the sense of architecture but high tech in its lifestyle and totally urban in its sensibilities. There's no sense of nature in the film at all; what little is there is incredibly manicured. Unlike *Boulevard Nights* which had a very realistic street look, I wanted the nighttime look in *American Gigolo* to look very manipulated. I wanted the light to look as though everything was artificial. There's a lot of arbitrary use of light and a lot of arbitrary compositions and camera moves in the film. It's a study in artifice finally. Richard Gere's lifestyle is a style of artifice, of packaging and presentation. Paul and I tried for a visual style that reinforced the superficialness of what you see is what there is.

Ordinary People was an exercise in restraint. It's a film of very intense, almost hermetic, human drama. It has a boiling test-tube quality to it. Test-tube in the sense too that there's a scientific, kind of detached point of observation. The camerawork and the lighting are self-conscious enough and remote enough so that you kind of sit back from the cauldron you see in front of you. Some of the most powerful moments with the actors have a detached feel photographically. Or, at least if not detached, then certainly a feel of not being obtrusive. It's the feeling that you're privileged to sit there and watch it but you're not thrown and pulled into it in a way that makes you feel viscerally distraught. It's an observed film; it has a certain coolness to it. I tried to color balance the film in a very cool way except for the opening montage which has an autumnal feel to it.

Honky Tonk Freeway was restrained chaos in the sense that it could have been a mishmash of unrelated incidents. But Schlesinger had a strong sense of how it should all weave together and how the sequences should dance. There's a lot of camera movement in the film, even more than *American Gigolo*, but it's camera

movement that is buried and tries to be seamless. It's restrained chaos in the sense
that I tried every way I could to keep things pulled together and unified and still be
faithful to the very strong eye that both Scarfiotti and Schlesinger had, looking at
the American landscape as two foreigners would look at the more visually bizarre
qualities in American life on the road. I tried to enhance that as much as I could. It's
so easy, in films of that scope, to be visually all over the place. But *Honky Tonk
Freeway* is a very disciplined film in a funny sort of way. The characters are so out
of control that you couldn't afford to have a film style that was out of control because that would just create confusion for the audience.

The approach to *Continental Divide* is what the title connotes: geographic seg-
regation. The whole point is that here are two characters that are just about as
different as they could be. You have a very urban being who is totally involved in
the world of newspapers and who would probably pass out the first time he
breathed fresh air. On the other hand, you have a woman who has very pointedly
escaped all that and has become a recluse high in the mountains. So you have the
contrast of the open expanse of the Colorado Rockies and the very closed, claustrophobic world of the Chicago Loop. I tried to juggle those two different visual
styles. I tried for a very strong sense of street energy around the newspaper office.
We did a tremendous amount of dollying. Michael Apted loves to move the camera
and the streets of Chicago are perfect for that. In the mountains, even though the
characters are hiking around a lot, the camera is hardly moving. The camera is
much smaller than the landscape. When you're looking at impressive mountains,
the only way you want to look at them is just stand back and look.

Cat People is a myth and a dream. Paul and I worked toward a style of photography that on the surface seemed to be real, almost kind of quotidian in its matter of
fact aspect. But it had an overtone, an evocation of a dream-like state. So the
camera, when it's moving, is floating. There are a lot of crane moves. So it just
wasn't a question of the camera moving laterally but on a crane, where it's up, down
and floating around. There's almost a detached point of view in a lot of *Cat People*,
where the camera is lighter than air. The characters are also kind of drifting. The
whole film is somehow in a cloud. That's not to say that the photographic style was
diffuse. We didn't want to get into a heavy fogged or diffused look. We used the
sense of movement and surreal lighting for that. There are a lot of low camera
angles and a lot of non-realistic lighting. It is expressionistic in the real sense of the
word not just in terms of long shadows but in terms of the colors. More than any
other film I've worked on, I really tried to go for a painterly use of light. In all my
other films I've tried to use a very realistic basis. In *Cat People* I tried not to.

*How would you advise a student who felt he had talent in this area? Would you
recommend the same route you took? Or are there many paths to the goal?*

There are many roads. I think that several of them can be pursued at once; it's
not necessarily just a linear progression. It's very important for everybody to explore the maze of his mind. Shooting, and the actual work of making a film, is very
important. Any kind of opportunity to shoot, to learn and to experiment is very
important. But I think there also comes a point where, if you're talking about

trying to get into the mainstream of the industry, you've got to make that commitment. I was basically very satisfied with the route I took. I don't necessarily recommend it for other people. But I think there is something to be said for the apprenticeship system. Assuming you've reached a point that you understand who you are and that you've spent some time working and shooting, you can try to get involved in mainstream film production at the bottom of the scale. You can start as a loader, become an assistant, become an operator and spend whatever it takes—six to ten years—to thoroughly learn all the elements. People are so impatient today. But you only get one chance, especially if you're a director. If he screws up on his first major film, it's going to be a long time before he's heard from again. Even more so for a cameraman. If you jump in before you're ready, you may get in way over your head and not work again for years. Preparation is really the keynote. You prepare and learn by watching other people. I learned from every cameraman I worked with when I was an assistant and operator. Because once you're doing it yourself there aren't too many people you can learn from because you're on the line all the time. I think a lifetime commitment to learning and studying still photography, painting and all the graphic areas is real important. It's a constant process. In a sense, you're a student for your whole career. It's important to keep that disposition. I think that the same kind of questioning that you do when you're first starting, where every shot is a new experience, is important to do all the way through. It's not a skill that you're learning where, at a certain point, you've learned it all.

I think that film schools are well and fine. I find that most of what you get out of film school can be gotten without going to film school. It's another link along the chain, though. I'm wary of film schools to the extent that they seem to foster a sense of arrogance more and more because of the success of so many people who have come out of film schools and become incredibly successful. There's a developing arrogance on the part of film students to think that they're going to come in and teach the industry how it's done. I think that's a mistake.

4

Bill Butler

"The day-to-day business of making movies is a matter of problem solving. You are constantly problem solving from the time you arrive on the set until you quit shooting in the evening."

Bill Butler has a habit of jolting people by casually mentioning that he's working on his third career. His youthful and energetic outlook tends to obscure the fact that he did a stint in radio, moved on to a distinguished career in Chicago television and then finally made the transition to Hollywood filmmaking in 1969. And while many creative people might have burned themselves out along the way, Butler is probably now turning out the most significant work of this three careers.

After receiving a degree in engineering, Butler worked in radio for a short time but quickly moved on to what turned out to be the ground floor in a similar but new medium—television. In fact, he helped to construct the first commercial TV station, WGN in Chicago. After getting the station on the air, he remained in an engineering capacity until one day, by some quirk of fate, he got behind the television camera. Ever since then Butler has been artistically hypnotized by that image in the camera viewfinder.

Working at WGN also laid the groundwork for an important personal and professional relationship that continues to this day. While Butler was a cameraman at the station, WGN hired a new kid in the mailroom, named Billy Friedkin. Friedkin showed some innate talent and was soon directing television shows there. Both men were interested in the dramatic power of film. At Friedkin's urging, they worked as a team, moonlighting on film projects for church groups and public service organizations. Several of their documentaries won film festival awards. Friedkin moved to Hollywood to test his directing mettle and Butler was to follow later.

Beginning with his first Hollywood feature, Francis Coppola's *The Rain People*, the number of directors Butler has worked with has expanded to the point where it reads like a Who's Who of Directors. Among the more prominent names are William Friedkin, John Boorman, Jack Nicholson, Phil Kaufman, John Korty, Francis Coppola, Irvin Kershner, Milos Forman and Steven Spielberg. Butler has also shot the first features of some younger, talented directors like John Badham and Randall Kleiser. His versatility has been proven in his ability to bring a specific style to "important" pictures like *The Conversation* and *Drive, He Said* as well as to lighter fare like *Alex and the Gypsy* and *Grease*. Two films photographed by Butler, *Jaws* and *One Flew over the Cuckoo's Nest* (co-credit with Haskell Wexler), have between them earned over a quarter of a billion dollars.

The secret to Butler's success is that he is a consummate professional in anything he does. After little more than a decade of shooting features, he has compiled a track record and a list of credits that any student cinematographer would aspire to and that even a veteran cameraman would envy. It makes one wonder what Butler is planning for his fourth career.

1968	*Fearless Frank*	1979	*Can't Stop the Music*
	The Rain People	1980	*It's My Turn*
	Adam's Woman		*The Night the Lights Went Out in Georgia*
1969	*Return of Count Yorga*		
	Vampire Blood	1981	*Rocky III*
1971	*Drive He Said*		*Stripes*
	Something Evil	1982	*The Next Sting*
	Hickey and Boggs	1984	*Big Trouble*
1972	*Melinda*		
	Running Wild	Television:	
	Manchu Eagle		
1974	*The Conversation*	1969	*A Clear and Present Danger*
	Jaws	1971	*TV Newscaster*
1975	*One Flew Over the Cuckoo's Nest* † (Shared Credit)	1972	*Deliver Us from Evil*
			Hernandez
	The Bingo Long Traveling All-Stars and Motor Kings		*Target Risk*
		1973	*Sunshine*
	Lipstick		*I Heard the Owl Call My Name*
1976	*Alex and the Gypsy*		*Indict and Convict*
	Demon Seed		*The Execution of Private Slovik*
1977	*Capricorn One*	1974	*Hustling*
	Grease	1975	*Fear on Trial*
	The Omen II		*McCoy*
1978	*Ice Castles*	1976	*Raid on Entebbe**
	Uncle Joe Shannon	1977	*Mary White*
	Rocky II	1979	*T. R. Sloan*

† Academy Award Nomination for best achievement in cinematography.

* Emmy Award for best achievement in cinematography.

How do you choose your film projects?

You try to choose from the best films available at the time. There's a choosing that goes on on both sides. A film kind of selects its cameraman and a cameraman sort of selects the films he wants to do.

I personally have tried to take as large a variety of subjects as I can possibly cover. Partly so I would learn more; mostly for my own education. And also because you can very easily get stereotyped, like an actor does, as only doing pictures, say, on a rushing river. Shooting the title and stunt footage for *Deliverance* probably helped qualify me for doing *Jaws*, which was on the ocean. I certainly learned things on *Deliverance* that I used in *Jaws*. But I would not just want to shoot pictures on oceans and climbing up mountainsides because that's not really the only kind of film I want to do.

On the other hand, a musical like *Grease* can be challenging. It was challenging because it was a small musical, not a large one. The story that it had to tell was not a great story, it was a light, little story and yet the musical on stage had such vitality to it that I thought it would be a lot of fun to try to get that feeling of movement and energy across on the screen.

I don't know whether I'm correct in the approach I took to the film; I took a rather straightforward, formal approach. I didn't go crazy with the camera as per *Jesus Christ, Superstar* or *Tommy*, which really relied on camera tricks a lot. I tried to keep the camera more subtle and still bring across the same amount of energy and the same ideas in a rather realistic way so that the story itself would stand out a little more.

As a cinematographer, it's really great to be able to approach an entirely different subject—to reason out what's really required to do that film properly and then to take that gamble and have someone take that gamble with you because whoever hires you is rolling the dice for several million dollars on your judgment. There's only a certain amount of planning and only so much a director and a producer can do when they go into a film. Once they get down to putting it into that little box and getting it down on film, then they're relying on you to get those pictures and to do it properly.

A cinematographer doesn't actually operate the camera, he really directs how it's to be operated and directs all the people that surround the camera. So really what they're paying you for is your ability to handle those people. You have to handle both their mood and approach so that it's the same as yours; their enthusiasm must match yours; and their creative inventiveness must match yours. Because the day-to-day business of making movies is a matter of problem-solving. You are constantly problem solving from the time you arrive on the set until you quit shooting in the evening.

This kind of problem-solving, of physical creativity, of building things for the camera, is very much a necessity with people who put this "trick" on film. And it is a trick. It's a mechanical trick; it's a mechanical machine that's making the image. You cannot separate that fact. And that fact may be overwhelming so what you must not do is to then let that fact overwhelm the artistic approach to making film.

And here's where some people get hung up; some people get so involved with the trick that what they do then becomes all tricks. They let the camera get in the way of what they're doing. It still may make a good show because it may be interesting to watch the tricks. But they may have, in the doing, lost the flavor of the soup they were trying to make. So then the story doesn't get told well but a lot of flashy photography gets on the screen.

There's a big difference though, between throwing up some lights and shooting it and doing a creative, artistic job, given those time restrictions?

That's the trick in my business. The trick you have to turn in this business is, given the time, to light the set and light it beautifully. It takes twice the effort to make it just a little bit better. It doesn't take just a little bit more effort, it takes twice the effort. And it doesn't get twice as good. You can do all of the things that are easy to learn out of books and by doing. It's easy to light a set to pass; no one but the most critical person might know the difference. You can light a set quickly when you have to but if you want to make it really striking to the eye, then you have to go play with the light and that's very time-consuming. I mean, it's time-consuming when the clock is ticking away at maybe $20,000 a day or $2,000 an hour. You know the money is going down the drain. And when it's you that's spending it, then the responsibility weighs very heavily on your shoulders. So you have to make priority judgments about how you want to spend your time, on what set, at what moment. When in the film will it pay off? So the wise cameraman then makes choices.

I don't know exactly why people hire me. It's foolish to think that you're hired *only* for the films that you've made that they've seen. That's what makes them give you the first call. But a good producer checks all over town; he checks with other producers. And they want to know a lot of things about you that have nothing to do with whether or not you can get the exposure correct. They already know that. They already know what your material looks like on the screen. If they're even thinking about you, they know that your type of photography is right for their film.

What are the things they check for? They want to know how easy you are to get along with. Are you going to give them trouble? Are you going to be a guy who waits for the clouds to roll by and until everything is perfect? Are you going to hold them up for time? How are you on speed? How good are you at going into a difficult lighting situation and how fast can you put it together in your head and figure out what to do about it? I mean, I'd have to name all the idiosyncracies of all the cameramen.

They're not checking you out to see if you can make the exposure; the director's already made that decision. He's decided your photography's fine, but in order to get your style of photography on the screen, what do you have to go through to get it? Are you some guy who's going to bring in fifteen arcs to light a street or can you light it with a few little lamps and still get it beautiful? They want to know a lot of things about you that affect the production. They are the producers. They want to know if you can handle it. Maybe it's a big show. Can he handle a big show, does he seem capable or is he a new kid on the block? Does he hit sometimes and miss sometimes? Some cameramen are that way. They'll be terrific on one show and turn right around and blow it on the next one. Their emotions sometimes get in the way. Is he emotional, does he blow up? Does he get along with the actors or does he give them a hard time?

But on some films you wish you had a little more input on why you're hired?

It would be very beneficial. But it isn't really essential. The only thing that's essential is that you be your own critic. Because if you listen too much to others, they'll mislead you. The harshest critic in the world must be yourself. And you'll be about as good as you are a critic of yourself. When you do something that someone raves about and you know it was a trick and it wasn't difficult, that anyone could do it, that you really didn't supply anything new, then you must tell yourself, in the harshest terms, that that is so and that you fooled them. When you come up with something that really *was* new, good and striking and you really made it on a particularly difficult shot—well, for instance, when I was hired for *Jaws* one of the most difficult requirements was that I could shoot day-for-night on the ocean. Now, shooting day-for-night on land usually means that you eliminate the sky because the sky gives away the fact that it's not night. So as long as you can shoot an area that has bright sunlight on it and dark shadows, you expose it low enough and the bright sunlight becomes moonlight and the darker areas become black. The grey and the shadowed areas of the sun, exposed down deep enough, become black. And you put a bright light in a window and suddenly people believe that it's night. It's easy. It's been done thousands of times. When done well, it's perfectly acceptable. But when you go on the ocean, there is no way you can eliminate the sky. I knew I could shoot day-for-night on the ocean and make it believable *if* they let me shoot it when I wanted to. I think probably that I have not seen better day-for-night shot on the ocean ever than I shot on that film. Yet I've never heard anyone comment on it. Only I know that it was as good as it was. In fact, *Jaws* was not even among ten films to be considered for nomination of an Oscar. Not even considered! Yet it was the top-grossing film of that year. Now, my own peers, other cinematographers who make these judgments, must have thought that those shots were done in the lab as a trick and therefore not worthy. I'm sure they're totally unaware that they were done in the camera with nothing more than exposure to pull the trick.

Apparently you did it so well that no one realized it was day-for-night?

Partially that's true. But, my point is, you have to know whether it was good or not. This is a business where everyone compliments you every day for reasons which have nothing to do with whether or not you're doing well. So sometimes it's difficult to measure and you stop listening very soon to what anyone says and you only listen to yourself.

You can also go very wrong because some people listen to themselves so much that they end up talking to themselves with film. They make interesting films where only they know what they're doing or what they're saying. So you can also go too far in that direction, losing your purpose in making the film and ending up not talking to the people, which is what I want to do. I want to communicate to people through the camera.

I want to be a popular communicator and that's one reason that I do television so much. Whenever a good television show comes along, I take it because I still have a great love for television. I've spent too much of my life in it not to realize that you can shoot a television show and be seen by more people than any one single feature. You can say a lot more in television to a lot more people, so I don't ignore it. I only try to pick the shows that I think are meaningful because I can do that.

You've done quite a number of excellent productions for TV, The Execution of Private Slovik, Hustling, I Heard the Owl Call My Name, Sunshine, *and* Raid on Entebbe, *to name a few. Do you find TV is more restrictive in terms of budgets and shooting schedules and does that limit your creativity more than theatrical features would?*

It limits how well you can make the picture because the bigger the budget, the better picture you can make. I've been fortunate in getting television projects that have good budgets behind them. However, television makes it possible for you to make pictures about subjects that wouldn't make any money in theaters. On television, they become the exceptional fare. I believe every television project that you've named is more important than any feature I've made, outside of maybe three.

Which three?

Well, I think *The Rain People* was one of them. Certainly *The Conversation* was an important picture. And you can't ignore *Jaws*, not that it had anything to say but simply because of the response that it got. It has become an important picture for that reason. As far as a message picture or a picture that had something to say, you know *Drive, He Said,* had more to say, perhaps on a deeper level.

But most of the pictures—well, like *Capricorn One,* for example, has a pseudo-message to it that all of the moonshots were faked on television or something. I mean, it's really a chase movie that's for fun. A lot of pictures purport to have a message; how important they are I don't know. They're almost like light television. They're more television fare, only done with a big budget. But you do a *Private Slovik* or *Raid on Entebbe*—that's heavy stuff because it's real and it happened; you want people to know about the story as accurately and dramatically as you can get it across. So I like television for that reason. It's really a great communicating medium. It hasn't even begun to be used. I think it's going to change a lot too.

All of the films you've done for TV are very well photographed. Most of the things you see on TV don't have that high-quality photography. I'm wondering how you do it, how you achieve that—since not many others do.

Part of the desire to make a picture look that good on TV came out of my frustration of having spent years, not only in television film work but in electronic television. I started when we were putting resistors together, before transistors were even invented. It was the day of the tube and the soldering iron. I helped build the first TV station in Chicago. All those guys who started out in television were dreamers and I was in that. So the early days of television was such a great dream and such a great challenge. Eventually the experimentation stopped. It got so all the networks and stations thought about was how to do it cheaper. That thinking still permeates television today and holds it back. Television could probably wipe the film industry out overnight if that thinking was to stop.

As it is now, to get something good on television, you have to shoot film. That partly accounts for my transition from the electronic into film work. I could do more and I could see where the quality was. So when I was offered this show (*Private Slovik*), my desire was to come in and make exposures not as the television people prescribe it. If you listen to the technicians at the television studios, they say that they have certain exposures they need and the densities they want and they're scared to death that this won't appear right on the tube (look good). I've been through all of that. I don't need a technician to tell me what it will take—I know what the tube will take. So I went into that show, I made the exposures that I wanted to make so it looked right, and the truth of the matter is, film comes out looking better on the tube than live cameras. You condense all the exposures and all the variations on the film and it goes right onto the tube in practically a one-to-one ratio. So if you make your exposures where they belong then you've got the quality on the film and then it'll transfer to the TV tube with no problem.

So basically you just shot it as you would shoot any other feature?

I shot it exactly as I would for the big screen, with only a few changes. You do handle some things differently for the tube, like close-ups for example. It's been figured out that if you shoot a person head to foot for a theather screen, he should look about normal because you're sitting so far back in the theater. But when you watch the small screen, you are not sitting halfway back in a theater. You're not viewing it from the same distance. The perspective is entirely different. You're looking at a small image and you're probably sitting much closer to it. They've found that close-ups work great on TV, but if you threw them on the big screen, a person's head would be a monster. Filmmakers today have gotten so used to television and to the effectiveness of close-ups that they now make much tighter close-ups than they used to. Also they err in that direction a lot; they do it at the wrong time or do it too much and wear it out.

As opposed to some other cameramen, you have no prejudices about working in TV. I think a lot of cameramen look forward to the time when they won't do TV any more.

Yes, it's used as a status symbol by too many cameramen who are being shallow about it. They don't realize that if you do a television show, in one night it'll be seen by more people than any feature you shot, at least most features. So if you feel that you're trying to say something with your picture, that you have a message that's worthwhile, then television is very good. Television is the height of communication today; it goes into every house. I can't imagine anything more communicative than television. So I can't pass that up. I mean, I won't become better known or more famous for it; you become better known for your features for some reason.

You shot Raid on Entebbe *on film and someone else shot a version of the raid on videotape; how did shooting the story on film enhance your version?*

I think it's generally agreed that the tape version was nowhere near as well done as the film version. Now there are a lot of other elements involved in the making of

BILL BUTLER   81

those two pictures that are important. It would be unfair to say that the tape version wasn't as good as the film version just because it was done on tape. However, doing it on tape, it had all the curses I've been talking about, trying to make it cheaper, faster, cutting corners; they were trying to beat someone out to the market with that story. If you were to have a fair test, you would let someone make a videotape at their own pace and no more budget limitations than we had. Even at that, we (on the film) were rushed. We were competing and we could not get it out as fast as the tape people could. But we got out a far better version than they did.

You've worked with a lot of younger and/or first-time feature directors?

For some reason or other, I've gotten a lot of first-time directors. Francis Ford Coppola wasn't exactly a first-time director but he was very close. I did *The Rain People* for him. He had done another feature before that and one just coming out of college. Spielberg had done one other feature before I did *Jaws* with him. I did John Badham's first feature, *The Bingo Long Traveling All Stars and Motor Kings*. I worked for Billy Friedkin when he first started. I shot his documentaries. I came in on his first feature and helped him finish that. So I've gotten into the vein of first-time directors.

But you enjoy it, don't you? I mean, the younger, first-time director is probably not set in his ways. He's more open, receptive and creative?

Yes, there's more creative freedom, I guess. There's a certain satisfaction in knowing that you just didn't go in and do the film the way somebody wanted it done without adding anything yourself. You know that you not only added a lot but you really carried the load.

I think it would be wrong for me to lead you to believe that I chose them anymore than they chose me. Let's put it this way: I don't object to working with first-time directors. I've done it so much that obviously it's not something I'm afraid of doing. On the other hand, it's not a preference, necessarily. Most of the first-time directors . . . take Spielberg, for example, he is exciting, full of ideas and imagination. I just like that element; the newness of his thinking. I like his desire to experiment. I liked working with Jack Nicholson on *Drive, He Said*. It was a challenge to try and keep up with his mind and try to get the show he's talking about on film. That's exciting. There are disadvantages; you build a better name as a cameraman working with the top directors in the field. But like everything in this business, you get typecast. And producers worry about their director making it through and they say, "Who is good with first-time directors?" Well, if after a while, you've worked with five or six first-time directors, all of a sudden your name pops up a lot. That's happened to me.

Working with first-time directors means more responsibility on your part.

Yes, a huge amount of responsibility. It gets wearing. After you do that a while then you really start looking forward to working with a really fine director who is well prepared and comes to the set every day knowing exactly the shots he wants. And all you really have to do is pull off what he's got in his mind already. You don't have to invent each and every cut, set-up and angle yourself.

What you like the best is when you do something well, knowing that the director

you're doing it for knows that it's good and can appreciate the fact that you've done
something very clever and very well. That's why I like working with Coppola because when I do something very clever and very well, he knows it and can evaluate it.

*Do you ever think that the cinematography can be so visually striking that it
overwhelms and overpowers the plot of the film?*

Certainly. Absolutely. It certainly can. See, if you're really directing the photography, if you're really living up to the title, you'll make that judgment carefully so
you're not making some large sweep with the camera when you should really be
standing still and not moving at all. That should be part of your judgment. You
must be more than the man who just gets the exposure right. It doesn't take much to
do that. Even if it's difficult, and sometimes it is, you must do more than that. You
must have some overall feeling for your subject matter. Then you must have some
opinion about what the style should be. And hopefully, if you're working with a
good director, you sit down long before shooting starts and you discuss the style.
Then when the shooting comes and the moment-to-moment decisions and problem-solving starts, you don't have to stop and hold a discussion about what the style
should be, what lens you should use, whether the camera should dolly, zoom or
crane. It's not the time for the discussion then; it should occur before shooting
starts so then, when those decisions are being made, they're coming out of a background of ideas that you already have.

Coppola is exceptionally good at this. You can sit down and discuss how to shoot
a film with him long before you start it. So when the heat of the battle occurs, you
don't have to stop then to load the rifle. You can take your shot and it'll be right.
That's the way I like to work. That's why I sometimes get weary of working with
new directors who don't have that background and that method of working.

One Flew over the Cuckoo's Nest *was a script you were really interested in,
wasn't it?*

It's a subject matter that I'm interested in and felt very close to. I felt I knew the
manner in which to approach it and I personally feel that a lot of the success of the
film is due to the fact that I did understand what they were trying to do. I knew that
Milos Forman understood what he was trying to do. Milos is a hard man to understand unless you take the time to get to know him. I think I helped Milos a lot in that
respect. I do believe that understanding the right approach to the level of humor
that was involved was important.

I had worked with Jack Nicholson before so that helped make it easier to do the
film. But it wasn't all that easy to do the film because working with Milos meant that
you had to understand what he wanted. His English, at that time, wasn't that good.
He spoke French very well and, of course, his own language. When the language
wasn't working for him, he might get upset about the language problem and not
about the problem you were discussing. Quite often these things would get crossed
in the minds of the actors. By recognizing that fact and being constantly aware of
it, I was able to short-circuit a lot of the problems they were having when I arrived.
I could communicate to the actors very often some simple little direction that he
wanted when they thought Milos was upset at them by the way they were doing

something. But he wasn't at all—he was upset because he couldn't say what he wanted to say. Many times I would just simply say (to an actor), "All he wants you to do is go there, take your medicine, walk back and that's all. All he wants you to do is to do it again." And that quick, the problem was solved.

One day Jack Nicholson was ready to leave the set because Milos and he didn't understand one another's needs in trying to do a fight scene. I had to smooth the waters, step in and talk to Jack because I could. And by making sense out of it, talking to both parties, I was able then to get Jack to choreograph the fight and do it. That day's shooting got done for no other reason than I stepped in between two very talented people who couldn't communicate that particular day.

I felt that I understood the film; I understood the right approach to it and that made a big difference. So it really had nothing to do with how to make exposures. Understanding the level of that kind of humor and what the humor was about was important. If you don't understand a film, you can go a long ways wrong. And that film was going wrong.

On Cuckoo's Nest, *Haskell Wexler and William Fraker were also given cinematography credit. How did you become involved with the film and under what circumstances?*

Billy Fraker came as a favor to finish the picture when I had to leave because of other commitments.

At what point did you come in?

I came in, let's say, because there was misunderstanding on the creative level between Haskell Wexler and the director. Put that any way you want, the bottom line was that Haskell didn't have the same picture in mind that the director had.

Very often a cameraman is hired who seems like he's exactly right for a film. I would have thought Haskell was and he wasn't. The same cameraman goes on to shoot *Bound for Glory* and wins an award for it because he was right for it. It's a difficult thing; I'd hate to be a producer trying to pick the right cameraman because who would know that my background was more complete in that area than someone else's unless they knew me rather well?

You were more complementary to Milos's personality and ideas?

Partially that, yes. Partially I have that ability to be a very flexible person. I have a great adaptability of those personal traits that make it possible for me to work with new directors. It's that ability to be plastic and still produce something—not being plastic to the point where you don't have a stand or a point of view. You have to be able to have a reasonable point of view, one that makes sense, and still be able to work within the artistic desires of other people. It's not easy because artistic people tend to kill creativity around them. The psyche tries to occupy the area. And a creative psyche is a killer sometimes. So to remain creative and work around other creative people means you also have to stay alive, creatively as well as literally. It's difficult. Creative people very often don't get along together when they have opposite views.

The secret of saving that show was photographic; and the secret was going tight enough with the camera so that the things and nuances that were going on in all the faces would show on the screen. They weren't doing that and without it the film would have failed. I mean, I don't know at what level it would have failed, but it would have failed. It would not have been the success that it was.

So if someone's looking for a formula about how to be a cinematographer, I'd advise them that one thing is to try to understand the director. I may be right or wrong, but I've found that each director really has one important thing that he's trying to say. I find that very often he's totally unaware of it. I try to find out what's in the man's gut. I try to find what he's trying to get out of himself and then I try to help him say it.

An early feature that you shot was The Rain People *for Coppola. I remember you saying* The Rain People *was shot with minimal lighting equipment; just a few quartz lights, etc. How did you get it to look so good?*

One thing I like a lot about Coppola is that he will gamble on a new idea and he likes to make little films with a small amount of equipment and keep them that way—feeling that he can spend more of his time and energy working with the actors, keeping the story simple and not letting it get out of hand physically. That was at least the theory.

So we put together a little equipment van, and when I tried to estimate what the lighting requirements would be to get the most amount of light I could on this little truck, I decided to go with the little quartz lights. They were not quartz lights with fennels in them and the focusing lights that you find today. These were like little tin cans with no lenses whatsoever. The quartz bulb could be moved in and out a little bit for a bit of flood and spot but they were open faced and uncontrollable beyond that. I estimated that if I had twenty 1,000-watt quartz lights I could shoot the film. I mean, I told Coppola that I could shoot just about any kind of scene that he could dream up. That was sticking my neck out a long way. He held me to do it and that's what we went with.

In the load, I put on a couple of 2,000-watt quartz lights and sacrificed some of the 1,000-watt lights. But I ended up with the equivalent of twenty 1,000-watt lights. In addition to that, we had some little inky dinks; I think we had four. And that's all the lights we had on the show. We did light every scene with them including one of the most difficult tasks I've ever had. I think Coppola did it to me to try me out very early in the film. It was a dining room/dance hall scene for the wedding. I had just these lights to work with. I thought the crew was going to quit; they thought it was unreasonable that he asked us to light this large room with them. The room must have been 100 feet long and 80 feet wide, something on that order. It was huge. But I looked at the room and thought if I spread the lights from end to end (the room had a beautiful beamed ceiling) I could fasten the lights to the beams, spread them all over the room and I could get enough exposure to make it. Coppola then came in and told me he wanted to shoot those beam ceilings 360 degrees. I think he was trying to make it impossible for me; maybe not, maybe he merely creatively wanted to do that. But it left me nowhere to hang the lights, absolutely nowhere. I went back to my room in the old hotel, sat down in the rocking chair and rocked away for about a half hour. And, as it will happen, a little light went on and I said, "Aha, there's one spot where he won't shoot that I can hang the lights. It's in the dead center of the room, directly over the camera." He could still pan 360 degrees and he'd have to pan straight up to see the lights. So we built a light ring that I could lift up right over the camera and we aimed all these quartz lights at various distances and then right overhead we put up an umbrella to bounce the light down so it would match the softness of the other light. We lit the whole room that way and shot all evening.

I think that trick sold Coppola on the fact that I was inventive enough to solve the problems of a major film and he kept me on the show. I think if I had not solved that problem, he might have decided that I didn't have it.

As I recall, The Rain People *was shot with actors and crew moving across country, caravan style, utilizing natural and realistic locations.*

The theory was that we would travel from New York to as far west as we wanted to go. We had this little van; Coppola had a large camper van that he had an editing table in and there were several station wagons. There were only about a dozen people on the crew and that was it.

Was that a crazy way to shoot a film?

It worked well. I enjoyed it. It wasn't unusual for me because I had just come out of documentaries anyway and I was used to working with small crews. To get good lighting out of those quartz lights the simple trick was, since they're hot in the center and not too bad on the edges, to hide the hot center. So that when you aim the light, you use the nice light that comes from the edge of them. You had to bury the hot center somewhere so that it wouldn't be seen, into something that would absorb it like a corner.

So you had to face those kinds of problems every day?

Right. But that was the trick that had to be overcome. You had to know the light, understand it and use it for what it was. If you were clever you could make good light with it. You had to face what you were dealing with and that was it.

In The Rain People, *you had several night-for-night sequences that covered large areas. What is your approach to night-for-night lighting, especially when involving such areas?*

On *The Rain People*, what I did there in the trailer park sequence was to go around to the various trailers and wherever there was a doorway, screw a bulb into whatever lamp they had there. And then where I had to, I'd use my quartz lights and set them around in little bushes or wherever so there would be little spots of light around until I got down to the point where we had to walk about half a block around a corner and play out a scene. I produced enough sources there to make that happen.

It's a real challenge when you have a minimum number of lights to work with and you have to do something like that. You really have to get inventive. I think, considering what I was working with then, that it worked really well. Maybe it would be better if cameramen more often did that. They might not overlight their sets so much.

Sometimes there is a built-in tendency to overlight just to show that you're doing your job.

That's true. That happens to guys who are just getting into features or just getting to the point where they're being handed lots of equipment. You get over that. You get to the point where you use exactly what you think it takes and that's what you should do. But you are also working against time and a budget on any film; you seldom get the luxury to play.

The way I beat the time in lighting for night is to prerig. So the secret, the real key, to lighting a street set for me is to be able to do it in the daytime. That is, to decide in the daytime where I want the light, where I'm going to throw it. I have my crew take the units and put them wherever they are going to have to be, rooftops or wherever. Usually they are on rooftops because if I have to throw a light, I like to throw it from high so it appears to belong up there where the streetlights live. So having done it enough times to know where those lights have to go, I tell my gaffer where to put those lights in the daytime, so that when nighttime comes and you hook up the generator and turn them all on, you see how close you've come for the effect you wanted.

That's interesting. That would really alter the way you might light it. You would almost light it the way you think it should be lit instead of how you might do it when it was dark already.

Well, you're working out of a lot of experience. There you tend to put up too many lights because you know it you're doing it for speed, you're going to turn them all on at night and then you're going to start turning them off. Anything that's too much, you turn it off. But by prerigging and working ahead that way, you can make night shots cost the producer much less because everybody who works at night makes more money. So you must have the ability to work fast at night. And nighttime shows no mercy; it's over when the sun comes up. So you're limited on how much time you've got.

There are a lot of tricks to night shooting. I think the people who shoot the best at night come out of New York. They've shot on the streets of New York so much, they don't use anything hardly in the way of light. But they've got street lights and store windows to do it there. I've shot on the streets of New York. I shot *Hustling* there and some of my best night street stuff was shot on their streets.

In improvisation, how difficult is that for a cameraman to follow?

It's difficult because if you and your whole crew are not ready for it, it will upset the working operation of an entire production company. Because essentially the cameraman gives the clue to the working people of what actually has to be physically done. It affects everybody if an actor has been rehearsing a scene a certain way and, at the last minute, they say, "What I'd really like you to do is go over by the mantle on the fireplace and light a candle." Well, all of a sudden, that means that a new dolly track has to be put down and the grips have to do a lot of work; it means that the lighting director has to do something with the lighting there. If the actor lights a candle, that's a little effect that has to be rigged with a dimmer. All of a sudden, a slight change by an actor can just throw an uproar into the entire working crew because they're just not prepared to create the effects that go with it. Now if you have a cameraman who knows that he's working in the kind of environment in which things may change rapidly and if he has properly prepared his crew to accept these changes rapidly and readily, then the show will probably go well for him. But if each time that happens, the crew grumbles and becomes dissatisfied because they've gone to a great effort making the shot the original way and they then have to undo all this work on what seems like a whim, it's very understandable that some crews can't handle that.

So it's difficult sometimes for directors and actors to really respect the amount of work that those people are putting into a show too. I think it's important that you do. I have a crew that I respect a lot; I respect what they can do and they do it for me. They use their talents for me, making my efforts look good. I also know that sometimes in a show it's important to be very, very flexible and I simply prepare the crew for that kind of show if I know that's what I'm getting into. I just tell them to stay loose and they do. That way they've been warned ahead of time so their mental attitude is adjusted to it.

You take great pride in the inventiveness of your crew and it's very important to you on a production. How do you go about nurturing that kind of relationship, that kind of inventiveness?

Well, it's a very personal thing of course, because the people that I work with are making the film for me, they're doing the work. They're carrying out my vision. If I step into a room with my gaffer, Colin Campbell, I know Colin is highly capable. I wouldn't even have to walk in the room; I could say, "Colin, go in the room and light the set; I'll come in later." But if I want to get my vision on the screen, then I have to have someone as capable as Colin is, who's willing to listen to what it is I'm trying for. So I can say, "Colin, here's what I'd like this scene to look like; here's my vision of what the light should look like. Now how do we get it, how do we go about it?" And then you find that there's no place to put lights here or there but still I want some lights there. But he'll walk back five minutes later and say, "What if we do this or that?" And suddenly he has figured a way to get the light to come from where I want it to come under impossible conditions.

For example, in *Raid on Entebbe*, we were shooting some scenes in the government building on Wilshire Boulevard and we were up ten or twenty stories. Now the sunlight is on the other side of the building. But I want sunlight coming through the windows where we're shooting because this scene is supposed to be in Israel, a land that has lots of sunlight and desert. I want that look; it's necessary for the story. So I hand this problem to George Hill, the grip, and Colin Campbell. Well, some guys would throw their hands up and tell me I'm crazy and that there was no way to get anything out there because it was a sheer wall of a building. They didn't. The kind of people I have, they take a couple looks at it, they get inventive and the next thing I know, they have taken some rigs used for car mounts and some tubular aluminum rods with fittings on them and they're running them out the window of the next floor up. They've fitted nine-lights on them and they tilt them down and, the next thing I know, I've got sunlight coming through the windows. Now that's the kind of people I've got working for me.

We were doing *Ice Castles* and the director wanted something that will race around the ice with the camera. Well, George Hill goes off with a hammer and a nail and pretty soon he comes back with the oddest looking rig you ever saw. But I can put a camera on one end of it and the guys can push on the other end with a dolly in the center, and that thing is spinning around the ice and fast. We could shoot low angles, high angles, anything we wanted and so suddenly we got a device to shoot on the ice that he invented in five minutes that made some very unusual and exciting shots for the show.

My operator, Jimmy Cannell, is fantastic. He's one of these people who if he says you've got the shot, you know you've got it. If he says we need another one you do not question him. You know that another one is necessary. If he says you need another one, someone has done something in that shot that no one else has seen or noticed, and because of that, it should be done again. Very often it's not his fault; very often it's because the actor did something that didn't work for the camera. But even if he misses the shot, he tells you so. The worst thing you can have happen is have an operator make a shot and say it's OK and when you get to dailies, you see that it isn't. And that's when you realize that the guy was under so much pressure that he deluded himself into thinking that he could get by with a bump or jar of the camera in a shot. Ideally you want a man who will tell you when it's wrong; that's as important as knowing you got it right. On top of all that, you want an operator who can make a difficult shot and get it the first time. With all of the guys, I respect their talent and I let them use their talent, which is highly important.

Who are the directors with whom you've had some of your best relationships?

I had a great working relationship with Irvin Kershner. I love working with that man because it was a highly creative experience. I've had a lot of great experiences with directors for different reasons. I love Nicholson because he is so full of energy and so full of ideas. He's so spontaneous. I enjoy being around that man because of what sparks out of his mind. There's so much going on. And I love to work in his kind of atmosphere too. I love working with Coppola because Coppola is heavy. The things that he's putting on the screen are heavyweight ideas. He gives you lots of freedom. He lets your creativity work for him. I like that a lot.

I've occasionally had to tell people that they've hired the wrong cameraman; that they're visualizing something that another cameraman does and they should really hire him. I have an idea myself about what's beautiful. I can't help but make my own judgment about something being beautiful. So if I approach a subject and I try to adjust the light and achieve a certain effect, it's because I think that effect is beautiful. It appeals to me. My taste prefers a certain look or something I've seen in my past that I like to re-create. So I try to go about doing that and if someone else comes along with a look they like that some other cameraman produced, I might not really like it as well. Thus I will not accomplish what the other cameraman did exactly because I don't know exactly how he went about it. I will end up getting a mishmash of styles. I've seen this happen to some really top notch cameramen. I know how it happened because I've had it happen to me. I was amazed when my work fell apart and then I realized that it was from getting into a situation where you were trying to do something you really didn't want to do for people who were probably confused in their own mind about what they wanted. They were making demands on you to produce a certain kind of look that they didn't understand thoroughly, that you didn't appreciate and, the next thing you know, your work falls apart.

In The Bingo Long Traveling All-Stars and Motor Kings, *I understand that you developed a theory of lighting black actors as opposed to white actors. Could you elaborate on that?*

It's a problem that any cameraman is going to have if he has a mixture of black and white people in the same picture. It's just the simple fact that a white face will reflect so much more light than a black face, which may be dark brown, dark blue, down to a skin tone that reflects very, very little light because it's such a deep color. It would be no different than a room painted a certain color or anything else; the problem is the same, the only difference is that when it's actors, they're walking in and out of your lights. If they were all standing still, it would be easy.

With anyone who's had this problem, the chances are that they've failed in a minor way in that their scenes probably all looked great, the room probably looked great, probably all the light-skinned actors showed up pretty good, but probably the black person didn't show up very well. So they get by with it and kind of glance over it. But that wasn't the case with *Bingo Long*. *Bingo Long* was a picture about black baseball players and they're the stars; they need to show up at every moment in every scene. I couldn't get by with letting them fall off too dark.

So I did some experiments with different kinds of light and I decided that what I really liked, when a dark face was lit properly, wasn't some of the old tricks that some of the old cameramen used to use. One of the old tricks, when you had a dark face in a picture like that, was to glance light off of them; kind of backlight them and glance it off the side of the cheek. And that dark face would always show up then but what you were getting to the camera was the pure light just reflecting off of the skin. It's not a very pretty look.

I soon discovered that you could light their faces well the same as anyone else, it just took some care with the exposure and certainly with the way the light fell upon their faces. I used a lot of soft light from the front which wouldn't be the way you'd normally go about it. I approached it from the philosophy of how you would light a person if you were taking his portrait. I just took a new approach on it and found that I got good-looking pictures.

The Conversation *was very claustrophobic, as far as both content and production logistics are concerned. What kind of problems did this present?*

For example, Francis found himself on the third or fourth floor of a little apartment building that he liked—he thought it was the right shape and size. But you can't light from the fourth floor of an apartment building very well if you aren't trying to put lights outside the windows. And that's what that particular look calls for; it's a very naturalistic look. So I had the crew make some huge brackets that would fasten to the walls outside this building on each side of the window. These brackets would hold nine-lights and then by ropes I could angle these brackets wherever I wanted them. If we wanted it to appear to be in the morning or evening, we could light the opposite nine-light on the opposite side of the window. They were slightly above the window too so that the light from the nine-lights would break in at approximately the angle that the sun would. Between using real day-light and substituting nine-lights, we managed to keep the same kind of lighting look in the room all day long. Again, I think Coppola was surprised with my inventiveness and he loves that particular kind of inventiveness anyway. I don't believe I've pulled off more special things for anyone than I have for him.

What can we say that hasn't already been said about Jaws? *When you initially got involved with the picture, were you aware or made aware of all the difficulties and physical hardships that went along with it?*

I think I was more aware of it than any other person. I don't think they were aware of it because no one I was working with had ever shot on water. I had, at least. I had experience that they didn't have. Shooting on the water is very difficult and makes logistics a problem that has to be dealt with. Motion picture production, like an army, hinges on the logistics of getting things there; the equipment, the vehicles and supplying the troops that have to make the picture. When they don't have experience on the water, you know that they're not going to calculate correctly exactly what the problems are. Therefore they got to Martha's Vineyard and rented a lot of boats that they should have bought because they ended up buying them later anyway. They destroyed most of them and bought new boats to replace them.

I realized that there were enormous problems that no one at the studio had any idea of. For instance, how do you light someone in the bright sunlight; how do you fill their faces with some light when the bright sunlight is hitting everything else which means your exposure has to be way down? What light are you going to get that's bright enough to light them from another boat? Because the actors are on a little boat away from you and you're on some other kind of device and you even have to figure out what that's going to be. What kind of boat or barge or what is going to hold you in the water? How big's it going to be? What are you going to work off of? What kind of platform? All of this had to be thought of before we left here so that I would take the proper materials for me to work with.

So I laid some requirements on them that really surprised and shocked them. One of them was that I would be working with arcs on the ocean because there's no other light bright enough and strong enough to reach far enough to do the job. If I was on the same boat that I was shooting on, then nine-lights would do the job, even though they're harsh and very hard to work with. But if I was to turn on a nine-light, I have to have a power source for it and, if I'm on a very small boat, there would be no way to put a generator on it. So how do I generate electricity for those lights? The answer was that I would have to have batteries that would work the lights for short lengths of time and I would have to be very careful about turning them on and off. I had to produce 110 volts with batteries. So in the hold of the picture boat, we used batteries as its ballast. That's what would light the nine-lights on the picture boat when we were aboard it and no other boat was close by. A lot of the shooting took place that way. When I was able to be on another boat—a barge next to the picture boat—I would then use arcs because I would have to throw the light further away and still reach it with a large amount of light in order to match the glare of the sun off the water. To do that I had a huge generator; that meant that the generator had to be aboard a rather large kind of tugboat. The electrical lines from it dropped down into the salt water and up onto the barge where were working and lit the arc lights. It all worked and the picture got made and made professionally. It looks good.

No one else was coming forth with the inventiveness to solve those problems?

No. Not only that, but I had to struggle to get the equipment I wanted. It looked like an entirely crazy scheme to them. When I told the director that I was going to hand-hold the camera, he nearly died. He thought I was out of my mind.

Didn't you have to hand-hold the Panaflex for a lot of shots because there was no other way to do it?

No, there were other ways to take the roll of the ocean out. But the best way to do it, from my experience on the water, was simply to use your body and hand-hold the Panaflex. Now the alternate way is to use a gimbal. A gimbal is this huge, heavy weight that hangs down the center of a tripod and, as the ocean rolls, this weight keeps you level. So if you work from a tripod, you must use some kind of gimbal. Today they have the Panaglide and other methods of keeping the camera straight. Again, with what is essentially a gimbal to keep the camera level. I still think that hand-holding was by far the best method for what I wanted to do. But the director insisted that we would not hand-hold it, that we would have everything on a tripod. I told Steve Spielberg, "You've never shot on water before, have you? You have no idea how seasick the audience would become if you did that." And he had to be convinced. We had to shoot some footage and show him what we meant. He soon came to love the idea. Not only that, I also insisted on shooting as low to the water as I could for the entire picture for the psychological effect that being close to the water would eventually have on people, knowing that there was a shark lurking under the water. That effect, I think, goes unnoticed perhaps.

So those were some of my contributions. The director had many contributions that I don't claim to take credit for because I think Steve did a fantastic job of timing in pulling the surprises in that picture. I don't think he receives enough credit for that; he certainly didn't from the Academy.

You used a water box a lot on Jaws. *How does that work?*

The reason for using the water box is that you then have the ability to get the camera right at water level. You can literally let the water level rise up to the bottom of the lens without getting the camera wet. That's the only reason: just to keep the camera dry. It's nothing more than a square box; it looks like a fish tank. It has a solid bottom and the front is glass so that you can set a camera down in it. With the top open, you can reach down inside of the glass and it's easy to operate especially the Panavision camera which has a longer viewing tube. Operating a camera that way is another experience you have to get used to. You guide the box as you would a camera.

We understand that you lost one of your cameras on a special effects shot involving the mechanical shark?

Well, we did get a camera dumped one day. The situation was one in which the special effects men were to bring the mechanical shark up out of the water and it was to land on the back deck of the picture boat. It's the scene where the shark hits the back deck and Robert Shaw falls and slides down the deck; then the shark grabs him and pulls him into the ocean. The special effects men tried the shot on a boat that was specially rigged in the water so the boat would sink just the amount they wanted and at the angle they wanted. The boat had no bottom in it and it had barrels of air and water inside it so they could control the buoyancy. They tried it; the water came up the deck to a certain level and then we set our cameras assuming that it would be the same when we actually did the stunt. We placed our cameras above where the water came to, but just to be safe we put the camera in the water box so that if some water splashed up, it wouldn't hurt it. That camera was flat on the back deck, above the level of where the water rose to. We put two more cameras inside the cabin where Roy Scheider was to fall and reach his hand out to try to save Robert Shaw. Of those two cameras, we put one on a shelf on what amounted to the upper deck and we had another camera beside it off to one side. There was no floor in that part of the cabin; you could look down and see the water because it wasn't a complete boat. We also had one other camera up above that was operated by an operator. Those three other cameras, though, were tied off, knowing that the kind of stunt we were doing might go awry.

I took a lot of care in pointing out to Roy Scheider the ways to get out in case something went wrong. I take as much care as I can when we're doing those kinds of stunts, especially when we're using actors instead of stunt people. You try to get them to think of how to save themselves in case something goes wrong. I'm glad I did because it did go wrong. The shark hit the deck and the water came up much higher than it was supposed to; the controls on the shark went awry somehow and the boat went much further down in the water than it was supposed to. The water did come up over the top of the water box; although we had plastic across the top so the water wouldn't splash in, it wasn't enough to hold back the weight of the water that hit it. So that camera went underwater. It made a nice shot actually, the effect of the water coming up over the camera with the floating debris in the water. The camera wasn't lost at all because it was fastened down but a very fast thinking assistant cameraman grabbed the magazine off the top, took it to the effects barge and immediately dunked it in fresh water to get rid of the salt water as much as possible. He kept the magazine underwater in a bucket. We handed that to someone who got on an airplane, flew it immediately to New York, took it directly to the lab and processed it right away. And the shot was fine; there wasn't a flaw in it.

If that happens to anybody, that is the way to save your film. You have to keep it wet and get it to the lab fast enough so that the emulsion doesn't get too soft. The important thing is not to let it dry so it will stick to itself and pull the emulsion off. Someone who hasn't shot on water might not know that but that's the procedure.

But when you're shooting under those kinds of circumstances, you know there's a great danger of getting the camera wet. Almost daily we got salt water on our cameras and that evening the assistants had to spend their time drying and cleaning them. The eyepiece, which got water in it nearly every day, was taken apart so much to be dried and cleaned that the screws wore out. They just got worn from constantly being disassembled and cleaned. Amazingly, we had little trouble with the equipment, considering the fact that it was always getting wet.

What are some of the things you think about when shooting a musical, like Grease?

One important thing is that you should pay close attention to the transition periods. If you're dancing and then you're going to start singing; if you're singing and then you're going to go into dialogue; if you're in dialogue and then are going to break into dance or song, if those transitions are not done properly, the audience is jarred and pulled out of the concentration that you've developed in the scene immediately before that and you've lost them and your musical will fail. Musicals have taken a downward turn; until recently nobody would touch one with a ten-foot pole. We had that working against us. So I said to myself, "We better obey the rules of musical filmmaking." Because the film didn't have a big theme. Take *Jesus Christ, Superstar*, it was a wonderful musical but it did not do as well as it should have. It was beautifully made. It had a message but no one, in my opinion, understood the message; the audience didn't know what they were going in to see and they came out disappointed. Then there's *Tommy*, which I didn't enjoy that much, but was, on the other hand, a very innovative film that broke all the rules. It was a well done abstraction.

But here I was with a musical that just had the energy of that time. It was a fun movie; it wasn't out to make a big statement.

What are the elements of a musical that a cameraman would find attractive?

I think cameramen who want to do musicals love the idea that there's the possibility of doing some beautiful photography in tempo with music. And, as a motion picture photographer, you're interested in compositions that are in motion. A still photographer can compose a still photograph and he can deal with his composition because nothing is moving or at least he's going to shoot when the composition is the way he wants it. A motion picture photographer learns to think in terms of things that are in motion. His compositions are alive and moving; the sweep of movement or the sweep of the camera are the elements that he is composing with. So it's an entirely different way of thinking. Well, a musical is full of movement; it's full of human dance form which is beautiful. Then you get a choreographer who can bring wild and exciting movement into a dance number, it has all the elements that a motion picture photographer is interested in.

Well, I didn't have all those elements to work with because of the type of musical it was. The budget was very small, which meant that most of the film was shot, not in the studio, but out on the street. Immediately, you're at the mercy of the sun and the weather, if the budget's so tight that you can't wait on it. And it was a very lightweight budget. Well, if you take the film on that basis, you're expected to deliver on that basis. So the light was not always kind to me and I lost some of the battles there. But when we did go into the studio, where we had more control, we were able to do some more interesting things.

With time and experience, you and your contemporaries are able to achieve more on the screen, getting better and more self-confident all the while.

A cameraman grows; the most fun I have in the world is watching my fellow cameramen work and grow every year. I know that I do although I can't see myself grow as well as I can see them. I've followed Connie Hall and Bill Fraker since I started in this business—as sort of idols. I like the way they work, I like who they are personally, so I've watched them closely. Both of them have done some amazing things but, on top of everything else, they've grown. They've gotten better.

What else happens to you is that, as you grow older, you grow in character as you spend more time working at the problem of making films. You're working also on the problems of the stories; you're getting emotionally involved in what the story is about because you're giving some of your life's effort to it. You're learning more not only about photography but hopefully about people and about yourself. You question what you're doing more. You see when you succeed and when you fail and you try to grow in the process. It's fun to watch cameramen grow and become more mature and do better and more subtle work. And not be so obvious or outrageous in order to be noticed.

Is that where the degree of skill really begins to show, when it becomes subtle?

Yes, call it taste; give it any name you want to. But the choices you make will be better choices. And when you see someone really making great choices, you know that he's arrived; he's there. Watch an artist who paints on canvas and you'll see depth come into his work, you'll see him do more sophisticated work. Now a film cameraman does the same thing; when he first starts, he's happy to have the exposure right and not have any dark corners in the room; when they get up where they're not afraid any longer of just getting enough exposure, then they go for the subtleties, the shadings. And if an actor walks out of the light they won't panic and throw ten more lights in and overlight the set, which is the tendency; they'll live with it.

You keep pushing yourself down on the quality of the film right to the very bottom of what it'll handle. When I was doing *Omen II* we had a shot in what was to be a totally dark room. My theory of lighting the room was to light it so that with the lights out you could still see something in the room but to do it at the very bottom of the capability of the film; so that it was so near black that if the person in the scene didn't move, you wouldn't see them on the screen. Only if they moved, would you know they were there; now that's a pretty low light level and that's keyed to what your key level is because they can print up and down and shift that on you, so you have to get it right in exposure. In the scene, the little boy is in bed and he rolls over; for a moment you don't realize whether it's a dirty screen or if there's something up there; it's that low. Then he moves and you realize he's still there. That kind of a thing is a challenge to a cameraman because every cameraman has had to contend with shooting someone in bed at night and making it believeable.

The director tells you, "Make it look like moonlight (as your source)." But there's no moonlight in there. What ambient light is there? You've turned all the lights out and now you want to see something.

One cameraman said that, without a doubt, that was one of the toughest situations to light, a scene where you have no light source.

It's a good test. One of my solutions to it is to drop down to something in the realm of four footcandles, then push the film a stop and then set the key that it came off of so that when the light goes out, it drops down and it's barely visible. And I mean not from a single source. The secret then is to have the light all over the room so that it is so dispersed and seemingly coming from no direction, that you just see something crawling on the screen. But you try not to light from a direction because then that's a source. It worked.

You have to have the guts to try something like that. If you're new on a feature and you don't have complete self-confidence, if you're afraid of it going wrong and you don't feel you can live through too many mistakes (and you can't), a cameraman might not try something like that. I'm not saying that's the most daring thing in the world, I'm just using that as an example. An inexperienced cameraman might play it safe and give himself a little source over there somewhere and he'd have moonlight coming in and it would be what you've seen a thousand times. He'd take the usual way out. So a cameraman has to gain enough self-confidence and enough status and power so he can try those things and feel that he isn't going to get a lot of static from the producer or director before he can grow, before he can even get to that point.

I expect a lot of that is just experience; knowing when and where, the right time.

Sure, it's like throwing a basketball into the basket. You do it enough times and you get better at it. Nothing's for sure. The variables when you go to make an exposure are so numerous that it's a crap roll. So it scares you to start with.

It think all cameramen go through a time when they think nothing is going to come out. I certainly did. You know that so many things can go wrong that you say, "Everything's going to go wrong." That's almost your attitude. It's a very negative attitude and out of that kind of fear you get very careful. And I think a number of cameramen work out of that premise. You also have to learn to deal with the human elements, the director, the actors and actresses, in addition to that piece of film, that you're sure is going to scratch in the camera. You're sure the assistant is going to forget to get the *f* stop exactly where you want it; you're scared to death he'll miss focus when people move. I mean, you're watching everything. You watch the front of the camera when the operator pans to see if it's smooth. There are so many elements that can go wrong that you try to watch everything. Your mind is racing, trying to keep up with all these elements, half of them mechanical, half of them human. On the set, all that tension, all that electricity is going all over the place. So part of what you try to do is to calm the director and performers. You might say, "It's not my job." But maybe it is.

If it affects you, it's important . . .

That's part of what being a cameraman's about too. It has to do with what kind of an aura you give off. One of them is that you're confident. If you give off a feeling of self-confidence, the crew picks it up, the director feels better and feels he's going to get a good picture. You can literally pull a production through by feeling confident and, of course, you have to deliver good photography. I mean, if you fail in that, then all the rest is just a facade. But if you're delivering at the same time, the rest of it really helps to get a production made. So when you say, "What do producers look for?" they look for those kinds of elements too.

You know, people don't realize how involved a cameraman gets in filmmaking. They think he only takes pictures and that's not true. I mean, I'm out there with Spielberg doing *Jaws* and I'm saying, "There's no element in the hunting of the shark where they show the *joy* of hunting." And if there's anything that man does as a hunter, he takes joy in it. So I asked where in the script was the joy of the hunt. The next day it was in the script. Now that's not the kind of contribution that you expect a cameraman has anything to do with. I doubt if there's a film that I've worked on where those kinds of suggestions haven't been made.

But frankly, all you have to do is deliver great pictures. It doesn't matter how you comb your hair, what you look like, how you talk, what your accent is or what your act is; if you produce, somebody will hire you. If you have talent, that's what really counts, that's the bottom line.

Since all the cameramen are using the same film, the same camera and the same lenses, do you think we're seeing a homogenation of look and style?

I think it makes for a sameness. The Panavision gear itself tends to make you shoot things the same way someone else using the same gear would shoot it. Because it will do certain things well. If you were to shoot with the Eclair, it slings differently over the shoulder, it moves differently, it gives a different feeling. So if you've got one guy using an Eclair, one using an Arri and one using Panavision, then you have three choices. You'll do slightly different things with each camera. But if they're all using Panavision, chances are that there will be less variation. There will tend to be a sameness about it.

I find that if you change any element in filmmaking, it will show up on the screen in some manner. It may be very subtle, but any approach you make towards making a film different—if you change the equipment, change the film or change anything—it will show up on the screen. It may be subtle; it may be a small variation. But when you get everybody using the same equipment, a certain mechanical sameness comes into what you do.

But somehow the best cinematographers manage to get something that's maybe a little bit different, a little bit more distinctive than the next guy, even though they're working with the same equipment.

Well, there you are. That's the tough part; that's where the little tiny fine differences come in. I mean, they pay a lot of money for that fine difference. How many Gordon Willises can you find? The man's got a touch that's an indelible mark. Of course, if you don't want that look, you shouldn't hire Gordon Willis.

Some cameramen strive not to just have one look but to be able to do a lot of different looks. I think cameramen go through phases where they feel they have to prove to everyone that they can do everything; they can do a Western, they can do something on a soundstage, they can light, they can do night shots. So after they've proven all of that, they settle down and let their own personalities take over.

Wouldn't you say that a cameraman, a person with your type of abilities, would be a logical choice to direct?

The cameraman is quite a logical choice, I think. But there again, you're talking about what capabilities it takes to be a cameraman; the capabilities to be a director are similar but there are additional things that he has to handle. A lot of being a director also has to do with what kind of power base he can operate out of. Does he have the personal strength to take this entire group of people through the film and is he charged up with an idea so that he can lead them through to the complete story?

There are a lot of things a good director has to be. He has to be a good story-teller; he has to know how to tell it visually. He has to know how to use the images and make the shots. And most of all, he has to have something to say. It doesn't have to be what's on the surface of the story. He has to have something to say that's in his gut. He has to be mentally disturbed about something, enough so that he will go out there and slip it into the story and the characters. So that when you've seen the play, maybe you've seen two plays. And you'll find that a director that does have something to say is successful and you will find that message in picture after picture that he makes; it doesn't matter what the title of the film is. But most important above all, is that he have something to say.

I have hesitated to become a director, and I've been offered directing shots before, but I want to be sure that I have something to say. I think I have. I've come to that point in my life where I think that there's quality to what I want to say.

You've made the statement several times that a cameraman literally has to see as a child does. Could you amplify that?

I think an illustration of that idea occurred to me when I was sitting at home in Chicago when my daughters were very small. One of my daughters was sitting at the table one day and I guess she'd had a Coke. There was an empty Coke bottle on the table and we were sitting there talking. Now I know a Coke bottle is a cheap piece of glass to be thrown away. I mean, it's cheap glass and it's very commercial so my mind automatically turns off anything that has to do with that Coke bottle. It's not a diamond. It's the cheapest kind of glass there is; it's got commercial messages written all over the outside of it so I don't even want to look at it. My sophistication is such that I know nothing good is going to come from that. And yet the child sitting there screamed all of a sudden, "Oh, look how beautiful." I didn't even know what she was looking at but the light was coming through the green bottle, diffracting and making the most beautiful green rays of light on this white table top. And it *was* beautiful. The child could see it and I didn't. And it was right in front of me, I mean, right in front of me. But I didn't look at it because my own prejudice shoved my eyes in other directions. Well, that's what happens to every-body as they learn what to look at and what not to look at. They end up looking over more than they look *at* anything.

We step on more than we look at. We do not see as a child. A child, who hasn't been told what's pretty and what isn't, just looks at everything and it's a new experi-ence. Because it's a new experience, the child sees it differently. It behooves one to try not to lose his vision, his objectivity and his interest in seeing things again. That's why photographers do well when they go to new locations, new countries. Because we tend to get bored with what we've seen before. We don't see it with a fresh eye and we miss a lot that's right in front of us. It's very, very difficult to keep your mind and your eye responsive, almost in a child-like way. We become so sophisticated that we become dull in our thinking.

5

Michael Chapman

*"You see, I wish I could have some more profound
things to tell you. I wish there were some great thing
dredged up from my psyche that I could say was the key
to all these things, but there isn't. It's a mechanical
medium and you've got to do the mechanics and let the
mechanics give the aesthetic pleasure."*

Perhaps the one of the most gifted cinematographers who now works only infrequently is Michael Chapman. He has shot just over a dozen films but has explored a great variety of styles and viewpoints. In a certain sense, he feels he's done it all; he now has no desire to take up the camera just for the sake of doing a film. So he does a film every twelve or eighteen months and then only when he feels he will be artistically and emotionally challenged by the project.

Once described as "a disciple of Gordon Willis," Chapman does not shoot like Willis or even have a comparable style. But he was Willis's operator for over four years, working on films including *Klute, The Godfather* and *Bad Company.* The most important thing he learned from Willis was not "how to" information but the philosophy that film is a mechanical medium of cameras, lenses and film stocks and the mechanics are the road to whatever aesthetics there are in movies. He also found that if you take your work seriously and concentrate your efforts, it will show up, sometimes even unconsciously, in the quality of your work.

On over half of his films he has worked with only three directors; these good relationships have formed the basis for a high level of visual collaboration. His three films apiece for Martin Scorsese and Phil Kaufman are indicative of his ability to view things with a fresh perspective: his off-center framing and garish use of bright colors to emphasize the pop-art, comic-book texture of *The Wanderers* is one example; his innovative use of variable-speed cinematography in the boxing sequences of *Raging Bull* is another. While *Raging Bull* challenged him with an opportunity to shoot in black-and-white, *Dead Men Don't Wear Plaid* required that he match, scene for scene, vintage black-and-white Hollywood films, a situation that called for a preciseness and a finesse that he had not achieved before.

The excitement of a new idea and the taxing of his creative energy to the fullest extent is what Chapman is looking for, a process that he describes as rejuvenating. It's not surprising, then, that he has taken on directing with *All the Right Moves.* Perhaps it's the ultimate filmmaking challenge.

1974	*The Last Detail*		*The Wanderers*
1975	*The White Dawn*		*Raging Bull* †
1976	*Taxi Driver*	1980	*Personal Best*
	The Front	1981	*Dead Men Don't Wear Plaid*
	The Next Man	1982	*The Man with Two Brains*
1977	*The Last Waltz*	1984	*The Clan of the Cave Bear*
	Fingers		
1978	*King* (TV)		As Director:
	Invasion of the Body Snatchers	1983	*All the Right Moves*
1979	*Hardcore*		

† Academy Award Nomination for best achievement in cinematography.

How do you view your role as a cinematographer? What are your duties?

The cameraman's basic duty is to get down on film a series of images which contribute to a coherent whole. Beyond that, it varies enormously from picture to picture. A cameraman negotiates—arranges—his function anew for each director. Some want you to light and be quiet; others want rather more.

But the bottom line is getting an exposure?

No, not even that. You can screw up exposure pretty badly and still see at least something. The most important thing is to get a series of images that convince emotionally and tell a story.

When did you work for Gordon Willis and what did you do together?

I was Gordon's operator from 1968 to 1971 or 1972. I operated all of Gordon's movies up through *Bad Company*. I operated perhaps ten films for him, *The Godfather* and *Klute* among them, and *End of the Road*.

What kind of teacher was Gordon Willis?

Gordy had an enormous influence on me. He's a remarkable man. Everything he made up and everything he did, he did on his own. I was a film buff and saw lots of foreign movies. I would see a film and say, "My God, Gordy, this is a wonderful movie; you must have seen it." And it turned out he'd never seen it. Anything you might think he was influenced by, Raoul Coutard for instance, he had never seen. He simply made it up. He's the most wonderful example of the American autodidact that I've ever met. He dredged it all up out of his own head, almost entirely.

Some people say he's almost obsessive?

Oh, Gordy's nothing if not obsessive! I mean I couldn't be fonder of anybody else in the movies. And I don't mean that as anything but praise. Obsession is a good thing. That is where aesthetics in cinematography lies: in those minute distinctions. You have to be obsessed enough to feel that there is reason for those distinctions and you have to be able to know in your mind what that reason is. I'm sure that you don't have to always consciously know why that distinction of a few millimeters or a little bit of exposure is important. I don't think you have to consciously be able to say exactly what the emotional difference between a key light here and a key light there is, but I think you have to trust yourself, your knowledge and experience to believe that there really is that difference. And by God, there is; over the years, all those things add up to a difference.

It's quite a subjective thing too.

The amount of unconscious material that you're involved with in shooting—I couldn't believe it, when I started shooting, how much there is. I always knew there was in operating, because I'd done a lot of it. Operating is very much a matter of existential choices; I mean, you're out there floating and you're making choices at twenty-four frames a second. But it's easier to demonstrate, in a way, how existential operating is. But shooting is too. And you deal with a lot of unconscious material. I can't explain why or how but it's true. I can't explain why, if I'm lighting your face, why the light being here or being there makes a difference but I do know it does. I do know if you have a firm view of the movie and you stay with it, it works.

Another thing that Gordy demonstrated by his work and his personality was that you have to have an overriding point of view. He's always very careful, in interviews, to say that you absorb that point of view from the director. But a lot of times you don't. Hopefully you do, but sometimes the director doesn't necessarily have one or he wavers in his point of view. But if you can be unwavering in your point of view, whether you got it from him or you made it up on your own, or, as inevitably happens, there is a combination of the two, if you can have that point of view for the length of the film and not allow yourself to waver, it's one of the most important things. It's the kind of discipline that'll get you through broken perfs, hangovers, lost raw stock and all the horrors that happen. If you can just have that point of view and fight and fight to keep it, it works. If you can't, that shows up too.

So you feel that Willis had a definite influence on your style?

On the way I think about things. I don't think style is quite the right word. He had an influence on my style in framing but that framing was something we agreed on from the very beginning, especially in the way scenes should play in a 1.85 to 1 format, which I always thought was a slightly awkward format. But, no, I don't light or shoot movies the way Gordy does; they're very interesting but that's Gordy. But he's certainly had an enormous influence on how I go about it. And I am thankful that I spent those years with him.

We've already talked about the fact that you operated for a number of years. What aspects of camera operating are most helpful in preparing you to become a director of photography?

Well, I tell you, I would operate all my movies if the union would let me. I'd do it for no other reason than to save time but also I flatter myself that I'm a really good operator. Operating allows you to think about angles. Once you know what you're doing and you're good enough at it so that you're not going to muff somebody's head line, you are forced to think about angles. You think about what angles do, whether angles are efficient, whether they work. Operating is great for that. Of course, it's also wonderful for studying somebody else's lighting, if you're stuck operating for someone who's not terribly good. In movies, I think angles are most important. And operating will teach you a lot about that. I operated the first two movies myself and I've operated parts of others.

I think most cameramen share that viewpoint.

If you operate the camera yourself, it saves time because you don't have to give the operator a rehearsal, you don't have to try to explain to the operator exactly what you want. You can take chances that no operator will ever take. I think I was a very good operator for Gordy but I know I was a better operator when I operated for myself. Because I would take all kinds of chances; I would let the actor's head get right up to the edge of the frame, where the operator wouldn't. And it would be a wonderful frame. I knew if I blew it, the director of photography wasn't going to come down on me because I was the DP. Even with the best will and the most trust in the world, the operator can't quite take those chances if he's doing it for someone else. So all in all, it's a better system. But it's an imperfect world.

You shot several films as a director of photography and then you went back to operating on Jaws *for Bill Butler. Why?*

I was stone broke; there just wasn't any work in the east at the time. I had a wife and two kids and I was getting down to the last few dollars in the bank. I heard about *Jaws* and I knew that Bill Butler was an old friend of Phil Kaufman. And I had shot *The White Dawn* for Phil. So I called Phil in San Francisco and asked him if he would call Bill Butler and let Bill know that I was available. And he did and Bill hired me. *Jaws* was fun and I loved it. It was a wonderful movie to operate on. Most of the end of *Jaws*, where they get on the boat and go out to sea, is almost all hand-held; it's the most expensive hand-held movie ever made.

The simplest way, in the end, to shoot on rough water is hand-held. If there's a regular motion to the waves and the boat, and you can get into the rhythm of it, I think you can do better than any gyroscope device or Steadicam. I've never tried Steadicam on the water and maybe it really works. But Steadicam takes up so much room around you that, on the boat, there just wasn't enough room to do it. I was cramped into all kinds of places. Besides I don't think Steadicam existed at that time. We just made the decision to do it hand-held.

Did you ever find yourself in conflict with Bill Butler, either visually or techni-cally?

No, I don't think so. We had a wonderful time. I didn't have any ego problems about not being the director of photography; I was having a good time operating. After a while, when the weather got warm, it was great. The damn mechanical shark never worked; we'd shoot one take and it would break down. We'd be anchored over some wonderful clam beds, and Spielberg developed a great passion for littleneck clams. So we dived for clams and kept Spielberg happy.

The environment was not so kind to you when you shot The White Dawn. *I believe you shot it up in Baffin Bay?*

It was done on Baffin Island around a little settlement there called Frobisher

Bay. It was done entirely on location. There was no studio work; nothing is faked. No, wait a minute, the interiors of some of the igloos were made in an old shed because we ran out of winter. A lot of the igloo scenes are in real igloos. But for some of them, we had to use igloos made out of styrofoam. We used them in the night scenes.

What were the temperatures there?

When we were shooting I doubt if it was ever below twenty degrees below zero. But with the wind, it feels a lot worse. We were not there in the dead of winter. I had lived for a year in Greenland, a good deal further north, so I knew what I was getting into but I don't think anybody else did.

What kind of problems does that type of weather present, technically? What are the things that a cameraman has to be aware of in that type of environment?

Well, the cameras have to be winterized but that's fairly simple. You have to take all the grease out of the cameras. We used the old Panavision camera, the PSR. It was a wonderful camera. It had a built-in heater system, just like a toaster really. As long as you kept a lot of batteries plugged into this heater system, you never had any trouble. In fact, I had used that particular camera before on *The Last Detail*. I had a complete matched set of lenses for it which I had also used before. It was a great camera. The dogs ran away with it on a dogsled and they took it for miles over the ice. It got dropped. It's unbelievable the things that happened. And it never, never missed a beat as far as I know. The Arriflexes froze all the time.

It's hard to explain. There were no shortcuts; there was no protection other than the obvious protection you can think of. We just did it. And it was an enormous amount of physical effort. What I found hard was that there was no direct sun very often. There would be a kind of very bright white haze over the whole sky, together with blinding white snow. And that the relative exposure of the film would have nothing to do with how you'd rate the film normally. I mean I was often rating it at about ASA 200 or 250. In those days I didn't even own a spot meter and so I did it all with a Spectra. And a Spectra is, of course, an incident light meter which is perhaps not the best with all that reflected light. Now I'd use a spot.

So I made a lot of tests while we were scouting locations up there. I worked out a system over a couple of weeks where I was fairly confident of what the exposure would be. But in the end, I did it by how badly my eyes hurt. I have never been able to wear sunglasses when I shoot; it just screws me up. So if my eyes hurt really badly I knew I would rate the film at about ASA 250; if they didn't hurt quite so badly I would rate it at ASA 125. And if my eyes were feeling pretty good I would expose it at the standard for that film, which was ASA 64, I think. And it worked out very well. I mean, there's more variation in exposure than there would have been under normal circumstances, but nothing that couldn't be corrected to acceptable levels. And that was really the biggest thing you had to work out: the enormous difference between the supposed exposure of the film and the actual exposure.

I would never do it again; I'm too old. But I'm glad I did it. We documented a way of life that has, more or less, disappeared. Even when we were there, they were doing it from memory; the young ones had to ask their elders how they used to do it. It's a very beautiful civilization and it's almost gone now.

How about the igloos? How did you light them?

In the daytime you don't have to light an igloo much. You can take the top off sometimes. Igloos are wonderful because you can take them apart as if they were the wild walls of a set. We would sometimes take the top three or four chunks out and let there be an overhead light, but in daylight you didn't have to do it. If it wasn't too overcast or too early in the day, you didn't have to do anything. During the day enough light came through the ice walls so that you could shoot with no lights at all. But if you live in an igloo for a month or so, after a while it gets all smoked up inside and is just essentially black. Then you have to have lights in the daytime. Our igloos, of course, were just built for a couple of days. So there's some wonderful diffused light that simply comes through from all sides and it was marvelous with the chinks showing between the blocks. It's beautiful, very blue and marvelous light, so we would just shoot.

You didn't do anything to enhance the light?

Not in the daytime. In the nighttime we had a generator. I mean, it was a full-tilt Hollywood movie, under circumstances where there was no reason in the world to make a full-tilt Hollywood movie. We had a 700-amp generator that we towed behind sleds and brought it out to where we had the camp. I had a very good gaffer from Hollywood, Timmy Griffith, and we had lights and everything. And again, igloos are marvelous to light; we used very, very small units and force-developed everything. Actually there was no alternative because we didn't have the generator for big lights and they would melt the igloo anyhow. As it was the inkies melted the igloo. But if you want a light here, we just had a little spear and we'd stick it in the snow and tie the inky to it. So you had this wonderful rigging all around you. You could put lights anywhere. We used the smallest possible light, and lit it so it looked like the light came from the two seal lamps.

So in the evenings the seal lamps were obviously not bright enough to do the job anyhow?

No. We used inkies and we used regular lights. But we made them look as if they were coming from the source. It was, in many ways, a very traditional Hollywood movie. I mean, we'd lay out dolly track on the snow; we made long, long dolly shots and then we would do long tracking shots hand-held in the sleds pulled by dogs. We did all the things that a regular big-time movie would do.

Do you have any advice for filmmakers who are going to shoot in a similar environment?

Well, don't. Don't unless you're a lot younger than I am, any more. Make a lot of tests, and once you feel you can do it, just trust yourself to do it. It's not impossible; you can do it, it's just like anything else, don't be afraid. If I were to do it again I'd use spot meters more and that would make life easier, so I wouldn't have to guess so much. But after awhile I knew I was guessing pretty well, so it was okay. Use a lot of neutral density filters to bring it down to an acceptable level and just do it, don't be afraid.

On Taxi Driver, *what kind of preproduction discussions did you have with Marty Scorsese? What was the visual style that you were kind of going for?*

Well, we looked at a lot of movies beforehand. Lots and lots of movies; I can't even remember them all. That's the wonderful thing about Marty; he sees all movies and we looked at things that didn't have a hope of having anything to do with *Taxi Driver*. Things that were in no way relevant and then things that were obviously relevant like New York movies, *film noir*, *Sweet Smell of Success* and things like that. Strangely we looked at a lot of black-and-white. But we looked at all sorts of movies and that was wonderful because it just made us sort of at ease with each other and confident that when we were talking about something we were talking about the same thing. And as far as a specific visual style, I don't know that we ever decided anything. Fortunately Marty and I and Bobby DeNiro were all New Yorkers, or had lived in New York. I felt a lot about New York and, I think, knew a lot about New York, and Marty and Bobby certainly did; a lot of the people who were responsible for making it be what it was had some passionate concern about New York. And I do think that *Taxi Driver* is enormously a New York movie and that we got the way New York looks. It isn't a terribly realistic movie, so maybe we didn't get the way New York looked, but we got some emotional equivalent, some vision of New York now, and I can't think of any other films that capture it quite that way. It sounds quite arrogant and I don't want it to be. Well no, by God we did, I can't think of any New York movies that get it that way. And I think that's what we went for more than a specific visual style, though Marty certainly has a visual style that all of his movies have. It's not my movie, by any means, it's Marty's. More than a visual style, it's the New Yorkness of it. I would come back to what Gordy Willis talked about: a point of view, some vision of New York that we did turn out to hold in common, some of it spoken and a lot of it unconscious. A lot of the unpleasantness of *Taxi Driver* is about a kind of paranoia that you can get in New York and that you have in New York if you live below a certain income level. And I think that, by whatever lucky accident or whatever you want to say, we shared some need about New York that we wanted to express.

Was the movie shot as fragmented as it seemed to be on the screen, or was that mostly in the editing?

Yes, I think it was, although it's in the script too. It's a great piece of movie writing. And an enormous amount of what you think of as that fragmentation, that sort of nervousness that begins to be one thing and then it is something else, is in the script. And Marty for once had an excellent script to deal with and he sure as hell dealt with it. I'm trying to remember; I wish I could think if Marty said some specific set of things about how he wanted it to look. You know, you say those things before a movie starts. You always say it's going to do this and it's going to do that, but after a while any given movie has a life of its own. It dictates to you and its style comes out of what happens, and if that style begins to come out, no matter what happens, then the only thing you can do is to let yourself go and let the movie go with it. If that unconscious material seems to be working coherently in some way, the best thing you can do is just let yourself go and just trust that impulse that is not quite expressable, and concentrate on the mechanics that will let that impulse be brought out. And I think that's what we did on *Taxi Driver* . That's what you do on a good movie that works, at least from my point of view. For what I do, I know that I work best if I concentrate on the mechanics of how. I mean, if the angle of the light, the way the camera moves, seem to be determined in some way I can't quite express, the best that I can do is concentrate on the ways to let those things happen.

There seemed to be a real difference between day scenes and night scenes; and the day scenes are like almost sort of normal for a city like New York. But at night, I mean, it was ominous; evil was lurking around that next corner. What kind of consideration went into getting that kind of effect?

I think that's quite true, but I think that the hardest photography in the world to do is day exteriors. I find it the hardest because you have so much less control. I'm only now beginning to think I have some clue of how to deal with it; how to impose myself on daylight rather than let daylight force itself on me. I mean, you never can. If you have a totally dark room and you have a night scene, it doesn't do anything, you do it all. You put the lights, you put the people, you do that. But if you have a day exterior, there's just plain less you can do. And the ordinary reality of the situation forces itself on you far more than you do on it. With all the elaborate camera moves and arc lights and scrims and things in the world, my God, there is just that ordinary daylight there. You can't get away from it. And I think it is the very hardest stuff in the world to do. In something like *Comes a Horseman* you have wonderful clouds and stuff like that, but that is something very different. I'm talking about the kinds of scenes where people are on the street and talking and there's all that light that's just there. And it determines you more than you determine it. It's the very hardest stuff in the world for me and I think for most people whether they even know it. I don't think there was a conscious attempt to make the nighttime scary; that just goes with the territory. That's the screenplay. It doesn't take any great insight to say that that's what you're going to do because that's what the movie's about. But I think a lot of it is simply the enormous recalcitrance of daytime. It's simply unavoidable. If it isn't I wish somebody would tell me because I struggle and struggle. I once did a western which was, as westerns are, filmed entirely outdoors. That was where I had to face that daylight, day after day.

How do you deal with that?

Well, it's mostly a matter of angles. It's a matter of using the angles. It's not just a matter of using back light, sometimes it's a matter not of using back light, but of letting it be a very elaborate pattern of flat light. A lot of it is in the locations, of trying to use the locations where some large contrast of light and shadow is there for you to play with, so that people can move from light to shadow and so that the screen is split up between heavy light and shadows. It gives you the equivalent of moving people say as in *Invasion of the Body Snatchers* where you can move a person into a light where it's shining like that, and then you move them into darkness and then into the light. It's a way of making the daylight give you some of that contrast, where you at least can, by playing with the actors and playing with the angles from which you attack it, achieve some contrast. It's hard.

What about that whole scene in, what was it, Columbus Circle? Having the political rally . . . ?

Yeah, Columbus Circle. A lot of the time we used people to create blockages and we kept inside the crowd. We took dolly shots with Bobby coming forward and reaching for his gun and then dolly shots of the candidate. We kept inside the crowd and kept it almost claustrophobic and jammed, so that kind of myriad of faces and the shuffling and the blocking and opening and blocking did some of that for us. And that has some of the tension that I hope some of the nighttime stuff had. And there's another big daylight scene where he's going to perhaps try and kill the candidate. It's a rally where he talks to a Secret Service man about some secret signal that the Secret Service has and then he makes up a goofy telephone number in New Jersey, and we tried to do some of that there, and also we did it from strange angles there. We shot them almost on top and we just did whatever we could. We tried to do it those ways but it was not as successful from my point of view, not from the movie and not from Marty and Bobby's point of view but from my own. That one just doesn't work as well as some of the others, because it's so bloody hard. You have to be able to force yourself and your will onto it the way you can on a set or you can at night. I mean, night is essentially a set.

You had all kinds of dolly shots in Taxi Driver.

Marty loves dollies, Marty loves to move the camera around and around and around, all the time. And I had been working in the movies in New York for years and knew the crews and things there. And by accident the town was very slow when we started *Taxi Driver*. And I got together, because of that fortuitous circumstance, a very, very good crew. Really wonderful. And Marty is a real charmer when he wants to be, like anybody who has real charisma. He really can seduce a crew if he wants to. And after a while they loved him. They made jokes about him. And so they really went out of their way to make all these elaborate moves, well and fast. So Marty just dollied and dollied and dollied and the guys did it. You know, there was the famous overhead shot and everything at the end after the killing takes place. We finally said, "Well, the only thing you can do is cut a hole in the floor of the next apartment upstairs," and so they cut. It was an old abandoned building and I drew a line where I wanted the opening and we just cut the ceiling out. Crews, if they're good, are a lot smarter than some people think they are, and they respond to something unusual if it is amusing. They're very sophisticated about movies. A good crew can be extraordinarily sophisticated about movies without having any theoretical background for it. They just are from doing it. And they got challenged and turned on by Marty.

And so the dollies just went on and on and I think by and large they worked. A lot of what you see is edited, and many of the moves were excessive and turned out to be excessive in the editing. But it certainly is a movie full of looks here and there and looks everywhere, like a walker in the city, you just keep wandering and looking. And I think appropriately.

With the student filmmaker in mind, what type of dolly equipment do you use?

Oh, nothing special, one of the early pipe track systems of dolly, and a lot of the time I seem to remember we used a western dolly with big tires. I made them get special big golf-cart tires that are quite large but are very soft so that you can dolly over small obstacles and things without even knowing it. Then we would put a sputnik on top of the western dolly and chain the sputnik down, and the sputnik has a great advantage in that the seat will swivel 360° around the central axis so that the cameraman, if he's good, can put his feet on any of the four little wheels of the dolly and swivel himself around and can follow action anywhere like that. In fact, all· that stuff in Columbus Circle where the candidate is walking forward was done exactly that way. We just built a little lip off the sidewalk onto the street and you never noticed that the track is bumpy as hell. The western dolly with soft tires absorbs so much and the operator, Freddy Schuller, was so good that you get away with it. While it's very good to be fussy about bumps in a track and things like that, if you have one of these systems of 20-foot lengths of pipe that are joined end-to-end, you know, and you have the little flange wheels that roll on them, you get a bump say at every 20 feet if they're not joined right. So it goes very smooth and then bump, very smooth and then bump . . . . Well, that bump is very noticeable. But sometimes if you have a western dolly with soft tires and you dolly down the street and there's a constant sort of slight movement and wobble in the dolly, you don't notice that at all. Especially if there are people, as there were for instance in that scene, surging back and forth in Columbus Circle, you can get away with murder, and you will never notice it. And sometimes trying to make a dolly too smooth to begin with just is an enormous problem. Sometimes it's better to do something like a thing with a soft-tire western dolly and some kind of pedestal that you can sit on or even sit hand-held on the dolly, rather than try and make it enormously smooth where you defeat yourself. Because you get it smooth and then each little thing shows up. But if you do allow a certain roughness, and especially if it's a scene where there is movement and there are things swimming in and out of the frame, it's better just to trust that the eye will absorb the bumps and not notice it. Now a lot of that you have to either be the operator yourself or trust your operator to know when you can get away with it and when you can't. It's very much a judgment call. When I did *The Last Detail*, which was the first feature I did and operated myself, we did a lot of it in Toronto in the snow in winter and we had one of those soft-tired western dollies with a sputnik on it. And we dollied over ice and off the sidewalk and all kinds of stuff. You see it, but you don't care. It was there and the interest of the scene gets you past it and you can go a lot faster and do a lot more. There's no sense pretending that getting a lot of work done in a day is not important; it is.

What's the most important thing or things to be aware of when you start setting up a dolly shot, as far as lighting and the physical aspect of carrying out the dolly shot and crew coordination, etc.

I don't know that any one thing is any more important than another. I would think strongly about what the sun is going to do for the length of time it takes you to set up the dolly, so that you don't have a dolly that starts out to be one thing and by the time that you've got it together, the sun's either gone or it has shifted. In *The*

Wanderers, which was God knows a big-time Hollywood expensive movie where I suppose I could have stopped and said, "No, let's wait and use something else," I would just ride the dolly. We got into a situation where there was an unavoidable delay. We laid up a big dolly shot in the Bronx by a high school, and originally it was all going to be in the sun. And by the time we got to it, halfway through the dolly they walked into total shadow and it was a three-stop difference. Well, I just rode the dolly and I changed the diaphragm. I didn't change it just like that, but I let it be a little over-exposed in the hot and then I slowly opened it up as it came into the shadow.

So know what you have to do and impose yourself on the reality. Make it work, make it do what you want it to do. The eye and the audience will accept all sorts of things if there is a continuity of your idea, if you know what you're doing. And even if you don't, as long as you think you know what you're doing and what you're doing is there; what you're doing may be even dumb, but any order is better than disorder. And any visual order inherently has a kind of acceptance in the audience because they want, or the unconscious mind wants, order.

What kind of problems did you have shooting on the streets of New York as opposed to shooting here [in Hollywood]?

Well, it's very different shooting here, there's no question. And Hollywood people shooting in New York tend to get freaked by the city, the people and the oppression. It's where I came from and where I learned to shoot, so it never seemed a problem to me. I mean, it is a problem, but it's just a problem like rain is a problem, or anything is a problem; it's not a problem of any special magnitude. Also there are production people who have grown up in New York and know how to work on the streets of New York. They do have to know that one New York fast-talking thing of how to deal with crazies in the streets, how to deal with people throwing bottles at you, how to deal with things that happen in New York. If two crazy people start making trouble, there is a way to come to them and talk to them and get them out of the way. New York's different, but I've never had those dramatic things happen on the streets of New York that people talk about. On *Taxi Driver* we shot on 13th Street between 3rd and 2nd Avenues every night for three weeks. That street is a very tough street and we didn't have any trouble. I can't explain exactly how you handle it but you just float, swim like a fish in the sea of people, to a certain extent; although it's hard because you've got lights and everything but to the extent you can, you cool it out quite a bit. New York is hard to shoot only in the sense that everything's very tight quarters, even 5th Avenue where everything is boxed in.

The Invasion of the Body Snatchers *was a really nice film visually. What kind of discussions did you have with Phil Kaufman beforehand?*

Well, I think we had a problem in that the first movie was a kind of cult classic "B" movie, and there was no way the new *Body Snatchers* was going to capture the absolutely appropriate paranoia. I don't think you're old enough to remember the first one and, even if you did, you weren't old enough to know what that meant. I was in college and I saw it at the old Nemo Theater on 110th St. and Broadway in New York, which is now a supermarket. I saw it with a girl named Irma Kurtz and when we came out, we absolutely knew that it explained a whole bunch of stuff and that a lot of people we knew were clearly pods; they had been turned into pods. And it was just a perfect movie for its time. McCarthyism, Eisenhower and all the things you read about the dreariness of the fifties were really captured in that film. And there's no way that the new one was going to have that absolutely perfect paranoia. So we had to do something else. The horror of our times is much more complicated, much more terminal, I'm afraid. So we thought about what we could do and we just said, "Let's just be outrageous. Be outrageous and have fun, have a good time." And I got a lot of old movies for Phil to look at. I made him look at one of my favorite horror movies, *Island of Lost Souls* with Charles Laughton as a mad scientist on an island. It was lit by Karl Struss, a great cameraman. It's extraordinarily good, amazing, wonderful and had a screenplay by a good novelist of the thirties, from an original story by H. G. Wells. In other words, though it was a horror movie made without a budget, it was a really class operation and it is beautiful. It's really scary, and the lighting is extraordinary. And I really as much as anything else thought I would try to do that. I would try to do an old black-and-white horror movie in color as much as I could. I just had fun. I made every kind of wonderful corny move I could think of and I was as outrageous as I could think of being.

Be outrageous but still move the story forward.

Yes, within what was going on. I mean, it's clearly a very self-conscious movie full of self-conscious photography. But I hope the good humor or amusement that we all felt in doing it takes the curse off the self-consciousness. There's a shot that begins like this, looking down, and the camera tilts all the way up like that and stops. It's full of disguised 360° moves in that room, the bedroom that Brooke sleeps in. It's full of moves that start here and then get blocked by part of the wall and then turn around here and then you see things in the mirror. I mean, it's full of every kind of trick and bit of bravado we could think of.

There's the crazy man running down the street, which you want to follow but the camera makes a pan and you realize why you're there is because you're following Brooke.

He's one of the early people being chased by a pod, but he's just there. It's full of all that stuff. We kept thinking of all the things that we could do to amuse ourselves and visually amuse the audience, and I hope it worked. You see, I wish I could have some more profound things to tell you. I wish there were some great thing dredged up from my psyche that I could say was the key to all these things, but there isn't. It's a mechanical medium and you've got to do the mechanics and let the mechanics give the aesthetic pleasure.

A lot of times the lighting seemed to be very expressionistic, in the German sense.

It was meant to be.

Like that one scene at the book party with all the weird lighting from underneath.

Well, there's also ultraviolet blue lights in the background and stuff. Those are supposed to suggest grow lights, as if they were grow lights for plants, i.e., for pods. I mean, we did have reasons for what we were doing; we thought about what we were doing, but it's mostly for fun, you know.

A lot of people take it seriously. I mean, more serious than you might imagine.

People make movies and other people find things in the movies that the people who were making them didn't have any idea of when they made it. Again, yet another example of reiterating that moviemaking deals with unconscious material far more than anybody has ever said. On the simplest level, you think you are doing something and you have a rational view, and in fact you are expressing other things. And you must never think about that. You must never think that you're expressing unconscious material. You should have a good, orderly workmanlike approach and you think, I'm doing this for these reasons. I'm doing this because we've only got a half an hour to do this and if I put the light here and it's the fastest way and other things come out. But you must never think it. If it's there, it's there. If it comes out, it comes out. But it's bad luck to think about it in that way. And it's death to think about it while you're doing it. I mean, it's okay to be Bergman, but believe me, *Body Snatchers* is not Bergman. Thank God. I don't like Bergman.

It really shows up in Body Snatchers *that you seem to like color a lot. Although, you go towards the dark end.*

Well, I under-expose a lot and it's a night movie.

But your blacks, they're right in there on the money.

Well, that's a mechanical thing. I learned it consciously on *Taxi Driver*, because we wanted to shoot on the streets at night in New York with as little obtrusion of the light as possible. I did some tests before we made the movie, and I found that you can in fact rate your film at night and push it a stop. And you can get at least acceptable results if somewhere in your frame you have something very bright. I don't care what it is, a headlight, whatever. You know, you can shoot with no lights at all in the taxi as we did, as long as there's some point somewhere in the frame that is over-exposed, really burned. If you do that then your blacks will be acceptably dense. If you don't, and you just go into a dark area and you have your meter and you read it 400 ASA and it reads $f1.4$ or $f2$, it's going to be grey mush; it's going to be nothing. I think in *Body Snatchers*, if the blacks hold up, and I guess they do, it is because I made sure that almost always somewhere in the frame although it could be very, very dark, there would be something somewhere that was bright.

I think this is important especially if you force develop. If you don't force develop you don't necessarily have to do it. The last movie I did I didn't force anything. I had a lot of lights and just decided not to. And I don't think I will now for a while. But even there I made sure that somewhere in the frame there would be something that would be bright. It doesn't have to be much, it could be one light. But if you do that kind of classic style—what you think of as New York style of one lightbulb in the john and nothing else and everything is dark and shadow—well, that one lightbulb should be there. And that's all it takes. If you have that, it allows the print to go for that. That's why if the blacks stand up in *Body Snatchers*, it's because I tried whenever I could to do that. I didn't always, and there are a few places where the blacks don't stand up because we were just pushed by the city of San Francisco.

Are you big on getting into the technical intricacies of the lab?

I wish I were, I wish I had the time to do it. I know there's a whole world of control that I could get that nobody gets, if I knew more about lab work and could make them do it, but it's not practical. If you go to Technicolor it would be wonderful to develop your own stuff and say, "Give me this printer, give me this developer, nobody can touch it, I'm going to print it myself." But it's not possible, you'd be working 26 hours a day, you can't do it. You are at their mercy. All you can do, and that again is something I've learned from Gordy, is to let them do as little as possible. Insist that they must print on the lights that you choose and that they must never vary the lights. If they vary the lights, how do you know if you've made a mistake? So I do that and think most good cameramen do that. To that extent, sure I have some control, and I have some interest and passion about what the lab does, but it's just not practical to become too involved. If you make a movie on your own, you can't. You're always doing the next day's work and literally working 24 hours a day.

You know what the lab can do and what the lab can't do, what the facilities are . . .

I wish I knew a lot more. I mean, it's a big business. They tag your film onto the end of somebody else's and it's going through the soup. I know there is a world of control that none of us have that does exist. For instance, still photographers who print their own color. They can do things that we can't do. But it's not that we can't do it, it's that for economic reasons we can't do it. If we could shoot a day and stop and then go to the lab and work it out or print it just right, movies would be a lot better. But it wouldn't be the same business that it is. So that's what I mean by the fact that you could get away without being a technician. I wish I were, but I'm not.

Body Snatchers was essentially a night film; how much do you push?

One stop for *Body Snatchers* and one stop for *Taxi Driver* too. There's no such thing as two stops. People say there is but I don't believe there is. I under-expose everything anyway. I mean, I under-expose within the one stop. If I say I'm pushing a stop, in fact I'm under-exposing a half a stop and then pushing a stop or roughly something like that. There isn't that latitude in the print with my stuff, so it really goes mushy if I try to go two stops. It's just that film doesn't have that latitude. You shouldn't do it, just use more lights.

Are you a proponent of using a great amount of lights?

No, I'm a proponent of using as few as possible because I get bored as much as anything else. Stylistically night exterior to me is, I don't know if it's easy, but you have control and it's very abstract. It doesn't have to be. You can have a whole lot of a thing, just let it be black as long as you're telling the story. *Body Snatchers* was also supposed to be ominous and black anyway. You just need the bare amount to get your image convincingly there and have it have the right emotional effect which in that case was obviously scariness and shadows and that what you can't see will hurt you. So that's what it should be for me. Also, I just get bored. I use as few lights as I need and no more. I am told, anyway, that I have more nervous energy than some other cameramen and that I have to keep doing things. I'd light a lot more if I could operate because I'd have that to do and it would make me a lot easier to get along with. But I can't, so I tend to get bored, I want to do something. I want to get on to the next thing.

Was there a time when you used a lot of lights?

No, no. But I guess I must not really want to, I suppose. I mean, even the first movie I did, which we have not talked about. Did you ever see *The Last Detail?* I haven't seen it since it came out. But when we were moving to this house I found a whole bunch of old notes I'd made for *The Last Detail*. It was amazing. I had written down all kinds of stuff. I was obsessive; I had every dolly shot written down in enormous detail. I'd love to see the movie again to see if the notes have anything to do with reality. But even in that, I didn't use a lot of lights. But again, that was supposed to be a street movie. That was, I guess, one of those films, when you speak of New York style, that was one of those gritty movies.

It had a scruffy look like its characters. It was like its thematic content.

We used very few lights in that.

Not all the way through the movie, but I remember vaguely where the grain was quite noticeable, which is a lot different than Body Snatchers.

Well, *Body Snatchers* is much slicker than *The Last Detail*. We were using a lab in New York which was having troubles, and the print really looked dirty and undeveloped. It was just really crummy looking. About two-thirds of the way through the film we got too depressed, we lost a day's work and things like that, and we just took it away from that lab and sent it to, I think, Technicolor in Hollywood. Suddenly it got a lot cleaner and after a while we realized we'd made a terrible mistake and should have stayed with the crummy lab in New York because it was just right for the movie. And by then it was too late, so there's probably a point in the movie where it gets cleaner and is not as gritty. But we should have stayed with it because it was working. I liked that movie, I'd love to see what I did on that. I don't have much memory of it other than these notes. I just remember that it was my first movie and I was terrified—as everybody is the first time out.

Well, how did you feel the first day?

I was just terrified. I really was.

You had all this experience?

A lot of experience in commercials and things, sure. But I mean, suddenly the guy was Jack Nicholson and it was the big time and I felt, as I guess anybody does, a total fraud. I felt that I was absolutely faking it. That's why I'm sure I just covered myself with these endless theoretical notes and diagrams and references to other movies. I mean, it was mostly just to give myself confidence, I'm sure. I was doing a hype job on myself because I felt I really wouldn't get through the day without making such a ghastly ass of myself that I'd be fired. Somehow I got through and it was terrible.

But I did have a point of view, and if I didn't know what I was doing, I knew what I wanted to do very passionately. And that point of view just gets you through. Point of view is far more important than correct exposure, no question about it. It's almost the only thing. If you have that and you expose correctly and do all the other things, wonderful. But the point of view is more important. I would say that from just the realities of the movie business. The next most important thing to really having point of view and confidence, is handling a crew. Exposure is maybe third or fourth in importance, although I must say that by now I do tend to get the exposure pretty well. There are other things. You know, it's a business. Moviemaking is a very expensive, high-risk kind of gamble. There's a whole lot of things involved that are enormously important. I'm talking about the politics of movies and I don't mean the politics of kissing a director's ass or not. I mean the hierarchical politics of the people who make movies and how they make them is enormously important, and I don't think that film students are aware of it or can have any awareness of it because they just don't live that life. It's a very particular kind of life that I fell into when I was young, with no background and no particular interest in it. Not that I was never interested in film, I had an enormous interest. But I'd always thought that films were made by sort of gods and I didn't realize they were just people who did things with dollies and lights. But I started as an assistant cameraman because I had a pregnant wife and no money. I had to earn a living. And so I did it the way you work in an office or at a construction job. I tried to learn it as well as I could because I needed to make money, I needed to support a family. And it turned out to be a very good way to learn the business because it allowed me to learn that whole aspect of it that has to do with how to get work out of a crew, how to face the realities of what a set is like and how work can get done, which is just as important, if not more important, than any theoretical knowledge. Grips know a lot about what film is. They know a lot about that stuff, and the energy that a crew pushes up into the higher echelons of a movie is enormously important. I know a lot of movie projects get completed due, in large part, to the energy of the crew who, if nothing else, just want to go to a bar and drink, or want to go home to their wives.

The art of the rock 'n' roll film or the performance film has been in decline since Woodstock. *What did you and Marty discuss for* The Last Waltz? *What were Marty's ideas on how to change that whole concept around? Most of these films are bland and not particularly well done. You guys wanted to do something different.*

I wasn't there at the very beginning; I was away shooting another film. I think, to a certain extent, it just grew. I think The Band just wanted to make a little 16mm movie of their last concert. And they knew that Marty was a big follower of rock. So they asked him to do a film. So then someone said, "Let's do it in 35mm." And they added more and more cameras. And it became this mammoth production. Although Marty had worked on other rock films, I think he always wanted to make one of his own.

And I must say he really did have it together in an amazing way. He had every one of The Band's songs entirely choreographed. He did ninety percent of them and I did a few of them because there were just too many songs in too little time.

Choreographed in what sense?

Well, let me explain that we couldn't move the cameras very much because Bill Graham [the concert producer] was very difficult and unpleasant. We used to have to negotiate our camera positions through lawyers; it was bizarre. We really did. We'd have to get the lawyers to negotiate whether I could put the camera here or there. So we couldn't move the cameras in a way that would hinder the audience's view. And since we couldn't move around much, Marty choreographed each camera's move almost down to the line of the song. Each camera was very elaborately orchestrated as to what it would do during the course of each song. Marty knew all of their songs and, quite by accident, I knew most of them also. And liked them. But most of the operators didn't know the songs. In fact, I can remember people screaming at me on the walkie-talkies, "Which one is he, which one is he?" when they were supposed to go to a tight shot of a certain performer. But most of the choreography was Marty's and certainly the entire idea and the original impulse was his.

So there was actually a typewritten script?

We had it totally drawn out; it was just like sheet music. It indicated what each camera would be doing at each line of each verse. We even had page-turners the way a pianist does. We had girlfriends and others to turn the pages in following the songs so that the camera operator could see what he was supposed to do. We had it for *all* their songs and really in enormous detail. The other songs we weren't sure about because we didn't totally know what songs the guest artists were going to do. So we couldn't do it anywhere near as specifically as we did it for The Band.

And we had colors. The way the film is cut, you don't actually see as much of it. But we had enormous color changes constantly. We had color keys for each song and in the middle of a song we might change the key lights from one kind of color to another. And the spots would change, depending on what was happening on the stage. And there were two huge dimmer boards. Those people had a whole set of dimmer cues to follow for the lighting.

Which was also choreographed beforehand?

Yes, all choreographed beforehand from the same things. We tried to practice as much as we could. We had some misses and one time a lot of fuses blew. But there were not quite as many horrors as you think. It was remarkably organized for a situation like that; it went five hours.

When it came right down to it, what was your function? You were the director of photography; how did you function with the other cameramen?

Marty and I had rigged up two different headset systems. One I had hooked up to the dimmer board people. Then I had another one hooked up to the cameras. And Marty had one to the cameras too. I was trying to supervise the lighting and see that it was going right. And I was trying to supervise the cameras too. It was like an army. There were seven cameras with thousand-foot magazines. We had a whole room full of camera loaders and black bags. I don't know how many hundreds of thousands of feet of film we went through in that one night.

If I didn't know any better, I would almost have assumed that there was no audience and that it was shot on a sound stage. Which it's not. But it looks almost that good; you had enough control of the situation and I guess that was part of the overall concept.

Well, we really did want to shoot it well. And shoot it in 35mm which immediately gives you a richer negative, clearer colors and images. We wanted to get the lighting to the point where we really could get a decent exposure. And to do all the things, I guess, that are not usually done in rock movies.

In quality, it was so superior to anything that had gone before in that genre. You even had Boris Leven to design the sets!

That was wonderful. Boris got a set from the second act of *La Traviata* from the San Francisco Opera and he just stuck it in there. It was totally incongruous and it worked wonderfully. Again, in some ways, I wish the film would have been cut somewhat differently so you could have seen more of it. You have very little sense of Boris's set. But it was always there and it always worked. It visually supported the music and the people.

It really was a kind of nightmare in a lot of ways. I was very angry though I was happy when it was over because I felt I hadn't had a chance to do it right. But we managed to pull it off. I was not rational by the end of it; I literally had not slept in days. I remember going back to the hotel afterwards and going to bed at about four in the morning. But I woke up at eight with incredible pains in my legs from having been on my feet for five or six days. I crawled out of bed and soaked in a tub for hours just so I would be able to walk.

Your tendency has been to go for a richer, darker look than most Hollywood cameramen. Do you know where that line is where things become too dark?

No, I don't think anybody does. Dark being dark is not any virtue in itself. Nor is being light. There are no rules except maybe that you shouldn't over- or under-expose so badly that the film doesn't work. It's just what seems right or looks right to you for what you're doing at the time. It's not an exact science. I suppose exposure is in some way but I'm no technician so I don't know. But from my experience, it really isn't an exact science; much of it is just fiddling around trying to make it look right. Nobody's really complained to me lately about my stuff being too dark. I feel less sure about what is aesthetically right than I used to. Five years ago I knew exactly what I wanted to do. I wanted to have all this nice cross light and this and that. But I'm not so sure now whether that isn't bullshit.

I can't say I really understand it all anymore. I used to think there were more clear-cut rules about what was good and what wasn't than I do now. I think if I were allowed to shoot entirely as I wanted without any consideration of studio policy or what the film needed, I think I would try to do things very, very differently from what I do. I think I would try to do stuff totally flat maybe, absolutely flat. I would like to make it much more abstract. I would like to make big patterns of color; totally flat red, yellow, green. I would change it around a lot. I mean, I've done all that other stuff.

Experimenting?

Yes, I would start all over again somehow. I think I'd try doing things like shoot Super-8 and then blow it up to 35mm so it would be like Seurat; all the grain would be that big. I would do things very, very differently. I would make it much more abstract, much more stylized and much less like reality. And no more of that pretty kind of Kotex-ad stuff that I did years ago with the pretty shafts of light. One of the things that made me realize how limiting that is was a movie called *The Duellist*. Everything in it is lit like Vermeer; everything is lit from the side. And for the first half hour, you think it's really wonderful but after you get further into the movie, you say, "If I see one more side-lit shot, I'm going to scream because it's so boring." And I realized that I was tending toward that kind of thing. A lot of cameramen were. It's not the answer to everything; it really isn't. A lot of times, luxurious lighting overpowers a movie and hurts it badly. There's a movie called *Agatha* with Hoffman and Redgrave that Vittorio Storaro lit. It's a very minor little tragic/comic, sentimental but very sweet little movie. It's absolutely sopped up like gravy by his lighting. The lighting is ruinously bad for the movie. It's very pretty but it's totally wrong. It burdens the movie down with a kind of weight that it shouldn't have. That's the kind of thing that I keep thinking of more and more. Somehow I would like to start all over again.

What you're saying is that the things you're doing are no longer challenging?

Well, fortunately I got to do a movie in black-and-white, *Raging Bull*, which is one thing I still hadn't done. Whether I've done it well or not, I have no idea. But at least I did it in black-and-white and I got an exposure and I began to understand a little about black-and-white. I wouldn't mind doing some more of that; that would be fun.

Do you like to work for directors who basically leave you alone to do what you have to do or do you prefer a director who says, "Let's all be involved in making this film. Michael, what do you suggest here?"

Either way. For example, Marty Scorsese is enormously visual but also extremely talented so it's wonderful to work with him. I've also worked, on a couple of occasions, with directors who want to be enormously visual and think they are but whose ideas are always terrible. That's really awkward and unpleasant for me. But when you work with somebody like Marty, who wants to be visual and in fact is, then it's a delight. Marty is incredibly rejuvenative somehow. He's so full of ideas and excitement. Then there are other directors like Marty Ritt who are not putting their energies into that and who will let you alone to handle the visual end of things. Either way is fine. There are good things about the one way and good things about the other. The awful thing is that middle ground where the director thinks he knows and thinks he should at least do something about the visual aspect but he doesn't quite know what to do. And then the whole thing gets confused. I can't really complain much though. I've been very lucky. I've had an awful lot of intelligent people to work with.

Whose choice is that, essentially?

It's just accident, you know? It really is. As a cameraman, you can't generate this stuff. You can't call up Stanley Kubrick and tell him that you want to work with him. You can only wait to be asked, like a maiden in the corner. Somebody's got to ask you to dance before you can dance. It's not up to you.

But after you've been a good dancer long enough . . .

Well, then better people tend to come and ask you. But I've been very lucky. I don't know why or how. Hal Ashby, Phil Kaufman and Marty are good people. In Phil and Marty's case, I've worked three or four films apiece for them. And they've been very good to me. If it sounds like I'm complaining about directors, I'm not. I've been given more than a good shake by almost all the directors I've worked with.

Let's talk a little bit about Hardcore, *which sort of came and went at theaters. I don't know what happened to it.*

It's not a very good movie.

It was interesting. All Schrader's movies are interesting.

Oh, sure. The original impulse of the script is very interesting and often very good. Sometimes there's a difference between the original script, the intelligence and energy that you find there and what comes across in the film.

Hardcore doesn't work for me. Bad choices were made somewhere down the line. But Paul is very bright and one of the most interesting people to talk to in Hollywood, which perhaps isn't saying as much as it should be. And he's a great movie writer. Whether he's ever going to be a great director, I don't know. So he's allowed a *Hardcore*. I didn't like what I did in *Hardcore* either. Some of it's okay but, by and large, I don't know what happened. The vibes, or however you want to say it, just didn't mesh right.

It's not Paul's best work and it's not my best work. It was once a wonderful script and when I was hired to do *Hardcore*, I already knew the script and I assumed that it was going to be an X-rated movie. Well, for various reasons, it was made as an R-rated movie and we got rid of all the anthropology and it's not very interesting. The real world of porno, which we lived in for a couple of months, is very bizarre and very far away from our ordinary experience. And it's very much worth dealing with absolutely straight; although it would have been an X, it would not have been an erotic movie at all. Quite the opposite. But it should have been, "Here we are in New Guinea and we're going to tell you about this extraordinary tribe that has rituals that you wouldn't believe." And there's none of that; there is no sociology, there is no anthropology. All you get is George C. Scott. It was a failure of nerve and a failure of imagination at a very basic level.

When you say you lived in that environment for several months, what exactly do you mean?

We shot in the real places and we used a lot of real locations. San Diego, apparently, is the porn center of the west coast. The Pacific Fleet is there; a Marine boot camp is right up the road. In other words, there are a lot of horny nineteen-year-olds there. And the city fathers and the military establishment have an unspoken agreement that a certain area of downtown San Diego will be straight porn. All of the horny nineteen-year-olds will be kept there and the rest of San Diego will be left alone. While we were shooting the film, they were cracking down on porn activity in L.A. and San Francisco. San Diego was where it was the most wide open—where there was the biggest number of massage parlors and skin flicks. So we spent a lot of time there. We used a lot of the real girls and real places. And they are inexpressibly dreary, sad and Quaaluded to the limit.

Was that depressing?

Very. I've never dealt with a crew where there was quite so much bickering, fighting and bad feelings. It was only because they were nervous and depressed by the whole thing. When we came back to shoot in Burbank, the word got around that we were shooting a dirty movie with George C. Scott. All sorts of people kept trying to sneak into our stage to watch us, hoping to see some hot stuff. You could always tell the real crew from the people who were trying to sneak in because all the real crew wanted to do was to get out. They'd seen so many naked women that they'd be hideously depressed by more of it. But the other people wanted to get in. You could tell the real crew because all they wanted to do was play cards or go home. They were so depressed. We never got that feeling into the film.

There're touches of it.

It's not enough. The sets aren't dirty enough. In San Diego, we did build some porn sets for ourselves and we had done some interiors back on a stage. They're not dirty enough; they're not sleazy enough. The actual places are so dirty they literally reek. And we didn't capture that; it never feels right. I remember some porn girls coming around to the set we built in San Diego; they didn't know we were making a movie. They thought we were opening up a new porn shop and they wanted to work for us. They said, "This is a lot nicer than the one I'm working in." They wanted to work there. It was true and it was our mistake.

In Hardcore, *when Scott goes into the theater by himself and sees a porn reel, how do you simulate the lighting, with the projection beam in back of Scott and the flicker of the image from the screen?*

You don't really. That's a terrible cheat. It's like making flicker for someone who's watching TV. In fact, when you watch TV, there isn't a flicker on your face. And if you're watching a film, there really isn't a flicker on your face either. So that's totally theatrical license. What I did was take a reflector and project the real film on the soft side of that reflector and let it bounce back on his face. It's totally a theatrical trick because it isn't anything like what it really is but everybody seems to accept it. Then later on Scott sees a snuff film and you can see the images on his face. There I used a real mirror because I wanted the image to be visibly on his face. I focused it so it would be sharp as it bounced back on his face. And, in fact, you can see arms swinging and someone being stabbed right on his face. And that's even more hopelessly a cheat. There's absolutely no way that would happen in reality. But it seemed like fun at the time, so we did it.

In Hardcore, Taxi Driver, *and* Invasion of the Body Snatchers *there are a lot of night driving shots. How do you go about rigging up a car for those situations?*

Sometimes I use two cameras and sometimes I use one. It's better to use one really. What you can do is mount two cameras side by side so you can get a wide shot on one and a close-up on the other, all of the same person. I often do that. But, and this is for night shooting, it's better not to have a camera in the front and at the side at the same time because some way or other you've got to put your key light in a way that's going to compromise the look of one of those shots. What do I do? You get a 110-volt battery pack in the back and you put an inky where you want it as a key light. You mount the camera on the front hood; I always use an Arriflex BL. I began using it on *Taxi Driver* because the lenses are very fast and very, very true in color. They're coated wonderfully so you don't get flares. The lenses are rated very honestly too. That is, when it says $f1.4$, it really is an $f1.4$ lens; it's not an $f2$ cheated to be an $f1.4$ on the theory that the lab will take up the slack for you. Usually, unless it's a dead black night with no lights in store windows, you don't even want to shoot at $f1.4$ because it's too bright. On those lenses you can shoot at $f2$ or $f2.8$ probably and it will balance out. It depends on what you're going to be driving through. When Scott is driving through the porn areas in *Hardcore*, it's not terribly brightly lit but it is enough, with movie marquees and things like that. So you just balance what you think the key light for the driver should be compared to what the background will be like. And it can be whatever you want it to be. In other words, it can be that the driver should be much less exposed than the background or more exposed or whatever. That's a matter of judging what it calls for.

I just mount the camera to a board and tie it to the chassis so that any bouncing of the car is the bouncing of the camera and you don't see it. I use just one light on the driver and no fill.

You don't use any gimmick lights in the dash? You don't put any lights underneath and shine them up?

No. It always looks like lights shining underneath to me. I just put a little key light and make that light dim enough so that as he drives past streetlights or as headlights hit him, they'll read on him. So his key light doesn't overpower him. It helps to have those good fast lenses to do that with.

But what about the background?

With a 25mm lens, it's going to be all right. It's not going to be really sharp but it'll be plenty sharp enough. And if you're shooting much tighter, you're not going to see that anyway; you're just going to see his face. Sometimes an out-of-focus background can look really wonderful because it flares and changes.

Are there any special considerations when working with neon lights or colored lights as you did in Hardcore?

I have a certain system I use for fluorescent lights. If it's at all feasible I replace the lights that are there with Sylvania Deluxe Warm Light bulbs. If I have close-ups of people's faces or if I'm mixing fluorescent and regular incandescent light, I tend to light through a chocolate filter. Or if that takes too much out, I put a couple of strips of chocolate filter over the light and I mix those up and make sure the lab prints on exactly the same light they always print on. It tends to look a little brown but it looks like fluorescent light. Well, it doesn't necessarily look like fluorescent light but it looks like a kind of light which is not incandescent light but which is not so ugly and green that you can't look at it. It's very fast and very simple. Again, it's an abstraction. What it says is, "This is a kind of light source which is not your ordinary light." The chocolate filter and the Warm Light are not as green and they overcome the green that is inherent in most cool white fluorescent light. There are elaborate systems for correcting fluorescent but you lose stops and stops in doing it and it's a big bore.

So it's a compromise?

Right. Why should fluorescent light look like incandescent light? It isn't. It doesn't look that way to the eye; why should it look that way to the film? So that's what I do. It's the simplest and the fastest I know of. And the rest of it is just a judgment of how much fill to use to overcome the fluorescent and how much not to use.

For The Wanderers *you and Phil Kaufman looked at a lot of old teenage movies. What did you get out of that?*

I did, yes. I looked at a lot of old AIP beach party movies. *Beach Blanket Bingo, Muscle Beach Party, How to Stuff a Wild Bikini,* and a whole bunch of them. A lot of that I did because I was in New York and there wasn't really anything for me to do except hold people's hands. I was going out of my mind with boredom. So I used to have them get me movies so I could fill up the day. And a lot of that was just my own perversity. I've always liked those movies; I've always thought they were innovative and influential in a way. So I watched a lot of them just for my own amusement and perversity more than anything else. There was a kind of feel that they have; a kind of teenage vulgarity that we wanted.

There are several things wrong about *The Wanderers* but there was an idea that could have been wonderful. It had the beginnings of making things much more abstract and stylized. If I ever have to do it again, I want to do it much, much more. So much more that anybody looking at *The Wanderers* would not think it was stylized at all. But there was just the beginnings of that in it. And Phil and I were consciously trying to do that; to make it look a little bit like a comic book. What we wanted was that the movie should be about how people remember being adolescents; how heightened and torturous adolescence is in memory. And we wanted to do that by visually stylizing and kind of pulping it, the way those beach party movies are.

You and Phil went so far as to talk about how certain comic strips were framed?

Sure, we did that. It's easier to say than it is to do. Because there is a rigidity in a 1.85 to 1 frame in films. You can't change it; that's it. Whereas in a comic, you can. You can have two small frames and then a big one. You are freer to change your frame and format in comics. But we did to a certain extent, try to stage and set things so that there would be some of that tension that there is in comics. We tried to get that funny snapshot framing quality that comics have. A lot of comics are framed like Degas, totally out of left field and balanced completely wrong yet somehow they work. It's very hard to do that in a movie. We did a little of it though. I would like to try much, much more of that.

Raging Bull *was the first film you've shot in black-and-white and one of the few films shot in black-and-white in the last ten years. What kind of problems did that present?*

It presented a problem in that I didn't know anything about it. I'd never shot anything in black-and-white. It made me feel young again, if being young is being inexperienced and terrified. On the simplest level, it's very hard to find a lab that will develop and print black-and-white. And if they do it, they don't do it well and there are terrible static problems and they just tend to screw it up. The technology doesn't seem to exist anymore, for some reason. The only people who could do it here, with any pretense of familiarity, was Technicolor because they do black-and-white for Disney. All the cells, in the various stages of animation, are done in black-and-white for money reasons. So they have a black-and-white film bath and they do black-and-white every day. Now Gordy had done *Manhattan* in black-and-white and he had terrible trouble; he had ruined negative and endless static problems. They had done it in New York and had a small lab do the developing and then Technicolor in New York did the printing. But the lab that did the developing just drove him crazy. People just do not know how to do it anymore.

He's very meticulous so he must have gone berserk.

Yes, he did go crazy. And I was going to use the same people because they had got their act together and he had beaten them into submission. But then, for various reasons, we came back here and we did all the fight sequences here. That took nine or ten weeks so there was no use sending it to New York. I sent it to Technicolor here and I stayed with Technicolor afterwards.

Black-and-white is just more complicated. You have to do the same number of things and there are fewer ways to do it. It's difficult and, as such, was interesting. I'd like to do more black-and-white. You know the reasons that it's more difficult: things don't separate by color, you have to separate them by light essentially. You can do it by backlight, or by having dark objects against a light background or by having light objects against a dark background. There are simply fewer ways to make things separate from each other. That's the essential reason. And except for the fight sequences, everything in *Raging Bull* is shot on real locations, which means low ceilings and no place to put the backlights that they used to have in the old days of the studio system. And we didn't have any of that because we were shooting in apartments and houses in the Bronx.

Do you think black-and-white is totally outmoded for use in features?

No, I don't see why. It's more abstract and thus, in some ways, more interesting to me.

How and who did Marty Scorsese have to convince on the black-and-white issue?

I don't know. He just called me up and asked me if I wanted to shoot it in black-and-white. I think perhaps Bobby DeNiro wanted to do it in black-and-white also. I think it was a very wise decision. I think that if you are above a certain age, you tend to think that real movies are black-and-white anyway. I certainly do. I mean the movies that formed me and that are deepest in my unconscious are black-and-white, by and large. And certainly you think of fight movies in black-and-white. *City for Conquest*, *Gentleman Jim* and all the classic fight movies I can think of, even *Champion*, which I don't like much, are all in black-and-white. So it seemed a reasonable thing to do. Anyone's memories of Jake LaMotta are black-and-white memories.

What are your favorite fight films?

I like *City for Conquest* and *Body and Soul*. But Bobby DeNiro is a better fighter than any of those guys. He looks and moves like a fighter. He has the punches and convincingness of a fighter, much more so. With Cagney or Garfield, you always have a sense that they are actors portraying a fighter. But Bobby is really a fighter. He spent a year not doing anything, just working out every day, obsessively. Finally he got to be a pretty good middleweight, I understand. He really can rock professionals with a punch. And he just looked and moved like LaMotta.

On Raging Bull *you did some different things as far as intensity, direction of light and stylization because it wasn't in color?*

Yes. We spent more time on the fights than the whole rest of the movie. In terms of screen time though, it doesn't play more than ten or fifteen minutes. So those scenes are very, very elaborate.

Choreographed?

Very, very choreographed. Just as *The Last Waltz* was. We had the camera inside the ring dollying around them. We were almost always shooting inside the ropes. We have huge crane moves that go through the ropes and come up and come down. It's done as if it were a dance. But, at the same time, they are really fighting and they're inside a regulation-size ring with a dolly, camera, grips and everybody pushing around. It's very elaborate stuff. And often it's very abstract. Things go from twenty-four frames per second to forty-eight frames per second and back to twenty-four frames per second in the same shot. Things like that. Most of the fight stuff is twenty-four frames per second. Everything else is at widely varying speeds; a man in the corner of the ring may be ninety-six frames per second. When people put water on him in the corner between rounds, it runs down his face at ninety-six frames per second and then you come out of that and slowly go to twenty-four frames per second when the fight begins again. You do this by changing rheostats and opening diaphragms and closing them down.

You're talking about doing it all with one camera?

Yes, and if you do it right, you don't get any change in density. We did things where Bobby would knock a man down and he would go to a neutral corner and that would be at forty-eight frames per second. When the other guy got up off the mat, Bobby would be standing there just like a raging bull, at forty-eight frames per second. Then as they began fighting again, it would switch back to twenty-four frames per second. We did all kinds of stuff like that. We had very elaborate light cues. Because if the camera does a 360-degree pan of the ring, and you always want to have back light and no front light, then you've got to dim the lights all the way around in sync with how they go. It's very complicated and it takes forever.

But there never have been any fight sequences even remotely like this. Some of them go into enormous abstraction, like when he's being badly beaten, the lights all dim, people are just silhouettes and there's smoke. There's also a great difference between his life in the ring and his life outside the ring. So they're shot in very different styles. What started out as a simple little black-and-white movie that wasn't going to cost much—it's just like *The Last Waltz*—it started out as one thing and ended up as something else.

You seem to be trying to move further into abstraction in your work. A bit of it shows up in The Wanderers *and now the stylization and abstraction in* Raging Bull.

Yes, that is true of the scenes in the ring, but the rest of *Raging Bull* is straightforward. It's as simple as we could make it. You shoot a wide master; if the character goes here, you pan here, if the character goes there, you pan there. If somebody looks at something, we pan over to what he looks at and pan back. We did the simplest kind of stuff on purpose.

But you personally are beginning to work more on a certain level of abstraction.

I guess so. But the other kind of shooting is also interesting too, which is *really* simple, like Renoir. You know in *Rules of the Game*, where they all arrive for the houseparty in the rain. And the butlers go out to them with the umbrellas. And the camera just follows the butler out and follows him back in again with the guests. And then he goes out to get more people. The camera does the same thing: back and forth with the people. It just couldn't be simpler; it would be impossible to be simpler. It's just a wide shot with a 25-millimeter lens and it pans back and forth. It's just one shot and it does everything. It has an enormous economy and it tells you everything you need to know about the people, the cars, the rain, the butlers and the house. That sort of ultra, ultra-simple shooting also is interesting. In a way, from where we have been, that also is something like an abstraction. It's so simple that it's back to 1926 and Buster Keaton. That to me, is really interesting if it could be thought out and pursued with real intelligence. It's just that you don't find many people, you know, who see far enough into films to know about that. Marty is one of them. Marty and I worked that stuff out and it could not be simpler. A lot of big scenes are done in just one master. There's no coverage; it's ultra-simple.

You've quoted Godard something to the effect that the choice of angle is a very complicated thing. Could you elaborate on that?

True, it's very complicated. I remember Godard saying that. I'm sure he once thought he understood them when he was the hot-shot moviemaker. He said he no longer understood angles anymore. They seemed much more mysterious to him than they had ten years before. And they certainly do to me too. They seem enormously mysterious.

In what sense?

Angles tell us emotional things in ways that are mysterious. And emotional things that I'm often unaware of. I think a particular angle is going to do one thing and it does something quite different often. I no longer have any sure sense that I have a grasp of it. Angles seem the most mysterious thing about movies to me, I think. I'm talking on a visual level. Occasionally you will hit an angle that is absolutely inevitable; it's just the right angle. But that only happens sometimes. A lot of times, what angles give you emotionally is puzzling and mysterious. I don't have any sense that I understand them.

Do you think there are a lot of subconscious things that go into the selection of an angle?

Yes. I realized that the first time I was a director of photography. If you were doing it as well as you could and working as hard as you could, there was a lot more unconscious material that went into what you did than you had any idea of. I thought it would be much more in the open than it is. I found that I was drawing on unconscious sources amazingly more than I would have had any idea I was. Anybody who was going to be honest about it would say the same thing. Unless they are just hacks. If they really are trying, and trying to do something for the first time, then you are using unconscious material surprisingly intensely. And I think one of the ways that that unconscious material reveals itself is in angles: in what it says about the relations of characters or the relations of characters to place. Or what it says about dominance and submission. It's genuinely mysterious. And I don't like mystery. You should never count on anything being mysterious or new or wonderful. Or that in the joy of doing something, you're going to create something new. I think the more planning, the more meticulous, the more anal-retentive you are, the better off you are. But there's no sense pretending that that mystery isn't there. I don't think you should ever count on it or ever even think about it until afterwards. This is all pretty abstract, I realize.

Are there other people who think the same way you do?

I have no idea.

Do you ever discuss this with anyone? With Scorsese?

Everything's unconscious to Marty; everything's mysterious to Marty. No, I've never talked about it to other cameramen much. I once had the opportunity to get together Gordy, Almendros, Nykvist, Ondricek and myself in one room because we were all in New York for some reason. And if I could have just worked it out, I could have got us all together just to talk. I was halfway to setting it up and I stopped myself because it was not going to be that interesting. I don't think that cameramen have a lot to say to each other, in a funny way. I mean, Gordy and I were the only two I knew who did talk to each other. But then I was his operator and we spent night after night on location with nothing else to do but drink and talk. So we talked. Other than that, I've never had a successful conversation about cameras, about cinematography with a cameraman. Nestor Almendros is a wonderful, sophisticated and cultivated man to talk to. And he's marvelous to talk to about literature or politics but we've never much talked about the mechanics or aesthetics of cinematography. But I know I'm right when I say that—I know I'm right for me, maybe not for anybody else. But I can't believe I'm not right about the unconscious things for someone who really is trying in some way to let some kind of energy loose.

Do you have any designs on directing?

Yes, I'd like to. I don't mean that I've done everything that can be done in cinematography. I just mean that, for me, I don't have the energy for it that I used to. And it's no longer as terrifying as it once was, even black-and-white. And therefore it's harder to deal with. I should do something else. Maybe I should be a grip. I'd like to run a bookstore. Something. But I'm not sure that I shouldn't leave it alone for a while.

I expect all cinematographers to say they want to direct.

Some cameramen don't. Nestor Almendros doesn't want to. Gordy's already done it. Lazslo and Vilmos, I'm sure, want to direct. It's inevitable in a way. Any good cameraman who gets passed from hand to hand, through a lot of different directors, ends up doing a certain amount of ersatz directing. And that's what cinematography is, a lot of it. I suppose you want to see your name or really have the chance to do it yourself.

6

Bill Fraker

"I think the criterion for separating the men from the boys is the fact that when you look at a cinematographer's work on the screen, you have to look at the consistency of the work. The consistency has to be there."

Like the narrow, winding street leading to his house high in the Hollywood hills, Billy Fraker's career has been a long and arduous climb to the top of his profession. Starting out in film school at the University of Southern California after service in World War II, he pursued a path which led him through a long apprenticeship in television on shows like *The Lone Ranger*, *Outer Limits* and *Ozzie and Harriet*. He moved on to become camera operator on Conrad Hall's first feature as cinematographer, *The Wild Seed*. They continued to collaborate on *Morituri* and *The Professionals*, both of which were nominated for Oscars. Since his first feature as director of photography, *Games* in 1965, his diverse credits have included *Rosemary's Baby*, *Bullitt*, *Looking for Mr. Goodbar*, *Heaven Can Wait*, *1941* and *War Games*.

You get the impression that Fraker has seen it all by now and none of it presents much of a problem. It's no wonder that many first-time directors call on him to shoot their pictures. Fraker's calm self-assurance and guru-like style are no doubt an asset in the frantic atmosphere of a film production. Although traditionally trained in the style of the old Hollywood cameramen, he successfully bridges the gap to the newer freedoms of the sixties and seventies. Having directed several features, he finds himself always returning to his first love, cinematography.

Unlike many of his colleagues, he is also actively concerned with enhancing the status of the cinematographer within the industry power structure. As two-term president of the American Society of Cinematographers (ASC), the by-invitation-only honorary fraternity of cameramen, he has lobbied hard for changes in the status quo. The proposals he has spoken out for include the elevation of the cinematographer to above-the-line status in film production budgets, the establishment of an international research council for the resolution of difficult technical and cinematic problems, an annual international symposium of cinematographers for the purpose of exchanging viewpoints and knowledge, and the formation of an international talent pool of cinematographers who would be able to shoot anywhere in the world without regard to union jurisdictions and national boundaries. While many individual cinematographers have been receptive to these ideas, the established system, propagated by fifty years of management/union relations, has been slow to change particularly with regard to the rank-and-file cinematographer.

Never content to be a follower, Fraker is an individualist who has established himself as an elder statesman of cinematography. He is a leader who is not afraid of innovation on or off the set.

As Director of Photography:
1965   *Games*
1967   *The Fox*
       The President's Analyst
1968   *Fade In*
       Rosemary's Baby
       Bullitt
1969   *Paint Your Wagon*
1970   *Day of the Dolphin*
1971   *Gator*
       Dusty and Sweets McGee
1975   *Rancho Deluxe*
       The Killer Inside Me
       Aloha Bobby and Rose
1976   *Exorcist II: The Heretic*
1977:   *Looking for Mr. Goodbar†*
       Heaven Can Wait†
       American Hot Wax

1978   *Old Boyfriends*
1979   *1941†*
       The Hollywood Knights
1980   *Divine Madness*
1981   *Sharky's Machine*
1982   *The Best Little Whorehouse in Texas*
1983   *War Games†*
1984   *Protocol*

Additional cinematography only:
1975   *One Flew Over the Cuckoo's Nest*
1978   *Close Encounters of the Third Kind*

As Director:
1970   *Monte Walsh*
1973   *A Reflection of Fear*
1980   *Legend of the Lone Ranger*

†Academy Award Nominations for best achievement in cinematography.

You're one of a number of early graduates of the University of Southern California film school who has had a good deal of success in the industry. Do you feel film schools are valuable for someone who is looking to get into the business?

I do believe that there is a very definite position for schools. I love USC because I consider it to be one of the foremost and best cinema schools in the world. I like the discipline and formal teaching at USC. I think it's very necessary and important, number one, to acquire some sort of discipline in filmmaking and, number two, to get a good basic knowledge of filmmaking. That's what I like about it. UCLA is a little lenient; good school, terrific students but a little freer.

A number of film schools are that way. It's the type of situation where nothing is imposed on you and you get out of it what you put in.

If you go in with the premise that you don't get something for nothing, you only get out of it what you put into it. It's basic. I love that formal education only because it gives you the discipline that you are going to need later on. Discipline comes not in making films but in working with people who have much more knowledge than you do; you have to sit in their wake a little bit to learn and that's where you need the discipline. If you want to go and explode the world, that's terrific but you want to learn as much as you can and then, at the same time, do what you have to do. Now I think you can find a marriage of those two things. It's very important to have the discipline. I know a lot of people don't agree with me; they say, "I don't have time for discipline." But it takes a long time to learn; it takes a lot of experience, a lot of heartbreak.

We've noticed a trend with talented young directors making their first film. It turns out to be a great film, tight and disciplined, but then the Hollywood hype machine starts turning them into stars and soon their work seems to suffer.

They begin to believe what people tell them. It's easy to fall for it, you know, you're only human. You start saying, "Hey, I must be pretty good." I don't know how you come out of that. I don't know how you hold your head straight. I mean, you go through divorces, you go through families, you go through fortunes. I don't know what brings you back down.

One cinematographer pointed out that every day people will compliment you and say great things about you for reasons that absolutely have nothing to do with talent. He says he just lets it all just slide by him. How do you handle it?

I have a basic rule that I go by. People say, "God, you did *Bullitt*, it was the forerunner of all the car chases, so to speak; it was great." As soon as they say that, *Bullitt* flashes through my head and I can name fifteen mistakes I made in *Bullitt*. I can't kid myself. I don't care who tells me how much they loved *Monte Walsh*, I know or I think I know where I blew it, where I failed. And that's what comes to mind; therefore I keep some kind of balance. When I reach the point where I do a picture and it's perfect and people praise me, then I'm going to say, "Hey, you're right, it's terrific." I don't think that will ever happen.

What was your first job out of school?

When I came out of school I tried to get into the union and it was useless. You have X amount of people in any union and you have so many jobs. Now it's the moral obligation of the union to protect its members. Therefore if you have more members than you have jobs, you have people in the union waiting to get jobs. The producers signed a contract with the union and their hands are tied because they have to get the people they hire only from the union. So it's a vicious circle and it's the same thing today.

I wanted to be in film so I worked in film but I worked non-union. (This was 1950.) I was cutting and doing insert photography to make a living more than I was shooting. Sometimes a producer would call me up and say, "Billy, I need a shot of three hundred workers coming out of a factory." I'd get twenty-five dollars for the shot; I supplied the camera and the film. I just gave him the negative. So I'd get into my Model A Ford and I'd go out to Lockheed at 3:00 P.M. and the bell would ring and out would come three hundred workers. I'd jump on top of the Model A with that Eyemo camera stuck to my eye shooting the shot. Then the guard would see me and say, "What the hell you doing over there?" I'd jump in my car and scream away. I shot everything, amusement parks, airplanes landing, whatever they needed a stock shot for. Finally I got a call from the head of the camera local, Herb Aller. He said, "I understand you want to get into the local?" I said, "Absolutely." He told me to come down next week and I said, "No, I'll be down there in ten minutes." When I arrived and received my application, he said, "I'll need three hundred dollars for the initiation fee." Well, I'd been holding that three hundred dollars for thirteen years. That's how long it took me—thirteen years from the time I started until the time I got into Local 659. That's how long it took but I got in and was admitted as a loader. And two days later I went to work as a loader on *The Lone Ranger*. They needed people at that time and that was the only reason I got in. That was only because of the advent of television. If it hadn't been for TV there would have never been this whole new group of cinematographers because there would have been no work for us. Television opened up the gates.

The reason many of us became directors of photography was that a whole new generation of producers and directors came into being and there was a tremendous generation gap. These people couldn't get into Hollywood from the bottom so they came in through the top. And suddenly you find someone directing a film at thirty with a director of photography who was much older. That's what really hurt and they wouldn't accept it. That's what blew it open for the young guys like Hall and Wexler to go through and become first cameramen. Otherwise it would have never happened. It's very interesting. For example, an older cameraman would say, "No, we can't do it this way." And we would say, "Well, you don't usually do it this way but let's try it and see what happens." There were other factors of course but that's a theory of mine as to why it happened. So now you've got a young bunch of cameramen who have come in, and have done terrific things.

How long were you working in TV and what was that experience like?

I spent about ten years in TV. I worked on *The Lone Ranger*, *Private Secretary*, *The Western Marshall* and others. In those days we worked six days a week and we did three half-hour shows in a week—one show every two days! Then I spent seven and a half years with *Ozzie and Harriet*. I moved out of being a loader to being an assistant cameraman and then moved to *Ozzie and Harriet* as a second assistant and I left that show as a camera operator. That was a great time in my life. Ozzie really created a family and an empire; he was on the air for fourteen years. He was very good to his people and he supported them. There were a lot of talented people who came out of that show like Chuck Rosher and Bobby Byrne who are now cameramen. If there's any success I've achieved or will achieve, I attribute the major portion of it to Ozzie.

So those years in television were well spent?

Oh, yes. I started to do some commercials. Then I did three pictures with Connie Hall; I was his operator. The first picture was *The Wild Seed*, which was a very interesting project. It was Connie Hall's first picture as a cameraman and my first picture as an operator. We had a terrific time. Then we did a film called *Morituri*, at Fox. The third picture was *The Professionals* with Richard Brooks directing. Connie was nominated for black-and-white photography on *Morituri* and color photography on *The Professionals*.

What was your first picture as director of photography?

My first picture was at Universal with Simone Signoret, Jimmy Caan and Katherine Ross, called *Games*, with Curtis Harrington directing and George Edwards producing. James Pratt, the production manager at Universal, called me and said that he had been watching me for a long time. He said, "You're a first cameraman and you did it on your own. You're the type of guy they need for this picture." Then I panicked because I knew I had to go in and run a crew and Universal had their own family like they do now. But I said to myself, "I don't care. I've got to do it anyway. I got to do it because you only get one or two shots in your whole life to become what you want." You have to keep preparing yourself for what your goal is and then when you get the chance to achieve that goal, you have to go out and do it. Right or wrong. That has stopped a lot of talented people. Anyway I did it and it didn't stop from that point on. For some reason, something generated a momentum and I don't think I had a week off from that point for three years. Next I did a picture with Mark Rydell called *The Fox*. I'm very proud of that film; it's one of my favorites. Then came *The President's Analyst* with Teddie Flicker directing. Then came *Fade In*, a film with Burt Reynolds, followed by *Rosemary's Baby*, *Bullitt*, *Paint Your Wagon*, and then I directed my first film, *Monte Walsh*.

When you were a camera operator what things were you looking for in hopes of that day when you would move up to that director of photography slot?

I think you really try to learn what becomes illusion and what becomes reality. To put it another way: what you can get away with and what you can't get away with. To put it another way: visual storytelling. I used to watch different people light and see what their approach was to the same basic subject matter. Everybody's different, so every time you turn the camera on, you learn something. But what really amazed me and what really turned me on, so to speak, was what you could really get away with. Not trying to cheat but whether you could spend more time achieving an effect and not spend the time because you know that the effect is already going to be there and go on to something else so you could move your time around, which is one hundred percent more valuable than anything else in making a picture. Light was phenomenal. I worked with Connie Hall who was a protege of Ted McCord. Ted spent more time with the backgrounds than any cameraman I ever worked with; Connie did also. In spending more time with the backgrounds, it gave you different planes and different levels of light to create whatever effect one would desire. Ted would just put a key light and a little bit of fill in the front and go. He used to spend hours on the backgrounds. And that's what created the illusion of all Ted's pictures. You see he worked very hard in creating a third dimension, to create that depth. Ted McCord was a major force and very influential to a lot of up-and-coming young cameramen.

Eventually there comes a time when you're not afraid of handling the wheels and following the people because when you got Marlon Brando and he says, "OK, this is going to be it; I'm going to do it once and goodbye," then you say, "Oh,

Christ, if I screw it up, I've had it." Once you get over that fear, and once everything becomes familiar to you as far as operating the camera, then you start looking creatively at what you're dealing with. You learn how far over you can move the camera, how much difference it makes if you can really see it with your eye when you can't see it through the camera. You learn to create a balance between light and shadow and also a visual balance. I think those things are the most important.

Would today's Bill Fraker shoot Games *the same as Bill Fraker shot* Games *then?*

No, absolutely not. I wouldn't try to do as much as I did and try to make *Gone with the Wind* on my first picture. I think what you learn through experience is that a twenty-five-day picture requires a certain amount of effort and a hundred-day picture requires another kind of effort. You don't know that when you first go into it because you're dumb, naive and enthusiastic. You try to do everything. And you waste a lot of time doing things that may not be in the picture.

The thing that struck me about Games *was that it wasn't a subtly photographed film; it was a bravado effort, you were showing off your stuff.*

Exactly. You want to make good so you really work hard and do all the things that you've seen in all the pictures that you loved. The things that you know are terrific, you try to copy them. And it takes you many years to put your act together in order to get to where you can do those kind of things naturally.

What's your personal method of running your career and guiding yourself around all the Hollywood traps and pitfalls?

It's spooky on the way up. I was fortunate because I didn't have the time to think about it and I really didn't care about getting to a position. I accepted each picture on its own merits. I attacked each problem day by day. I got so involved with what I was doing that, before I knew it, people were calling me for pictures; I was making good money and everything was happening. But all that stuff has to be secondary. You have to make what you're doing the most important thing. Your output becomes the most important thing in your life once you become a director of photography. You're working day and night; there is no such thing as eight-hour days and five-day weeks.

Is there any particular reason you've chosen to work with a lot of first-time directors?

That's very interesting; other cameramen have asked me the same thing. I don't see anything wrong with working with first-time directors. Most of them that I've worked with have been very knowledgeable. They know their craft and they know what they want to do; they just have never directed a feature. I seem to be able to get along with them for some reason. We're all human and we all have egos; it's what position and where you put that ego that matters. Any man who feels that he's right all the time and that there is only one way to do anything is wrong. I think there are fifty thousand ways to do everything. And they're all correct if they work.

So therefore my approach to working with first-time directors comes back to what I said about USC and the discipline. The director is the overall boss, he's the man you're working for. Your job, as cameraman, prop man or whatever, is to get into that director's head and put what he wants on the screen. What you have to do is look at that person and really study him, try to understand what he's about and what he really means. I think it's a marriage between the cameraman and a director; you're going to have your ups and downs just like a marriage. But you want to go on and be happy like in any marriage. In filmmaking, living happy is having a good film on the screen. That's the goal.

I guess it all boils down to the person who puts down his five dollars to see a movie.

Exactly. My approach to working with a first-time director is that we're here to make a film. So I don't give a damn if you work with someone who's made twenty films or just making his first; it doesn't make any difference. Sure your approach is different. You work with people like Richard Brooks who has directed films before but the input and approach to that man's position is to elevate him and give him the support he needs. I've directed and I was a first-time director and I know what people need. I was a cameraman who made set-ups but when I directed I found you still need that help. You still need that input. With first-time directors, I adore their receptiveness. What I'm saying is that you have to help them. And what happens is that you come out with good films because you've had the input of two or three different people instead of just one.

Let's talk a bit about technical things. How did you set up the chase sequence in Bullitt?

The chase sequence sort of established a genre for automobile chase sequences. I got a lot of notoriety and a lot of acclaim for it. I give all the credit to Peter Yates, the director, and Frank Keller, the editor, who won an Oscar for the picture. The chase took three to five weeks to film. We could only tie up certain streets of San Francisco at certain times. We would do the chase periodically whenever we could get a clearance on a location; sometimes one day a week, sometimes two. Every inch of that chase sequence was choreographed; we literally drove each shot and then we got out and we walked the shot. We talked about each problem we felt we might have and then Peter and I would set the camera where we wanted. I think the success of the chase was the result of the placement of the camera. Because the audience actually felt that they were participating in that chase. They were no longer observers. In old chase sequences, you would take a camera and pan as the car went by. Peter got the idea of placing the camera inside the car subjectively. So you got a feeling of participation. Also it gave you an outlet to take an automobile and smash it against another automobile; things that you always have wanted to do ever since you started to drive a car. And now you finally got a shot to do it. The secret of *Bullitt* is that we shot it at twenty-four frames per second but the cars were actually going 100–120 miles per hour. There was no cheating; we didn't speed up the camera. Also, as I say, putting the camera inside the car and letting the audience participate was important.

What were you doing for exterior lighting on that sequence?

For the exteriors of that sequence, there were no lights at all; we just shot. That was another innovation at that time: moving away from Hollywood and taking equipment up there, like arc lights and such, but then not using them. People said it couldn't be done but I had been doing it for years on commercials. But you see, at the time, it was a transitional period. We were just getting started as young cameramen. You would go to work for a major studio and they would hand you your equipment list. And you'd say, "What's this? I didn't order this." And they'd say, "This is what you're going to take." And you'd reply, "I don't want this equipment." And they'd say, "If you do a picture with this studio, you take this equipment." That was always a big fight and it still is today. It's the bureaucracy horseshit that I can't deal with. I don't want to deal with it and I won't deal with it. With the studios, you've got that overhead system so that you never get dollar-for-dollar value. The production ends up being charged twenty-five to forty percent overhead. And for what?

In Aloha Bobby and Rose, *you shot a lot of night exteriors. Could you comment how you approach those types of scenes?*

The interesting thing about *Aloha Bobby and Rose* was that we did it for $670,000 total, above and below the line. It grossed about twenty-five million and did terrific business. We shot it in thirty-six days and we shot it on Fuji stock. I liked it very much. Fuji was good stock but Eastman to me is still the best and most consistent. And that's what you're looking for, that consistency. You are constantly trying to match something. I place value on a cameraman who can maintain the consistency of a look he uses on a picture so that the picture doesn't jump all over once you get that look established. A good example is *Julia*. Once Doug Slocombe locked in the look of that picture, he held it all the way through. Owen Roizman's *Three Days of the Condor* is the same way. Connie Hall's *Day of the Locust* is another one that comes to mind. The cameraman, in turn, looks for that consistency in the equipment and film he uses.

Aloha Bobby and Rose was a gratifying experience. We shot in the rain on actual locations. We stole locations. Floyd Mutrux, the director, is extremely creative and allows a tremendous amount of input from people around him. He has good taste and he's very, very funny.

Did you have to force the film much on that picture?

As far as forced development goes, Fuji could go one stop with no trouble. Forcing two stops doesn't work one hundred percent of the time; only about seventy-five percent of the time but the forcing has to be honest. The philosophy people use when forcing film is, "I don't have enough exposure so I'm going to force it." Well, with Fuji, it has to be calculated. If you're forcing it one stop, you have to be short one stop exposure; you can't be short 1¼ or 1½ stops. With the Eastman stock you have more latitude and you can play with it but with the Fuji you have to be completely honest. That's not anything negative about the film; it's just different and you have to realize th.... I think the film responded very well.

Is there any difference between cameramen on the East Coast and their contemporaries on the West Coast?

Yes, there is a difference in philosophy and approach to photography that New York and East Coast cameramen have. You see, we've had everything we've really wanted out here on the West Coast. That's because this is really the capital of the motion picture industry throughout the whole world and we were born and raised with it. Hollywood is still Hollywood and the East Coast was sort of like a sister. Their innovation to photography was, "We can do without. We'll make do with what we have and we'll show you we can do as well as you." And they have. The innovative geniuses that have come out of New York have been phenomenal and have had a major effect on Hollywood. They're the ones that developed the realistic style, visually and photographically. They had $f2.3$ lenses but they wanted $f2$ or $f1.8$ lenses and they worked on it and they got them. They went into Penn Station and shot with no lights, they went into the subway and shot with no lights. They did these things out of necessity because they didn't have the money and the backing of a Hollywood studio to give them the equipment. And they didn't care anyway because they wanted reality and realism. Shows like *Naked City* made a tremendous input to us out here on the West Coast. So they developed that style of a visual look as opposed to a Hollywood look that we were all educated and raised to get on a sound stage.

What has happened is no matter where there are filmmakers, Hollywood still maintains its hold on moviemaking throughout the world. I don't know why. Maybe it's the heritage, its history or the studios. Those New York cameramen may have developed all those things we talked about but Hollywood gets the credit. It's because of the New York influence that I can make the statement we don't need lights for exposure now. We need light so we can do what we want to do, to create the image we want, the look we want. A good example of the old Hollywood studio lighting is *Heaven Can Wait*. We went back to the forties look because the look of that picture was really dictated by what we wanted to do with the main characters, Julie Christie and Warren Beatty. The rest of the picture achieved its look because of that. The look of a picture is inherent in the material. That's where you find what the look of the picture will be.

How do you get good skin tones?

Well, I think it's a combination of things. Things that are inherent in the film itself, the processing method and also the color of light being used today. The lenses are supposed to be color corrected. The color of the room and the ambient colors bouncing off the walls will be picked up on the faces. Skin tones are a very funny thing to deal with. You can achieve good skin tones by bringing your key light up to key and keeping it up to key and exposing for that key. Someone who is tan will photograph differently than someone who is pure white. If a scene like that occurs, you have a major problem. You try to bring the dark person up and take the light person down so that you even out.

I thought some of the skin tones on the close-ups of Julie Christie and Warren Beatty in Heaven Can Wait *were great.*

What we did was develop a key light for Julie and kept it throughout the whole picture; it worked terrifically for her. We developed a key for Warren too but it was a completely different one. Now you bring them both together and you have a helluva time. You've got people flagging lights all over the place during the scene. So that's why you fight to get people on the crew who can handle certain jobs. And the studio doesn't want them because they get paid over scale. But if you have a man on the dimmers who can work double key lights and he makes a switch so good that you can't even see it, well, that person's worth a million dollars. But you can't get the studio to believe it.

You have to have a close collaboration with the lab to get the effects you want too?

The labs really dictated to you what you could do and what you couldn't do. My philosophy is I don't really care about the film, I don't care about the lab, the lenses, the cameras. Now don't misunderstand me; I need them all and I have to deal with them. They're all very, very important but I consider all of those things tools. We have to become masters of those tools, we have to learn how to use them. I don't care if I have to take a brand-new Panaflex camera and dunk it in the ocean; if that's required by the shot, I'll do it. Some cameramen would never do that in a million years. Equipment is just a tool. Once you become master of those tools, then you can do anything that you want to do.

What kind of collaboration do you have with the labs? What makes a lab enjoyable to deal with?

The individual attention that you get at a lab makes the difference. All labs primarily do a terrific job and they all do about the same thing. When you're a cameraman shooting a picture, that's the most important thing in your life at that time. I personally want service. I want to be called up at six in the morning and told, "Hey, Billy, there's something wrong with your negative," or "It's really beautiful, Billy." Also I want to be able to call them and say, "Did you see such and such a scene and how did it work out?" I want them to know what I shot and I want them to care about what I'm doing. That's all I'm asking for; just that service. The one who spoiled us all was Giff Chamberlain at Technicolor. Every morning you got a note and a copy of all the printing lights or he would call you, no matter where you were. That's service. You start a scene in the afternoon and you may continue it the whole next day. You want to know if you made the right or wrong decisions.

Why is that service so important?

What we do today is establish a printing light where we want our negative to print and then we shoot for that printing light during the whole picture. This begins to give us a little bit of consistency. So when we go into a scene and the negative is down a little because we have this pre-established one light daily, we know that something isn't working. That we aren't getting enough bounce, that we aren't getting enough fill. So you work to your own printing light. A lot of people do that; they just don't expose their film and send it to the lab and say, "OK, give me a print." We work very carefully with our printing lights and if we're off a little bit a guy like Skip Nicholson at Technicolor will call right up and tell us.

Do you believe that there is an optimum f-stop at which you receive the best possible photographic quality?

That's an old theory. Lenses were made a certain way and you had an optimum everything; exposure, color and everything was optimized at a certain f-stop. Those lenses were ground at that f-stop as a basis so therefore they thought that that would be the optimum f-stop. I don't really believe that. I think the look of a picture comes from what you're doing with the lenses and the lighting. If you're shooting at $f2$, you'll get a different look than at $f5.6$. Maybe there is an optimum look; I don't know if there is or not. Now when I start to shoot at a certain f-stop, I try to continue that. On exteriors I hate to stop down past $f6.3$. I think lenses are too sharp. I try to diffuse some of that sharpness with filters.

You don't think it's essential to always have a very sharp negative?

No. Although in *1941*, we tried not to put anything in front of the lens. We tried to put all our filter color on the lights so that the negative would be very sharp because there were a lot of special effects and it had to go through a lot of opticals. Normally I have a filter packet on the front of my lens about two inches thick.

Why do you think the lenses are too sharp?

Lenses are just too sharp today and the sharpness builds up the contrast. I don't like that contrast. I want the blacks to be really black but I don't want anything sharp in there. I don't want a sharp black line in the shadows; I want it to fuzz off a little.

Do you prefer working on location or in the studio?

I prefer the studio, preferably on a sound stage. I think locations are marvelous; they present different types of challenges and I have fun on them. But I really like the stage because when you walk on, the whole thing is black and you hit the first light, the second light and the third. To me it's a little more creative approach to cinematography. You look back at the old films and that's the way Hollywood was built. Everything was on sound stages; they seldom went outside. The most important thing is the control you have. If you shoot outside exteriors, God gives you the control and that's what you have to deal with. You can deal with it much better in the studio.

Do you feel that cameramen sometimes get too enamored with the mechanical aspects of the profession?

Well, when something comes out that's really marvelous like the Panaglide or the Steadicam, everyone goes crazy with it at first. Then everyone settles down and uses it only when they have to. We always do that. When the zoom lenses came out, the same thing happened. Now very seldom do you see a zoom lens shot. I don't use them at all. Someone recently asked me about an automatic focusing system. The creative art of selective focus is a tremendous art; to be able to move your focus where you want it. If you have an automatic focus system, it will be just like an automatic spot meter in still cameras now. It will always give you the average. You don't want the average, you want to be very selective in what you do. I work under the principle of using one light to do one job; we don't use one light to do three jobs. If I want a key light, then I set up a key light. It's the same with focus; you want it to do one specific job.

How closely did you work with Roman Polanski in establishing a style for Rosemary's Baby?

I think that Polanski is a cinematic genius. He commands his own space. He developed the style and look of *Rosemary's Baby* as much as anyone else. *Rose-*

mary's Baby was shot in fourteen weeks: two on location and twelve on sound stages. We re-created the Dakota apartments at Paramount. It was the first picture Paramount had done where a blueprint was drawn for the electrical department for developing and scaffolding, building special equipment for the picture. They said that it had never happened to them and that they had never been brought in so early in the planning stages and they loved it.

Dick Sylbert was our production designer extraordinaire who copied the Dakota apartments to scale. So that meant that we actually had eighteen- to twenty-foot ceilings, four-and-a-half-foot hallways and three-by-four-foot closets. So in order to light and get exposure — at that time we were using 5251 which was much slower and also we didn't push film then — you'd have to go to 10Ks, the larger units to get that amount of light. So we developed what they call a "trombone" for each size light. A trombone is a steel wire hooked on the edge of a set that had a lip on it and had a pipe that ran up and down. You could put your lamps on there and adjust it to any height that you wanted. So there was actually very little rigging in the scaffolding above the set. We had all the physical rigging and the power lines up on scaffolds; there was nothing on the floor. The sets had no nails in them like they normally do. We had set walls with interlocking bolts. That gave us the versatility of pulling those walls in and out a hundred times a day if we wanted to. If you had nailed them together, after three weeks, you would have chewed up all the walls.

We devised that every room have a different look in the apartment. The kitchen was yellow and always had a cheery, bright look. The living room was the only room that would change its mood. The bedroom worked high and low, although a little different than the living room. The baby's nursery was always down, never really very bright. The hallway was always down because a lot of things happened there. The whole picture was shot with two lenses, an eighteen millimeter and a twenty-five millimeter. We devised an H-bar (Roman's idea) which was a device to allow a lot of hand-held camera movement without the disturbing walking motion. About forty percent of *Rosemary's Baby* was hand-held. We shot all the hand-held with the twenty-five millimeter and with the actors constantly pushing and crowding the lens. Roman wanted that perspective, even on inserts. I once did an insert with a forty millimeter lens in a telephone booth and he said, "Billy, it's wrong, it's terrible. Shoot it with the twenty-five." So we went back and shot the insert. It works and he was absolutely right. Polanski's power, as a director, is that he is very strong. I'd put him in a category with Richard Brooks. They lead an audience. You can go to a Richard Brooks picture or a Roman Polanski picture and you can see the intensity on the screen and the effect it has on the audience. They direct with a heavy hand and you can feel the pressure. I love it because that's what they are; they're storytellers. They take that audience and they move it to where they want to move it.

Let me give you an example of that from *Rosemary's Baby*. In the film, Ruth Gordon needs to make stronger contact with Mia Farrow. The kids have fixed up the apartment and now Ruth comes over during the day and knocks on Mia's door. Mia opens the door and says, "Hi," and Ruth looks past Mia's shoulder and sees part of the kitchen and says, "My God, you kids have finished the apartment." And she forces herself in. Mia looks a little quizzical and Ruth takes over from the doorway and starts to push the camera down the long central hallway. She's walking and she comes to the front room with Mia following her and she says, "Oh my goodness, you've done a marvelous job." She's in the front room now and she turns around, with Mia in the background—now this is all still one shot with a twenty-five millimeter lens—and she says, "The bedroom, is that the bedroom?" And Mia says, "Yes, but . . ." Ruth says, "Do you have a phone?" and Mia says, "Yes, in the bedroom." So Ruth takes off exiting for the bedroom and Mia steps up to look at what's happening in the bedroom.

Now we're in the front room and Roman says to me, "Billy, now we need Mia's POV of Ruth on the phone." I said, "OK, terrific." I had to solve one window problem in the bedroom and that was easy; so after fifteen minutes I told Roman we were ready to go. He comes over and looks and says, "No, Billy, it's wrong." Now what I had done was that I was shooting from where Mia was standing. There was an archway from the front room to the hallway. And there was another archway or doorjamb from the hallway to the bedroom. The bedroom door was open. The bed was right there and Ruth was sitting on the bed and talking on the phone. Now I had her framed through the doorjamb from the hallway. It was terrific; I even had a little breeze coming through on the curtains. But Roman thought it was wrong. And he began to move the camera to the left. Now, by doing this, he began to cut Ruth off by the bedroom doorjamb. He cut her in half. Then he said, "Stop the camera, this is it." I looked through and all you could see was Ruth's back and fanny sitting on the bed. You don't see her legs, her shoulders or her head; all you see is just part of her but you hear her talking on the phone. I said, "You can't see her!" Roman said, "Exactly, exactly." So we shot it that way. Now, months later, we go see *Rosemary's Baby* in a theater. We watch the picture and then we come to the scene I've just described. Ruth goes into the bedroom; Mia looks on from the hallway. Then you cut to see Ruth and you cannot see her; you can only see half of her and fifteen hundred heads in the theater lean to the right to see around the doorjamb. Now, *that's* the power that Roman has. And that is the thought that's behind it. I think that's the best example of how he commands an audience. Richard Brooks does the same thing. It's phenomenal and tremendously exciting.

Rosemary's Baby was a tremendous experience for me because I really grew up as a cameraman on that picture. In all aspects, from really realizing what contribution you can make to understanding the complete marriage of a cameraman and director. I realize the gratification of really working hard and then seeing it happen on the screen. The love of filmmaking that Roman and Richard express, once you begin to accomplish what you set out to do, is great. The satisfaction that comes from, "God, it's working and it's beautiful; let's keep going, let's keep going," drives you on to extend yourself. It's marvelous. That's the turn-on in movies.

I guess having a director who can instill that is important?

Those are the directors that can bring you up to one hundred percent of your capacity. I've been fortunate because I've worked with several directors like that.

There is no wasted effort with Richard Brooks; everything you do is going to be on the screen and you know that when you see it, it'll be terrific and you get a lot of gratification.

I thought that Rancho Deluxe *was a really well-photographed film. You really captured those wide open spaces. What cinematic concepts were you concerned with there?*

There was a very definite cinematic concept; whether or not we pulled it off is something else. It was "big sky" country and it was absolutely gorgeous. We were shooting in Livingston, Montana, which is the northern entrance to Yellowstone; we were surrounded by 360 degrees of mountains, big billowy clouds, changing weather, blue skies and snow. I tried to develop some sort of an idea for a look and I didn't come up with anything until I shot the tests. When I saw the tests, I said, "My God, we should postcard this picture." In other words, it should be just like you see on a postcard. You shouldn't try to make it washed out or flat; you should take advantage of the beautiful natural scenery that's up there. And that's the whole concept that went into *Rancho Deluxe*. To postcard the whole picture, using heavy filters and so forth to bring out all the clouds and to make the sky blue; plenty of saturation. I wanted to make it like the great old Technicolor films. I thought it worked very well.

Before you started shooting, did you read any of Tom McGuane's books and did they have an effect on the way you looked at the picture?

Oh yes, very definitely. Having taken a different track than he has taken now, I very definitely believe that he would be one of the strong and great American writers of today, in the mold of Hemingway. He really writes sensationally. There really hasn't been anybody to translate his stuff to film; I think Frank Perry has probably come the closest. That's an entire art itself: transposing the written word to the screen.

As a cinematographer, it would seem that the better written the script, the more input you have to work with.

Primarily I think you're right. I think theoretically all that works when you're all sitting around talking about it. Theoretically, as a cinematographer, that's exactly what you're supposed to do. You're supposed to take some printed material and be able to transpose it onto the screen. I would love to teach a class about that at some university. Because I think it's very, very important and it's one of the things that is not taught. How do you say, "World War II began," in context with what the rest of the material says? Very, very few people can take a sentence and put it on the screen. It's difficult, it's tough. Most cameramen are really concerned about exposure; you know, putting a light on a person or a set and saying, "That's $f2.8$," and working from there. We work just the opposite because we work with what we feel should happen insofar as what our eye sees. We use one light to establish a key and then everything else is done by eye. You train yourself and you learn to do things like that so that you can move into any situation, anyplace, and do the same thing. As soon as you walk into an actual location, you see what light exists and you have to control it. Then you decide your lighting from there.

You shot the last ten days or so of One Flew Over the Cuckoo's Nest, *after both Haskell Wexler and Bill Butler had worked on it. Isn't it difficult to come into a project like that with little or no preparation?*

It's extremely difficult. What I do is I look at a lot of the dailies and literally try to match what the previous cameraman has done. I followed up shooting for Bill Butler on *Lipstick* too. And no two people shoot the same. So therefore I wouldn't have done what Bill had done but at least I feel that it's one's responsibility to help each other when we can. So therefore I literally tried to match what he did as best I could.

On Aloha Bobby and Rose, *you had a small budget as opposed to other films you've done. As a cinematographer, where do you feel the pinch of a tight budget and how do you get around it?*

We did *Aloha Bobby and Rose* for $670,000 in 36 days. After working in the business for a number of years, you become known as a professional. And I have to say professional with quotation marks. In other words, you pretty well know what you can do and what you can't do with an amount of time and amount of money you have to work with. Because almost all the pictures run the same amount of time on the screen; they run between an hour and a half and two hours. Therefore you have to shoot a certain amount of pages a day in order to meet that schedule. All the scripts generally run from 110–125 pages. So all that is pretty much standard. The budget and the schedule give you a good idea of how you're going to have to perform. With *Aloha Bobby and Rose*, you had to do six, eight, ten pages a day in order to meet your schedule. If you have a lot of moving around during the day, you can't take all the equipment out of the truck and still meet a schedule. (With that type of budget, you usually don't *have* a lot of equipment.)

If you basically use the principle of making almost every shot an effects shot, then I think dramatically you can bring off a helluva lot more, faster, in a shorter schedule picture. You don't have time for a lot of visual exposition. In other words, you're going from an interior of a motel room to a diner. So there's no way to lead up to the two. You may cut right from the motel room to the diner. Both are interiors; your approach to the interiors has to be different so that visually the exposition takes care of itself and tells you exactly where you are without leading into anything or being subtle about it. You just more or less automatically know, through experience I guess, what that approach has to be.

I realize this is a hard question to answer when you're not talking about something specific, but I'm concerned with where you decide you can sacrifice on a lower budgeted film. Do you say, "I can take the time here, but I can't take the time over there"? Is it from scene to scene?

Well, I think the criterion for separating the men from the boys is the fact that when you look at somebody's work on the screen, you have to look at the consistency of the work. The look of the film has to remain the same because I feel that the look is inherent in the material. The look of the picture does not come predetermined as some cameramen feel; I don't believe in that. The consistency has to be there. Also involved is that you don't have the luxury of shooting a master and covering everything twenty-five different ways. You have to do it in one master or maybe not even that. Richard Brooks, as much money or as little money as he may spend on a picture, never shoots a master. That's his philosophy. So if you have an eight-page scene, he may do it in seventeen shots or in three shots depending on what he wants the actors to do. He never shoots a master because he knows where he's going; he cuts in the camera.

Naturally you have to have help from the director. If you have a neophyte director or a director without too much experience, naturally he wants to protect himself and get a lot of coverage but you just don't have the time to do that. You either have to talk him out of it or you have to compromise someplace. And it's a matter of who makes the compromise. Chances are that you do because you're the cameraman and he's the director. But if you get a man that's absolutely fair he'll want everything that we put in the film to be the best we can do at that moment in time. Some directors aren't like that at all; they want everything but they can't have it.

So that your primary consideration, no matter what the budget, is that the film be consistent. That's where you draw the line.

Yes, absolutely.

If you achieve that but lose some of the subtleties around the edges . . .

At least it's up to a certain standard, right? There are pictures I haven't done because I didn't feel that the picture would be given a fair shot by whomever.

Because of the budget involved?

No, because of the producer or director or actor involved. And you say to yourself, "You know you're never going to do it with them," and you walk away and forget about it. You know, every time you do a picture, it's a helluva lot of work. You leave a little piece of yourself on the screen. If I were thirty-five years old, I guess I wouldn't care; I'd do everything in order to get the experience and keep going and keep going. Because every time you do a picture, you learn. I don't care what you've done or how much you've done.

The thing that's really interesting and marvelous about our business is that we've all done certain things that came out terrific and we've received praise and all that baloney. But if you don't progress each time you make a picture, if you don't move into another area, if you don't try to extend yourself each time, then why kill yourself? You might as well just do a show where you can stay in the city and get paid five days for three days work. I'm not putting anybody down. What I'm saying is that it's not any easier but it's nicer. Let me put it that way.

Paint Your Wagon *was quite a large budgeted film for its time and that type of project doesn't really seem to fit in with your other work. How did you come to shoot it?*

I got *Paint Your Wagon* because John Truscott, who was the art director/production designer, had seen my work on *The Fox* and said, "That's what we want this picture to look like." That's exactly the reason. Because by rights, somebody like Jimmy Wong Howe should have done it; that type of a cameraman. Or Leon Shamroy, who had done *South Pacific*.

Was that the most expensive picture you had worked on up to that time?

Yes, definitely.

Did you feel a big weight on your shoulders?

No. And the reason is that we approached the picture like any other picture with a certain budget. So I measured the weight of the picture by the amount of equipment and the size of the crew, at that time. I figured it was a twelve or thirteen million dollar picture. The thing that devastated me after we started shooting the picture was the fact that they told us that the production costs were eighty thousand dollars a day. There were some days that I had to make decisions not to shoot and that was just like throwing away eighty thousand dollars. That was the toughest thing for me to do. But I didn't know what else to do because we'd started shooting a sequence that was going to last twenty minutes on the screen; we'd got about six or seven minutes into the sequence and that was shot in sunlight. Then the overcast came and I didn't know what to do about it. So we waited. That was probably the toughest thing about the film. We shot up there until we were snowed out and had to go home.

That almost killed the studio, huh?

Well, that along with *Darling Lili, Catch-22* and a whole group of pictures that were being done at that time at Paramount. It's funny but almost the same thing is happening at this point now in Hollywood. Studios are making big pictures now and the pictures are going for anywhere between ten and twenty million dollars. They're going to big theaters, big screen, big sound; the same thing that was happening at that time. I don't know if there is a resurgence of that same philosophy. You take a look at a picture like *Grease* which cost eight or nine million dollars or *Heaven Can Wait* which cost ten million but those pictures are still pulling in seventy or eighty million. I don't know what the answer is.

Most of your films have moderate to large budgets and you obviously have a choice of doing those kinds of films. But yet you've shot three films for Floyd Mutrux without the benefit of those type of budgets. So there must be some other attraction involved there.

Yes, there is. A major attraction and that attraction is ownership, which is awfully nice and also sets a precedent. But more important is Floyd. He's the real attraction. Floyd is marvelous to work for; he gives you complete liberty. He makes horrendous demands which are impossible to meet but again it's a sort of stimulation to work above your capacity or at least to a hundred percent of your capacity. And that's all you ask for. In a sense it's the reverse of what Richard Brooks does but it achieves the same effect. I love Floyd. He's been very good to me and we have a lot of fun making films. He doesn't like to spend a lot of money on films; it makes him nervous. So he likes to shoot in thirty-four days. And he keeps saying, "Well, why can't it look like *Day of the Locusts?*" Well, terrific, it could, but we don't have an eighty-day schedule or a hundred and ten days. You just can't walk into a beer joint and set up six nine-lights and bounce the light in and have an actor go through twelve pages *and* have it look like *Day of the Locusts.* It just doesn't work that way.

On Looking for Mr. Goodbar, *you said that you were shooting at two and three footcandles, you were printing dead center on the negative and you had a very solid negative with rich blacks and good skin tones. It was really interesting that you were working at such low light levels yet still getting such detail. You said you devised a system that worked for you. Could you explain?*

Normally I think we were shooting a little closer to six or eight footcandles. The theory that we used was that no one gets black by taking the light off of a subject. The film itself requires that the silver halide crystals, which give you an exposure, receive an exposure. So therefore if you want to go to true, rich blacks, you have to give the film some exposure. Then the low level of the low end of the film or the black part of the film can get an exposure and when you print it at a certain level, the black comes out. Does that make sense? Well, that was our philosophy. In other words, if we want a corner of a room to go black, we put one or two footcandles in that corner so that the silver halide crystals in that part of the film receive an exposure; then we print for our key, whatever we decide that may be. The corner goes black, good and rich, because it's got an exposure. If you don't do that, then that area starts to milk up a little bit. I don't like to play with the negative because I feel that the people who are making the final print, most of them, aren't that well versed as to what a film should look like. They're more interested in just printing the film so it takes care of the average. I like to give them a full negative so that they can still move it up or down and we can still have what we intended the picture to look like.

When you are shooting at such low light levels, is it harder to keep the look consistent?

Very, very definitely. It's more of a problem because of what ratio you work with, as far as fill light to key light goes. You really almost have to do it by eye; you can't measure a two to one ratio of key to fill light, or four to one or five to one in that type of situation. When you get into low light levels, it has to be what you see. So the consistency really depends on what you're looking at and how far you want to go with it. You really have to stay on top of it because the low light levels will fool the hell out of you.

Why is that?

Well, because you're dealing with the difference, right or wrong, of one footcandle. In other words, if you have a key of five footcandles, one footcandle gives you a five to one ratio and it's like shooting daylight. So if you're working at five or six footcandles, you can't have a footcandle to fill it for your fill light; you've got to have one-tenth of a footcandle or so. And there's no way to measure that, you have to do it all by eye. So you do have to stay on top of what you're doing.

You certainly were on top of it in Looking for Mr. Goodbar. *I thought you did a terrific job.*

We, I mean all of us, did. Richard Brooks was phenomenal. You know the one great thing about working for him is that nobody sees the dailies. Only Richard, and whoever he permits, see the dailies. Nobody at the studio sees them. And therefore, going into the project he said, "Billy, we've got something to do and it's going to be up to us to create an illusion and tell a visual story very, very dramatically. And we have to extend ourselves; so therefore if we do extend ourselves and we miss, nobody's going to know about it but you and me. So let's really reach and really extend ourselves and if it's wrong, we'll come back and shoot it again. You and I are the only two who are going to decide whether we do it again or not. If you don't like it, I promise you we'll go back and do it again. If I don't like it, I'll ask you to do it again." That's our whole relationship and it worked out very, very well. We did not shoot anything over again as it turned out.

What kind of lights were you using in her apartment in Looking for Mr. Goodbar*?*
We used regular studio lights.

Very small units?
Mostly all small units—nothing larger than a baby and also some inky-dinkies and nook lights. We had regular 150-watt bulbs in the actual lamps. We used an overall fill light which are called "coffin boxes." It's an overall fill light that works in the middle of a set. It's a shadowless light and it gives you an overall ambient light. In other words, when you're working at low light levels, you need an ambient light that allows you to see what you want to see, depending on how much you use. And it worked very well.

I'm not a soft light advocate. I don't necessarily believe in soft light; I'm not against it, I love some of the stuff I see. I usually don't use it because I don't think that pictures should achieve any sense of realism; I think pictures should be fantasy, should tell stories, take you out of a realistic approach to life, move you to another level. That's my philosophy; I'm a romanticist and I think movies should be romantic. I think people on the screen should look pretty; I don't think people with a forty-foot face up there on the big screen should be ugly. That's my whole approach.

It should be stylized.
Right. There are a lot of people who disagree with me but I can't help it; that's the way I feel about it. I like the romantic approach to making movies because I think that it's tough to get somebody out of the house, who faces that realism all day long and then comes home and faces it with the kids, and expect them to leave the house and spend five bucks to go and see some more realism. No, I want to escape. That's one of the great things about *Heaven Can Wait*. It brought back people who were forty and fifty years old to the theater, who weren't going to the picture houses anymore. That picture, more than anything, proved that you could bring those people back. It took it out of the hands of the eighteen to twenty-five year olds and brought back to the forty and fifty year olds.

Do you think Looking for Mr. Goodbar *was "romantic," as you say?*
I think *Mr. Goodbar* was very definitely romantic and that's the biggest thing I was criticized for.

In what sense?
Because the situation and the scenery weren't realistic. We shot on the backlot of Paramount so therefore I was criticized because the streets didn't have a New York look but it had a Hollywood look. It was said that the discotheques didn't have a realistic look but had a Hollywood look. We knew that going into it but we decided to do what we did and it was talked about at length with the director. And we

decided to romanticize this picture because it was a picture about somebody who was real but the girl herself was a marvelous-looking girl, Diane Keaton. She had a romantic look. So we decided to "romanticize" that whole thing, in a sense. And I say that with quotation marks. We were trying to keep it somewhat real and believable and I think we achieved that. I think the fact that it was shot on a Hollywood stage is an achievement. I give credit for that to Richard, I really do.

It was important to care about her but it was real easy not to care about her.

Exactly; exactly the point. And we discussed those things. Those things were put out on the table and hashed over.

It would have been easy to say, "To hell with this character, I don't care about her."

You've got to get into her. You've got to tell a story and yet stay in context with what's happening visually too. I thought we reached a happy medium between the two. But that's where I got all my criticism. And they don't let up, I tell you. You do a picture and your peers are on it right away; your phone starts ringing.

Your peers wanted it to be much more realistic?

Exactly. But then only one-tenth of the people would have ended up going to see it. The picture would have died in ten days if it was too real. As it was, it was horrendous anyway.

Originally, how dark did Richard want the film?

Well, he doesn't care how dark you go as long as you can see the people's eyes. As long as you can see their eyes, he feels that you can do anything you want to do. Now, in *Looking for Mr. Goodbar*, as far as dark goes, he did not want to show any pubic areas, penetration, fornication or anything like that. He wanted us to create an illusion that you in the audience thought you saw. And everybody did; we achieved that. There was nothing shown. You never saw a thing. That's the brilliance that Richard brings forth in planting an idea in your head. We even shot tests of how far we should go here and even where the shadows were going to fall. We shot tests of the movement and where the shadows would go and what they would look like when they were on the bed. It's all well designed and well planned; and you never did see anything. You saw a breast twice and a fanny once or twice. But that's it. You never saw anything else; and it worked. People only see what they want to.

The final murder scene in Mr. Goodbar, *how did you shoot that?*

That was shot with a strobe. One day we quit early and spent about an hour and a half doing tests. We shot at different speeds and so forth. The next day we looked at our tests and we saw that the strobe was completely out of sync with everything. It seemed, on the screen, that instead of exposing a full frame, we exposed about two sprocket holes and the line in the middle seemed to be shifting all over. It would expose one frame beautifully and then eight frames would go by without an exposure. It was erratic. We looked at it and said, "Well, I guess we screwed up. We're going to have to call in the strobe specialist." And Richard said, "No, let's run it again." So we ran it again. And the sporadicity of what was happening seemed to create its own thing. And we thought maybe it's better to go that way. Because in shooting it, if you had one black frame between two exposures, you could add two feet of black if you wanted. Or you could add ten frames. So, in cutting you could change the rhythm of what you wanted to do.

So the strobe is the only light you're using there?

Yes, the strobe is the only light that's working. But what happened is that we used three strobes. I used a key strobe, a fill strobe with a lot of stuff in front of it and then a kicker strobe. So maybe when the key and fill strobes were out, the kicker was working so that's the frame you get for that moment. Then maybe just the fill; then maybe the key; then maybe all three together. But that type of confusion really worked for us. Then they moved the frames around in the cutting and put in the black frames where they wanted.

Yes, because you would get into a rhythm there and just about the time you adjusted yourself to it, the rhythm would break.

But you notice when he reached down to pick up the knife off the floor, you definitely see that. That's a story point. Richard put a lot of frames together so you could make that distinction.

It's a very controversial film; it was very well received outside of Hollywood. And I do believe that Diane Keaton won the Oscar that year because *Annie Hall* and *Looking for Mr. Goodbar* both were released in the same year. It showed the complete scope of her ability, which is magnificent. It was a marvelous experience. I was nominated for the cinematography.

On Mr. Goodbar, *whose idea was it to stylize the ending like that? It was really horrifying, actually more horrifying than presenting it realistically.*

Exactly. Richard conceived the idea. The strobe light was set up earlier in the picture. So it was thought out even before we started to shoot; that's the way Richard works. He leaves nothing to chance; he knows totally the direction he wants to go in. He's one of the last real filmmakers who works it all out and has it all in his head. Not that he won't change anything; he'll change in a minute. But he has a very strong sense of what he wants to do.

I know Connie Hall feels the same way to have worked with Richard Brooks. Richard makes films a different way; I really feel that he is one of the great, great filmmakers of all time. I feel very complete now that I have made a film with him. I think it rounds out my career as far as films go. I've made films with lots of directors but Richard is extraordinary.

Then how about working with a new director like Warren Beatty in Heaven Can Wait?

He's terrific but we fought like cats and dogs. But the end result is what counts and Warren cares. You can live with almost anything as long as someone cares, as long as you can see that the effort you have put out can be seen on the screen. The moment of truth is on the screen. I don't care about anything else. You can bullshit, you can go to cocktail parties, you can dance, you can drive fancy cars, you can look terrific in expensive clothes and all that crap but it doesn't mean a thing, until everyone sits down in that theater and you put it on the screen.

That's the bottom line?

The bottom line, and that's where it all ends.

Your work on The Heretic *was widely praised by your peers. You were among the final ten in nomination for the Oscar, which is unusual because the film was generally regarded as a disaster. It was a film that must have had a lot of challenges to it. Can you single one out as the most difficult?*

Probably the biggest one was trying to reproduce the Ethiopian desert exterior on an interior set. We were using one hundred and twenty arcs to give us that sunlight; I don't know how else to do it. I guess other people would have done it with ten arcs. I don't know how you simulate an exterior intensity without stopping down. So how do you stop down? You put the light in so you have to stop down. You sure as hell can't shoot an interior that looks like an exterior if you're open at $f1.4$. It doesn't work the same; the whole look is different. That was our philosophy and that's the way we went into it.

That was extremely difficult—extremely difficult because, number one, when you're working with large crews, it's difficult to get the same people back day after day. You get somebody to work the way you want him to work, the next day he's not there; then you've got to break in somebody else, so it takes that much more time. When you say, "Trim your arcs," one hundred and twenty arcs should go off but it would take ten minutes to turn them off and ten minutes to put them on. And when you want them back on, you have nothing but inexperienced people up there and they never put the arcs back in the same place. Therefore you have to rebalance the backing and the foreground again. The backing was eighty feet high by five hundred and fifty feet around. There were horrendous problems. For example, getting dust in the air and working with dust in the air with everybody complaining, moaning and groaning. Trying to put that whole act together is, logistically, as tough as running an army.

That set was probably one of the toughest and I doubt if I would ever try to do anything like that again. It just takes too much out of a person. The other set involved all the special effects that were required for the picture; the deterioration of the Georgetown house, the reflections in the train windows which are just so time consuming and very difficult to achieve.

What about the sequence where you had the two different scenes going on at the same time in two different locations?

Where we re-created the original Georgetown exorcism and the present time lab? It was shot through a transmission mirror, a fifty percent transmission mirror, which we call a ghost glass.

What is that?

It's a piece of glass that has mirrors mixed in the glass, a special glass called transmission glass, which allows you to look through and reflect, at the same time, fifty percent of each scene—what you're seeing fifty percent and what you're reflecting fifty percent. Depending on which scene you gave more light to (with dimmers), you could bring one scene up and take the other one down. That's exactly what we did.

Are you shooting on the mirror or through it?

Through it and on it. What we did was we re-created the entire original exorcism scene of *The Exorcist* with Linda Blair and Max Von Sydow and at the same time, we were shooting Linda Blair in present time. We had a double working on that scene with her back to us. We did no opticals on that at all; it worked on one piece of film. It took all of one day to do it but the scene covered six pages so we were way ahead.

The Heretic, all the way through, was a very difficult picture to do. Because we tried to do something that wasn't being done in Hollywood at the time; it had been done in Hollywood years ago. We were trying to bring back the old craft and the old art without the departments that used to do those things; they don't exist anymore. We had to rebuild whole studio departments in order to do certain things, like backings and set designs. If the studio isn't set up for it, it costs a helluva lot of money. We'd shoot it, it wouldn't work, and we'd have to go back and do it again.

The gratification of doing a picture like that came at the end of the year when it made the top ten in the preliminary Oscar nominations for cinematography. Which proved to me that my peers felt it was extraordinary enough to be one of the top ten pictures photographically, even though it didn't work commercially. I felt very good about that. There were four pictures that I was associated with that year that made it in the top ten: *Mr. Goodbar*, which I was nominated for, *The Heretic*, *Islands in the Stream*, which I did some second unit work on, and then *Close Encounters*. So that was a good year for me.

You're the exception. You're the cameraman who has directed and who doesn't seem all that taken with the idea.

I want to direct another one but I've been waiting for the right property and the control. I've been through the directing part; now if I'm going to direct, I want the control. Then I can really direct. I've done it under their terms, now I want to do it under mine. So that if I fail, which I haven't proved to myself yet, I want it to fail totally because of me, not partially because of me. I don't want any cop outs.

For your directorial debut, you chose to do a western, Monte Walsh. *Why?*

I was born and raised in California. I grew up in the days when you went to the movies every Saturday afternoon. Westerns were the big thing then and western lore has always been sort of an interest of mine. So when I had the chance to do *Monte Walsh*, especially because the book was written by Jack Schaefer who wrote *Shane*, I jumped at the chance. Westerns are probably the last of the great romantic periods left. It's probably one of the most romantic periods in the history of the world. In sixty years time, one man's life span, a lot of things happened. I love that period and that's why I did it.

Looking back, how do you feel about Monte Walsh *now, considering all its trials, tribulations and its lack of promotion? Would you do anything different if you were doing it today?*

I still believe in *Monte Walsh*. I still think it's a helluva Western. I still get letters and comments about it even today. I'm not going to compromise my position or anyone else's position. I'm very proud of it. If I had it to do again, I'd do it differently. I think I would improve it but it would still be in the same style. Some of it was inherent in the material; it was a little episodic and I would bring that more tightly together. I would work on the relationships a little bit more too. But I love it.

What's the most difficult thing in making the transition from cameraman to director?

To disassociate yourself from the visual storytelling. I think you really have to get into dramatic storytelling and you really can't rely on anything or have any kind of crutch in order to make a picture. You have to go out and do it. Cameramen are so specifically trained that it's hard for them to move their heads over. It's a natural transition, and I'm not saying that it doesn't happen, but it's difficult. Most cameramen who have tried to make the transition have difficulty in succeeding.

When you did direct on Monte Walsh *and* Reflections of Fear, *you had David Walsh and Lazslo Kovaks, respectively, as your cameraman. As a cinematographer yourself, what were the talents and abilities you were looking for in choosing a cinematographer?*

Number one, David Walsh was made a first cameraman on *Monte Walsh* because he was my operator and we had worked together for three or four years. David's very sensitive, has a great eye, was a marvelous operator and is a lovely guy. I felt that on my first picture as a director I needed to work with somebody that I had a great rapport with and who understood what I wanted.

Number two, *Reflections of Fear* was a picture that probably should have been shot in Canada, something with a foreign look. We couldn't move it out of Hollywood; we had to shoot it here. I decided to go with a cameraman I thought would give it the best, so-called "foreign look," which was Lazslo. It's probably one of the best pictures Lazslo has ever photographed; it's absolutely exquisite. It's a shame the picture didn't do well because it was so exquisite. It's a terrible picture and there's a lot of reasons for that. I'm not copping out. Lazslo's a romantic; he's soft and sensitive. And this film needed that type of approach. So I thought Lazslo was best suited for it and rightly so. We did it in thirty-five days too.

What do you think makes a cameraman worth what he's paid?

What do you think makes a cameraman worth what he's paid? Well, let me ask you something; what is a cameraman paid?

It varies.

Do you think he's paid too much?

No. I think the Hollywood adage is that you get what you're worth or what people think you're worth. It's pretty nebulous. If I were to talk to you from a middle-class, Middle America standpoint, I don't think anybody's worth what they get paid in Hollywood. Nobody's worth that much money.

It's all relative.

Certainly it's all relative to the business.

OK, that's the question. How am I going to answer that? Now we take the writer, we take the director, we take the performers; then who do we take next? The producer? No. The film editor? No. The musician? No. It's the cameraman. I don't think the cameramen are paid enough. You can have the best story, the best performers, the best director and if it isn't put on the screen correctly and quickly, I don't think it works. You have pictures that are photographed very badly that are very successful. Correct? And you can have pictures that are acted, directed and written very badly, but are photographed beautifully that are successful. You'll find that ninety percent of the time, when you have a first-time director, the producer or whoever will put a heavyweight cameraman behind him. That's a general practice although it doesn't happen all the time.

The one person who runs a set on a production is the cameraman. He's the one who really controls the time; he's the one who can bring you in on schedule or put you over. That doesn't mean that all those other variable factors and all those other things can't happen with or without a cameraman. It's a visual medium. The symbol of motion pictures is the camera. I think cameramen are extremely important to a motion picture. The sad part is not only do I think they're worth the money that they get, but I think they should not be categorized; they should be put above the line in costs. I think they should be put in the same category as a writer, a director or a performer. I don't believe that they should work for a weekly salary. I believe they should do a picture for X amount of dollars just like the star.

I believe what happens, and this takes its course in any business, whether it's movies or not, is if a cameraman is paid a helluva lot of money, it's because he's well worth it. If you aren't worth that money, nobody's going to pay it to you. If you perform and merit that kind of money, you get it. Most cameramen are asking for percentages of a picture now. And rightly so. I'd much rather put my money where my mouth is and take a shot at making it in the end, while keeping the production costs down. If only we could find some way to keep the studios honest. Not that I think that there's anything wrong with them. But if you could get a fair accounting of the profits, then I think you could make many more pictures and you could keep the price down. There is no other way to keep the price down.

I really feel the professionalism of a cameraman, the years of training and experience, is where his value lies. We were talking about fifteen million dollar pictures and six hundred thousand dollar pictures and it all works. We do all of them. *Old Boyfriends* was done for 1.6 million. We had a thirty-six day schedule, so I knew what I had to do and I did it. The next time, you do an eleven million dollar picture and you know what you have to do there also. The fact that it's an eleven million dollar picture doesn't mean that there's more money being put in your pocket. It means that what you're trying to do and how you're trying to do it costs more money. That's all.

7

Conrad Hall

"I think one of the reasons people quit is because they're afraid they won't be able to get better and better; that they have come to a zenith of some kind. You feel like you've done everything and all there is left to do is to just do it well each time. But you know you haven't done it all because you know everything keeps evolving and changing; and you know you can evolve with it if you grow and develop as a human being. But the increments are smaller and smaller. I think everybody has that problem whether they're cinematographers or farmers."

Conrad Hall didn't necessarily intend to pursue a career as a cinematographer. It was more a matter of fate, luck and a little ambition. The son of James Norman Hall, coauthor of the *Mutiny on the Bounty* trilogy, he had originally wanted to be a writer like his father. But while attending the University of Southern California, a less than adequate grade in a creative writing course gave him other ideas. As he describes it, he picked up the USC arts and science catalog and went down the listings alphabetically: Astronomy, Biology, Cinema. He went no further than that. Filmmaking intrigued him, and although he had no photographic knowledge at the time, the more courses he took, the more passionate he became about film.

After graduating in 1949, he and two associates formed their own production company. When they decided to do a low-budget feature, they drew straws to divide the responsibilities of producer, director and cameraman. As fate would have it, Hall drew the cameraman slot.

Later, after this company dissolved, he paid his union dues and worked as an assistant cameraman and camera operator for respected traditional Hollywood cameramen like Ted McCord, Ernest Haller, Robert Surtees, Hal Mohr and Burnett Guffey. After a stint in television, he broke into mainstream features with *The Wild Seed* in 1965. As his craft and artistry developed, he was able to take many photographic risks in the features that followed. A five-time Academy Award nominee, Hall won the Oscar in 1969 for *Butch Cassidy and the Sundance Kid*. His cinematography on *Day of the Locusts* is widely considered by his contemporaries to be a perfect example of visual mood wedded to dramatic content. Although he hasn't shot a feature since 1976, Hall's fellow cinematographers consider him one of the best in the business. Their respect and admiration for him and his work indicates something about his staying power as a cinematographer and, more importantly, as a human being. Although he occasionally directs and shoots television commercials, Hall now devotes his time to writing and negotiating the opportunity to direct one of his own scripts.

1965	*The Wild Seed*	1969	*The Happy Ending*
	Saboteur: Code Name Morituri†		*Tell Them Willie Boy Is Here*
1966	*Incubus*		*Butch Cassidy and the*
	Harper		*Sundance Kid**
	The Professionals†	1972	*Fat City*
1967	*Divorce American Style*	1973	*Electra Glide in Blue*
	Cool Hand Luke	1975	*Smile*
	In Cold Blood†		*The Day of the Locust*†
1968	*Hell in the Pacific*	1976	*Marathon Man*

*Academy Award for best achievement in cinematography.
†Academy Award Nominations for best achievement in cinematography.

You're one of a growing number of cinematographers who wants to direct.

Filmmaking is like a compass; it's a circle with a lot of points. Each one of those points are the crafts that make up the whole film. I feel that once you're inside that circle, you can be drawn to any one of those points and still stay in the business. They're all interesting points and you hit as many as you want to hit and have time to hit in a lifetime. I just get interested in other points. I mean, I love cinematography. It was accidental that I began at that point. If fate was different at the time, I might have been a director or have changed from that and become a cinematographer if I hadn't been suited for it.

Going back to your beginnings, I see that at the University of Southern California you studied under Slavko Vorkapich. I wondered if you learned anything specific from him?

He's like a parent to me, a true teacher and someone who was inspirational in revealing to me something that I knew nothing about before. I'd been studying journalism at USC and I had done badly in a course and I didn't want to take it over again for credit so I switched majors and took up cinema for all the wrong reasons: money, fame, glamor and all the star-struck things that were publicized about the industry. But once I got into it, Vorkapich instilled in me—and probably all the people who studied with him—the wonder and the joy of being able to communicate in a new language. He helped me to learn to communicate in that new language and he taught me that it was not a business kind of language. But that this language should be learned and developed into communicating wondrous things and not to make money. So he gave me what I consider the spirit and soul of an artist. And I don't mean that in any kind of egotistical sense. I mean, the way I approach film is what I feel he gave me.

He never taught me anything but the principles. He never told me what to do with them or anything else—except that you should deal with them in an artistic way rather than in a functional way of some kind. But he taught what happened when film ran forward and backwards, upside down and inside out. I learned the principles of my craft from him.

What about Ted McCord? I understand he was one of your mentors?

You're talking about all my fathers. Ted is dead now. He was a cinematographer, an artist and a wonderful man. We met on a project that Leslie Stevens directed, wrote and produced. I operated for Ted on that film and then I became his operator for a number of years until I became a first cameraman on *Stoney Burke*. I learned a number of things from him about cinematography and filmmaking. But again, what I really learned from him was the approach to your job, the approach to the way you look at film and how you think about it.

In other words, there's not really anything specific that you can point to; it was more like a philosophy or way of looking at things? An open-minded, open-ended approach?

Absolutely. That's it. It was his non-closed-off sense about his job. He approached each picture as if he knew nothing when he began. And it wasn't that he didn't know anything; he knew everything that he knew. But he approached it as if he was always frightened to death and he was always trying to bring something unique and special to that piece of material. It was the search for that uniqueness and that specialness that embodied his approach. He was always searching for the best way to express that piece of material. That's the kind of artistic sense I'm talking about. He was trying to find precisely the right kind of thing rather than imposing techniques indiscriminately on the material. He wanted to find the way of telling that story correctly using everything that he knew or finding out new things and experimenting. Those are the things that I learned from Ted. And that attitude is what I cherish.

Let's talk about your first film as a director of photography, The Wild Seed. *It was interesting in that it was a "road film," as we've since come to term that genre of films. How did you arrive at a photographic style for the film? What were you influenced by?*

I was probably influenced a great deal by Ted McCord because I worked with him for a number of years. Although I know on the day I took over from him on a *Stoney Burke* segment when he got ill, I said to myself, "I get to do it the way he does it." But I couldn't do it the way he was doing it. I didn't believe in the way he was doing it and I changed everything all the way around. He was into really controlling light; I was into using light and controlling it. He was into cutting it out and starting from scratch; I was into using it and controlling it somehow. I learned my black-and-white craft basically from Ted. And his ideas about contrast and lighting are still probably instilled in me.

As I remember it, there were three new people on the job in *The Wild Seed*. There was Brian Hutton as director, Al Ruddy as producer and myself as first cameraman. And as I recall that film, it involved just doing what you knew how to do. I don't remember having any real conceptual idea about doing the film in moving shots or whatever. I don't think I was thinking that much about the philosophical elements imposing on the style to tell a story. I was more concerned with just getting it out and done.

It's a helluva little film; it shows up on the late show quite often.

Yes, everybody did a great job on it. We did it for $286,000 in twenty-four shooting days, if you can imagine that. It's something I'm very proud of.

Harper was the first film you shot in color. You've said previously that you shot it just like you would shoot a black-and-white film. Does that mean that you didn't pay any special attention to shooting in color?

I didn't. On my first color picture, I shot it just like I would if it were black-and-white. In *Harper* I was more interested in movement rather than lighting. Sometimes the lighting area just gets out of hand. I remember on *Harper* we had a night shoot and I requested a crew and the electrical department allocated forty electricians. And I gulped hard because I had never worked with more than two or three! So the budget department came tearing down and wanted to know what was happening. So I automatically cut the crew to twenty people. It was the first time I learned that small is not beautiful necessarily. And that big is unmanageable and uncontrollable and unless you have all the time in the world, it is tough to get what you want and keep your sanity. You learn that sometimes you just settle for getting it done when it becomes unmanageable like that. It taught me how to manage things and not let them escape your grasp. I think probably some of the lighting on that film escaped me. It just got done by itself, by the gaffer, by other people and I just sort of accepted it in order to get the job done. I don't like to do that now.

You really weren't too concerned about the color then?

Well, yes. I was learning and it was my first color job. I was learning how much you could overexpose the film and things like that but I didn't feel that I was bringing any artistic eye to it other than treating it like black-and-white ostensibly. I was not doing any flat, overall lighting; I wasn't using color to separate, which was a style I got into later on.

I once read that you said you didn't like color; that you hated it. I don't know if that was in jest or not. Could you explain?

Well, color produces such inaccuracies. We are dealing in a realistic medium and whenever it's inaccurate, it's offensive. You know, if you look at a Caterpillar tractor and you know what color that kind of tractor is, and suddenly it's an awful color of orange, you know that it's wrong. You know what the ocean looks like. And if it's the wrong color, it's terribly offensive. So it introduces a whole new element that didn't exist in black-and-white. That includes the lab and the control of that print to get what you feel it should be. It doesn't pose an artistic decision; it's a mechanical thing. I mean you have to go to the lab and play with filters and talk to somebody and tell them how you feel it should be. You do this much later after the film has been shot. It's a much more complex area to deal with. I think maybe that's what I was talking about when I made that comment about color. I don't dislike color as a means of telling a story.

Do you or did you prefer black-and-white?

Not any more; I think they're both useful. I think the unfortunate part is that black-and-white has been phased out so far that it now draws attention to itself like the first color film did when it came out. So if you want to make a film in black-and-white, everybody says, "Oh, he's trying to be arty." Or "What is this?" I consider black-and-white photography like reading: you supply the colors, you supply the sensations of reality in your mind to a greater extent. You work harder, as an audience, in black-and-white. I don't think that's a bad spirit to have between the film and the audience.

Do you have any basic rules of thumb that you follow when you're shooting in black-and-white?

Black-and-white only concerns itself with the grey scale from white to black. And separation has to do with depth and using these values against one another creates depth. You have to understand that you want to create depth to get reality. And that gives you what I consider the "color" of black-and-white photography.

So that's the primary consideration when you're shooting in black-and-white?

Yes. You need that. You don't want things to blend into one another. So you have to create separation and depth.

For your work on The Professionals, *you were nominated for an Academy Award. You said that, at the time, you liked your work on the film, but that you don't now. Could you explain?*

I saw a lot of things I did that were offensive to me when I viewed it again. But I like it; it's not a badly photographed picture, I don't think. There are certain things though that I had a hard time dispensing with: things that came from my black-and-white days. For example, liners—you have to use them very, very carefully otherwise they create unreal light.

What is a liner?

A liner is a light that comes from a reflecting angle. This highlight on my cheek right now is a liner from that window. You would use this in black-and-white in order to help separate the background from the foreground. It's a technique you don't have to use in color because color will separate itself. It's also valid to use it in color; however, you can overuse it in color.

I think you were concerned about the color saturation also.

Yes, the blue skies and things like that. Blue skies are something that I have trouble dealing with. Blue is a tough color for me; I don't know why. It's probably because the sky is something that we understand so well visually and when it's not quite right, it's offensive to you.

Has there been any film that you've shot that you've been totally satisfied with?

Well I'll tell you the ones I'm happiest with. *In Cold Blood* is one; *The Wild Seed* is another. I haven't seen it for a long time but I remember being happy with that. I also like *Day of the Locust*. I think those are my two favorite films: *In Cold Blood* and *Day of the Locust*. And *Fat City* for sure. *Fat City* would be the best of them all. But, you know, I'm never happy with anything totally.

Is it because you've changed as a cameraman?

I've changed as a person; that's what causes my change in visual things. I don't say, "I'm going to do a film like this cameraman or that one." It's how you emotionally perceive life and how you want to portray it. It comes from living. I read somewhere some comments that Francis Coppola made and I think they're quite precise. He had started to make *Apocalypse Now*, and it started out as one film and then it kept changing and changing. And the reason is that he kept changing and the people involved kept changing. So that it became an entirely different film than it was going into it. He spent a very long time on it. And, as a human being, your perception about life changes with your experiences. They changed as they made the film. So that's kind of what I'm talking about but in photographic terms rather than directorial terms.

On Butch Cassidy and the Sundance Kid *and* Tell Them Willie Boy is Here, *you did a great deal of overexposing the film and then printing it back down. What factors led you to use this technique on these films?*

Disliking saturation. I was struggling with the primariness of color. I didn't like blue to be strong blue, you know? I didn't like pure green or those vivid kinds of colors. I didn't see light that way and there's always atmosphere between color and me in the form of haze, smog, fog, dust. There's a muting of color that goes on in life. There was none of that in certain kinds of printing colors in film. And so I objected to that. I couldn't stand that kind of primary color and I tried to change it. I experimented with filters and fog filters. I used desaturation when we had imbibition printing. I tried all kinds of things: underdeveloping, overexposing and various lab techniques. The overexposing was, I felt, a way of destroying the color. Without the use of filters, you could overexpose so radically that when you printed it you barely got back anything. But it was enough to be in color and it wasn't vivid anymore—because it had been destroyed so far. Not only would it destroy the color value but it would destroy the sharpness value. I felt film was too sharp; I didn't see life that sharp and I don't like it that sharp actually. So I always destroy sharpness. It may have to do with my own personal vision—my eyes, I mean. In other words, I know a tall man sees life differently than a short man; the angle is different, etc. There are a lot of psychological factors involved in how you see things and why you are specifically that way.

What sort of reaction did you get when you started overexposing the film a couple of stops and then printing it back down? Was it accepted by the people at the lab?

No, it frightened the hell out of everybody, as a matter of fact, even though I made very careful tests. Unless you have backing and help, you can get shot down. Anyone can make it tough for you, especially somebody who doesn't want to change. It's a terrible thing to fight and struggle against but it exists; you do what you can and I started to do what I could on *Butch Cassidy* but I didn't do it totally. But I started to do that kind of work. Then I went off to do *Hell in the Pacific* and I decided that I didn't want the picture to look that way. But all the time while I was shooting *Hell in the Pacific*, I was fascinated with the idea of overexposing. I would make tests, overexposing to certain degrees and then seeing how it would come out. Now I don't overexpose every film I shoot. Overexposing is a technique, just like underexposing is a technique. It's another tool, that's all. But I knew it was going to be a valuable tool and I'd use it well some day. And I got a chance to do that on *Fat City*. When I started to shoot the film and employ this technique, the director liked it real well, the producer didn't like it so well and the studio hated it. So again there was not a lot of backing. But I persevered anyway and got it done. I can't say I would have done it better if I had had some back-up. I did it anyway and the only thing they could have done was fire me.

What's the first thing you do when you come on a set? When you start lighting, what's the first light you set?

The first thing I do is quake in my boots; that's the first thing I do. I sit down and I get a camera set up and I probably lean my eye against it as a sort of security thing like the character in the "Peanuts" cartoon strip who sucks his thumb and holds the security blanket up to his ear. That's about what I do with a camera and my eye. I put my eye up against the camera and close the other eye and be totally alone. Or I can blink and see if anybody is watching. And everybody *is* watching because you have to decide what you're going to do and you have to communicate that to somebody. After you get rolling, you pretty much have it all well in hand what you want to do. But the first day I come on the set, I usually don't know what I want to do; I feel like I've just graduated from USC, I feel inadequate. It really takes me a little while to get rolling and to get my courage and spirit up. Not too long, but it takes a while. Then what you do is, if you haven't done it the night before or the week before, you decide how you're going to light it. In other words, you don't decide whether it's going to be rough or slick, real or naturalistic. But you have to decide how to produce that effect that you've already agreed upon with the director. And there are a lot of different ways of accomplishing it. So you just go about doing it; there's no formula.

You have no routine that you usually follow?

No, you really determine those things beforehand. You don't just show up and start doing everything. You've had the chance to walk the set with the director and the art director and talk about what and where the action is going to be. You've probably seen a rehearsal the night before. So you should know whether you're going to light through the windows or whether you're going to use some overhead light. All of those decisions have been made. But if you didn't have a set-up the night before, you'd sit down and you'd watch the director rehearse the actors and they would move about. Then the director would communicate to you that he wanted to go so far in this scene and you would figure out how to do that. You would choose the camera placement and/or movement. You decide upon that with the director. Then after you've done that, you would mark all the people and know where they are going to be within the scene. The script dictates whether it's night or day and you produce night or day in whatever way you want to. So that's what you do when you come onto the set.

What you're really saying is that every situation is different and your approach depends on what the circumstances are.

Yes. And the only constant is the fear of not being able to do it well. I worry about that.

In a previous interview, someone asked you about lighting and you said, "Well, there's front light, back, cross, bottom and top light. What else is there?" I don't know if you said that in jest, but is it really appropriate to think of lighting in such simplistic terms?

In order to overcome the infiniteness of the variations and possibilities, you've got to know that there are only so many. It's like when you sit down to write a script or a story. Where do you begin? What to decide to do? There are all those infinite decisions that you're facing. So in a story you get people who are role characters for you and so you simplify it. It's the same way with lighting; you simplify it. You know that you can light it all from overhead; you can light it all through the windows. Knowing this gives you the courage to make a decision of some kind on how to do it. It's like a compass; it comes from all around you. Whether you want the light to come from one direction or all around you, those are the decisions you have to make. You make it almost something mechanical so that you can deal with it rather than wonder about where the light comes from. It comes from the top, it comes from the side and it comes from the bottom. Okay, Conrad, now get in there and light the set. And light it where you want it to come from and how you want it to come. How strong do you want the light to be? How weak? You have to make all those decisions. It gives you courage to get out there and do it if you know that it's really not that hard. You have to tell yourself that the light just comes from all around you. It's a way of conceptualizing it.

Say a director came to you and said, "Connie, I really want this to look slick." What would you do and how would you go about it?

I'd ask him what he meant, first of all. Because that can mean a variety of things, depending on who you're talking to.

What would that mean to you?

I means to me what the cliché of the term means. The cliché of the term is a kind of photography that was done in the thirties, forties and fifties that kind of typified the Hollywood look. It had a beautiful, unreal and romantic quality that was not the way life was necessarily lived. But if life were lived like that, wouldn't it be slick? That's what I think of.

How would you communicate that to a director?

I'd ask the director what film he meant. He obviously is talking about something he's got in his mind. I like to get right at what they're talking about. I don't want generalities. Then I can give them something different but something that's good too. If he wanted a *Citizen Kane* slickness, I'd give him a Conrad Hall version of *Citizen Kane* slickness. To me, slick means flawless; that's what I mean by slick. My initial understanding of that term is "without flaws" and that's the kind of photography I can't give anybody because I don't see life that way. But I can come pretty close to it; I can give my version of it.

As in Day of the Locust?

Day of the Locust is the closest I've come to flawlessness, I would say, in style.

You say that sometimes you have a tendency to overlight. You mentioned a couple night scenes in Butch Cassidy. *Why and how does that happen?*

Well, that's when it gets away from you. That's when somehow or other you have not learned to control the elements that go into lighting so that it gets away from you. And suddenly things can get very complex. When I say there's top, bottom and side light to simplify it, that also indicates how complex it is because it comes from everywhere. And when you finally don't know what's causing something you don't like, then you're in trouble. But you might just roll the camera and live with the knowledge that it's overlit and hate yourself for doing it. But maybe there's no time to change and simplify it. I think the better I become at lighting, the less I'll say that it's overlit. I don't want to overlight anything. It's when it gets out of my control that it happens.

What are the tendencies that cause a cameraman to overlight?

It's not understanding what light really does and knowing how it will affect the film and that kind of thing. It's really knowing your craft. Somebody who really knows his craft will not overlight a scene, unless it's intentional. When something is overlit, it looks wrong.

We've spoken to several cameramen who were noted early in their career for working quickly and using a small amount of light. But as their careers progressed, they began to use more and more light to the point where they realized they were using too much. One cameraman, in particular, wants to get back to using less light, as he did earlier.

Well, it's the same question you would ask a painter, "When do you know your painting is finished?" Now that's the same question you've asked me about lighting and overlighting. "When is the canvas finished?" is what you're asking. You know that, at one point in your life, you might have ended the canvas earlier and it might still have looked rough but that may have been a pretty good style and everybody seemed to like it. Then maybe later you get much more elaborate and you look at it one day and say, "This is bullshit; I'm using too much." It's how you feel about the reality of what you're trying to do. It's being able to quit when you think the job is done. It's not trying to please others or trying to please what you don't know. The more you understand about your craft, the more precise you can be and the freer and simpler you can be also.

One of your contemporaries said that one important aspect of In Cold Blood *was your decision to use anamorphic lenses. He felt that it placed the picture just slightly outside of the documentary style and therefore it was able to involve people deeper with it on a dramatic, storytelling level. Would you be inclined to agree with that?*

Absolutely, I agree with that. It's definitely a dramatic film rather than a documentary film. But Richard Brooks's concept of that film was to make it very real. So he chose to shoot it in the actual locations where the story took place to bring realities to it that were outside normal film realities. Normally you go to a set and shoot it there or you find a location that's like where it happened. But to shoot a film where it actually took place, especially a murder story, is quite an unusual and innovative concept. So the documentariness of it was wanted and was thought of in those areas. It's real. But that had nothing to do with the framework of how you mount this reality. We originally wanted to shoot it in a 1.85 to 1 hard-matte format. I particularly wanted to shoot in this format so that there would be no way that anybody could project the film differently. Because I didn't want too much head-room or too little headroom. I wanted people to see exactly what I wanted to show them. Now Richard Brooks was all for that but Columbia wouldn't let us do that. So we decided to shoot it so that the precision of the top and the bottom was unchange-able in Panavision. There's no way you can show too much top or too much bottom; you have to shoot just exactly that. You can cut off the sides a little bit but we didn't mind that. We knew that the sides would probably be cut off but that would just bring it back down closer to the 1.85 to 1 ratio that we had originally wanted to shoot the picture in. That was the main consideration. It was not the perception that was stated in your question; we were trying for that, although I didn't think of it exactly in those terms. Although it's quite right that using the anamorphic lenses makes for a dramatic proscenium for a documentary.

It takes it one step out of that documentary format and brings it closer to . . .

It's like going to the L.A. Coliseum to see a Little League baseball game. In other words, it's not normally what you'd be accustomed to seeing this style in; it's a different proscenium that makes it more dramatic.

Again, you were shooting on the actual locations where these real events took place. How did you go about lighting the locations for that dramatic effect?

I chose dramatic lighting—lighting that was clean and uncluttered. But I think the basic technique or idea was to be very precise about what you were lighting and what you were showing. I tried to let blackness or non-visibility be a very dramatic element. I tried to use the blackness as a character in that film.

So then you didn't stick to source lighting–I mean, your primary consideration was to create an effect. So I guess you deviated from the normal source lighting that you would find in a farmhouse.

Well it all depends on what you think source lighting is. Is source lighting some-thing in which you see a source in the frame or is it light that you know where it comes from but you don't see the source? Do you see what I mean?

Whether it's justified or not?

Yes, and I think I'm basically always justifying light. There's no question about that; that's the only way I can understand it: to know where it comes from. Then I can know what to do with it. To dream up places that light doesn't come from is an exercise in despair for me. I don't know how to think that way. I can't organize it unless I know it comes from someplace. But whether the place the light comes from is in the frame or not, that's not important to me. For example, I could have a lamp next to you and it would not be the major source of light on you. Now is that source lighting or not? But obviously there's a brighter source someplace else; if you had a chance to look around in this room, you would see that source and it would be justified.

Speaking of source lighting, could you explain how you did the sequence in In Cold Blood *where your single lighting source appeared to be a flashlight that Robert Blake was holding as he was roaming through the dark house?*

What a wonderful opportunity it was to have a picture like that. Of course, I love working with Richard Brooks and that film was a wonderful experience for me. I was working with people I really respected and admired. To be together with people you like and have a chance to do something like that is a great experience. But to answer your question, it's hard to do that. If you get a flashlight that's strong enough, it has to be electrical and connected via a wire up the guy's pants. But it always has to be connected to some kind of umbilical cord. We invented a flashlight that was battery-operated and that had enough power to produce an adequate amount of footcandles at ten feet. And it would produce a strong enough light to mean something lighting-wise.

Now when you come into a darkened room, there is still some visibility there. There is never no visibility except in the total absence of light. And unless you close off all the cracks and crevices, there's hardly ever that. You have windows and, even with the blinds closed, you still have light seeping in from outside. So, first of all, in lighting that sort of thing, you create the visibility. You have to do that quite precisely with certain kinds of lights hidden around the room. Now after you've set up the amount of visibility you want, you bring the flashlight into the room and it produces a different visibility. When it produces that different visibility, it's not just where it shines that produces the visibility. The lip of that flashlight, when it's held in front of you, is lighting that person's face from underneath. The flashlight is also hitting the wall and that's a grey area so it causes a certain kind of reflection. But when it passes across a fireplace, it's white and suddenly the illumination blooms back at you. And that bloom, if you're the camera, is occurring out of the frame but it's still having an effect on the frame. And the lighting is changing every second depending on where that flashlight beam is hitting. Every second the level of visibility is changing and so it was a beautiful opportunity to do something like that. I would love to have the chance to do it again because that was the first time I had done it well, I felt. But other people could improve on that and I could too now.

You probably had the tendency to use less light on that film because you were on location and you were using the fast black-and-white film stocks.

Yes, I didn't use much. The thing about lighting that cameramen have to face is budgetary problems. In order to have the kind of light that you really need, you need a big budget. To use less light, you need a bigger budget than you do to use more and have it do less. You need precision in lighting. To create the different kinds of light that exist, you need arcs; you need the right kind of lights to create soft light. You need certain types of lights to create single sources sometimes. It takes money and very often you have to do without it and use another way. I had everything I needed on *In Cold Blood*. And thus maybe I used the precise light in every situation. Instead of using two lights to do one job, I used one light to do the job, which makes it simpler and better.

Bill Fraker said that the experience of working with Richard Brooks (on Looking for Mr. Goodbar*) made him a more complete cinematographer, a more complete filmmaker. Have you ever worked with any directors that you feel the same way about?*

Yes. Brooks is somebody I love very, very much and who I admire a lot and disagree with tremendously. It's like I loved Ted McCord but when it came time for me to do it and become a first cameraman, I had to do it my way. I couldn't do it his way. And I can't do it Richard Brooks's way. I don't always like it his way and he understands that.

With Richard you really pay attention to your job. I worked very hard for him on all his pictures. I really tried to do the best I could for him. And they were all wonderful experiences and they're all wonderful films too. I think *The Professionals* is a wonderful film; *In Cold Blood* is a wonderful film; and although it's not my favorite of the three, *The Happy Ending* is a wonderful film. In any event, Richard Brooks is a person I really like working with. John Schlesinger is another. You like directors for different reasons. But the ones that I like and respect both, are Richard and John.

What about John Huston?

He's a guy that I started respecting before liking. He used to come down to USC when I was a student and he would talk about films that he was making. He was a god, an alien being for us students. Then soon, I was making films with him, which shows you how fast you can get to work with your gods in this business. And when you work with your gods, you find out that they're human. You know, for a long time, I blamed him for not making *Fat City* a better film. What a terrible thing to blame somebody for! I wanted that film to be seen by people. I guess I blamed him for no one going to the film. And that he didn't work hard enough to make it a film that people would go to and have it still be a wonderful film about that subject. That's what I blame him for: for not being perfect! Whenever I'm asked to speak at a university now, I always bring *Fat City* with me. I take it with me to study why nobody went to see that film. From the students, I'm getting just as much out of them as they're getting out of me. I'm trying to learn to do what didn't happen on that film. But I've long since forgiven John and I know what a wonderful film it really is. So now I respect him and love him as a human being and forgive him for not being godly.

One of the best scenes photographically in Fat City *is the opening scene in that dump of a hotel room where you learn so much about the main character in a short time.*

Isn't that a wonderful shot! I love that shot. It's one of my favorite shots of all time. It's such perfect cinema. It's such a beautiful way of telling that man's story at that moment in time. It's so precise. It was not overlit.

It looked like you were using only the natural light.

Well, I have to cheat and say there was a light in that scene. There was a nine-light out on the window with only one bulb lit. I had two lit to begin with but that wasn't precise enough; it produced a sort of double shadow. So I killed one bulb. In that part of the scene when he finally walks into the foreground and goes through his jacket, I needed to light the wall behind that jacket so he and the jacket would stand out a little more. That's the only reason that light is on. I think I even had that light cut off at the beginning of the scene until we were over at the dresser and then when I panned over at that point, the light was on. So during the first part of the scene, there's nothing lighting it except the light from the outside.

Did you just look at that room and decide you could do it with the available window light?

Actually it was more a camera movement problem than a lighting problem. I thought about using a crab dolly but I threw that idea out. I put a white card up in back of me in the hallway, on the wall opposite the doorway in the hall. I took a light and hit it into that white card so it would fill the room. But before I went with that shot, I just knew it wasn't right. I knew that pushing the film would allow me to see enough into the dark areas. I knew that the light coming through the window, which was six or eight stops overexposed, was enough to create like a fog filter. My craft was pretty precise at that moment, you see. Eventually I told my gaffer to kill the light behind me. He killed it. We looked at each other and we went without it. Now that would have been overlighting; I didn't need it and I knew, at that moment, that I didn't need it. But until then, I thought I needed it.

Maybe that's a symbolic way of showing what's happened to me with respect to lighting. I mean, I might start to overlight to begin with, but now I'm killing this source and killing that one because I'm getting better at it. I know what it'll do and what it won't do. I know how it'll do it, why it'll do it and, most of all, I know how to get what I want.

When you're using natural light and you have to augment it, how do you do it? Do you use ratios, do you do it by eye?

You do it by eye. And you do it very carefully and simply. That kind of lighting should be done very, very simply. You try to augment the realistic light. If you're in a bar and you have a couple of beer signs or a popcorn machine, you make those things actually do the lighting. You make them so that the film will recognize them the same way your eye recognizes them. And that they will have the same effect on the room that they actually do have on the room at night. It's not using 10K's and inky-dinks and things like that necessarily if there are other actual things available; it's making the beer sign do the lighting for you.

How do you mean?

You pump it up. You can put those lights on a rheostat and control the brightness up and down that way. Or you can take stronger bulbs than what are in the beer sign, and put them behind the sign. What you want to do is make the film see it the way your eye sees it. It's the same way when you light a room with daylight; you take the basic daylight and you pump it up to actually do the lighting. I'd put some material over the windows and then pump lights through them so that it comes in soft.

Fat City *had a real nitty gritty look to it, with the seedy town and the low-life characters. What did you do to bring that out photographically?*

Photographically speaking, I tried to make it real. I tried to make it the way it is. I tried to not make it look like a motion picture; I tried to make it look like a social study of down-and-out people rather than a slick way of looking at down-and-out people. I didn't want to beautify it in any way that would make it seem attractive. I made it abrasive; I tried to make the photography abrasive just as their lives were. I had overhot things and dark areas and the contrast between those, not in the same scene but from scene to scene. But I didn't do it the way they did it in *All the President's Men*, where you cut from a bright room to something very dark. That's an effect and it was done for effect rather than for abrasion. I did it for abrasion and I kept doing it throughout the film.

To throw the eye off balance.

Exactly. To let you know that this is not beautiful. I got a wonderful start on that picture. Huston called the production designer and myself into his motel room to have a talk a day or so before the picture. And he asked me and the production designer, Dick Sylbert, what we thought the picture was about. I don't remember my answer but I remember Dick Sylbert's. He said the film was about life going down the drain before you had the chance to put the plug in. That's all I needed to know precisely what to do or to know precisely how I felt about it. I had known that but I hadn't vocalized it. Sylbert vocalized it and Huston agreed with it and that was a very valuable experience in helping me to do my job. For three days after that I went out and shot some title material. They were tearing down part of the city where the bums lived to put a freeway through there; I think the only reason the city fathers did that was because they wanted to get rid of the bums but they didn't know how to do it. So they decided to put the freeway there and get rid of them, right? But instead of getting rid of them, the bums just move three or four blocks on either side of the freeway. You don't eliminate that element of despair in humanity by building a freeway and cutting out their habitat. Anyhow, I got a camper/truck and put black curtains over the windows. I put a tripod at each window: the back window and the two side windows. I had a camera and a quick-change mount and I would just lift the camera and the head onto the appropriate tripod if I saw a piece of action. We cruised the streets looking for life running down the drain. I got some of the most marvelous stuff you ever saw! It was wonderful stuff. Then the first day we started shooting with actors, it all came back into perspective. You see, for three days I had been shooting by myself out of the back of this camper. And then we had a full crew and started shooting the actors. What a difference between reality and drama! I was fascinated with the difference in lighting between doing a movie and just shooting what was happening on the streets without any lighting at all. Shooting out of the camper, there was no lighting. And that allowed me to do that naturalistic lighting more precisely by actually seeing it. Seeing what happens with no lighting at all really allowed me to be better at it, to really see what it looks like and produce it.

It was a wonderful experience for everybody, especially the actors because they saw how much they overacted. They sometimes don't act like real people at all and they could see that in that environment. We tried not to be filmmakers at all; we just tried to follow life around. I think seeing those first three days helped everybody be more precise in their jobs.

If the cast and crew had just gone up there and hung around in Stockton for a couple of days, it wouldn't have been the same as watching it on film.

No, it wouldn't have been the same. Because with film, you are able to select what you want to show. Maybe a few people went to see *Fat City* but nobody would have gone to see the film that I did for the first three days. It was about human despair. And I don't think we should be despairing of humans. I think we should try to make despair a palatable emotion to go to movies for. We should somehow show a way out. I don't mean to be cornball but there must be an escape. To me, despair is a wonderful subject for motion pictures because it's such a common plight of man. We all know despair; it happens all the time. And I just want to be able to go to a movie, pay five dollars, despair for two hours and not go out and shoot myself afterwards. I want to have a good despair; it's like people wanting to go have a good cry or a good laugh. I want to go have a good despair. I want to line people up around the block to see despair; that's what I'm trying to do now. That's why I take *Fat City* with me whenever I'm asked to speak. I want to find out how to make despair palatable because it's a worthy human condition and one that fascinates me. It's a condition I want to dramatize but I want people to go see it too. It's not an easy thing because nobody seems to be able to do it too well. It's a condition that you should be able to deal with. I mean, what we, as filmmakers, offer is two hours of vicarious living for X amount of dollars.

Talking about despair, there was the same kind of problem with Day of the Locust. *The people involved with the film were afraid to make the film too realistic-looking for fear that it would be horribly depressing. Because of your experience with* Fat City, *you also felt the same way. Looking back on it now, do you think that decision helped or hurt the film?*

I think it helped the film. Choosing to couch the proscenium of the characters' lives slickly rather than abrasively made it more powerful. The proscenium of *Fat City* and the choices made there were intended to match their lives. The choice in *Day of the Locust* was to cover that, to show what their dreams were about and to let the audience see how they felt about themselves. That's as opposed to how they actually were, you see. So we all decided to do it this way and go against the material. Karen Black's character, when she's thinking about movies, always sees the glamorous aspects of it and always sees herself in it even though her life is nothing. So the visual approach was one that coincided with her dreams to make it more palatable for the audience. That's precisely the reason for that approach. Because to me, the obvious best way to tell that story is to match the despair of it. But then again, if you did it that way, you'd have to somehow make despair palatable at the box office. I think it's possible.

That film didn't make despair any more palatable at the box office either; it took the opposite attack.

Right. And it might have made it more palatable if it were more real or true! It's a goddamn dilemma; what do you do?

It's hard to say. That novel is really a depressing one, especially if you're anywhere near Hollywood, because all those things still go on.

It will always go on. In Hollywood, maybe only ten percent make it and the other ninety percent try. This elusive dream of making it and being on top is the same story as the moth being drawn to the flame. The flame and its attractiveness is something you'll never eliminate. Some will learn how to live in that environment and others will burn in it.

On Day of the Locust, *you wanted a toasty, golden look. Part of the technique of that required the use of silks and nets. Could you explain a bit about that?*

Yes. After we had decided that the style of the film was going to be romantic rather than austere and naturalistic, I had to go about achieving that style. One of the ways is to use diffusion to change the sharpness of the image so it becomes softer-looking and somehow, more comfortable. It's like the texture of cloth: some are slicker and others are more abrasive. It's the same kind of thing here. So this technique is one way of achieving romanticism.

Now I thought that this was a story that involved everything that was golden, not only the times but the money, the sunsets, the era and the idea of the moth drawn to the flame. All of those things made it sort of a fait accompli as far as what the dominant color tone was to be. The only difference that John Schlesinger and I had was that he didn't want it to be all golden; he wanted some contrast and I wanted it to be all golden. And he won. There is a blue scene in it. It's the one where they go to the bar and there's a female impersonator dancing; I wanted that couched in golden tones too but he wanted it blue. We disagreed but he got his way because he's the director. And his point is very valid; he might be right and I could be dead wrong about it. It's pleasing his way and I'm not against it, I just had a different opinion about it. But basically it's a golden picture.

The golden tones certainly predominated in the picture.

Yes, but he felt that happened if you contrasted it more. I feel that you just draw attention to it by doing that. It's like cutting from black to white; if you don't do it all the time so that it becomes a style, then it becomes something that stands out. I don't like things that stand out. So I would have rather had that scene consistent with the rest of the picture. But as we talked about before, there's a lot of ways of achieving something and there's no one right way. I respect John's decision and we agreed to disagree on that scene. That doesn't make him right or make me right. It's just that he's the director and he got it his way, which is fine with me. Because when I'm the director, I want it my way.

The great scene around the campfire, when you were up in the hills—how did you shoot that scene?

It's great that you say "up in the hills" and point to the hills! That was shot on Stage 14. Richard Macdonald built the Hollywood Hills on Stage 14 at Paramount. Stylistically, the campfire is doing the lighting. But what happens when the fire goes out? You have no light then. So you have to create the light that is there the rest of the time. I've got a little bit of starlight and also light reflecting from the city below. I had a lantern because the characters had to go look for something and it would be too dark where they were doing the looking. So I produced a lantern with a gimmick light behind it which, as you move it about, does the lighting. I did that rather than taking a light and shining it on the person and the lantern and what it's supposed to be lighting. It's so much simpler to let the actual light do the lighting. So I put a little gimmick light behind the lantern, ran the wire up his sleeve and down his leg and you don't really notice any of the hardware.

There's a lot of different ways of producing a fire effect. There are different kinds of fires too. I chose to make it a flame fire. One of the better ways of doing that is to project the look of flames on a person's face. It's like Robert Blake crying in *In Cold Blood*, that's the look of rain on a window projected on something. If you do that through a fire, it won't project through flames. But if you have a smoky fire and you project your light through the smoke, then the smoke creates the flame effect. When we started that sequence, we had a beautiful stage with girders and nice woods, but when we finished shooting in there, that stage was totally black. Every day after work our noses were rimmed with black soot. But that's how I did it. I shot light from a low angle through material that's been soaked in thick diesel oil; I also had some bits of crystals that they use in bee burners in with it. You extinguish that and you use the smoke to create the effect of the fire.

The art director and set designer make enormous contributions to a film. How important is it for you, as a cinematographer, to work closely with these people?

Very important, especially on a film like *Day of the Locust*. That's where you see the talent of a Richard Macdonald, the set designer, and John Lloyd, the art director, creating these exciting things. Richard created that Cinderella bar and all that kind of thing. He used a lot of mirrors and that's a cameraman's nightmare. But I love nightmares. They don't get in my way at all; I love the challenge of it. And I know that nightmares make me do it precisely. There's no way out for me not to be precise. Mirrors create precision; I mean, you can't put a light where someone will see it. And there's only so many places you can hide lights in that kind of situation. Richard's not doing it to cut down on light, he's doing it because he knows it will create an effect. And I accept the challenge and do it. It's nice to work with good people and the cast and crew on that picture were wonderful.

How do you achieve consistency from set-up to set-up, especially in a film like Day of the Locust?

Memory of concept. Now once you decide how you're going to shoot some-thing and you begin to do it, you obviously have a concept of how you're going to achieve it. For example, let's say we're talking about this room and the light is coming from these windows. Now I'm going to put up backing; and I have to light that backing. I have to bring lights through this part of the window over here and the way to do that is put material on the window and pump light through it or even move it back ten feet so the far wall isn't overlit and so on. You know what your conceptual viewpoint is in shooting something this way. But then you go on loca-tion for a week and shoot something else. And when you come back to this room, you shoot it the same way again. You remember how you lit it conceptually and that allows you to do the same kind of lighting in the rest of the scene. But it's memory; it's remembering your concept. Oftentimes, as a cinematographer, you'll work with the script supervisor very closely. So when you're working on a film where you are shooting out of sequence, you'll ask her to help you with your memory of the light-ing. On *Day of the Locust*, I shot at $f3$ all the way through; that was a concept. I never shot at $f5.6$, I shot at $f3$.

You tried to maintain that predetermined f-stop or level of footcandles.

Exactly. Or you may change from set to set because each set is a different problem. One set you may shoot with a fast lens, another set you may use a zoom lens. There are many different ways to solve these problems and it depends on whether you have the money, backing and time. But as far as consistency, it's memory that does it. The script supervisor can be a valuable person to you. If you tell her, "I'm working at fifty footcandles here; I'm pumping lights through the windows from ten feet back in order to keep the interior walls down," then when you go back two weeks later she can read your notes back to you to remind you.

For you, what determines a good frame, a good composition?

The way you're photographing the picture. In other words, do you want it to be slick? Do you want it to be unreal and help to tell the story by making light unreal or do you want to help tell the story by making light real? That affects your composition. All compositions have a function and you choose the composition based on the concept of your story and how you're trying to tell your story.

I learned what painters know about composition; that was taught to me in school. You can learn that very easily in a quarter or a semester. How to use it effectively is something else again. But the actual principles of composition can be picked up in a short period of time.

There are a few basic rules.

Yes, and the rest of it is trying to fit it into what you're doing. If things are off-centered or unbalanced compositionally, it's probably producing an emotional effect that a balanced composition is not producing. It's learning how composition affects you emotionally that allows you to learn how to use it.

I suppose someone could learn a great deal about composition as a camera operator?

Yes, operating teaches you a lot about composition because that's exactly what you're doing. It's so hard to talk about composition. It can be difficult just communicating the type of composition you want to your operator. It doesn't lend itself easily to words.

The visual nuances are always hard to talk about.

You can teach someone the rudiments of anything but you have to learn how to use them for yourself. I mean, we do have within us that something that allows us to be different from somebody else. That's how composition is; it's quite individualistic. As a result, it's hard to teach. When somebody says, "This is the way it's supposed to be," and you can do it another way that works, then it's easily refutable. So what are we talking about? You mean there's somebody who can teach precision in that field? Is there anything precise about composition? I don't think there is. And therefore I don't look for it.

It's like what you said before about lighting: there are five different kinds of light and what you do with them either makes you or breaks you. I guess it's the same thing with composition.

Well, I think it's valuable to learn how to compose the way Michelangelo or other great painters did. But you're composing the way they composed. In other words, you're giving the world their compositions. And if that's what you want to do and if you want to make it look like that, it's perfectly valid. There's nothing wrong with doing that; they're wonderful, they've had the test of time and they've survived. They're great artists, no question about it, and worthy of duplication, I'm sure. But hell, you've got to be able to do it yourself. You've got to be able to do it the way you want to and know why it is that you're doing it. And at least if you don't know intellectually, you know emotionally that it's right. It feels right to you. There are a lot of different levels of people working out there. And there are a lot of different ways of validating to yourself how you feel about things. To me, when I worked as an operator, my validation about rightness or wrongness was always an emotional one. It affected me emotionally when it was wrong. When it was right, I didn't pay much attention to it. That's how I tell about composition.

Has there been any major change in how you perceive your work from your early work until now? Would say that the use of desaturated color was something that you began to like more and more as a style?

I don't think you can tell. I don't think I have a style. I know I don't want one. I know that I have a way of doing something probably because I started in black-and-white films and evolved from there. That's got to have affected me fairly deeply. It's a bottle-fed baby versus a breast-fed baby. Sure, it affects you without you really knowing why or understanding why. I feel that the fact that I started in black-and-white has had an influence on my life as a cinematographer. Naturally everything that you do counts: the pictures I chose and why. You could probably partially trace the kind of person I am through those films, sociologically or psychologically. But visually I feel I'm somebody who knows nothing and starts learning over again according to this new set of circumstances at this new stage in my life. Now whether that makes for any foreseeable continuity or not is something I have never noticed. I don't perceive that there's any kind of consistent thing to my work except that I try to do it well. And when I don't, I'm pissed off at myself.

Let's approach the question from another angle. Is the cinematographer who did Day of the Locust *a better cinematographer than the one who did* The Wild Seed? *And if he is, why?*

Yes, but it's hard to define. I hope to be able to get better and better. I think one of the reasons people quit is because they're afraid that they won't be able to get better and better; that they have come to a zenith of some kind. Sometimes you lose interest in your work when it ceases to become a challenge. You feel like you've done everything and figured it all out and all there is left to do is to just do it well each time. I think everybody has that problem whether they're cinematographers or farmers.

If you do something well and you're really good at it and you put a lot of effort into it, I guess there invariably comes a time when you feel you've done it all.

But you know you haven't done it all because you know everything keeps evolving and changing; and you know you can evolve with it if you grow and develop as a human being. But the increments seem to be smaller and smaller. At first they were big increments and right away you saw your improvements in this area and that area. Pretty soon you do know how to do it all and now it's just figuring out how to do it best each time. That's a wonderful challenge for a while too but eventually you want to try something different because it gives you the chance to improve and develop differently. And I want that chance. I've developed as far as I'm going to go—as far as my interest is keeping me at this moment, photographically speaking. I want to develop in other areas. I want to develop in the area of dealing with human beings and not so much with light, composition and movement and how that affects showing the life of human beings. Do you know what I mean? I want to get into life dramatically. I want to write; I want to direct. I'll always love shooting and I'll always come back to it. But then if you don't do it for a long time, you have a chance to really feel new about it. You can bring a freshness and excitement to it.

I want to do other things. I'm not satisfied doing one thing in life. I'm a filmmaker and I only became a cameraman by accident. In my student days, three of us got together to make a film but all three of us couldn't direct it. So we wrote "producer," "director" and "cameraman" on three pieces of paper and I drew the piece of paper that said "cameraman." Once you get started, you get good at something and people don't let you back out of it. Not only that, but you don't want out of it because you want to develop and see how good you can get. Then once you've found out, that doesn't mean you can't get better. But it almost becomes the same thing over and over. Once you know you've done well, it's nice to try something else if you know you've got the interest for it. I'm interested in other things and I want to try them. If I find that I'm not good at it, that it's too much work, that I'm not suited to it, that I don't have the talent for it or all of the above, I'm sure I'll recognize it and go on to something else or come back to cinematography.

You can see a lot of directors who have nothing more to say; they've burned themselves out. Fellini used to make incredible films but he hasn't done anything noteworthy in years. I guess maybe once you get to that level, there's nowhere else to go unless you can pick up and move to another field.

The problem with that is that a man's experiences are not infinite. And a good director can only bring something special to what he really knows about. So once you've dealt with life, death, love and all the things you want to deal with maybe or the things you know about or are interested in, it seems to me harder to just find other things. I know quite precisely what I'm trying to say. Except that in my desire to make films, I have a hunch that I don't want to make more than about four. I may change my mind about that but at this moment, judging the time of life I have left at maximum productiveness, I've got time for about four interesting subjects. I want to deal with love, passionate love. I want to deal with obsessive sex. I want to deal with death. I want to deal with my family; a film about family like *Amarcord*. There may be a couple of other things but these are subjects that are fascinating to me; subjects that I want to learn about or already know something about. I want to find a story and delve into these subjects dramatically. You know, there are ways of living and learning about life in areas you're certain you want to move in, rather than just make it because you want to make another movie. That doesn't mean I wouldn't make a musical or a comedy. Because I do want to make all these subjects palatable. I want people to line up around the block to go see them. I want to communicate.

I think film is something quite special. Painters don't have the same kind of economic sanctions that we have in film. Each artistic equation is a different equation. The film equation is quite a unique one because of its costliness. That's a very special equation that the painter and many other artists don't face. Films are quickly forgotten and have an immediate turnover; those things are part of the equation special to our art. And we should know them, accept them or struggle against them if we don't believe in them. But we're responsible to them.

In filmmaking your film is never really finished until you sit down with a group of people and watch it. And that happens in no other art form.

Yes, the communication of it. What a wonderful night it is when you go to see your film with an audience.

In college, I used to envy the students in the creative arts department who were painting or sculpting; they could get physically and totally immersed in their art. They had a one-to-one relationship with their art. With filmmaking it all starts with a little idea and then you have to go through this big and involved process to arrive at the finished work.

It's a big trip. So you might as well use it to help yourself; to grow, develop and prospect in the areas that you're interested in. That's what I use film for. It's a wonderful medium. It's like a circle and I'm an atom in that circle. These things like cinematography, drama, music, etc., which are all part of that circle, are variously attracting from time to time. So I move around but I never have to leave the circle.

With your production company, you've shot and directed a lot of commercials over the last couple of years. One reason is to pay the rent. Why else?

I'm not worried about time but, on the other hand I'm fifty-two now. Your time is limited; you don't have those first fifty-two years anymore. You have the next fifty-two and you have to use it more wisely if you want to get anything done. What I have done by starting the commercial company is buy time. I live in an economic world; I have a family and I have to provide a living for myself and them. And if you quit cinematography and that's what you know how to do and that's how you've been making your money, you're suddenly left without a means of livelihood. So I have chosen commercials as a means of making money because it allows me to pay for the economics of my life with the least amount of time expenditure. So thus I have time to pursue this transitional thing, which is getting a film to direct. I don't love commercials but I don't abhor them. They're pieces of advertising to me.

Do commercials allow you to be a bit more experimental?

No, there's less experimenting going on now. But advertising people are experimenting because they want to teach themselves how to get into film. They're learning. It's like Jim Guercio using *Electra Glide in Blue* to learn how to make films. It was a multi-million dollar learning experience for him. Now some kid gets out of film school, he gets a job in an advertising agency and he becomes a producer. He produces a commercial. He's experimenting to find out what he wants to know.

But does that allow you to keep up with the technical developments in the industry?

Absolutely. That's a nice way of allowing you to keep up on technical developments and to keep your hand in at what you know how to do well. I haven't really learned much from being involved in commercials actually, other than that the restriction of time allows you to learn how to manage film fairly well. You have to be precise in your storytelling which I consider a valuable thing to work at and develop in. I'll be able to transfer that ability to my feature if that's what it calls for.

Michael Butler, the cinematographer, said that one of the most important things he learned from you was that a cameraman should be financially stable so that he will have the freedom to choose his films without regard to economic necessity.

What I'm talking about is being free. I want to always be free to not have to do something. I want to not have to take a picture for any other reason than because I want to or for whatever reason that I want to take it. I don't want to take a picture because I have to. That's how despair begins; when you don't have the freedom to say no to something that you don't want to do. Suddenly you get locked into not being free. So it's good to be financially stable or even independent so you can do what you want to do. That's important. It's a concept I've always had because I'm sort of like a cowboy. I'll take my saddle and blanket and move along. Your horse may die underneath you but you just get on another horse and you can still be mobile and free. And still do a job. You partake of all of life but you're not dependent on anything. You don't get suckered into all the things that make you dependent. I don't allow myself to become dependent. And I was lucky. I was born with a silver spoon in my mouth, sort of. I was born with an island almost. I was given one when I was four and a half years old. That's when I think that concept started for me. That's when I became a cowboy; when somebody gave me an island. I've never had any money; I bet I have just as little in the bank as you do, honestly. But I have this instilled philosophy that if something happened to me, there's always this island I can go to. It's a concept more than anything else. It's a concept that you have a place to go to; a place that doesn't make you have to do what you don't want to do.

You said that you've done four or five great shots in your life. One of them was in The Wild Seed. *What constitutes a great shot? How do you define it?*

What allows me to arrive at feeling that way about a shot is when the marriage of everybody's job, connected with what you're doing, comes together perfectly. It's when the story is being told so wonderfully by the actors, the cinematographer, the director and everybody else. It's when it all comes together so right that it hits you and you realize that it's right. It's an emotional thing. In *The Wild Seed*, it was a shot where she was reading a letter and he was feeling the effect of it. And we panned from one character to the other; we panned as slow as it was conceivable to pan. In fact, we didn't want anybody to notice the camera was moving. There was nothing to look at in between the two characters and you didn't actually realize the camera had moved until you got to the other character and then you felt that it was such an emotionally right thing that you knew you had done something wonderful. And that's film at its happiest form. But all the effort in between is all necessary too. But that was such a moment. It happens in other areas too. It's Bobby Blake in *In Cold Blood* talking about his father and the rain is on his face. That to me is pure cinema. Using light, acting, drama and all the other elements. In *Fat City* you've seen the life of the main character when Stacy Keach gets up out of bed, looks for a cigarette, gets dressed and leaves. You know him well, all in that one shot. You know it's hopeless for him.

You know the other eloquent scene in that film . . .

Eloquent, that's the right word. It's when the factors that go into making a picture are so eloquent that they effect you profoundly. That's a precise answer to your question.

8

Laszlo Kovacs

"You can't photograph a piece of paper that has a bunch of lines written on it. That's not life; that's not drama. You have to bring that alive; you have to visualize it."

Laszlo Kovacs tells one of those mythical, almost clichéd, American success stories: the immigrant boy driven from his native land comes to America and makes a name for himself. It's part of our collective folk culture.

Just over twenty-five years ago, Kovacs was a young filmmaker in Hungary. When the Hungarian Revolution exploded and was ruthlessly put down by Russian armor, Kovacs along with Vilmos Zsigmond took to the streets and chronicled the revolution on film. They smuggled thirty thousand feet of documentary footage out of the country, achieving freedom for themselves in the process. Kovacs immigrated to the United States and eventually ended up in Hollywood, lured by the opportunities he thought existed there. But the only thing he found was odd jobs to support himself, while he shot, in his words, "no-budget" features on the side. But he finally scored his big breakthrough with *Easy Rider*. A watershed film that crystallized the feelings of the burgeoning youth movement, it also changed the way Hollywood made films. No longer confined by studio sound stages, filmmakers rushed out to shoot in the streets, seeking a kind of authenticity impossible in constructed sets—a concept that continues to influence Hollywood today.

Inevitably, *Easy Rider* changed Kovacs's life, giving him deserved recognition and high visibility—and eventually his union card. He easily made the transition to big-budgeted, studio-financed films, and has been in constant demand ever since.

A self-confirmed workaholic, Kovacs has worked with a great variety of directors. The one thing, however, that remains constant in his work is the organic matching of a visual look and style to each specific film. He constantly emphasizes that each film has its own character and that the cinematographer's approach to it must come from the material. That's why none of his films look the same. His slight European accent gives his voice an air of artistic authority and indeed he has a different way of "seeing" than a native American. His mind does not work on an assemblyline basis but on a loving, handcrafted level.

It's a long way from Budapest to a cool bungalow overlooking a lush green canyon in the Beverly Hills. But Kovacs has overcome many obstacles that would have doomed an ordinary man to failure. Once a stranger in a strange land, he persevered and succeeded through ability, talent and confidence.

175

1963	Mark of the Gun		Paper Moon
1964	A Man Called Dagger	1974	Huckleberry Finn
1967	Hell's Angels on Wheels		For Pete's Sake
	Targets		Freebie and the Bean
	Rebel Rousers	1975	Shampoo
1968	Psych-Out		At Long Last Love
	The Savage Seven	1976	Baby Blue Marine
	Single Room Furnished		Harry and Walter Go to New York
1969	Blood of Dracula's Castle		Nickelodeon
	Easy Rider	1977	New York, New York
	That Cold Day in the Park		The Last Waltz (camera operator)
1970	Getting Straight	1978	F.I.S.T.
	Five Easy Pieces		Paradise Alley
	Alex in Wonderland	1979	Butch and Sundance:
1971	The Marriage of a Young Stockbroker		The Early Days
			Heartbeat
	The Last Movie	1980	The Runner Stumbles
1972	Pocket Money		Inside Moves
	What's Up, Doc?	1981	The Legend of the Lone Ranger
	The King of Marvin Gardens	1982	Frances
			The Toy
1973	Steelyard Blues	1983	Crackers
	A Reflection of Fear		Ghostbusters
	Slither	1984	Mask

Tell me about your early life in Hungary.

I went to cinema school in Hungary from 1952 to 1956. It was really a great school. The whole program of the school was not really to teach anybody how to be an actor, director or cinematographer. Basically the school was designed to discover your talent and ability and how to bring that out of you in the best way. I met Vilmos Zsigmond in cinema school; we became good friends and have been ever since. In the Hungarian Revolution against the Russians in 1956, Vilmos and I got involved in covering the revolution and we accumulated about thirty thousand feet of film in black-and-white on 35mm. It's really a long story, but what it amounted to was that we smuggled the film out of Hungary. We arrived in Vienna with the film and we discovered that we were really latecomers because newsreel footage of the uprising had already been seen all over the world. We had a really detailed story of the revolution on a day-by-day basis from the beginning. It was terrific coverage but the irony of it was that no one really wanted the footage. We couldn't even give it away. Its news value was gone. The revolution began on October 23rd and we left on November 20th. By the end of November there was no more news value. But we finally found somebody who took the footage and wanted to make a feature-length documentary about the revolution. A year later, on the anniversary of the revolution, CBS was looking for some footage. They somehow contacted Vilmos, who was in New York, and he referred them to the man who owned all the footage. And I understand he sold the footage to CBS for around $100,000.

What did you do when you first got to this country?

At the very beginning, I somehow ended up in upstate New York in a maple forest making maple syrup. Then a cousin who also left Hungary and was living with a family in Seattle arranged for me to live with another family there. So I took the bus there and it was really an incredible ride. I ended up in Seattle and remember, I still couldn't speak English. Finally I got a job working in a lab processing newsreel and kinescopes. I had learned enough in cinema school about processing so that I knew what I was doing. After two weeks, the owner gave me a raise and kept me on. I was working there for about a year and Vilmos was working in New York in a color lab. We decided we should come to Hollywood and try our luck. I know it sounds very clichéd but we really wanted to come to Hollywood to see what all the magic was about.

You had seen a lot of Hollywood films in film school?

Not too many. You must understand that Hungary was behind the Iron Curtain and was very isolated from western culture after World War II. It was a gradual process of isolation that was absolutely completed by 1948. Until then, we were able to see American, English, French and some Italian postwar films. But after 1948, that ended. I remember the first time I saw *Citizen Kane*—it was moments before the isolation when we could still see some western films. It happened to be playing only one week and, through some strange luck, I was able to see it.

You had heard of Citizen Kane?

No, absolutely not. It just came in like any other movie. There was no history, background or publicity that came with it. It was really a longlasting impression and experience for me. In 1948, I was a teenager basically; I wasn't inclined toward photography or anything like that. I just loved movies and so I saw anything I could. Later on, when we were in cinema school, we were able to get some of the western films. So I saw *Citizen Kane* again with a little more direction and focus. Because the first time I saw it, I saw something different in the film; it was a magical impression. When I saw it four years later in school, it came as an incredible shock. "What a film this is," I thought. At that time in my life, I was interested in lighting and composition and this film just blew my mind. I just couldn't believe that anything like this could be done. It was done on such a great scale and yet it was still very simple. It was a great way of telling a story. The other memorable film was *Casablanca*. *Casablanca* and *Citizen Kane* were the two films we could run over and over at school. Due to the political climate, they didn't want you to be too exposed to western films. We had a steady diet of Russian films. And we were fascinated with some of the older films of Pudovkin, Eisenstein and Dovzhenko. But we were very curious about what was happening in the west.

So you finally made it to Hollywood; what year was that?
1958.

What did you find when you got here?

Disaster, it was total disaster. When you come here, you don't even know where God lives. You don't know who to talk to and you get the cold shoulder from everybody. Vilmos and I went down to the union, which was a very funny experience. We didn't know anything about what was going on or what the system was. We told them that we would like to join the union. These two guys at the union office looked at us like we were crazy and all they said was, "Come back when you speak English." After we did learn English, we slowly found out that the system just doesn't work that way.

So I had some crazy jobs here like being involved in the home portrait photography business. That was a sad business because it took advantage of people who couldn't afford it anyway. So I quit. I worked for an insurance company for four years in a darkroom making prints from microfilm documents. I got to the point where I really had to decide what I was going to do with my life. So I just walked away from it. By that time I knew some cinema students at UCLA and some of our friends were studying there. I would come and watch and help. I met Francis Coppola and got to know some other people there. At that time, there were a lot of low-budget, independent, non-union pictures being done. I got involved with some of them. Vilmos was going his own way and finding some contacts—people who couldn't really afford to pay you. We really didn't care about the money but we wanted the experience. So those were the learning days. I worked on some films where Vilmos and myself were the whole crew.

So when you started doing these low-budget films, you started as a cameraman basically?

Yes. We used to call these pictures "no-budget" films, not low-budget films. It was very exciting because we learned from our own mistakes; we learned how to overcome some of the limitations we were up against. We tried to use our ingenuity to overcome the budget limitations. Those were very interesting and colorful days as opposed to today because that whole climate doesn't exist anymore. It's kind of sad because there are a lot of cinema school students and people from other walks of life who want to get involved in filmmaking and they really have no chance to practice and learn from their own mistakes.

When did you move up from the no-budget films to the low-budget films like some of the motorcycle films?

Wow, those were the big epics for us. It was a word-of-mouth thing that these two crazy Hungarians were pretty good and they worked cheap. These producers just wanted somebody who could get an image on the screen and show up every day on time. We tried to go beyond those requirements and better ourselves. We tried to hire good people and we built up a nice group who were really into it. They were all enthusiastic and in it for the love and excitement of making films. One thing led to another and each film was a bit better than the previous one. By the time we got to doing the motorcycle pictures, we were working with $60,000–$80,000 budgets.

Is that all?

Oh, yes. And they were considered legitimate films. Let me try to remember some of the titles. One was called *Blood of Dracula's Castle*, a very hokey horror film which was probably done for $30,000. There was one called *My Soul Runs Naked. Nasty Rabbit, The Traveling Salesman* and *The Fakers* were some others. But we made these movies awfully fast, in ten or twelve days. We had practically no equipment. If we had to shoot an interior, we rented a kit of quartz lights and plugged them into the wall. Of course, we didn't have any fill lights or even reflectors on any exteriors. I once did a picture and all I had was four reflectors and one set of master lights. That was it. The producer had a blimped Arriflex and three lenses. But I was very happy that I could have that much. I remember later on that it was a big day when they let us rent a zoom lens! It was a constant battle. On a different level, it's exactly the same today. Even if you make an eight or ten million dollar picture, it's the same hassle. It's just on a different scale. When you hear about an eight or ten million dollar picture, it's not really because the above-the-line people walk away with five million. And what it really amounts to is that they leave you fifty cents to make the film! Really. I told them, "I used to work with Roger Corman and he cared more about what showed up on the screen. He really didn't cut the wire so close." It's crazy today; it's really unbelievable. If you don't foresee the need for a particular piece of equipment but you decide you would like to have it for a particular scene, you have to have a work order before you ask for it if you're working for the studio. Suddenly you're making paperwork, not film. That's why I like independent filmmaking because if you need a piece of equipment, you don't have to waste your time and then wait for approval. On an independent production, you send somebody off in a car and inside of twenty minutes, it's there. You have that freedom there while the studio charges you for overhead. I grew out of no-budget/low-budget films and you had to be very budget-conscious. That's why what's happening in the studio system today really goes against my grain.

So after no-budget films, low-budget films, then came Easy Rider?

No. Actually, there was a transition period between the no-budget films and the low-budget films when I was working indirectly for some of the Roger Corman productions. I never worked directly for him or with him but I was involved in several of the films he financed and put together. Films like *A Girl in Daddy's Bikini*. Roger would start a film with a union crew and he would shoot with them for a week or two. Then he would announce that the picture was completed. He laid off the union crew and he would hire a completely different non-union crew to make it look like a totally different film. And we would finish the picture. It was marvelous for us; we didn't care as long as we had the opportunity to work. During this period I met Richard Rush and he was preparing a little film called *A Man Called Dagger*. He was looking for somebody he could afford and he wanted certain things from the cinematographer in terms of quality. That was the beginning of another long association with a particular director. Together we went on to bigger and better pictures, in budget and quality. A totally new direction opened up for us. I had done a couple of films with Richard when a total unknown came out of left field and wanted to make a film called *Targets*. That was Peter Bogdanovich. He was also looking for somebody he could afford. He also wanted something very special and very specific from a cinematographer. He only had a certain amount of money and a certain amount of days with Boris Karloff. We had incredible experiences on that film; we had to use a lot of ingenuity to solve the budgetary problem. Polly Platt, the art director, would revamp one set and make it look completely different inside of a few hours. We worked incredible hours, sometimes eighteen hours a day. So this film started Peter and me off on another long-lasting relationship.

What kind of training ground were no-budget/low-budget features for you? How did that help when you moved up to larger projects?

That was enormously important. It provided me with such an incredible training ground where I could make my own mistakes. The next film you might make another kind of mistake but you never committed the same mistake twice. So it was a learning process. In the early sixties, there were a great number of low-budget, exploitation pictures: the bike pictures, the flower children pictures and the horror pictures. For the new and young filmmakers it was important that they were able to work on these films. In the last five to eight years, that spectrum of filmmaking has disappeared. But I think it's coming back again in the form of horror and exploitation films that will give other new talent the same chance we had ten or fifteen years ago.

Without that experience and learning process, I couldn't be where I am today.

It was basically your training ground before you got your union card and started moving up to major features.

At that point, the card wasn't that important. That was one of the future goals. Several contemporary filmmakers like Alonzo, Zsigmond, Roizman and Willis went through that kind of experience and it was just vital to us. Now those opportunities are coming around again for the new guys. So there is a little light at the end of the tunnel. Union status comes later; you have to establish yourself first. Suppose they bring you a union card on a silver platter without you having the experience, knowledge and the art refined. What are you going to do with it? Nobody's going to hire you.

You probably wouldn't be able to handle it at that stage in your development.

No way. So it's necessary to go through it. I am not specifically talking about the stepladder structure of the union. I'm talking an individual artist developing his or her talent. That takes years and a lot of experience. No one can teach you experience. Once you have a reputation, you can become a member of any union you want. If you have the merit and the weight behind you as an artist, then there are elements that will be going to bat for you. For instance, I couldn't have gotten into the union by myself. I had a lot of help from different producers because they felt that I was good and was worth the fight. They thought I had talent. But if you don't show that quality, nobody's going to help you.

Tell the story about how you came to be involved in Easy Rider, *which was a landmark film in many ways. It was particularly a turning point in your career.*

It came at the end of a long succession of no-budget/low-budget motorcycle pictures and other kinds of exploitation films. I did *Hell's Angels on Wheels, The Savage Seven, Rebelrousers,* and so on. When *Easy Rider* came along, it was a time when I really felt I had done my share of those kinds of films. I was ready to move on to bigger and better things. I didn't feel like doing another motorcycle picture and I felt that if I heard another bike roaring, I would go crazy. The first approach came from Paul Lewis, the production manager, with whom I had done a lot of these pictures. He said, "There's a picture coming up, a motorcycle picture (he made the mistake of saying "motorcycle" to me) with Dennis Hopper and Peter Fonda. This is not the conventional type of motorcycle picture that we have been involved with. This is different." I said, "I don't care if it's different or not, there are motorcycles in the picture and I don't want to do it." Now this was still in my pre-union days. There was still enough independent production around that I thought I could move on to something better. But Paul thought otherwise. He said, "Listen, have enough courtesy to listen to Dennis Hopper's story. He wants you desperately for the film because he saw *Psych-Out.*" So I agreed to listen and we got together in the production office where we were all waiting for Dennis to come from the airport with the completed script in hand. Suddenly the door of the office slammed wide open and Dennis comes in as Billy the Kid, dressed in the same hat and leather gear that you see on the screen later in *Easy Rider*. He has a bunch of rolled up papers under his arm and he shouts, "Here's the script." And he throws it across the room and the pages go flying everywhere. We are all in bewilderment; we don't know what's happening. Dennis said, "Don't worry about the script. I don't want anybody to read the script. Everybody sit down and I'll tell you the story." He began telling the story and, as he went on, I got more and more fascinated with it. And when he finished telling the story, I said, "When do we start? How do we go about it?" Well, as soon as we could, the art director, the production manager, Dennis and myself got into a car and traveled from Los Angeles to New Orleans, scouting out the kinds of things we wanted to do. We flew back to L.A. and really started preproduction. And the rest of it suddenly became history.

After the film was a success, a lot of people felt that you just got lucky. That you just went out on the road haphazardly, turned on the camera and accepted what you got. But that's not true is it? The film was totally prepared, wasn't it?

It was totally planned. On top of that, a lot of people said we didn't even have a script. We had a very specifically written script by Terry Southern, Dennis Hopper and Peter Fonda. It was an actual shooting script. All the scenes were carefully followed, especially the dialogue sequences after the Jack Nicholson character joins them. It wasn't just a bunch of stoned guys sitting around a campfire and improvising that. It was charged that we lucked out, that we just turned on the camera and suddenly we captured the actors at the right moments. We did get lucky but our luck was that people were receptive to it at the time of its release. If the timing was wrong, the picture would probably still be on the shelf somewhere. But luckily the timing was so perfect. A lot of young people could associate their own problems with the search for freedom. We were addressing some really contemporary problems facing young people. It made people think.

As you know now, *Easy Rider* drastically changed the way films were made. I'm not saying *Easy Rider* was the first because that movement had started years before; it was a movement that I was part of but other cinematographers and filmmakers were equally part of it. In the beginning we were forced to work on location because we couldn't afford the sound stages. So we had to go out and find the real thing and put that on the screen, which gave a new freshness and new reality to the dramatics. That's the advantage of the no-budget/low-budget films: that you are forced to do things that you wouldn't normally do. That's the reason that I'd like to go back to it again: to refresh that memory, to refresh that feeling. Now we tend to do films with many trucks of equipment—and sometimes that is necessary—but suddenly, with all that commotion, the film itself sometimes gets lost. You lose sight of the main objective. *Easy Rider* is considered a milestone now.

Easy Rider *was the film that was the most recognized, even though all these other things came before. This film was the culmination.*

Yes, everything peaked in that moment. I was, again, lucky to be part of that project and to be part of that moment that really changed a lot of people's lives, not only from a filmmaking viewpoint but also from the viewpoint of communicating with the audience. I still keep meeting people who tell me that *Easy Rider* changed their lives. The technology of film changed too. We got faster film stock, smaller cameras and more portable lighting units.

Filmmakers were freed from the traditional system of using twenty arcs on a sound stage.

Exactly. It still affects my present day work, technically speaking. And that era affected our thinking and philosophy. Both Vilmos and I came from a different country and culture; we came here and went through culture shock in adapting to new ways of doing things. I can still remember the first major reviews I got were on *Hell's Angels on Wheels*. The reviewer didn't know who I was but he said, "This person obviously comes from another country. I have never seen photographs of the American countryside and the American road like these. I have never seen it in exactly this way before; it shows us how we really look."

Interesting.

That was basically the theme all the way up to *Easy Rider*. Even past *Easy Rider*—*Paper Moon* is a road picture. Look at the Western; it's part of the great American folklore, whether it's true or not. Basically filmmaking is magic because you create something the way you see it. How do you see? That's what is so important because that's when your own artistic statement gets stamped on a film. How you do it and where you set your exposure doesn't matter, it's where it's coming from that's important. You can't photograph a piece of paper that has a bunch of lines written on it. That's not life, that's not drama. You have to bring that alive, you have to visualize it. You don't do it alone either. Film is a collaborative effort.

*Let me ask you this. You were obviously a good and competent cameraman when
you shot* Easy Rider. *What nuances and subtleties have you picked up and developed since that time that's made you a better cinematographer?*

It's a very difficult question. Your artistic statement doesn't stop with a certain
film. You start from somewhere and you grow. You progress a little each time you
do a film. A lot of people called *Easy Rider* a milestone. But I don't consider it a
milestone in my artistic development and career. It was, however, a major force
that really changed my life. But artistically, I didn't stop there. That whole process
of thinking and philosophizing continued to grow and it still grows to this day.

You cannot let yourself be categorically put into a pigeonhole. I was accused of
only being able to do exterior, road pictures. If there were too many interiors on a
picture, I might not get the job because they didn't think I could light interiors.
Then I started doing interior pictures like *At Long Last Love* and *New York, New
York.* So when I wanted to do a western, they wondered if I could shoot good
exteriors. Well, that's insane thinking. They don't understand your total commitment and what you're made of.

It's not just making pretty pictures.

No, that has nothing to do with it. Because all those moments and all those
elements dictate what the format, texture, mood and style of the film should be.
You can't create a beautiful format and then try to squeeze what you want to say
into it. It's not going to fit.

It has to come from the material.

It's organic; it has to come out from the material. Shakespeare said, "The play is
the thing." That's still valid. If you don't have the play, if you don't have the dramatics, if you don't have something to say about people, then what have you got?

*What determines your choice of lenses for a particular shot, scene or a whole
picture? It becomes an artistic decision even though you're dealing with the
mechanics?*

Yes, it is a very mechanical thing but it points out a major artistic question: how
do you use your tools? I'm talking about lens, camera movement, composition,
different lighting equipment. It's how you combine all those elements into an effort
to put what you want on the screen that makes the difference. The choice of lens is
of incredible importance. Because, with a choice of lens, you can change reality,
you can change perspective and even the relationship of people to each other. Your
choice of a lens has to relate very strongly to the dramatic content. It cannot be an
arbitrary choice. For example, *Paper Moon* was black-and-white and it was also a
deep-focus picture. That meant that everything in the composition, no matter how
close or far away from the lens, has to be sharp. It had that wonderful, exaggerated
perspective of the American countryside in Kansas. If you think about it, Kansas is
not really too scenic; it doesn't have beautiful mountains and valleys. It's flat as this
table top. And that was an element in the film and I had to make it work for the film.
Now in the choice of lenses, you can't shoot close-ups, especially of a little girl,
with a wide-angle lens. Particularly when the director is staging background action
behind her close-up that he wants to be just as sharp as her face. The wide-angle

lens would distort but it would carry the depth of focus. But you don't want to distort the little girl's face; you don't want to give her a blown-out face with an ugly potato nose. So these choices are very important.

Getting Straight, with Dick Rush, was exactly the opposite of that. We experimented with the long lens and the critical rack-focus technique. He deliberately wanted to work with a very narrow depth of field, a very shallow focus. He wanted only one particular actor in focus until the other actor behind him talks and then you change the focus. He didn't want anything else to visually interfere with those moments. We were criticized for using that technique. But if film is an art form, then as filmmakers we are obligated to explore our tools and push them to the limit. We are not just recording a story. The camera, lens and composition are instinctively a major part of telling a story. The real trick of it is in how you apply all those elements.

How do you achieve consistency from set-up to set-up, from scene to scene?

That's really basically a technical skill. Generally, you try to retain a pictorial quality with your lens and your f-stop. But the problem comes in when you have to either create or destroy depth of field. So then you have to build up your stop, either raising your lighting level or pushing the film one more stop. You can use longer lenses. You can knock down the light level with neutral density filters. When you have a wide master shot, medium long shots, some over-the-shoulders shots, and some close-ups all in one sequence, the images must flow visually and look like they belong together. Each shot shouldn't look like it's from a different movie. Technically speaking, it's a matching problem. Your major element in matching is lighting. I'm talking about interiors now where you have the control. You are one hundred percent in control on a sound stage. The worst problem of matching and continuity arises in shooting exteriors. Let's say you have an exterior sequence scheduled for five days. The first thing you want to know is what the weather report is for the next week. So you start shooting, probably out of script order, and you shoot in the early morning, high noon, afternoon and early evening. And you have to have the same lighting quality for all of them, no matter what time of day you shot it. It's very hard to control the big gaffer in the sky. The sun is a given but nevertheless you have to twist it and control it to make an entire day's shooting look like it took place in five minutes. Again, knowing how to do this comes from experience. Those bloody low-budget films taught me that there is no mercy. At that time you learned how to do those things by your blood, sweat and tears. Even now, you learn every day. I have students and young filmmakers asking me, "Should I do this or should I do that?" I think you should do everything you can. As long as you have film in the camera, shoot anything. Because the next day you can screen and see what you did right and what you did wrong. Where are you going to learn something like that? You keep doing it and you keep learning from your mistakes.

What you're saying is that through experience you get the knowledge and control of your tools.

Absolutely, that comes from having a vast experience to draw upon. Let's say that the young filmmaker doesn't have that vast experience but the requirements of the project are very high. The producers are not going to tailor their needs to your experience. It doesn't work that way. You have to bring yourself up to that level. Nobody should be afraid of doing that; you have to give it your best effort. That's how you collect all those little bits of technical information.

You have to be an observer of life because that's what you're dealing with. Right now I'm watching your face, which is changing by the minute because the sun is setting. Even as we talk, I can't help but observe it. I see it and it gives me a certain emotional feeling. Now later when a scene like that is required, you have to be able to put it on the screen. The director has his own problems with actors and others. He can't worry about you. That's why he hired you, that's why he trusts you. The next day at dailies, he's going to see what you did and it better be what he wants. Good directors are always looking for your contribution and input beyond the call of duty. There's no excuses; you can't say to him, "I knew what you wanted but I didn't really know how to do it." You can't say that because then you shouldn't be there in the first place. And the director will find somebody else who can.

What determines a good composition? Is it balance, symmetry, focus or lighting? What are the important elements?

The major criterion of a good composition is whether it supports emotionally the scene and the dramatics. The composition has to serve that purpose. You can achieve that with a balanced or an unbalanced composition, a symmetrical or an asymmetrical composition; it's proper if it emotionally supports the dramatics. Again, the play is the thing. You don't make beautiful compositions just for the sake of making compositions. You can't because if you do, you're working on some other picture. You're not working on the same picture that the director is working on. You have to serve that same emotional and dramatic level that everybody is working for. An actor has to work hard to capture the character and the scene; you are a visual supporter of that.

You have to be flexible in your vision in order to know how to treat all those elements. In the last few minutes, we've talked about a hundred different problems—lenses, compositions, lighting, color and camera movement. You can talk for weeks about any one of those things.

It's almost like talking about each of those things individually is to take each one out of context.

Exactly. And it's all in your hands; it's all in your control. On the set, you are the juggler. You are playing with all these elements and you are making choices in order to serve a particular purpose. Nobody else is making those choices for you. It's your artistic responsibility to decide how you want to see that story, above and beyond what the director wants. It's not enough just to give what the director wants. It becomes only an average effort then. You must contribute beyond that.

Sometimes it really blows my mind when I see some of the earlier pictures I did. I start to analyze why I made the choices that I did. Why did I photograph *Heartbeat* this particular way, *The Runner Stumbles* another way and *Shampoo* another way? What guides me to make those choices? All I can tell you is that it always comes back to the same starting position: your instinct. Your relationship to the

material gives you an incredible emotional feeling. You feel the story, you see it in
a way that no one else sees it. For instance, when I read a new script, I see it and
visualize it even as I read. You can't see it the way the director sees it at that point.
You see it your own way. You wait until you sit down with the director and let him
tell you how he feels about it. If the director asks me, "How would you photograph
this picture?" I would get up and walk away. That's a tremendously unfair question.
If you are the director, I want to know how you see the film first and then I'll tell you
what my ideas area. If you trust me, it's my responsibility and obligation to help,
instigate and inspire you. And vice versa. That creative atmosphere is so important. Without that, you just become a mechanic.

*What kind of different visual references do you have with various directors? Do
you use paintings, photographs or other movies?*

Yes, it's of major importance. I have been involved in several pictures where
directors have dug up photos or prints from the old masters. "See this picture," one
of them said, "This is how I feel the whole movie should look." You look at it and,
knowing the material to be filmed, you understand what he wants. Then you bring
in the images when you read the script without any outside influences. You can see
either how close you were or how far apart you were from the director's vision. It
doesn't matter really because the idea is to bring those two images together. In the
process, you may even improve upon it.

It's like a visual shorthand.

Yes. But sometimes you can't find an appropriate visual reference and you are
forced to verbalize it. And it's almost a cruel, impossible task to translate visual
images into verbal ones. How do you describe a picture or a painting that I have
never seen? The visualization is one of those elements that are just as important as
the choice of lenses or the choice of camera movement. Once you have that image
in your head, you know you can create it. It comes with experience and technical
expertise.

*With everyone using basically the same cameras, the same lenses and the same
film stock, you would think that it would lead to a more homogenized look. But it
hasn't.*

By logic, maybe it should. We are creating magic and magic is not necessarily
wizardry. If you really feel that something is right for a particular film, you can
torture and twist that film and camera in order to really get the exact result you
want. It just somehow gets on the screen. And now you ask me, "How did you do
that?" I don't know because you should have been there at the moment it happened
and watched. Even if you watched, you would never know what I'm doing and why.
It's something I just can't explain. If I do one thing this way, then you do another
thing and so on. When you add it up together, it equals something else. There's no
formula because this is an art.

*That's where the talent, imagination and creativity of that particular person
comes to bear on the situation.*

That's exactly right. You're working with very lively material that you've recorded for the future with your own eye and vision. I interject that you are working

independent of the director's vision. You have your own function. Nevertheless everything is filtered through your heart, brain, eyes, taste and choices. That's how the audience is going to see this particular story. I think today is the fascinating era of cinematography. The form and the final shape of that film is going through your eye. You want everybody to see that film in this particular way. That involves very strong convictions and choices. The assistant director will ask you, "Are you ready yet?" And when you say, "Yes," then you have a rehearsal and take one and take two, with maybe a few minor adjustments between takes. But when the director says, "Print," it becomes history. That moment is history; it's there on that piece of film for future generations to see. It's part of yourself there too, especially on an emotional level. What's fascinating is that you have that incredible power and you better use that power for the right purpose.

Do you think storyboarding is a useful tool?

Up to a certain point, I can see the value of storyboarding, especially in an educational situation where film may be a totally different language. In dealing with film students, you have to force them to think visually. So storyboarding can be very useful for that but afterwards you have to drop it; you can't carry it around and live with it. You're imposing limitations then.

Students want to know why directors don't use storyboards. They think it's a sign that the director doesn't know what he wants to do. Lack of a storyboard doesn't mean that at all. He knows what he wants to do in his heart and mind already. But he's not going to totally know it until tomorrow morning when he and the actors come onto the set. He's going to get everybody moving and see how the actors feel. He's not necessarily imposing anything on anybody; he's waiting for suggestions and ideas. He wants to see what the actors will bring to it. He's not going to go home the night before and draw out a floor plan. No. You have to wait until the human elements come in and the actors start creating the characters. Real artists, whether they be directors, actors or cinematographers, realize that they are dealing with human beings and their emotions. The actors are creating what we have come together for. The performance brings the characters alive. Good actors bring fabulous ideas to the film. They come up with things that aren't on any storyboard.

The key word is flexibility. But you will admit that it's much easier to work with someone who comes prepared every day.

But it would be the most boring thing. If you don't have any openness, it becomes routine. You suddenly realize that it has nothing to do with filmmaking.

You're not suggesting that you shouldn't be prepared?

No. You have to emotionally know the relationship between the characters, where they are coming from and where they are going. If a director knows that, a cinematographer understands that and the actors try to portray that, then I think you are on the same wavelength with everyone, creatively speaking.

There are times, of course, where you have to storyboard certain things. For instance, in *F.I.S.T.*, we had a strike sequence that was incredibly involved. Now you could just jump in and start shooting that sequence but it would take you two months to figure out who is where at what point in the scene. So we sat down and storyboarded it. That storyboard was extremely important because it enabled us to shoot that sequence in six or seven days without getting totally lost. We were also able to shoot it in chronological sequence otherwise we might have gotten into the problem where the enemy was behind you when he was supposed to be in front of you. So, for certain things, it is important to storyboard. But when you're dealing with straight dramatics, you don't really need to storyboard.

From the no-budget/low-budget days, you gained a reputation as a very fast cameraman who did quality work. What is it later on that slows a cameraman down?

A good question. How does it happen? I think we lose our momentum. You never like to do that; you want to keep going because that flow of activity creates excitement and a certain quality of work. Now when you get to bigger films, the physical problems of staging some scenes are enormous. You may have four or five hundred extras plus the principals; plus you have very intricate blocking. You, as a cinematographer, can't really start working until the director has worked out what he's really happy with and wants to put on the screen. In some instances that takes an enormous amount of time. When that's worked out, the director usually says, "Okay, it's yours now. Call me when you're ready." Now twenty minutes later, the second assistant director comes to you and wants to know how you're doing. You know that such a complicated scene is going to take an hour and a half to light. But the physical pressure is right there so you tell him that you'll let him know. Five minutes later the other assistant director comes in and wants you to give him fifteen minutes notice before you're ready so he can get his extras on the set. In the meantime, you're driving and working with your crew, rushing to get things done. Unfortunately the cinematographer is always treated a little bit like a stepchild on the set. I mean, the most important thing is the actors and their performances and I agree with that one hundred percent. If you don't have the right elements in front of the lens, then what are you doing there? The people who control the money complain that you're taking an hour and a half to light. But they discount the fact that you're working on the largest sound stage in Hollywood, that you're dealing with five hundred extras and so on. Unfortunately things take time. I don't think it's out of line to spend up to two hours on a set-up when the director has spent the whole morning with rehearsals and communicating with his actors. It is necessary for him to do that and I support that. He must find out where the heart of the scene is. As a cinematographer, I'm right at his ear so that we can talk about it as we go along. He must be able to work that out.

But, by the same token . . .

When I spend two hours on my job, they say I'm slow. All the responsible cinematographers want to do a good job. If a good cinematographer is only doing three set-ups a day, it's not really his fault. I guarantee that if the scenes were ready and worked out, he would be able to do ten set-ups. In other words, the cinematographer is not the one who is slowing down the process. My philosophy is to give the director the most time possible without compromising my work. Because if I compromise in my work, I cheat him out of something that he expected from me. If I can't give him that on the screen, I'm a thief. But I need some time to do my work also. So who do they come down on? Who do they blame? They have to find a scapegoat. But let me tell you that you are only as fast as your director is. So this is the kind of pressure that you have to deal with as a cinematographer. You have to be responsible; I learned that on the low-budget pictures that I did in two or three weeks. I knew I couldn't lounge around on the set; I never had time to sit down. I have never seen a cinematographer sitting in a chair on a set, except for lunchtime or a story conference.

Outside of the creative realm, you also have to be a great personnel manager.

You're running a huge company. They are ready to do what you tell them. But I can't tell them what to do until I know what's happening from the director. When the director is working out the scene with the actors, you are part of that discussion. Then when the director turns the set over to you, you know exactly what you have to do because you've already witnessed the whole process taking place. The next hour and a half is the hard labor to put that image on the screen. You know, when you are prepping a film, the closer you get to the shooting, the more you see the film in your head—not the specifics of it but the general approach and the visual style.

Do you always control the camera position? Or have you worked with directors who like to exercise their control in that area?

No. I don't think it works in that dictatorial way. I have worked with many directors and I can't remember the last time a director told me, "Put the camera right here and put a 28mm lens on it." It's a very close collaboration and you work it out with the director. The actors understand what the camera means and they work for the camera. Intelligent actors are aware of this and can tailor their performance to that level. Therefore the camera placement is determined organically as you watch the actors work through a scene; it automatically tells you where the camera should be. So no one says, "Hey, put the camera over here," because we all discover at the same time where the camera should be, where the focal point should be and where the audience's point of view should be. It's not like the theater where you're sitting in the eighteenth row and watching the whole thing from the same point of view.

Many of Bogdanovich's films have these incredibly fluid camera movements. How much of that responsibility was yours and how much came from him? What goes on in that kind of collaboration?

First of all, it always comes from the director's concept or desire. He sees a scene in movement and fluidity and he wants to have one continuous long take. He would always say, "I only want to cut to a close-up when the actors are bad." That's when he would break up a long, designed movement. He expressed that feeling to the actors because the longer takes demand a little bit more. Now the director is always working out the movement of what he wants the actors to do. What was always so wonderful with Peter was that you would be next to him and he would give you a jab in the ribs with his elbow and say, "Do you see what I mean? Do you follow me?" I would be right behind him, making chalk marks on the floor. He would move, almost subconsciously, as the camera would move. He became the camera. He would ask me, "Do you think we can do this?" I told him not to worry about any of that. He should just work out the scene and we'll see how we can do it later. In other words, I never tried to impose any kind of limitations. It's the director's desire to move the camera or not. In *Five Easy Pieces*, Bob Rafelson never moved the camera on an exterior; on the interiors, we did move it. It's a conceptual thing. It's his film and that's the way he believes it should be done. That doesn't mean that it's bad or good. Because another director would direct the same film in a totally different way. It's a concept that comes from the director. I personally like long, continuous scenes because I feel the less the interruption of the actors and the performance the better. Unless of course, a new angle is required dramatically. What it all comes down to is how you want to tell the story. Do you want to move the camera or not? That's basically the director's choice and you work it out with him.

What you're basically saying is that the camera, the technique and all the mechanics of it are really subservient to the director, the performers and what the whole concept of the film is.

Right. Everything has to serve one purpose. When you turn out the lights in a theater and the image comes on the screen, that's it. Everything has to serve that. It's what everybody is there for.

You know, from what I've been able to determine, directors in the thirties and forties were the slaves of the cameraman because the technology was not that advanced.

But that's not so anymore. We have lightweight, portable equipment. Everything depends on how you apply those tools. When you see some of those old musicals with all the movement in them, you have to realize that they had 400-pound cameras and you just wonder how the hell they ever did some of those things. So they overcame all those physical handicaps in order to let their imagination soar and prevail. Today it's the same; that part hasn't changed. One important thing though is that the tools cannot overpower and distract from the story. I'd rather have the camera lie back and record the story when it needs to and find a moment when it can be part of the storytelling. But when the audience is involved in the dramatics and suddenly they're drawn out of context by a real interesting shot, then you're out of line.

But it happens. On the other hand, some films are merely recorded, as if they were a weekend snapshot. There's nothing added to the story by the camera.

Or the cameraman puts on such an incredible bravura display that it takes your breath away. But the next second you have to ask yourself what it all meant in the context of the story. And you realize that it didn't advance anything in the story. You try to always find a good balance. Great filmmakers instinctively know and understand where that balance is.

Many times today films are recorded with a total detachment. There seems to be no personal involvement; there's a certain distancing involved. Many times the cinematographer tries to inspire the director. You try not to do things in such a pedestrian way; you help him look for a more unique way of saying something. Or sometimes a director will try an extremely complicated way to say a simple thing. It's your responsibility to tell him that there is also a simple way that might be more effective. You're responsible for saying that but the ultimate choice rests with the director. You're one of the few persons on the set that can have that kind of influence. If the cinematographer doesn't open his mouth and air his convictions and beliefs, then that collaboration goes down the tubes. There's no spark, no interaction. I need to be stimulated too. I want that inspiration from the director. If you disagree, you still have to express your opinion. But the ultimate decision is always the director's.

You've shot several films for Billy Fraker, who is also a cinematographer. When he's in the director's chair and you're his cinematographer, do you ever feel intimidated by him?

We had a wonderful relationship on *The Legend of the Lone Ranger*. He has total trust and I never let him down. He gets so involved in creating the film with you as his closest visual helper. If he asks me to photograph his picture, he has a complete trust in me. You have to have a camaraderie with the director; you have to be very close. That goes for any picture. If you see the expression change on a director's face, you can't just walk by and avoid it. It means something and you should get with him to see if something is the matter. He may not be sure if his instinct about a scene is right or wrong. You can see that he's bothered and you have to help bring those thoughts to the surface. After all, he's a human being, not a god.

Do you approach a six-million-dollar film any different than a fifteen-million-dollar film? Do you approach Inside Moves *any differently than* The Legend of the Lone Ranger?

The answer is no and yes. It should not influence your artistic input; you can't buy that. But at the same time, you must be realistic enough to realize that you only have so much money and time. With my background, I always had to be conscious of it. In the early days, a director would call me and say, "I have an eighteen-day picture. Can you do it?" In other words, when you approach a film, you must know what your economic limitations are. Because that will tell you what your financial responsibility is. That's what I mean when I say the answer is, "Yes." You definitely have to consider those things. But artistically it shouldn't be affected. You may have all kinds of economic and logistic considerations but one thing that shouldn't be affected by that is the quality of the film.

What's your relationship with your crew?

Basically I believe in a repertory company. I've been using the same camera crew for many, many years. I've worked with the same gaffer since 1964; the same key grip since 1972. You have to find creative collaborators. These people also personally know and understand me and that cuts down on a lot of unnecessary explanation and dialogue on the set. For example, if we're working a scene out, I want all the key people there watching it so that they understand what the dialogue between the actors and the director is all about. To me, it's very important to have those kind of people that you can trust picture after picture. I can't go lay a dolly track by myself or light a set by myself. I need people who understand what needs to be done with the least waste of communication. The pressure is on you and your crew to perform when you have the set. Otherwise, they say the cinematographer is slow. I don't want to spend half an hour to explain the shot to everybody and how I want to light it. I have to in a certain sense . . .

But you don't have to give a dissertation on it.

No. They have almost a sixth sense about it and right away they get into gear. Suddenly lights are being set and dolly tracks are being readied. You can only do this with a crew of really qualified, talented technicians who understand you. These people believe in film and work very hard. While my crew makes a living at this, they also enjoy making films very much. Having these people around is so important; without them, you can't exist. The level of excitement that the actors put out should be carried on right through to the crew. I can't work with a crew that doesn't get excited about what's happening.

You're one of the few cameramen in recent years to have shot a feature in black-and-white (Paper Moon). *Is it outmoded for theatrical use?*

I don't think so. I still strongly believe that there should be room for black-and-white. For commercial and theatrical reasons we lived through a period of time when black-and-white was looked down on. I always felt that if you really believed that film was a form of art, then black-and-white was one way of expressing your art.

People argue, "We see in color." But that doesn't justify that everything has to be in color. Black-and-white does create a certain kind of abstraction visually. If the subject matter is right, it helps you to create the dramatics of the story more effectively. Black-and-white should have a place in filmmaking. I couldn't visualize *Paper Moon* in color, especially the way it was shot. If it was done in color, it probably would have been shot quite differently.

Did you light Paper Moon *any differently than you would have if it had been a color film?*

No, even today I always light color like it was black-and-white for separation and creating depth. Color is more effective in doing that. Black-and-white is difficult because you have the grey tonalities from black to white and you have to create an image which includes depth and separation. In color a brown head will separate from a beige wall naturally but in black-and-white they may run together. You must create a lot of simple compositional elements in black-and-white. I always treat color as if it were black-and-white. You use your discretion; you never really ignore that you're working in color. Our problem in cinematography is really controlling colors. The lighting creates everything: the tones, images, texture and mood. It is so important that those elements are harmoniously put together in order to serve the visual impact. That's true in black-and-white also. I don't think color and black-and-white should be opposed to each other; I think they should be living side by side. Each one has its own value and merit.

What kind of filters or diffusion were you using on Paper Moon?

No diffusion but I did use colored filters to create a deep sky look. It really helped to bring that deep blue sky to almost black. That's the filtration I used and I had no diffusion. My philosophy about diffusion is changing. I like to see less and less glass and nets in front of the lens. You can create hardness or softness equally as well with the lighting. You can create a soft image without using a crutch in front of the lens; it depends on the quality of the lighting. Diffusion helps and it has its place. I'm not saying categorically that I'll never use it again; I will use it when I feel it is really required by the feel and the texture of the film. One of the first things young filmmakers want to know is, "What shall I put in front of the lens?" I tell them, "Forget it, that comes last. Don't use it as a crutch. Try to see the light and make distinctions between the qualities of light." If diffusion is used well, the audience will never even know it. Even I might not know in someone else's work if it gets me into the visual language of the film. Then I accept it. But most of the time it gets in the way of that.

What about the use of diffusion in photographing beautiful women? Did you use any diffusion for Liza Minelli in New York, New York?

That's a problem. Because if you elect to use diffusion on a woman, then gradually you have to use diffusion for the rest of the picture too. I used a very slight diffusion on *New York, New York* and I tried to use the softest possible quality of light on her close-ups. I did the same thing with the scene leading into it because, in post production, you never know when they are going to cut to the close-up. You don't want the close-up to stick out like a sore thumb as they did in those Doris Day pictures. If the scenes are not gradually diffused, it will end up looking like that.

Do you have any aspirations to direct?

Not really. I have been asked to direct specific projects. And it's really good for your ego. But you have to be very careful when you make a decision like that in your life. First of all, I love what I'm doing right now too much. I decided when I was eighteen that I wanted to be a cinematographer; it was like a dream for me and that dream came true. I enjoy every moment of it and I don't want to leave it. Secondly, and this is more of a sobering comment, if you want to be a director, you better be a damn good director. It's not good enough to direct traffic; anybody can direct traffic. There are a lot of traffic directors in this business. If I am going to be a director, I want to be one of the best; but I don't think I would be. So I really like what I'm doing and it's exciting for me. On a day-to-day basis, it's so exciting to work either for or with a director. It's such an exciting, creative process to go through his pain. Good directors go through a lot of pain, believe me, you don't just come in and say, "Roll it, boys." I see the pain of their creating and trying to get out of themselves whatever they want to express. It's like giving birth; it's not easy. The director has some very hard moments. So you try to help him and give him ideas and when one of those ideas works, you are very gratified. It gives you great satisfaction when you are able to contribute. I wouldn't give that up; I think that's too precious. Those are the wonderful moments.

9

Owen Roizman

"Style really comes from taste. If you try something and you don't like it, you better abandon it because otherwise you're going to find yourself in a rut that you'll never get out of. If you like it, then you just have to perfect it and make it work for you. You also have to be able to vary it and apply it to the material at hand."

Long considered one of the finest cinematographers working in New York City, Owen Roizman packed up and made his move to Hollywood in the late seventies. And while he was never at a loss for work before, he's now constantly in demand by producers who recognize his wide-ranging versatility.

Early in his career, Roizman gained a solid reputation for the documentary type of realism that he brought to two urban-street-life dramas, *The French Connection* and *The Taking of Pelham One Two Three.* His use of low light levels on real locations was a revelation to some of Hollywood's more conservative cinematographers; subsequently many of them moved in the same direction, avoiding the look of backlot studio sets.

For a time, producers thought to call Roizman only when they had a gritty street-life drama to shoot. But a cinematographer of the stature of Roizman is not committed to a specific style for its own sake. So, just to prove his greatest admirers and his worst critics both wrong, he showed them he was as versatile as any world-class cinematographer by shooting a studio comedy (*Play It Again, Sam*), a location comedy (*The Heartbreak Kid*), a special effects-laden studio drama (*The Exorcist*), and a western (*The Return of a Man Called Horse*).

With the large number of scripts coming his way, Roizman's priorities in choosing a project include the director, the script itself and the opportunity to do something visually. He achieves a great rapport with the people he chooses to work with, as evidenced by the fact that directors like Sydney Pollack, William Friedkin, Ulu Grosbard and Harold Becker rely on his taste and judgment in film after film. Now no one pigeonholes Roizman, except to place him high in the ranks of contemporary cinematographers.

1970	*Stop*	1976	*Network†*
1971	*The French Connection†*	1977	*Straight Time*
	The Gang That Couldn't	1978	*Sgt. Pepper's Lonely Hearts*
	Shoot Straight		*Club Band*
1972	*Play It Again, Sam*	1979	*The Electric Horseman*
	The Heartbreak Kid		*The Black Marble*
1973	*The Exorcist†*	1980	*True Confessions*
1974	*The Taking of Pelham*		*Absense of Malice*
	One Two Three	1981	*Taps*
1975	*The Stepford Wives*	1982	*Tootsie†*
	Three Days of the Condor	1983	*Visionquest*
	The Return of a Man Called		
	Horse		

†Academy Award Nominations for best achievement in cinematography.

You spent a number of years shooting television commercials. What did you learn from that, what did that give you that carried over to your work in features?

Well, you have to understand I started out in the business in TV commercials. My indoctrination in the film business was through commercials as an assistant cameraman, later as an operator and a first cameraman. Back East you do your own operating as a first cameraman so you get the experience of doing both at the same time. So I really learned my craft from commercials. My technique and everything I learned about lighting all came from working with commercial cameramen while I was an assistant and operator. Then I developed my own style once I was on my own. Working in commercials, I had a great opportunity to experiment and try different things. I learned a lot about special processes like blue screen, infrared, rear and front projection and other kinds of matte work because we were always doing trick things in commercials. I learned the use of every type of lens because you go to extremes in commercials. You use lots of long lenses and you use lots of wide-angle lenses. You go through phases where either one of those looks is the in thing. There have also been different fads for lighting styles. These have varied from very "hard" to very "soft," from theatrical to natural.

As a commercial cameraman, did you learn to work on low budgets?

The budgets are now a lot tighter. However, I don't notice any difference between working under the pressures of a commercial and working under the pressures of a feature film. Every producer is concerned about money. When they make a budget up, they want to stick to the budget if they can. There were a great many commercial directors who took advantage of them and went way over budget. And the same thing happens in features. There's really a great similarity between the two, the biggest difference being merely the amount of time spent on either one.

Are you freer to experiment in that context as opposed to feature work, where I guess there's really no time to?

It depends. I don't really draw any great distinction between the two in that respect because if I did, I think it would be taking unfair advantage of one or the other. I can't say I'm going to do a commercial and use it to experiment because that would be unfair to the people I was working for. Also they come to expect my work to be good; so if I go try something that doesn't work out, then it's not good for me either. On features, I'll gamble. I've found myself gambling a little less the last couple of years than I used to. When I first started, I would gamble with anything. But maybe that's because I didn't have all that much experience and what I thought was a gamble was really something that somebody else would know inside and out. Now that I know a lot more, it doesn't seem like a gamble anymore.

You have to stretch for your gambles.

Right. You have to look for something to gamble on. I like to experiment. And I would use a feature film to try out something new. There's no reason not to. If you don't try something new, you're not going to learn. You have to keep trying all the time. You have to look for new techniques. You have to gamble but what you're doing is you're gambling a lot with greater percentages because you have more experience each time. So it's not so much a gamble as it is just trying a different artistic approach to something. Whereas when you're inexperienced, it's a gamble.

We understand that you like to shoot everything wide open. Why do you do this? That seems different from what other cameramen do.

It's funny because I don't do it as much now as I used to. Because you have to make sure you have the right assistant cameraman if you're going to do that. The focus is so critical that if it is off by inches, you're going to have a different effect. It may not look out of focus but it's not going to be crisp. I like things to be crisp. At the same time, I like a shallow depth of field. That's why I shoot wide open. I like the focus to be on the subject that I'm trying to bring out. If there's an actor speaking in the scene and you want the audience to be riveted on him, that's what should be in focus. Anything else that may be in focus may be distracting. It also makes it easier, in many respects, to do nicer lighting. Because as soon as everything is crisp, then everything has definition, and everything has to be lit with a definition of some kind. If the background is out of focus, you can infer that it's there. You can make the audience feel it but they don't necessarily have to see it clearly and it doesn't have to be lit precisely. It can be a general kind of a mood that can be added to an area when it is out of focus. So that's why I have the tendency to want to work with a shallow depth of field. And I like lenses towards the longer end; from medium to long as opposed to wide-angle lenses. In wide angle you see everything. Now in commercials, I go just the opposite. I stop the lens down much more and often work with wider-angle lenses. Usually, in commercials, you want to see everything. Because anything you put in that little area on the TV, you want to show something. You want to see each element that's enhancing the product you're selling.

So you didn't shoot wide open to get a thinner negative or to reduce color saturation?

That has nothing to do with color saturation or a thinner negative. If you work wide open and, at wide open, you're underexposed two stops or a stop, then you're thinning out the negative and changing the color saturation. But if you are correctly exposed at wide open, it doesn't do anything but change the depth of field. The quality of the lenses also makes a difference. The spherical Panavision lenses are so crisp that you can shoot almost any of them wide open with virtually no problem. When you go to the anamorphic, high-speed Panavision lenses, they are really best in a contrast situation at night where you have strong contrast to aid in the focus. All of the high-speed Panavision lenses offer an extended range to work in. You can use them wide open at night without any extra lights at all, or you can use them stopped down under normal conditions during the day or in lighted interiors.

Have you incorporated the newer, fast lenses into your shooting style?

It's almost what I just touched on. When I shoot spherical pictures, all I get is the high-speed lenses and that's all I use. I'll generally shoot not totally wide open but at $f2$, which for some of them is almost wide. $F1.9$ is probably the slowest of the high-speed lenses. So to shoot at $f2$ is a good safe number to keep them all in the ballpark. Then you can go down to $f1.4$ or $f1.1$ if you have to if the situation dictates.

Some other cameramen have claimed that these lenses are too sharp, too good. The lenses don't give them the kind of look that they want and they have to break down the sharpness with diffusion devices. What do you think?

I think it's a matter of personal taste. But there is definitely a difference between those lenses and the old Cooke lenses. There's a softness that Cooke lenses have that Panavision lenses don't have. However, I would rather have a lens that can do anything and then have it be left up to me to get the look that I want. I would rather go with a Panavision lens any day and have it real crisp; then I could figure out a way to soften it if I so desired. If I had a Cooke lens and I wanted something really sharp and contrasty, I would have to take a totally different approach to try and make it work. It's pretty hard to add sharpness to something that's not there but it's easier to take it away.

I suppose, at one time, you used to force-develop everything as a matter of course. Now, in your last few pictures, you've stopped doing that. Why?

I was going to start *Three Days of the Condor* with Sydney Pollack. And we had some long talks about the look of the picture. He said, "I'd like to have New York look real and I'd like the picture to have a realistic look, but I don't want that dingy kind of realism. I want it to be 'pretty' real. I want to see good rich colors." He also added, "I hate forced developing; anything I've ever seen of forced developing looked terrible." I argued back that if you force-develop properly and expose properly, you really can't see the difference unless you run both prints side by side on matching projectors. But I said, "OK, I'll do the picture without forcing it and I'll learn something too." I forced all the night scenes in that picture and I didn't tell him about it. I finally told him after two or three nights of shooting when he said something like, "Look how good this looks." Or I think he said to me one night, "Can we put a zoom lens on the camera?" I said, "Sure." And he said, "Even if you have to force it, do it." I said, "What do you think I've been doing? I've been forcing all the night stuff." He was surprised but from what he had already seen of it, he had nothing to complain about. All the rest of the picture, we didn't force-develop. I got to like the look of it. I really did enjoy the little difference in quality I did start to feel. I felt it would bring a certain texture to the film; I felt that the blacks were richer. With forcing, in areas where you were off a little bit on the exposure, it didn't look so good. Now, without forcing, even if you're off on your exposure a little bit, it still looks good. If you're underexposed, you can print it up and it'll still look nice.

So I've got to liking it and the last few pictures I've done, I've not forced, except on certain occasions where I felt I needed a little extra exposure. I've even tested that and found that half the time I did it due to a little insecurity on my part. You feel you need a little bit more exposure so you go to forcing it rather than printing up. And you could probably get just as nice a picture by printing it up as long as you're not too far underexposed.

Why did you start forcing the film in the first place?

The first picture I forced was *The French Connection.* I had never really done any forced developing up until then because everything else I had done was commercials. I had done one other picture that was never released and it was a high-key, pretty picture that didn't call for anything like that. For *The French Connection,* I wanted a dingy look. I wanted to have a lot more latitude in available light situations. The fastest lens I had was $f2.3$. We were shooting very late into daylight and trying to match it with the middle of the afternoon. It was winter and the days were short. We were shooting in subway stations and various different locations. So I needed as much out of the film as I could get, using as little light as possible. I forced it all and I underexposed it all and then printed it up. So I used both techniques there. I liked it and I found that I shot some stuff that was overexposed and forced developed but when it was printed down to normal, it looked great. So I felt that if it looked good with that kind of processing, why should I shoot it normal? I started pushing everything with every picture and I was happy with the look.

You've worked in a lot of low-light-level situations like The French Connection *and* The Taking of Pelham One, Two, Three. *Is there any one situation you could pinpoint as the most difficult low-level lighting problem that you've run into?*

There was a scene I did in *Network* that was probably the most challenging as far as low-light situations are concerned. It was the scene between Bill Holden and Faye Dunaway in Holden's office at night. He's sitting behind his desk and she comes into the office and verbally seduces him and gets him to ask her out. We shot it in the MGM Building in New York. We were shooting out windows that were very dense (tinted) because of the sunlight during the day. In other words, the windows all have an added neutral density filter. There were office buildings in the background and we wanted to register the lights on the office buildings and still keep the room moody. We needed to keep a mood and still keep the light level low enough to see the people's faces *and* the background out the windows. Now that in itself is a problem. But the big problem was that the three walls we were looking at were all glass. There were the two outside windows which formed the corner of the office and then the inside partition to the rest of the offices was glass. And we were panning with Faye around the room. We had to take her from one side of the room all the way to the other side. And then, on top of that, we had to make Faye look good. Being a star and an actress, she always required a little extra special lighting.

I didn't want to force-develop the film. I had a look going for me on the film that was kind of clean and I was afraid to force it because I didn't want to dingy it up at all. We worked at twelve footcandles or something like that. We used 25-watt bulbs as key lights. We tried to hide them so you didn't see the reflections in the windows. It was difficult.

You just dropped these little lights in wherever you could sneak them in?

Yes, we'd hang them on the ceiling and then try to mask the reflection in the window. Hide them behind the desk and block the reflection from the window. Any light that you'd aim towards the wall, you'd see a reflection in the window. So you had to shade it off the window. But then you had to deal with practical ceilings; there really wasn't that much room. So it meant that each light had to be very carefully placed and each light had to do a specific job. You couldn't just bounce a light off the ceiling and say, "Okay, let's shoot."

Do you prefer working on location or on the sound stage?

I like them both. I like the control of a stage. I think I can get a more realistic look on the stage than I can on location. People go on location and they think they'll get the look of realism. But what they forget is, if you're going to go out and shoot one quick scene that's going to be done in one take, it doesn't make any difference what the light is. But if you're going to shoot a long scene with matching cuts, you have to control the light. You can't shoot with available light because it's going to change throughout the day. If the sun's out and the clouds roll in, it's going to change the whole quality of the light. So what you usually do is you overcome the light that's outside anyway; you make your own lighting. And once you make your own lighting, you might as well be on the stage because it's the same thing. Outdoors you have the constant problem of balancing to a background that's changing throughout the day, if you want to see out the windows. Once you balance for the outside, you have to use filters on the window to knock that down and then you can't bring any strong light sources through the window because you have to double the intensity of the light source to come through these heavy filters. And you're also trying to keep the color balance the same. It's horrendous. Whereas if you have a very good backdrop on a stage, you can make that look more realistic than the real thing. It's like the bedroom in *Straight Time*. I was really happy with that because it looked real to me. I kept the background bright and it was almost blown out but you could see detail in the buildings. Now the girl's room in the film was exactly the opposite. It was a location. We used available light but it was calculated. We happened to be there on a very clear day; we placed this huge white reflector outside the window and let the sun hit it. It bounced into the room and gave us the most beautiful soft light. It was a clear day and the sun looked pretty much like it would hold for the whole day and we just went with it. As the sun got a little bit weaker, I had to keep opening the exposure. The color temperature will change slightly also but that can be corrected as long as it's one light source.

What type of problems do you really hate to come up against generally? What one thing really bothers you?

I'd say the most difficult thing, at least difficult for most guys, is the "no light look." That's where you're shooting in a room that has absolutely no light source and yet you want to see everything. That's probably the most difficult situation one could run into. There's no particular situation where I say, "I hate to do this." That's because if it's different, I like the idea that it's challenging.

In a situation where you have no source light, what do you do? Do you create your own source?

You call in sick. Yes, you have to create your own source but you have to make it look like there's no source of light. You have to light and expose in such a way that you get the feeling that you're in a darkened room.

What film did you do that in?

In *The Exorcist* I had one scene like that. Most of the time what we do is create some kind of a source; like we'll assume that there's a street light outside. But if you're in a closet, that's something else. I haven't faced the problem that much. Somehow we always come up with a source. But I've seen pictures where obviously somebody was faced with that kind of situation, like shooting in a closet.

Realistically, if you can see in a room, then there's some light source in that room. The human eye really compensates quite a bit. To re-create what that effect is, is what's difficult. However, if there's any kind of light source, you just have to ask yourself, "What is this light source? Where is it coming from? What kind of effect does it have? How can I re-create it?"

Do you think there's a "New York style" of cinematography as opposed to Hollywood? I mean, from the perspective of Hollywood being the center of filmmaking and you were outside that center. Therefore you didn't get the feedback and interaction that cameramen in Hollywood got.

Filmmaking in New York is not really any different than it is here. The crews there are excellent; there's not as much depth but some of the guys are wonderful. But as far as filmmaking goes, it's done the same way. The directors are the same, the production department is the same. And you have the same pressures to get the job done. There was a tendency for New York cameramen to generally be kind of sloppy, I think. I don't mean it as an insult when I say sloppy; I mean sloppy in the sense that they didn't have to make everything super-pretty. They could go for realism and go for a natural look and people would accept it because they'd say, "Well, the guy's from New York." Whereas if a Hollywood cameraman did it, they'd say, "This guy doesn't know what he's doing."

For whatever reasons, the way of doing things and shooting evolved differently in New York. And Hollywood has borrowed from it extensively.

I think it came from commercials. In my case, one of the great influences on me when I started shooting was the lighting used by still photographers. It was an era where many of them were being brought in as "photographic consultants," as they were called, on certain jobs. And they were introducing still photography type lighting, which was bounce light, diffused overhead light, general soft light and a much more naturalistic look. It wasn't the typical old-fashioned studio lighting kind of look, what people referred to as "the Hollywood look." My style developed a lot from that. I found myself starting to try things and gamble; then once a style evolved it carried forth. They weren't doing as much of that in commercials in Hollywood. Then from that, another style developed which was an approach to making features using that type of lighting. You could hear all the feedback from the gaffers. Every time you'd work with a gaffer who was not familiar with soft light and you told him that you wanted to bounce the light, he'd look at you like you didn't know what you were doing.

The cameraman I worked with most of the time was working with direct light. So I didn't learn it from him. The directors I started working with liked bounce light. They'd bring in a photograph they liked and wanted to re-create that type of lighting. I'd get excited about it and try to figure out how to do it because it wasn't something I had been doing. I worked one day with a still photographer and I saw the way he wanted to light the room. I couldn't believe it and I thought it was going to look terrible. But when I saw the results, it was beautiful. So I started doing it. Then I found I didn't totally like that approach. So I threw in some variations. I changed, adjusted and experimented with it and developed something that worked for me.

Apparently it's very important where a cameraman's roots are. Because in the first four or five years of shooting, the basic style is developed. It changes and improves but basically the style forms at a certain point and it's all building on top of that from there.

And then it should just be improvement from there. Because style really comes from taste. If you try something and you don't like it, you better abandon it and go on to something else otherwise you're going to find yourself in a rut that you'll never get out of. If you like it, then you just have to perfect it and make it work for you. You also have to be able to vary it and apply it to the material at hand.

Since you shoot wide open a lot, you have to have a sharp crew. What type of relationship do you have with your crew? Do you have the same crew from picture to picture?

I wouldn't want to be my assistant. It's difficult sometimes. However, in the past, I've been very lucky; I've always had very good assistant cameramen. I try to keep a family-type relationship with my crew. I'm very close with them usually. I not only pick guys that I consider good but also people I get along with on a social level. Usually my assistant, my operator and I and our wives are very good friends. I like to keep my crew interested in the work. I don't like to be a dictator and say,

"Do this, do that." I'll take a suggestion from anybody. I like to give the crew creative freedom, my operator especially. I try to keep the interest up to the point where they come to dailies all the time. Because if they come to dailies every day, then that shows they're interested and they'll do better work. They'll watch their work, they'll watch my work and we'll all criticize one another. We'll all talk about it and I think it only makes for a healthier atmosphere on a film.

The scene in The French Connection *where Popeye grabs a guy in this bar and takes him back to the john to shake him down–I understand you lit that with just a photoflood. Now there are a lot of cameramen who wouldn't do that. Just because they're so used to lighting, they maybe would have made that scene and the light- ing of it more complicated than it had to be. Do you think that there's a tendency for cameramen to overlight a situation?*

I think there's a great tendency to do it. And I'm as guilty as anybody. I probably overlight more now than I used to. I used to think I underlit; now I think I overlight sometimes. I don't know if I'd light the scene the same today if I had to do it. I might. I have a feeling I would. I have a feeling that I'm going to lean towards that way of working again.

But again, it's a judgment that one has to make on the spot with regard for the material. My basic feeling and approach to lighting is probably the same as most cameramen. And that is: you should keep it as simple as possible, use as few lights as possible to get an effect. You really shouldn't use more lights than are absolutely necessary. If I can light something with one light, I'll always try to do it that way. Or if I can use no lights and just turn on existing lamps in the room—if it looks good, I'll do it that way.

We've noticed that many cameramen who were noted for using very little in the way of lighting have gotten away from that and now they shoot the same way Greg Toland shot, with the arcs and all the equipment. Several years ago when these cam- eramen had to go out with one equipment truck and shoot a whole feature, they did it and did a good job. Now they don't have to and they use as many lights as it takes.

When a producer and director hire you they usually expect the cinematographer to produce the best image that he can, using whatever equipment is necessary, within budgetary limits. The reason why those cinematographers worked the way they did is because those were low-budget pictures. Now that they have proven themselves and have done good work, they are asked to shoot bigger films. When a producer pays his stars a few million dollars to do a film, he expects them to look as good as they can, so he doesn't expect the cinematographer to try and save a few pennies on equipment if it means sacrificing any quality that will affect his picture. I sometimes find myself coming home at the end of the day and thinking that I could have done a particular scene a lot simpler. But maybe it's something in the subconscious that says, "They hired me to give them something special, so I better use a little extra." I know when I did *The French Connection*, I worked with spit. I mean, I used a lot of lights but not big lights. I still prefer to use mini-moles, inky-dinks and things like that. I sometimes hide them behind a table, a lamp or almost anyplace. On *The Exorcist*, that's what I used in the cold room. Inky-dinks were the biggest lights. I know if I was out here and I said to a gaffer, "Let's just put up some inky-dinks on the wall," they'd look at me funny. They'd want to put up juniors or seniors.

Right. It seems unconventional. Some cameramen have to throw up a lot more light than that. So probably your lighting seems unconventional to a lot of the older cameramen.

But pictures that I've done in Hollywood, I've used bigger lights. The last one I did in New York was *Network* and that was the smallest amount of lights I ever used. I literally used bulbs, 25-watt bulbs.

But lately we're seeing 20 to 40 million-dollar films where the cameraman has a big responsibility. I guess the films have really changed.

I don't know. I know that the cinematographer has lately been accused of becoming a superstar. I don't ever consider the cinematographer as a superstar. But I do consider any gain in prestige as one that is justified. Some of my peers have done some absolutely exquisite photography and they should be highly acclaimed. And many have been. They should get every bit of the recognition that's due them. And some of that recognition has now come in the form of accusations that they've become superstars. These guys are artists and they're doing good work. They're not superstars; they're conscientious artists. They just want to be treated as people of their responsibility and talent should be treated.

We've noticed that many times when things are going badly on a picture, the powers that be blame the cinematographer and fire him. Why is that?

I think that often it's a scapegoat type of thing. But I think you have to analyze the overall production and the people involved. If you have a strong, top-notch director, you're not going to have problems like that. Because, first of all, he knows who he's hiring and he's going to shoulder any responsibility for anything. If he feels that the cinematographer is slowing down his production, he's going to know it right away. The director is going to go to him up front and tell him he is unhappy and that he would like him to move faster. But that's something that can be determined very early on and a director should know it early on. There's no reason for it happening at all if you're dealing with a top director and a top cinematographer.

And conversely, the director will go to bat for you if you're having some particular difficulties with a situation.

Right. Also you have to understand that the decision on how much time you take has to be one of mutual agreement between the director and cinematographer. The director is the one who lays the guidelines down. If he says, "I want the quality of this picture to be spectacular," then it's usually going to take longer. If he's going to sacrifice and accept things that are less than perfect, then you can go faster. Working with Sidney Lumet, we finished *Network* two weeks ahead of schedule. Lumet said one day, "Let's face it, and most people won't admit it, but it's up to the director to set the pace of the picture." I agree with him. It's the director who sets the pace and he does it in two ways. One, in his demands for quality, and, two, his own preparation.

Knowing what he wants?

Right. Being prepared, knowing what he wants and being able to move quickly himself. And if he sets that pace himself, everybody is going to keep with him. Invariably where you run into problems is if you have a director who is inexperienced or incompetent—he will rely very heavily on the cinematographer to not only do his own work but the director's work also. Because if he didn't have somebody to lean on and get help from, he'd be floundering. Now that is going to slow the pace of the picture down unless they're both going to do just schlock work.

If I see that the director is sloughing off, the production manager isn't doing his job and the producer doesn't give a hoot, then it's very hard for me to push the whole thing along. Because you know what's going to happen: you're going to try to go fast and your work is going to suffer. And that's because you're trying to do more than your own job. But if the director is moving fast and doing a good job, you can keep with him and still do good work. When he's prepared, he can tell you ahead of time what's necessary and then you tell your crew what's necessary and you can all be prepared. But if you have somebody who doesn't know what they want until the day they walk in or until the moment of the shot, then there's no way for you to be fast and be ahead of him.

I understand that in a couple of scenes in The Exorcist *and* The French Connection *you used available fluorescent light. Using fluorescent light doesn't seem to bother you, while a lot of other cameramen shy away from it. How do you deal with fluorescent light?*

The first thing is that I've done a lot of experiments with fluorescent lights. None of the shooting I've done with fluorescent light has been accidental. I've shot many tests. There are five or six different types of bulbs made; each one puts out a different color. The trick, to me, is to never mix any other kind of light with fluorescent. Only use fluorescent with fluorescent.

What about daylight?

It depends on the bulb you use. For daylight, there's a special bulb that's made that you can mix with it and it'll give you perfect color temperature. You can also mix an HMI light with it. That's the way I shot most of the scenes in *Network* in the office buildings. So you don't really have to worry about daylight and fluorescents as long as you're using this particular bulb. Although you may run into a problem with it if you're going into a place with loads of fluorescents and daylight. Normal fluorescents in most buildings are called "cool white bulbs" and they have a green tint to them on film. So if you're mixing daylight with fluorescent, if you correct for the fluorescent then the daylight is going to go red. And if you correct for the daylight, the fluorescent will go green. You really can't mix the two. So you have a choice: you block out the daylight and go with the fluorescent alone or you have to change all the bulbs. Wherever I can I opt to change the bulbs. If it's too big a place or building, then you have to take a different approach. At night, there's a light you can use to mix with tungsten light. There's a bulb called a "warm light deluxe" and it's slightly greener and bluer than tungsten. If you mix the two directly, you can get away with it. If you really want to correct it properly, there's a combination of filters that I came up with that will perfectly correct it. To the eye, it looks green and horrible but on film it's a perfect match.

So then it's a matter of trying to mix those lights to what you're using.

If you're balancing with tungsten and fluorescents, then you'd use warm light deluxe. If you're shooting daylight and using fluorescents, then you'd use vita-lights. You can also use HMI lights. . . .

Why are the HMI units so advantageous?

HMI is a type of daylight-balanced light. It's a cool-burning light. It runs off a special ballast and it runs only on AC current. It's absolutely perfectly color-day-light-balanced. You can shoot indoors with them without the problems of the faces going red and the outside going green. It's a cool light, so it doesn't give off a lot of heat.

There's never been anything made, other than an arc light, that really matches daylight perfectly. They all have their problems but an HMI matches perfectly. They're really small for the amount of light they give out. A 4000-watt HMI light is almost as powerful as a brute.

Around the time of The French Connection, *you said that your theory about film, if you had one, was that you wanted to record a scene on film as it should look rather than you might want it to look.*

I think what that related to was going to look at a location. The reason why one picks a location is because of the way it appears by eye. If you walk into a bar at night and it's dimly lit, dingy and funky, and there's also something about it that you find appealing for the story that you're telling, then that location works for you. Now if you go into that location and, all of a sudden, start to light it up and change the characteristics of the place, you may change the whole look of the location, the whole mood of it. So if you can capture on film the way it appears to you in person, that's optimum. Now how you go about doing that, technically, is the challenge. In other words, if you go into a dimly lit bar at night and you turn all the lights on, all the lights that would be on during the day when the janitor is cleaning up, it proba-bly looks like a totally different place. In fact, it usually looks disgusting. You see all the details in the shadows, you see all the crap, you see what the furniture really looks like and it doesn't have any look at all. But in a dimly lit situation, it looks wonderful. That's what I want to capture on film. That's what appeals to me.

With the 5247 stock, do you have to use a lot of fill light? Or do you when you shoot at low light levels?

At low light levels, you usually don't have to add fill for anything. Usually what you see by eye is what you get on film. It's closer than at high light levels where you really have to judge what you're doing once you start getting up in exposure and pumping a lot of light in but still want it to look dark. The film never ceases to amaze me. It's really all in how you expose it. I have a tendency to overexpose film. It's a safe way of doing it but I also like the effect that you get. I like a rich negative. It used to be when I started shooting and when I was doing *The French Connection,* I liked a very thin negative. Now I like a very full negative; I find I have much more latitude. And if I want to desaturate, I can do it with filters rather than underexpose or things like that. If something requires underexposure, I guess I underexpose as much as anybody does. But I overexpose because I like the richness of it.

So you have the tendency to overexpose and print it down?

In general, I like film a little bit overexposed. I like to print on a little higher print lights. It gives both me and the lab more latitude. I don't have to be as critical with my exposures. I mean, it's fun to be critical and it's a great challenge to be very, very critical with exposures but there are so many variables in exposing film that it's impossible and very time-consuming if you try to take the time to make sure that every frame was exposed exactly right. You have to go for a general ballpark thing, give the lab a set of print lights and just judge to see if you're staying in the ballpark.

Do you go in for a really constant lighting ratio? Are you always watching your lighting ratio or do you more or less do it by eye?

I've almost never measured a lighting ratio.

That's one of the big things they teach you in film school.

I think it's a great basic to know because it gives you technical knowledge. It gives you a background to proceed from. Once you learn the rules, you can expand from that. But I go by eye as far as lighting is concerned. I'm very strict about working at a certain exposure or key light level throughout a picture. I'll determine that I want to work at thirty, forty or fifty footcandles in a picture and that's what I expose most scenes at. Or once I start a scene and the nature of the scene calls for me to expose it much greater, I'll make sure that each time I do a shot or an angle, I keep it consistent.

You keep your footcandles at a certain level and therefore you probably have an f-stop that's pretty consistent also?

Yes, generally I get into a pattern on an *f*-stop for a film and that's what I stick with. And usually that's determined by the slowest lens that I have—the widest opening for the slowest lens I have. That's so I can put on any lens at any time without relighting. If my slowest lens is *f*2.8, guess what I shoot the picture at? If my slowest lens is *f*2, I'll probably shoot the picture at *f*2. If I was working with a zoom lens, I'd be shooting at *f*3 or *f*4, whatever the stop was for that zoom lens. That's so I don't have to relight.

I can see where that would save a lot of time.

You can get stuck real easy. Say you start a shot with a *f*1.4 lens and, all of a sudden, the director wants to go to a long lens, then you have to relight the whole scene. That's no fun.

How do you approach the lighting of large locations such as the big Georgetown chapel in The Exorcist? *Do you have a particular approach in lighting that type of situation?*

No, lighting any big practical location really depends on the architecture and the location itself as far as the light sources that are there. If you have good light sources in there that you either augment or brighten, you may have to do very little. But the church in Georgetown required quite a bit of lighting. We had arcs on parallels and through the stained glass windows. It was some pretty involved lighting.

But you still maintained the look of the church—it was dim and had kind of a warm glow. Do you light a big area like that the same as you would a small one, just on a larger scale?

Yes and no. Because whenever you're dealing with a large location, you do have to think in terms of economics to a degree. You know, it would be wonderful to say, "Give me six cherry pickers with brutes on them outside each window." If you're going to ask for a lot of equipment, it should always be for a very good reason. Sometimes using large equipment can result in a time saving which would balance the cost. Whereas if you're shooting in a small room, you know you have all the equipment on the truck to deal with it. If it's going to hinder you by not getting what you want, you won't get the look. So you have to speak out up front and say, "This location is not going to work; we have to find something that's more practical." Or you say, "We can do it, but it's going to cost you a fortune." You have to be in a position to tell the production department that.

I always like to think small first. I always like to think of what I can get away with and then work my way up from there. If I can change the bulbs in a room and nothing else, I'm going to do it. But if that doesn't do anything, then I've got to think of what's the next step, what else will work.

In The Exorcist, *even from the beginning when we didn't know what was to come, there was an ominousness that pervaded the atmosphere. What did you do visually to help create that feeling?*

The theory we subscribed to was to go for realism in the picture. But we were going for a slightly enhanced realism, leaning towards the mysterious. In other words, the lighting I used throughout the picture was all bounce light; it was soft light. But where I might have normally used my lighting at eye level or from above, in this case, I used it very low. Now, you know it's a cliché that mystery lighting will come from underneath. But we didn't want to go for that; the kind of thing with shadows and lights up the nose. So just be lowering the light sources below the point of reality, we achieved an effect that added a little bit of mystery.

You were throwing the light a little off center of what you normally would?

Very often we'd light from straight overhead which is not necessarily normal, say, if you're in a room with lamps. It's not normal to have a light source overhead in that situation but it's also not ominous. But if you put the lights down very low, it starts to get a little more ominous. That was one way we did it. The other technique we used was slight camera movement. When the camera really shouldn't be moving we'd have it move in slowly or move to the side slowly. Things like that are something you don't realize; they're not obvious but they make the audience uneasy.

Also there's something in the looks of the performers' faces and in how they speak. There's a lot of subtleties in that picture; there's a lot of wonderful acting in it. There's a lot of nice subtleties in it that you notice when you see it the second or third time around that you missed because of the shock value the first time.

What about the special effects involved in that picture? Most of the special effects involved actual physical things that had to be photographed as opposed to something that was going to be done in the lab later.

Well, the only thing you can do with mechanical effects is shoot them in such a way that you don't see the mechanics. You have to make it work. The hardest shot was probably lighting the levitation because of the wires. You have to shoot it so the wires don't show. There's an old trick that I learned when I was doing commercials that I applied to this situation and it worked very well. And that was painting the wires in like a dotted line. Instead of just letting them be solid, one color or other, whenever they show up against a background, they're going to show the opposite tone. But if you paint them in a dot/dash fashion, light and dark, all the way up, then they'll disappear visually. And it worked pretty well. The only problem we had with it was that we had a solid color wall and we had a bright light effect on it. Part of the wall was very bright and part of it was dark. It made it a little more difficult to do. If we had a patterned wall there, it would have been perfect because you'd never see it.

So the most difficult effect in that bedroom was the levitation effect because of the wires?

No. The most difficult part of the effects was the breath. Showing the frost on the breath was the most difficult thing. And that's because we decided not to work with back light. The reason for that was because we were always looking up so many times. We didn't want to get too involved and have to constantly change lights. So what we had to do was have an electrician control a light, which was hidden behind an actor most of the time, and project it to catch his breath as it came out of his mouth but without hitting the actor's face.

By physically turning it?

Just masking if off mainly with a piece of card. And panning with the actor. The actors moved a lot so it was a matter of staying with them. We'd rehearse it, getting a feeling for it and do it. There's a lot of little, difficult, tricky things in that movie that people don't realize.

If memory serves me correctly, the only practical lighting you had in that bedroom were the two lamps on either side of the bed. And you had to simulate all the lighting from that; how did you do that?

Of course, every shot and every angle dictated a different approach. You couldn't make any particular lighting set-up work from one shot to another because sometimes you'd see the ceiling, sometimes you'd see three walls at once.

Did that set have wild walls?

Oh yes, it was totally wild. The whole set was on gimbals so it rocked and rotated. I just tried to maintain the source of light whenever possible. I would use many small lights. I'd hang inky-dinks off the side of the set; I'd hide them behind an end table where a priest was kneeling. I'd hide one between the table and the bed.

The Exorcist *went several times over budget. What kind of pressure does this put on a cameraman? How does it affect his work?*

Well, there's pressure on everything. There's always pressure to stay on schedule. It was obvious, going into that picture, that it was never going to be done on schedule. It seemed obvious to everybody but the studio. I know it was obvious to Billy. The attitude was one of "let's get it right" and that started from the top with Friedkin. It was a difficult story to tell so we had to make it effective otherwise it could be a big joke. We didn't grind it out. Billy wanted to make sure that every effect worked. And when you do that, it takes time.

The French Connection *really has an available-light look to it—the "let's go out in the streets and shoot it" look. But it's not really that way because you did do a lot of lighting. Can you explain what your approach was there?*

The lighting approach was to enhance or augment what struck us about the locations. It was a matter of finding a location that really felt right and then asking ourselves, "How do we capture that look?" I didn't have fast lenses then so I couldn't just go in and shoot available light; I had to build up the light level to a point where we could photograph it. Sometimes you can do that just by changing bulbs. Often what happens is that you can burn out light fixtures if you put in bright bulbs because most of the places we shot in didn't have enough electric capacity in the wiring. Each place naturally dictated a different approach. But the approach usually was to try and get the flavor of the place as we saw it and add whatever lights in whatever areas were necessary. I used mostly small lights; I mixed a combination of bounce lighting and direct lighting, whichever one worked best. I didn't stick to any particular format for the picture.

It was basically an enhancement process. You didn't want to pump a lot of lights into it and destroy the whole mood of what you saw?

Right. Now, on the other hand, in each picture and in each instance that I ever tried to do that, there are some locations that you go into and, even though you like it, you can make it look that much better if you do something a little different with the lighting. Maybe the lighting in the place makes the room look great but the faces don't look that interesting. So what you would do then is adjust the lighting for that and make the faces more interesting and try to still keep the same mood in the room. That's why I've always said many times before, "If the lighting looks good, I leave it alone. But if it doesn't, I'm going to change it to where it looks better." Or at least to where I think it looks better. And that's the approach I always take.

How concerned are you with skin tones? If you're shooting on a stage where you have more control, it's easier to deal with it. But if you're shooting in a situation like The French Connection, *where you have less control, it would seem to be more of a problem.*

To me, the thing I always go for is skin tone. To me, it's the most important thing you can go for because anything else in the shot can be a color but skin has to look like skin unless you're going for an effect. If you want someone to look like a ghost, then you want their skin to look blue. Or if the scene is supposedly in moonlight, their face can go on the blue side. If you're by firelight, the face can go a little on the warm side. But it's all relative skin tone and it's the skin tone that's the most important. When you have trouble with release prints in the matching from cut to cut, it's always the face that tips you off. It's either a face or a white wall; those are the two dead giveaways. Anything white or anything skin color would be a dead giveaway for a color mismatch. Almost anything else you can get away with—clothing or colored walls because they don't show up as much.

I'm very finicky technically. I'm very strict with myself and my crew technically. Because you have to have the technical aspects down pat before you can create something artistically. I like to make sure the lenses match colorwise because they very rarely do and you have to correct them. I like to know what's going on with the cameras, lights, lenses, etc. I know some people who don't do that and, on the other hand, I know a lot of people who are even stricter than I am.

I had not noticed inconsistent skin tones in any of your pictures. I was just curious if that was something that happened normally or if you put extra effort into that.

I think you have to make a conscious effort. I had a print that I was terribly unhappy about and the thing that bothered me most was that they let the skin go blue in the interiors. There was no reason for it. And the release print was made with blue skin tones in a couple of sequences. I was furious with the lab for not changing it. To me, that was a gross error and it was strictly the lab's fault.

That gets us into the subject of labs. Generally what should you expect out of a lab?

I expect two levels of performance from a laboratory. One is in the production stage and the other is in the finishing stage. In the production stage, all I require or hope to get from a lab is good communication on a day-to-day basis. I like to pick a set of print lights before a picture, through some tests, and say, "Let's stick with these print lights." Then I'll adjust to the print lights. If you're on a one-light print, it's a lot easier to make adjustments if you have all your technical things down pat. There's no reason why you can't keep your negative and your print quality on a pretty even level from day to day. I like to have everything printed on the same printer because printers vary. Even though labs will say that they don't, they do, in fact, vary. I like to be able to call up the contact man at the lab in the morning—well, first I like to call him at night after I finish the day's shooting and say, "Here's what I shot today." Then I describe the scene, the look I was going for and what I felt it should look like on film. Then the next morning I call and what I hope to get back from the contact man is, "It's just as you said," or "I think you're a little overexposed," or "something went a little too green in this scene."

The other level is the finishing stage or the answer print stage. They should really try to get it done the best possible way they can and the fastest they can. They should give you every benefit of the doubt, not argue and just do what you wish. They have a responsibility to not let that print go out unless it's right. What invariably happens is that they tell you, "There's not time. The producer needs the film in a week. That's not enough time to make an answer print; we'll do the best we can but that's it." Now while you're shooting a picture, if you say, "This shot doesn't match colorwise with this other shot," then the answer is, "Well, that's easily correctable. We'll fix that in the answer print." Right? Now you get to the answer print and you tell them now's the time to fix that color mismatch and they say, "We don't have time." Those are the frustrations that drive cinematographers clear up the wall. You've got to get those things straightened out up front. You have to make sure you have the time at the end to do it right.

I am fairly articulate with laboratories. I can tell them what I want. I can talk technically with them on any level: printers, timers, densities, etc.

Have you found that to be important?

I've found it helpful. Any time you communicate anything in this business on any level, you have to be as clear as you can be. Because if there's any room for personal translation, it'll come out different. It's going to be, "I thought you said," or "I assumed you wanted" and that's not the case. The whole key is being specific. And if you're specific, you should get the job done. If you still don't get the job done, then there's room for anger.

I have to mention the name of a man and I'm not doing this to compare him to other people. But there's a fellow by the name of Otto Paoloni who works for Technicolor in New York. He used to work for Deluxe Labs and he processed *The French Connection* and another picture for me. He's the most wonderful, most conscientious, most perfect example of what a laboratory man should be. He worries as much as the cinematographer does. Laboratory men could all take lessons from him. There are many other good ones, but Otto is the king.

Straight Time *was a really interesting film. It was shot in Los Angeles but it didn't look like TV shows that are shot here; I thought that was really a great achievement on your part. I wonder how you made L.A. look different than what we see on* Adam-12 *or* CHiPS.

Number one, we set out to make it not look like L.A. That was a preplanned thing. We wanted to shoot the areas of L.A. that have not been seen on TV all the time. Because it's difficult to shoot L.A.; every place you go, there are film crews working and many places have been see on TV. So those areas had to be carefully filmed. Once that was done, it was a matter of determining the look. I wanted it to look gutsy so I went for that look. I didn't want to make it look like *The French Connection*. I wanted it to be a step above that as far as the look because it was still supposed to be Los Angeles, the land of sunshine. But it was a matter of just capturing the right areas, shooting them at the right angle and showing what you wanted to show. It also involved the right wardrobe, the right colors down to the colors of the cars. Each element was chosen for color. We had a wonderful production designer on it, Steven Grimes, and he did a super job; he totally understood the look. He provided the elements to photograph and once you have the elements, I think it's rather easy. If you have to fight the elements, it's hard to achieve anything.

The film did have that seedy look. It's hard to make L.A. look seedy because of the sunshine. How did you overcome that?

We shot a lot on overcast days like today. We shot most of it in the spring, the time of year when you get that early morning cloudiness. But you try to choose the right light and you shoot in backlight. The filter pack that we picked for printing the picture was of such a color that it was not bright, beautiful or colorful. The interiors lent a lot to it. They lead the mind too. You shoot an interior under totally controllable circumstances and make it look seedy, then the outside appears to have been the same.

It's really a matter of choosing the colors you photograph; that's the first thing. Then there's exposure, lenses and so on. But it's basically choosing the palette. The palette has to be right.

Regarding the night exteriors on that film, did you shoot with available light or did you supplement them?

Hollywood Boulevard was available light with certain exceptions. When Dusty made a phone call from Hollywood Boulevard, I put a little red light on his hair to make it look like it was coming from a neon sign. But you could never tell; it looked like a glow and I thought it was a good touch. It filled out his face.

What about the scene in the motel parking lot?

That was all lit. I think that's one of the best lighting jobs I've ever done at night.

All the night-for-night sequences in the film were really impressive.

Yes, I thought that was some of my best work

There was all that depth in that scene and a great attention to detail. It really captured the mood.

We lit the motel room up, we lit the motel, we lit the car. It was a totally dark area. The available light that the motel had was nothing so we had to make it look that way. And that was an area where Dusty and I got into all kinds of arguments there about the lighting. In the end it was a compromise. He was right about a lot of things. I changed some of it. I had too many areas lit up when we started, not the faces, but the background. I had too many areas in the background lit up and he found it distracting. I looked at it and I killed some of the light.

True Confessions *was a period piece. How did you adapt your style to the period set in Los Angeles? Did you do anything special with filters, gels or lighting?*

I had a look in mind when I started the picture. I didn't want to do it as a cliché period picture. And when I say "cliché," I mean that it seems like every period picture is highly diffused and colored in a coral or sepia tone. I wanted to do something a little different than that. Also the director, Ulu Grosbard, wanted the picture to look like it just happened. He has a theory that if you make something look old, you're removing the audience from the reality of what's happening. I didn't agree with him totally on that. So I shot the film straight. I put nothing on the lens—just straight photography. The only thing I did was that I kept the lighting on the contrasty side. It was soft but contrasty. I tried to work with great black shadows. I didn't do it all the time because I don't necessarily feel that you have to carry an exact look throughout a whole picture. I feel that each room, each set and the time of day dictates its own lighting style. On a realistic level, I felt that later, if we desaturated the film and possibly flashed the print stock, I would get rid of that contrast or at least neutralize it. And if I like it, then we'd keep it. But we ended up releasing it exactly the way I shot it. Frankly, it came out so good that I was a little

shy about desaturating it because, from an ego standpoint, I hate to see it deteriorate my work. It had such a richness to it in the way we did it that to desaturate it
would somehow remove some of the quality from it.

Have you had any experience with the higher speed Kodak film stock 5293?

I shot *Tootsie* with 5293; it was the first picture entirely done with 5293. And I'm
doing *Visionquest* with the newer, refined film stock 5294.

Compared to the 5247 stock, what do you like better about the 5293?

Well one thing is that it's much faster and you need less light. The color in it is
not as rich as 5247; it's a softer color, a little more desaturated. It's not as contrasty
as 5247 so you have a lot more light in the shadows. It's great for shooting available
light situations in low key areas, especially at night.

It seems this film stock would fit right in with your philosophy of lighting.

Well, it depends. In the last five years I've changed a bit. I've gone more for a
brighter look and for a little more depth. I've been working at deeper stops lately.
And the film stock allows me to do that. On *Tootsie*, I shot everything around $f3.2$
or $f4$, where I used to shoot at $f1.4$ or $f1.8$. So actually I was using about the same
amount of light but the increased speed of the film let me stop down more instead
of cutting down on the amount of light I used.

That's the big advantage right there.

Getting more depth, sure. But it doesn't take opticals as well as 5247; it doesn't
lend itself to desaturation either because it's already desaturated. So I wouldn't do
that with this film unless, for example, I was doing a period picture and I wanted
that kind of look.

You've flashed film before; have you ever used lightflex?

No, I personally have no desire to use lightflex. I saw the demonstration reel and
not only wasn't impressed with it but I didn't even like the results. If you're shooting a big night exterior, they claim that you can open up the shadows a little bit by
using lightflex. But what it does is it adds a milkiness to the film and it adds a grain
structure that I found ugly. I like rich blacks and depth and this thing just flattens
everything out. But there are guys that swear by it. It's just like any other tool.

What about a tool like the Panacam?

No, I haven't been doing any video. Maybe it's Panavision's way of trying to get
into the video field. Sure, it offers you the opportunity to work the way you're
accustomed to but maybe that's not what's required. Maybe what's required is adjusting to a different way of working.

The feeling is that you can bring more of a film look to video.

That'll never happen anyway. The only way that will ever happen is when video
gets to the same resolution that film is. And when they can figure out how to
override the electronics so the electronics don't burn out highlights and things like
that. That's the big difference between film and video and the method of getting it
won't make any difference.

Are you familiar with Garrett Brown's Skycam?

It's fantastic. You can make shots over areas where you might have had to lay dolly track. The best way I can describe it is that you can make helicopter shots starting from the ground up in ways you could never use a helicopter. You can glide up over cars, objects and buildings and drop down on the other side. It's like combining a crane and a helicopter and a Steadicam together in one unit. It pans 360 degrees and tilts 180 degrees; it goes from ground level to as high as you set these wires that control it. So any place you can put these wires, the camera will be able to go. It's quite incredible.

Are there any other recent technological developments that have impressed you?

There is a new lab process that Technicolor does that is terrific. It's something that Storaro, Rotunno and a lab technician at Technicolor in Rome came up with. What it does is it desaturates color. In fact, it's exactly what I wanted to do on *True Confessions*. I did it on *Tootsie* on all the release prints. What you do is flash the print and then you redevelop the film in a black-and-white bath so that gives you back the blacks. So you end up with rich blacks but desaturated color. On *Tootsie*, I flashed the interpositive so instead of flashing all the prints, I only had to do one. Storaro is flashing each print; it gets flashed and then developed in that bath. That runs into some expense and is also time-consuming. On *Tootsie*, we were in a bind to get the picture out for release. But I felt that the release stock was so bad, so contrasty, that I wanted to do something with it. So we tried this which I don't think had been done before. We flashed the interpositive so that the flash was built into the release print and then they just develop each print in this extra bath. It's called ENR. It's a new process for desaturating. It smooths everything out when you're going into the dupes for release. The dupe stock is terrible, very contrasty, and you end up with a whole different-looking picture than you started out with.

You've worked with Sydney Pollack before; what was your stylistic approach on The Electric Horseman?

We were going for a very real look but "pretty" real. Sydney's basic theory, and the way he likes all his pictures to look, is not necessarily to go for the reality, because he would go for more of a theatrical look than I would. He likes reality but he likes a prettiness to the reality. He doesn't like things to look dingy and funky. So that's the approach we took for *The Electric Horseman*. We were just capturing the places we were in but always trying to keep them looking pleasant and a little above the dinginess of reality.

Did you do anything special as far as a filter pack or diffusion?

Basically not. I used nets a lot because the story and locations, along with Fonda and Redford, dictated that it needed to be enhanced slightly by something. In that case, I found that a light net was the most interesting method. It made it just a little bit prettier; it softened it just a little bit.

There was not quite that total sharpness of reality?

Well, there were many scenes that I shot totally sharp also. You can mix the two and I don't think anybody can tell the difference. In fact, I recall that from the time the picture starts until Fonda and Redford are out in the wilderness together, we kept more of a sharp and detailed quality to the picture. Then when the love story starts, we tried to get a little more lyrical with the photography. To do that we shot as much as possible in back light and I used the nets on a regular basis.

Does it occur sometimes that people go into a film with a preconception that they want a certain type of look and then they change their mind or they're not willing to give you the time to give them that look?

Very few people ever stick to what they say up front. You go into the picture and there's always the monumental meeting between the director and the director of photography. You sit down and you say, "What shall we do for a different look on this picture?" Then the first day on the set, the director says, "Okay, let's do this over here, put these people over here and why don't we shoot it with a wide lens." And you say to him, "Now wait a minute. That's not what we talked about." And he says, "Yeah, but I hate to throw away the background and it's so interesting this way." And suddenly your look is out the window. So the only way you can do it is if you get somebody that's really conscious about a look and cares very strongly about it. And frankly, I prefer not being that locked into something because if you are that means the director is not really paying attention to the performers and the story as much as he should. He's getting so involved with worrying about satisfying the look and satisfying the cinematographer, that he's losing control of getting a good story told.

When I did *Three Days of the Condor*, Sydney Pollack and I had long discussions about doing the film with all medium and long lenses. And the first shot, the very first day of the picture, he says, "Why don't we put on a 30mm lens?" which, of course in anamorphic, is a very wide lens. And I said, "A 30mm? What happened to all those discussions we had?" He said, "I have to show the set. Steve Grimes did such a beautiful job with the set, why don't we show it?" From there, I knew the tone of the picture was set and that was: do what was necessary for each shot. Which is really not a bad way to work. The only thing that I like to be real strict about and that I'll fight for is the palette. You can't be working in earth tones and then have somebody all of the sudden walk through the scene in a red vest. It's jarring visually and it's inconsistent.

Then you must work very closely with the set designer, the art director and the costumers?

Yes, as closely as I can. There are certain things I don't go for. I don't like bright whites and I drive wardrobe people crazy with that. I find white difficult to handle for the type of lighting I use. I'd rather have the palette right and then I can do the kind of lighting I want. I don't like bright, vivid colors either. But I may some day want to do a picture where I want people to be dressed in white, red, green, blue, yellows and all the colors that I would avoid normally. It depends on the nature of the story.

My favorite sequence in Network *is the scene in the long conference room with Finch and Beatty. It's got all those bluish-green lights along the wall that give it an eerie glow. Could you explain how you approached that scene? It had a really dramatic effect.*

We shot that in the New York Public Library and it was a room that was dressed as it is except for the lamps on the table; we added them. We could not rig any lights in there. I knew what was involved with the scene and I must have spent three different days just sitting in the room, in the corner by myself and looking at the room, trying to figure out what to do with it. I knew it was going to be difficult. We wanted to bring out all these wonderful tapestries, chandeliers and things that were in the room. So I tried to figure the simplest approach. The way we did that was we took those lamps and we put them on the table; I think I ended up using 25- or 40-watt bulbs in them so they didn't look too bright. I hung one light on the chandelier—that much they allowed us to do—that I used as a spotlight for Beatty. I used a couple of lights from the floor just reaching across to the tapestries and that was it. That was the only light I used; the rest of it was just available light. We had the sconces on all over the room. He turns down the lights and when he does that what he's left with is those sconce lights that were plenty bright, all those lamps and the spotlight on Beatty. And I had just one light on Finch. Then when Beatty walks down the length of the table, where he was against a totally black spot on the wall, I edge lit him and then when he went back against a light spot on the wall, I silhouetted him so you just feel him in the shadows. And when Beatty came into that position with Finch at the end, I had a light directly behind his head so that as he came into his position, we brought the light up to its full intensity in order to make his head glow. Then we had a little light off a white card bouncing into his face. It was kind of simple actually.

But as simple as you say it was, you spent three days before that thinking about how to shoot it?

To me, lighting is an engineering problem very often. With Lumet, for example, you know what you're going to shoot in advance, so you can think about it. It's not like going in and finding out that all of the sudden the director has turned the camera around and all the places you've engineered the lights to be are no good. Now you have to redo everything. That's a problem you run into a lot. But with Lumet, he says, "The angle's going to be here and it's going to be this way." And you know what you're going to have to face. It's wonderful to work that way.

How do you choose your projects now? Does it require a challenge, money, points? What turns you on to a project?

Well, a couple of things. One, I like to work with a director that I know and have worked with before or a director that I feel I would enjoy working with. Number two, I like to read a script and see if it's something that I really feel will be a good movie. It's always a difficult decision. I've been partly lucky and partly selective in what I've done up to now. I've had really good pictures to work on. I've made some mistakes in my choices and those mistakes usually came from letting personal things get involved with my choices. Personal reasons like home life and being in town rather than going on location. And sometimes I'm willing to make sacrifices like that because I like being around my family. But it's just a matter of getting good scripts. If it's a good script but a director I don't know anything about, I would meet with the director and let my instincts dictate whether or not I think I could work well with that person. So I really go for the script as the number one thing. Unless it's a director that I've worked with before, then I would usually accept the picture on the basis of the director without even seeing the script. I've done that with Sydney Pollack; I just like working with him.

When you say "good script," do you mean artistically, dramatically, commercially or what?

Well, I like to judge it on all three levels. If I think it's just going to be a great art film, I don't care much about that. I like to do something that's commercially successful also. I like to do something where I know the story line is good, the acting is going to be good and where there's a chance for me to do something visually. Most comedies I shy away from. Because I did a few early on in my career, and when I finished the last one I said, "That's it, I don't want to do any more comedies." And I haven't done one since and I'm happy about that.

That's interesting, we didn't even talk about any of your comedies.

Play It Again, Sam was one of my favorites. I think it was really a good picture. I'm not known as a comedy cameraman but I did three of them and I just find that you end up shooting it a little bit brighter and using more light.

There isn't much you can do.

It doesn't make that much difference even if you do. *Annie Hall* looked terrific but *Annie Hall* probably would have been just as funny even if it didn't look so terrific.

What films have you done that you're the happiest with and why?

Well, I don't really think that there's any that I've done that I can say I'm the happiest with. I can't really pick any one out. It's very difficult. I used to think *The Exorcist* was and *The French Connection* was, but seeing them again after many years, I don't know. There's something about each film that I like and there's probably things about each one that I don't like. I get really excited about some of the things I've done in some of the pictures and then there are other scenes that make me want to crawl under the seat when I see them.

Will you ever get to the point where everything in one film is perfect?

If I do, I think I'll retire. Because then all the challenge is gone. You know, I did another picture that we didn't mention here. It opened and closed real quickly and nobody really had a chance to see it. I'm talking about *The Black Marble*. I was very happy with my work on that and I also liked the picture. It was the first low-budget picture I'd worked on in a long time.

Were you aware of any budgetary restrictions that you normally wouldn't have to work under?

Only in the sense that I knew we had to get done a certain amount of work on a certain schedule. And that it just would require an all-out effort from everybody to get it done and get it done with as much quality as we could. I don't feel we sacrificed anything at all. In fact, we brought the picture in a day ahead of schedule. It was a very nice experience and I enjoyed it immensely. It was something that I would do again in a minute for the same people.

As far as the stylistic approach, Harold Becker, the director, and I decided on that. Joe Wambaugh had plenty of confidence in Harold from his work on *The Onion Field*. I'm sure he had confidence in me from my past work. So he never really bothered us when it came to the look of the picture. Harold and I decided what we would do with it.

What makes a cinematographer worth what he's paid?

That's a pretty ambiguous question. I mean some cinematographers get very little money and some get a lot.

But when we're talking about people on your level, we're talking about the top people in the business. So what in your contribution makes you worth as much as you get paid?

Next to the director, on a responsibility basis, I think the cinematographer has the greatest amount of responsibility. There's a great deal of skill involved in making sure that scenes match from shot to shot within the scene, that scenes flow together in the picture. There is definitely a flow to a film that must be maintained by a cinematographer. There is great technical knowledge required as far as dealing with a lot of elements that one may run into, for example, photographing video screens or using rear screen projection. I feel what determines your salary is a combination of experience, of knowing how to handle all these things so that the producer can have a fairly safe bet that he's not going to have any reshoots because of the cinematographer's errors. All errors aside, the producer should feel that when the picture is done, it's going to be representative of high quality. And the quality of the look on the screen is something that is felt by an audience. The general audience does not know, really, the difference between good lighting and bad lighting or good composition and bad composition. But it's a psychological subconscious feeling that's transmitted to them by the cinematography. And if it's not very good, the audience walks out feeling that it was average. If there's something really special about it, they can feel it. They may not know what it is, but they can feel it. And I feel it enhances the film. I know that I charge what I charge based on what I think I can do or what I can contribute picture after picture, on a quality basis.

If you were just starting out in the film business today, especially in the field of cinematography, how would you go about it? How would you advise a student?

That's a tough one. I really don't even know where I'd begin. It's an industry that seems to have more and more filmmakers than ever before. There are more film students; they're more intelligent and more alert. They've learned more at a younger age. They're more ready now, at a younger age, than we were. And the competition is probably fierce out there. I really don't know what I would do. As a guess, I would try to make contact with a cinematographer, somebody whose work I admired. And just see if you could get permission to go watch him work day in and day out. Just sit and observe and try to learn as much as possible. As far as earning a living goes, I wouldn't know where to begin.

10

Vittorio Storaro

*"There is no question that any moment you make a
design, shoot a picture or photograph a movie, it is a
representation of all two thousand years of history,
whether you are conscious of it or not."*

Born in 1940, Vittorio Storaro, the son of a motion picture projectionist, was encouraged by his father to formally study photography at the age of eleven. At eighteen he
was one of the youngest students admitted to the Centro Sperimentale di Cinemato-
grafia (the Italian national film school). And at twenty-one, he was already working
as an assistant cameraman. To be a cinematographer, to "write with light," as he
terms it, is something Storaro has been preparing for his entire life.

Storaro is one of the cinematographers most respected among his peers. This is
primarily due to the intensity, passion and love Storaro invests in his work. Somehow, through the magic of chemicals and celluloid, these qualities get transmitted
to the screen. At the age of thirty, when most cinematographers are still maturing
and learning their craft through the apprentice route, Storaro was shooting Bertolucci's *The Conformist*, a film that is a unified masterwork of style, form and sub-
stance. His continued collaboration with Bertolucci produced some of the most
intriguing films of the seventies, including *Last Tango in Paris*, *1900* and *Luna*. But
widespread international recognition of his talents did not come until Coppola's
Apocalypse Now was finally released, for which Storaro won a well-deserved
Oscar in 1979. In this project, probably the most physically and emotionally gruel-
ling experience of his career, he nevertheless achieved and maintained a visual
look and style that was entirely appropriate to the mood of the story.

His most recent films, *Reds* (another Oscar) and *One from the Heart*, indicate
the wide-ranging palette his creativity and imagination encompass. *Reds* is a sol-
idly mounted dramatic, epic-scale picture, that is indicative of traditional Hollywood filmmaking at its best. *One from the Heart*, on the other hand, is a cream puff
of a whimsical romance, almost a fantasy, accentuated by his unconventional and
highly color-coded lighting. His camera is always moving in a way that can only be
described as hypnotic.

These are two very different films—each in its own way superbly realized by a
man with a specific, creative vision. Storaro is only forty-four now and is already
working at a level that many cameramen never achieve in an entire lifetime.

1968	Youthful, Youthful		Giordano Bruno
1969	Crime at the Tennis Club		Identikit
	The Spider's Stratagem	1974	Footprints
	The Bird with the Crystal Plumage	1975	1900
1970	The Conformist		Scandal
	Adventure of Enea	1976/	Apocalypse Now*
1971	'Tis Pity She's a Whore	77	
	Bad Day for the Aries	1978	Agatha
	Body of Love		Luna
1972	Adventure of Orlando	1979/	Reds*
	Last Tango in Paris	80	
	Bleu Gang	1981	One from the Heart
1973	Malice	1982	Wagner
		1983	Ladyhawke

*Academy Award for best achievement in cinematography.

How and why did you first become interested in cinematography?
Well, the decision wasn't mine. I was pushed by my father to study photography.
And what did you father do?
My father was a projectionist for a big company in Italy. I discovered later on that photography allowed me to express myself. Today I can honestly say that I don't see myself doing anything else but trying to express myself through light in cinematography.

So that's where everything started. My father tried to encourage me into the kind of school that was teaching photography. And at fourteen years old, you don't really know.
Did he have some inkling that you were talented in this area?
No, I believe he was thinking about himself. It was something that he himself thought he might do but never did. So he pushed one of his sons into it as a continuation of himself. I'm glad for that because, in the last several years, I've really discovered something about myself.

Photography, for me, really means writing with light.
Painting with light?
No, not really. For me, it's writing with light in the sense that I'm trying to express something that is inside of me. With my sensibility, my structure, my cultural background, I'm trying to express what I really am. I am trying to describe the story of the film through the light. I try to have a parallel story to the actual story so

that through light and color you can feel and understand, consciously and unconsciously, much more clearly what the story is about. For several years I thought that the light and only the light was the main thing. I was really concerned with the fact that I was using elements that came between myself, my use of the light, and the audience. I'm talking about different lenses, different cameras, different film stock, different developing, different printing, and different screenings. These things were a kind of obstacle to really expressing myself clearly. These things got in the way of what I was trying to say in a story to an audience.

So I had a very interesting experience in the theater with director Luca Ronconi. He asked me if I would do some work with him in the theater. So I stopped working in the cinema for one season and worked in the theater. You know, in the cinema sometimes you build a kind of light in interiors and, according to what kind of things are done in filtering, that tonality, that color and that brightness will be changed later on. I really would like to show an audience exactly what I am doing. This was one of the main considerations for working in the theater. Plus I wanted to know why, in theater, the story of light had not changed for a long time. It was rare to find an opera interior lit in a new way.

I did *Kathchen Von Heilbronn* by Kleist and *Oreste* by Euripides. And what I discovered through them was that my total expression wasn't just with light. The light was the main thing; it was the start. The lenses, the camera, the negative stock, the positive stock—any single element that would affect the final positive image—that's what my expression was about. When I discovered that, I really understood cinematography.

So this experience in the theater really helped you?

Yes, you know, we are talking about light. Light itself is energy. So it is very difficult to transmit your feeling in pure energy. You have to translate it into something. This energy is being stopped by an object or the human figure and being registered on film through a kind of glass and then it's developed and printed. It's like the paper and pen for a writer or a canvas for a painter. These kind of elements are not something that is going to be an obstacle to my expression and what I want to say. It is really the brush, the pen of artistic expression. That was something important I discovered about myself.

You had also studied a great deal and did a number of short films while you were working your way up to first cameraman.

Yes, I had studied photography and cinematography for nine years. After that I right away became the youngest first assistant cameraman and camera operator. Then for a few years I was a camera operator. Then there was a big film crisis in Italy and I stopped working for a couple of years.

That was 1963–64. There was a production lull and a financial crisis within the industry?

Yes, production started shutting down. The cinematographer I was working with was not working anymore. That lull gave me a chance to research and study, on my own, anything that I didn't develop during my student period. Particularly because at that stage you are learning because you have to learn. Your knowledge is limited to

names and dates and things that you have to learn. Mainly you gain technical knowledge. So I used this slack period as a kind of development and formation of my
cultural background. That gave me concepts of how to use all the technical knowledge that I had before. And this was one of the most important moments in my life.
Like everybody, I don't think you just start at point A and go straight to point B. You
always go up and down in the way the energy is moving. So the more you go down
and escape into your roots and your background, the further you can climb up the hill
afterwards. There will be important moments and I have had these moments
throughout my life. There is a moment after I have done something very important,
something that I think was an incredible expenditure of energy, when I really have to
stop and recharge my battery. Or go back and study some more or do a movie that is
totally opposite than what I've done. I try to get involved in an involution to myself to
create new energy. Even the idea of starting from the beginning again is very important in our lives. After this stage, I started working again as an assistant cameraman
and I met Bertolucci on *Before the Revolution*. And after that meeting, he called me
back again and that started a totally new era for me. So if I had never had this crisis, if
I was never able to start from the beginning again, I would not have been able to have
this evolution later on with him.

In his early years, Connie Hall worked with Ted McCord. And Connie said that
every time Ted started a new film, he came onto the set as if he'd never shot a film
before.

I think that this is one of the most important feelings that we should have. I
remember every first screening of every picture I've ever done. I remember my first
picture specifically. The moment that the screen is going to be lit by an image,
there is an incredible emotion in my heart. You can see an image moving and the
magic thing is happening again. At that moment it doesn't matter which kind of
image it is; just the fact that you can see an image is something very magical. It is
really painful until this moment; until the light going through the positive stock
breaks the obscurity of the room and you can see an image. Afterwards you can
analyze and discuss whether it's good, bad, or whatever. But that moment is a
wonderful moment.

I must say that on the first few days of each new picture, I am so frightened.
Because each time I'm trying to take a step forward. I try to have the strength and
energy to do it because otherwise you just get bored doing the same things all the
time. The first days of a new film create an incredible pain and suffering until you
establish what you want to do. Once it's clear and you see it on the screen, you go
forward. And you never stop. Day by day, you must concentrate intensely on what
you are doing because otherwise you will become distracted. As soon as I read the
script and I speak with the main auteur of the film, the director, and I have the first
direction about where the movie should be going, I try to find a way to understand
how to conceptualize an image, from the photographic point of view, of the story
itself. I try to find what is the main idea and how it can be represented in a symbolic, emotional, psychological, realistic and physical way. That's my approach.

That's your role as a cinematographer?

Yes. And if I don't find that first, I don't think I can do the picture. Because I wouldn't know what I was doing. After I find this kind of specific direction, I contrapropose to the director what I think can be done in the photographic area. If we agree, this will be my way, my structure. It's very clear from the beginning. Of course, as there is an evolution of things around us, each movie can change with us day by day. So this main plan or structure is very important because it will lead you through anything you think can attract you. Sometimes you see something that can be more beautiful than what you want to do or say. But it would be wrong because it would be something that would distract you from the main idea. So you should be very strong in selecting only that kind of light, that kind of tonality, that kind of feeling and that kind of color that you think is right for that story. When you are writing a book, each chapter of the book is not as important as the book itself; but if each page doesn't help your understanding of the following page, then that page didn't contribute to the whole.

You're talking about a unity?

I am talking about the unity of the work itself. So from the moment that you have this idea, this intuition of what you can do with the movie, you try to make it clear so you can talk about it. Sometimes you can have an idea but it is difficult to express. That's why, in the last few pictures, I've tried writing out these ideas. I do this to make my ideas very clear. Because after you work your ideas out, you have to be very concrete with the director, the production designer, the costume designer, etc. Everyone needs to be going in the same direction. And from that time, moment by moment, day by day, during the realization of the film itself until the answer print, it is all one arc. You never stop. You always can add, you always can continue until you have the answer print. Only at that moment can you say, "I've done it. It's there; it's on the screen." Through the lab, you can use a technique to reveal an image or to represent an image, from negative to positive, in a particular way that you need for this particular picture. I do not usually do two pictures the same way at the lab. Each one is different. But there are some basic things I do, which is part of myself, part of my expression that you can recognize in all my movies. And that's just the particular kind of person I am, just like any other person trying to express themselves through something.

My first picture in 1968 was an incredible moment in my life. It was like my first love. It was the first time I had the chance to express myself in a complete "opera." I had previously done some short films, but a feature allows you to be more solid, complete and specific. I was trying to be present every single moment of every single day. I told myself, "Vittorio, be careful, because this moment will never come back again. You will do hundreds of pictures that will be bigger, smaller, better or worse but this particular time in your life will never come back again." After your first film, you can add and develop certain things but it will never be like the first time. I remember that two days before the end of my first film, I was crying like a baby. A friend of mine didn't understand and wanted to know what was going on. And I told him what I was thinking: that it was a beautiful moment in my life. I was going to lose something very, very important; that is, the innocence to do something for the first time.

Everything I have done since then, like *Spider's Stratagem, The Conformist, Last Tango in Paris, 1900,* and *Apocalypse Now,* is sort of a branch of things that were born on my first picture. I just went on to develop this main idea. I think my first film is like an imprint.

Everything is there in that first expression?

Everything. It is like my fingerprint. After my first film, I just took any single element that was there and tried to evolve it. I tried to make it clearer, bigger, more evident. It evolved especially in the translation of black and white and color. Because the dialectic of the conflict between artificial energy and natural energy was always one of my concepts. The conflict between day and night, shadows and light, white and black, technology and energy; these are things that you can always recognize in myself and my work. The dialectic between two different things, two different poles are in conflict only because they are separated. And the moment the two poles are reunited, there will be balance. It will be the most beautiful thing that can happen.

In fact, you may have noticed one of my symbols that I used in *Spider's Stratagem, The Conformist,* and *Last Tango in Paris.* Any lamp that I was using in those pictures was round; it was a globe. It is the image of two half things put together. Any circle has always been my symbol. I think I developed this kind of area, between these two energies, from my first picture up to *Apocalypse Now.* With *Apocalypse Now,* I wanted to express the main idea of Joseph Conrad (*Heart of Darkness*) which is the imposition of one culture on top of another culture. I was trying to express the conflict between natural energy and artificial energy. After I had done such a huge "opera" as *Apocalypse Now,* I felt I was going to close the first chapter in my life. It was very hard for me to start again after that because nothing was able to give me an idea or enough energy to start something new. So I stopped one more time in my life and I tried to escape into my past. I escaped into all my books and any knowledge that I had before in school. I did research into what "color" really meant for me. I researched all the meanings of color, all the theories of color. I wrote about my research and this turned out to be a very important moment in my life again. It was beautiful to go back as a student, it was beautiful to go back into myself and it was beautiful to know where I was at that moment. Because before that I didn't know where I was. I knew where I had been but I didn't know what was in front of me or which direction I should be going in. That research on color once again gave me the strength to continue in a specific direction. *Luna* was the first movie I did in this new chapter of my life, using mainly the symbolism of color. Luna is the symbol of the mother in psychoanalysis; so when I understood that, I tried to use the symbol of the color of the character to express the character itself. Concerning the light, I tried to surround the character in a kind of way to give it depth. I tried to give thickness to the characters; I tried to build the volume of them up; I tried to give them such a presence that you could touch them physically on the screen. I'm not talking about having three dimensions, I'm talking about giving volume, about something that is more a personality presence. But mainly I wanted to develop the symbol of the color in *Luna*.

What do you mean by "the symbol"?

In psychoanalysis, every color represents something specific in an emotional sense. It's not something that I made up; it's something that scientists and researchers have studied. In other words, if you dream something in yellow and red, that has a specific meaning because of the colors involved. So I used this kind of theory of the symbol of color to represent the emotion of the characters in *Luna*. The second application of this is in *One from the Heart*. In that film, I was concerned with the physiology of the color. That is, in what ways the human body reacts to color. Now the human body has been exposed to light and color for thousands of years. And since the beginning of time, the body reacts one way: you expose the body to light (or yellow), you get activity, you need to work. Each time you expose the body to darkness (or blue), you need to rest. Since the beginning, the human body has made this kind of journey into night and day. Today scientists have proven that your body changes in the presence of a particular color. Your body reacts differently to different colors. You become more active or more relaxed or more depressed. Even your blood pressure may change. So in *One from the Heart* I tried to establish the emotion of the character through the emotion of the color.

How did you train yourself or become able to think in these unique terms?

For example, when Francis Coppola talked to me about *One from the Heart*, he told me the story which was very simple and realistic. It was set in Las Vegas. So we went to Las Vegas and I was astonished with the way Las Vegas was built. Las Vegas has such an incredible amount of light and the reason it does is to regenerate your energy or your body. We were talking about this exact thing before: how your body reacts to light and dark. In Las Vegas, you never have to feel it is night or late.

The lights basically replace the sun.

Exactly. Being inside the hotel or casino you don't see the sun outside so you want to go for a walk or have some fresh air. But you see that each window has been painted blue so you feel that there is no sun outside and you want to stay inside and gamble. They were using these color principles to have a particular unconscious stimulus to the human body. Having the story set in Las Vegas and being based on the passion and emotion of people, I had the idea to use the physiology of the color itself to establish the mood of the film.

I remember that I didn't know why Bernardo Bertolucci titled his film *Luna*. But suddenly it hit me that Luna means mother. And that was the key. So I tried to represent, in color and light, the story through the symbol of color. When I read Conrad's *Heart of Darkness*, in preparation for *Apocalypse Now*, I asked myself what the book was about. The main concept was about one culture on top of another culture; it was a conflict between two different cultures. I asked myself how I could represent that. I felt it was the difference between natural energy and technological (artificial) energy. That's where I started from. On *The Conformist*, the period that it was set in was a very claustrophobic period. It was a time of dictatorship. One of the ideas we had for *The Conformist* was to use a location for every single interior. And outside the window, we would never show the reality. Because at that historical time the promises were very great but their fulfillment in reality was very little. So, outside the window, we have something phony, something unreal, something painted. In fact, the sequence on the train was done with rear projection. We wanted to show the kind of conflict between the stated reality and the real reality. I wanted to show through light the idea of claustrophobia, of being caged. I used the idea that the light could never reach the shadows. So that there was a distinct separation between the shadows and the light. That's why I was using the kind of technique to give very sharp shadows and very sharp light in the first half of the picture. Now when they were going to Paris—Paris for us was a free nation; it was where everybody was going to escape from the dictatorship—I expressed this sense of freedom by letting the light go into the shadows. I completely changed the style of the light and I gave the audience colors that they hadn't seen in the film before. *The Conformist* is almost a black-and-white picture in the beginning. But in the last half in Paris, you see differently. You see the light going into the shadows. It's like two sections that are united once more.

All the night sequences of *The Conformist* are blue. At that time I didn't know specifically why I chose blue; I just felt that I should. Later on, I understood the kind of symbol blue intellectually is. When we were talking about *Last Tango in Paris*, I went to Paris for the first time in the winter and I saw the lights of the town all on. The natural light was so low that the town was used to having all the artificial light on. The conflict between these two energies (natural and artificial) gave me the different wavelength or vibration, the different grade of Kelvin that can be represented, the different color that you can take. So I was starting to understand how it can be important to represent the story in this kind of town. I used the color of orange. Once again it was the different wavelength or energy that gave me the idea; the high level of that wavelength was giving me the impression that it was about passion. We started to paint that empty apartment orange; we started to use the winter sun, which was very low, during the daytime. The light of the sun gave us very warm tones. And the color of the artificial light next to the daylight suggested this color too. It (orange) was the color of the passion, of the emotion. So that's how the idea for *Last Tango in Paris* came about.

On *Spider's Stratagem*, the main idea for the approach to the film was suggested by the story itself. It was something that didn't exist but we wanted to represent it as a real story. So the idea was to show this little country as an enormous stage because the story is set in a little town. The kind of color we were using was very strong and very pure. It was the first film I did with Bertolucci. On that film, it was an incredible moment to come out of a big city like Milan or Rome and, for the first time, go out into the country. In town, the smoke and fog act as a kind of filter so that you really don't see the true color of things. You don't really see the red of the sunset, the blue of the water or the green of the field. So it was an incredible and impressive emotional experience to see, in the clear air, the pure color of nature. It was incredible to hear without the filtering of the city noise. You know, when you constantly hear the noise of the car, of the air conditioner and of the TV, you lose the ability to really hear. But if you take away that noise level, suddenly you hear the leaves fall, the wind move through the trees. And that was a very important discovery. The look of *Spider's Strategem* came from this kind of experience.

As a generation of cinematographers, we represent all the cinematographers that have gone before us. We are at the present moment because of all the work that has been done up to now. Without them, we couldn't be here today. There's no question about that. But even before that, there is a whole history of painting. Since the first graffiti was scratched on the walls of the caves, since the first Egyptian drawings, since Piero della Francesca, we have had ways to express emotional stories and emotional figures in a particular style. There is no question that when you make a design, shoot a picture or photograph a movie, it is the representation of all two thousand years of history, whether you are conscious of it or not. So I think we should be conscious of what has been done before. And I think it would be wrong to take a painter and ask him to paint in a certain style from the past. It would be wrong to ask a cinematographer to photograph a film in the same style as another picture because you can never do that. And the reason is that the same elements, the same history does not exist in the same way as it did previously. But you can have reference to past work in order to be more clear with yourself about where you want to go and what you want to do.

It exists purely as a reference point?

Having a reference allows you to decide that you want to move into this direction rather than that direction. So that the knowledge of culture, history and your own experience is very important. At this moment, it is not only painting that is important but the theater and even our conversation right now. The kind of shadows that your papers are making on this table right now is a background for me. It's something that may be affecting my mind; I don't know how, why, or when but it's something that will come back to me.

What you're saying is that there is a lot of unconscious expression in your work?

Not only in my work, but in everybody's work.

Yes, but some people won't admit that.

Because it's unconscious. Otherwise it would be conscious. You realize it's unconscious because you can't explain it or you don't know where it came from. I mean, why suddenly do I have an idea and then turn off this light rather than the other one? In making that decision, there are so many millions of elements that push me to make that choice. You may choose green instead of red, black instead of white.

But maybe sometimes you don't know why? But you look at it and you know it's right for you.

Maybe sometimes you don't know. But you know that this is what you want, that this is what you feel. You know that this is what you want to achieve. Some time later you may discover why. Honestly, I didn't know why I did all Paris in blue tones for *The Conformist* and then two years later I did it in orange for *Last Tango in Paris*. At the time, it was the feeling I got through these kind of wavelengths and through these kinds of color. Eight years later I discovered what these colors represent and so maybe I know why I made the choices I did. At the time, it was something emotional and something that I felt.

It's something that you can't explain rationally.

Sometimes you really can't explain it. It arrives to you by intuition and you do it. It may be difficult to talk about, especially if you are in a creative state. I gave you these two pages to read about my concept for *One from the Heart* because I'm finished with the shooting. We have some retakes but I am basically finished. Ninety-nine percent of what I was doing is there. So it is easy to talk about now. When you are in the creative moment, it is very hard to talk about it. If you already have in your bones everything that you are going to say, it means that you are already done. Only if you know what can be done and which, in your opinion, is the right way to do it, then day by day, step by step and moment by moment, you do it. You have the realization of the thought that you had. Afterwards, you understand that you are right or that they can even be pushed and developed further or that they can be realized exactly the way you thought. Afterwards you can talk about it. Before, it is only an intuition; you don't know if it works or not, you don't know if it can be done or not. You know rationally, being a professional, what your odds are; it can be ten percent or ninety percent. But it can never be one hundred percent. If you produce an image and you want to do it over again exactly as you did it the first time, it is impossible because it will never come back again in the same way. Never.

But do you really know what you've done until you finally see it, until it's finally projected? Right now, you say you're finished with One from the Heart *and you know what you've done. But do you really?*

I can really say that it's ninety-nine percent done. This is a function of how confident you are of your technical knowledge, how much experience you have in this field and how much concentration you have at the time you produced that image. I think I know enough that from the moment I think an image to the time I realize that image, I know how it will look on the screen. And I think I know how I can put it on the screen. There is no question that percentages will be involved; sometimes there is one percent and sometimes there is ninety percent that is new. These are things that you didn't expect. It's something that maybe you felt inside yourself but you couldn't describe what it was. I never believe anyone when they tell me, "I knew it was exactly like that." It can be in the same direction and it can be like the same thing but it can never be exactly like it. Never. Technology changes and comes between your thought and the screen. And in technology, you have choices. Some items are variables. For example, the standard of the lab changes each day. The tolerance changes each day, the structure of the emulsion changes each day and the screening changes according to each theater. The light, the bulb itself, is changing every single moment because every moment that it is sending out energy, it is not being replaced in time. Day by day, you have a different image. I feel that the emotion of the people who are going to create and build an image will change the image itself. The film is so sensitive that it can register the emotion of the people present. When you see a movie, you can feel if it was done with joy, anger, or passion. And if you change one element of the crew, the movie will be changed. The collective emotion will be different. Because each one of us, whether we have a very small job or a very big one, makes decisions every moment. Pushing the dolly a little faster or a little slower changes the movie. Putting the flag in front of the light a touch lower or a touch higher changes the movie. And I'm talking about something very simple. I really think that a picture is not just a picture and that we put all of ourselves into it as human beings.

But how do you try to control these things? Or do you?

. The only control you can have is in choosing to have the right people next to you and then try to put the right energy into it. So, in a sense, you can control, you can give direction. That's the only control you can have. Otherwise the more control you exert, the more you limit emotion and the more you limit freedom. So you end up having a movie made by prisoners. That's what happens when people are not allowed to think, to tell an idea, to tell an emotion to someone. Maybe there will be nineteen ideas that aren't very good but maybe there will be two or three that are. So I don't think you can control it; people try to do it. The form of control you can exert is to try to push in the right direction. And when anyone is going in the wrong direction, you try to persuade him and make him understand which is the right direction. Sometimes that's not easy.

For example, what is your relationship with your crew?

I've had my crew forever. I've had the same crew since I did my first picture. It is like my family, my professional family.

Are you dictatorial? How much freedom do you allow?

Well, you need a captain, you need a conductor. If you just let everybody do whatever they want, you will be doing a hundred different movies at the same time. I think you need a leader to give the right direction and that's what I try to do. In their own specific field, I think they should be allowed to express themselves, i.e., as a camera operator, as a key grip, as a gaffer. At the beginning of a film, you try to be as specific as possible about the direction and the way you want to go. Because you don't know if other people will go in a different direction. That's why, step by step, you get closer to the right direction as your people come to get to know you better. It becomes easier to be freer among us. We just talk at the beginning about the type of style we want to establish on the picture and we develop from there. After that I don't have to check anymore on the way the gaffer set the lights, on the way the operator made a pan. I don't have to check and see if the camera has the right filter and if it's set at the right aperture. That's something that has already been established. It's like a language between us. So I can concentrate my energy on the film. Otherwise, if you change your crew on each film, then you have to start at the beginning with them again.

To establish the ground rules.

We've had enough time to establish the ground rules and now we can fly.

You wouldn't want to operate your own pictures?

No. For several years, I was hand-holding the camera because it was part of something that's difficult to explain. It was part of making photography more specific and building an image, more so than just operating on the tripod or dolly. But no, I don't do that anymore.

You believe in very strong controls at the lab?

I started my collaboration with one particular lab. It's not the lab itself, it's the man at the lab. I had a good relation with this man at the lab and he was so involved that he was almost part of my crew. In the beginning, I remember the difficulties I had with whether he was going to understand me or not. When I was doing *Last Tango in Paris*, he felt I had too much yellow and orange. It was because he didn't understand what we were doing and why. So I called him to the set and explained everything to him. Afterwards it was much clearer to him what we were doing. We have worked together on several pictures now. And when I'm going to go in a new direction, I'm very careful and try to be very specific about what I'm trying to do. One of the most important things is how he reads what I wrote. There is no question that when he chooses a printing light that this is a particular choice that is part of his personality. So any image that I'm going to see will be my emotion, my involvement plus all the technical things plus his emotion. He puts his emotion on top of my emotion and knowledge and so this image becomes a new image.

For example, on One from the Heart, *you didn't use a Hollywood lab?*

One from the Heart, started out to be an MGM picture so I convinced MGM people to allow me to bring in this same gentleman from Technicolor Rome to print the film. I am very particular about this. And on this film I was trying to do certain things with color and I couldn't start from the beginning with another lab man. So I brought this man in and we started the film with a lab in Hollywood. But we discovered that here they use high-speed machines in the lab, which is different than what we were used to in Rome. In Hollywood, which represents the most important center of the movie business, the lab companies have the new machinery to develop the negative at a very high temperature in a high-speed machine. There is no doubt that whenever you're going to gain something, you're going to have to pay for it somewhere. In essence, the lab saves time and you lose on the quality of the image. In the last few years, we have been considered very lucky as a generation of cinematographers. Today we are really able to be free in relation to what the cinematographers of the past were able to do. We are free to use light and just deal with the main concept of light without worrying about all the technical details of exposure for balance and so on. Today, the new films, the new lenses, the new cameras, the new lighting equipment, really give us an incredible freedom. But here in Los Angeles you are starting to see an involution. The way the high-speed processor has been built and the way it is being used here, the variation of tonality that you can register in a positive print today is less than yesterday. That's one of the reasons I stopped using a Hollywood lab on *One from the Heart* and switched to an out-of-town lab that still used the old system. It was ridiculous that I wasn't able to do what I wanted in a lab here. I think this situation is very bad and something should be done about it. It is important for a lab to meet the desires and requests of the cinematographer. Since the beginning I have felt strongly about the lab because when I start one particular thing, I try to continue with it. That's why I was using the same man with the same lab even when I was doing *Last Tango in Paris*. I would send the film to Rome. When I worked in London, I would send the dailies to Rome also. There is another thing that is very difficult for a modern lab to do and that is to get them to try to do something different. They find it hard to change the way they do things. But that little change in treatment gives your own personality to that film. It allows you to better express yourself in that particular picture. Today, with the new processing and the new technology, they try to have no change at all between my piece of film and another cinematographer's piece of film. They try to level everything out at a mediocre standard. This allows the lab to process and develop the maximum number of feet per minute. This is very damaging because there will be no distinction between one film and another film, between one cinematographer and another cinematographer. We will be stuck on a standard level and all work will be like a flat line; there will be no variation. They will not allow you to use your personality which is the most important thing that we have. We should be able to be different like writers or musicians are.

Let's talk about Warren Beatty's picture, Reds, *which you've invested so much time and energy in. And now you're not being allowed to shoot the last five days of the picture because you're shooting in Hollywood and the union is objecting to your working in their jurisdiction. This is exactly what we are talking about here. The union is telling you that someone else can finish up the picture and it won't make any difference! It will look the same anyhow!*

I wrote the following letter to the American Society of Cinematographers: "If it is true that one is an 'author,' that is, one who has the creativity to transform an idea or an intuition into literature, art, music or photography; if it is true that photography is the literature of light; if it is true that the cinematographer is a writer who utilizes light, shadow, tonality and color, tempered with his experience, sensitivity, intelligence and emotion to imprint his own style and personality on a given work, it is then incomprehensible how a union that represents cinematographers of one nation can, in good conscience, impede the final critical week of cinematography by a representative of another nation—on a work which has been in progress for over a year.

"It is like refusing a writer permission to finish the final chapter of his book, or stopping a painter's last strokes of the brush, or denying a composer the opportunity to complete his 'finale.'

"This issue strikes at the heart of efforts made to date to advance the art and status of cinematography. It leads us backwards into the past, in which the director of photography was considered simply an obscure technician, interchangeable with any other technician at any moment and thus, a helpless witness to the sudden violations of his creative efforts and the individual vision he brings to a film.

"It is an act against the cinematographers of all nations as authors of their own work; an act against the very membership of the union in question; an act against the magic of the 'literature of light'—photography."

Eloquently stated.

I think it's crazy to think that you can defend the work of cinematographers and, at the same time, believe that we are interchangeable as a piece of machinery. This has been one of the most discouraging experiences of my life. I was not able to hold my light meter, I was not able to look through the camera on a movie on which I had collaborated for thirteen months before.

11

Mario Tosi

*"A cinematographer's style of lighting is how he ex-
presses himself. That's how the individual personality
comes out."*

Mario Tosi, unlike many of his contemporaries, had never given much thought to a career in cinematography. A native of Italy, his initial creative leanings were towards drawing and painting, an influence that is now invaluable to him in composing the motion picture frame.

His first filmmaking experience came when he assisted an Italian cameraman and, from that point on, he began developing his skills from behind the camera. Never having formally trained as an assistant cameraman or an operator, Tosi started shooting documentary films independently as a way of learning the technical aspects of filmmaking. His first major film was a South African documentary, *Tears on Johannesburg*, on which he assisted the Swedish cinematographer.

Oddly enough it was the 1961 Jerome Robbins/Robert Wise production of *West Side Story* that helped give Tosi the final impetus to seek his career in America. He was so impressed with the size of the musical's sets that he had to visit the United States if only to see how they did it in Hollywood. As naive as it might seem now, Tosi wrote to a number of veteran Hollywood cinematographers, asking their advice on how to go about breaking into the Hollywood system. Much to his gratification, many of Hollywood's professional cameramen replied to his request, among them Hal Mohr and Arthur Miller.

After a few false starts, Tosi broke into the business working for veteran Fouad Said's production services company, first as an assistant and later as a cameraman. While the time he spent with Said taught him little creatively, he did acquire a professional confidence and a working sense of the industry. He later became a freelance cinematographer, adopting Said's Cinemobile concept by packing a Volkswagen bus with a couple of Arriflex cameras and all the lighting equipment needed to shoot a feature. He shot quite a few low-budget films out of the back of his bus; in fact, *Buster and Billie* was shot entirely on location this way. As Tosi's reputation increased, so did the size of his budgets and the importance of his projects.

Although quite a few of Tosi's early films were done in the shoot-and-run environment of network television, he gets greater satisfaction from the relatively leisurely pace of theatrical features, to the point where he picks and chooses his projects carefully now, doing no more than two a year. But no matter what the medium, Tosi's overriding concern is to infuse any production with a certain visual quality that will contribute to the overall enhancement of the film.

1971	*The Killing Kind*	1976	*Judge Horton and the*
	Some Call It Loving		*Scottsboro Boys* (TV)
1972	*Frogs*		*Sybil* (TV)
	The Marcus Nelson		*Carrie*
	Murders (TV)		*MacArthur*
1973	*Reflection of Murder* (TV)	1977	*The Betsy*
	Summer without Boys (TV)		*The Stunt Man*
	The Stranger Who Looked	1978	*The Main Event*
	Like Me (TV)	1979	*Resurrection*
1974	*Report to the Commissioner*	1980	*Coast to Coast*
	Buster and Billie	1981	*Whose Life Is It Anyway*
1975	*Friendly Persuasion* (TV)	1982	*Six Pack*
	Hearts of the West		

Why and how did you first become interested in motion pictures?

I got started in the business in a very casual way. I never intended to become a cameraman. I went to art school and I painted for several years. Growing up in that artistic field, I was seeing very little money as a painter. I had a friend in motion pictures and he introduced me to the business. I learned the mechanical aspects of the camera on my own. I found that my artistic background helped me in the area of composition, depth and the use of color. I discovered that motion picture lighting was very similar to painting. I did a lot of tests and experimenting in my own darkroom with still photos until I became accustomed to photography and then I did my first little film. It came very spontaneously and it was easy for me.

You mention your background as a painter. How does that help you visually? Does your conceptualization of a painting transfer over to the camera frame?

Immensely so, I think. It is very helpful to have a background in drawing and painting. You see, I have to build my composition and my lighting to that camera frame. In painting, using charcoal, you study depth, composition, shading and form. And it's the same thing here. When I first started motion picture lighting, I just started building the composition until it looked good to me. That's why I didn't need any photographic training. Technically, you know, photography is very simple. After you learn the potential of film, the only difference between an amateur and a professional is that the professional imposes his creative ability in the process of becoming a good cinematographer. A creative cinematographer gives his own personal expression to the material. Whether it's better or worse than another guy, it is still his own.

I love lighting and I think the look of my pictures is due to my background in painting as well. In painting I learned how to compose, how to build up the depth, especially in black-and-white, which I love. I also learned taste and how to apply color.

What do you consider the function of a cinematographer?

The function of a cinematographer is a very involved one because he must function both in the artistic area and the mechanical area. He has to be in contact with all the various departments that make up a motion picture production. One of the chief responsibilities is the handling of the camera crew; sometimes you have a little crew and sometimes a very large one. When it is large, it is easy to lose control, especially on a large set where communication is difficult. At times I feel like a general commanding an army; you have to be a tough general too. You have to make sure, without denying anything to the artistic achievement of the film, that everything goes smooth and fast enough to remain on schedule. The other function is the artistic function. The cinematographer has the responsibility to create the strongest mood the script requires. Whether the script is a comedy, drama or thriller, you have to govern your actions accordingly and do your best to achieve the desired tone and mood.

What is the difference, in your opinion, between a purely mechanical cinematographer and an artistic, creative one?

The difference between these two types is very definite. The motion picture business is a commercial industry that has a goal of entertaining vast audiences and making money on it. There are hundreds of films produced and some of them require more or less quality than others. That applies to everything, script, sets and all down the line. So a majority of films are struggling against a certain limitation due to the aim and requirements of the market for which they were made. Most cinematographers are selected according to the quality that the story, schedule and production calls for. Most cinematographers are mechanical. They are very good at the mechanical aspects of cinematography; they can set up shots quickly, use two or three basic lights, shoot it in a couple of minutes and get the story down on film. The creative cinematographer is basically an artist. He studies the shot with the director and he works with the motion and mood of the shot. He is after quality so that the story will consciously or unconsciously come alive in the mind of the audience.

What kind of cooperation should there be between the cinematographer and the director?

There should always be a great amount of cooperation between the two. The director is the boss of the set while the cinematographer is trying to express his visual feelings on the screen. In Italy, where I started, there is always a lot of conversation about everything, both before the production starts as well as during it. In the United States, some directors work differently and you, as the cinematographer, have to work differently as well. Some directors like to concentrate on the story and the handling of the actors; they leave the cameraman much more freedom to work on the cinematography. But generally the cinematographer should be concerned with the composition of the picture, the camera movement and the lighting, which is the main responsibility. Other directors like to work and play with the camera themselves; some of them are very good at it. For example, Joe Sargent is good at lining up very complicated shots. Richard Rush is very good behind the camera also. So there is merit in both types of cooperation. On one hand, you get to exercise your mechanical and artistic skills and, on the other hand, when the director takes more of a part in it, you really have much more time to concentrate and enjoy the detail of the lighting.

What are the most common problems that you encounter in making films today?

The bigger the film, the bigger the problems associated with making it. There are always compromises with time. The schedule is always hanging over your head and it is a constant battle for the creative person to try to do the best he can under the restrictions of time. Just because you are shooting a twenty-million-dollar picture, you are not exempt from the clock and the pressure of working under it. This problem affects the entire production but particularly the cinematographer because he is the chief user of time on a production. People are always waiting for us and if we are rushed it shows up on the screen.

How do you think the average audience reacts to the photography of a given film?

There are two different kinds of reactions on the part of the audience. One is the conscious reaction by knowledgeable people, that is, people in the industry or the photographic hobbyist. They are aware of what's happening. They admire something that is photographically well done or interesting. If you are an artistic cinematographer and you create that special look for the story you are trying to make come alive, you will get a conscious reaction from this audience. But that, I think, is only a selected group of individuals. The larger audience is the audience that goes to a movie just to enjoy the show; they are not aware of the photography at all on a conscious level. But still, good photography will make the story come across with more impact for this audience as well. They will gain from good photography in a subconscious way. If I had shot *Carrie* with flat, TV-style lighting, I don't think the film would have had the same power that it did. Whether the audience recognizes the photography or not, it doesn't matter. It still helped them get excited about the drama. The photography helps with the mood and feeling of the film. The drama is heightened and this is the most important thing. I think photography adds to a film immensely; that's why it is so important to settle on the right photographic style at the beginning and stick to it for the entire film. A good cinematographer can give a film a look that has impact even though the audience may be unaware of it.

Do you prefer working on location or on a sound stage?

Being artistically inclined, I like working on the stage the best. If you have a good art director who creates a good design, and a good set has been constructed, then you can have the best of both worlds: a beautiful set and the comfort and facilities of working on a sound stage. It makes it easier to achieve the effect you are striving for. Now that is not to discount location shooting; it still has great appeal. In exterior location shooting, you have the ability to go to some of the most beautiful places in the world to create the atmosphere that you need instead of being on the back lot of some studio. Exteriors are obviously better shot on location. For interiors, sometimes it's advantageous and sometimes it's not. For example, they might want to shoot in some dingy little motel room where there is hardly room to put the camera and hide the lights. So it becomes difficult for a cinematographer to achieve any kind of quality in that situation. On the other hand, sometimes you can find a castle or a mansion that cannot be reproduced on a stage. Europe is great for this because they have two thousand years of history. So obviously you go on this type of location and you can get the greatest visual impact. On *The Betsy*, we did a lot of location shooting in beautiful, old, well-preserved mansions in Newport, Rhode Island, that are now museums. They had fantastic interiors with big windows to let natural light in. They would have been hard to duplicate on a stage.

On the stage, you start from black and you can create anything you want.

Right. On stage, you start working a long time before shooting. You work with the art director and tell him where you need windows or light sources. You prepare the set for the shot. And if you want to use a long lens for a different mood, you just take the wall out and move the camera. The stage is best especially when you have an art director who knows how to create a mood and give some shadings to the environment.

You mentioned your cooperation with the art director. What is your relationship with him?

I like to prepare with the art director far ahead of our shooting date. It depends on the budget as to how many weeks of preparation we get. We scout locations and study the script. I have always had a very good relationship with the art director. I believe if he gives you some good things to shoot, then you can do some very good things with it. But if he gives you just a plain wall, what are you going to do? So I always try to work with the art director and usually he is very interested; he usually gives me a lot of good environments to shoot in. Especially when you consider that for my kind of lighting, I need a lot of light sources. You can't give me a room with just four walls. I need lots of sources: stained glass with lights behind it, a door with glass, two or three windows so that you can leave the set dark but the actors can go through the sources. That's the real beauty of it.

Let's talk about your style of lighting, particularly your use of bounce light.

A cinematographer's style of lighting is where he expresses himself. That's how the individual personality comes out. It's the most important thing an artistic cinematographer should concentrate on. In the last few years I've been experimenting with more natural ways of lighting. After experimenting with materials which you put in front of the light to soften it, like spun glass or velveteen or even sheets of fiberglass, I found that bounce light is the most beautiful, efficient and natural.

Now I'm not discovering anything because that's the way our grandfathers were making photographs. They didn't have much equipment and they were just getting a spill of light coming out of a window. And they photographed the subject with that softness, lots of good strong modeling but no shadow. Bounce light produces this type of softness. So I bounce lights into a card or foamcore and, when the light is put at the right angle, it creates a softness and beauty on a subject that you can't get using any other type of light available today. That's the way I photograph ninety percent of my films now, no matter whether it's a master shot, a medium shot or a close-up.

Bounce light is not very popular because it is a very hard light to handle especially on the modeling in the background, due to the fact that the lighting tends to spill all over. It's very difficult to control. So to use it, you have to work with big teasers and enormous flags. And unless the crew has been working with you for a while and are used to that style of lighting, they may have a hard time understanding it.

The beautiful thing about bounce light is that sometimes you need only one source instead of twenty different lighting units. You just set one source and it does everything. That source has to be studied though so that you can put it into a key position to maintain all the modeling on the subjects and in the background as well. The background area is the most difficult to control because it usually looks flat. That's when you have to shape the light and struggle with it.

Don't you have to use a lot more light because you're talking about reflected light. You maybe use twice the light you normally use?

Yes. You use twice the light or more because it's reflected. And the bounce light tends to drop off very fast. So if you have a large set, you may put up a four by eight foot or more sheet of foamcore and pump two or three 10Ks into it. But that's it. If you have the light well placed at the key point, that's all you need.

No fill light, nothing more?

Maybe a little fill. But, you see, if you light a set conventionally from the catwalk overhead, you use maybe up to twenty lights and more. Bounce light looks so natural; it's so soft. It gives a completely different feeling from conventional lighting. It looks like it's not lit; it looks like you are filming a natural environment and that's the biggest achievement.

To make it look natural?

Yes, whether it's high key or low key—just make it look natural. And, as I say, it is difficult. But because it's difficult, it doesn't necessarily take more time.

What about a scene where you're going to have a lot of motion, where performers will be walking back and forth in a room?

That's a good question. The motion is the other thing, besides the background, that makes bounce lighting difficult. This is due to the intensity of the bounce light dropping off very quickly. If there is a lot of motion, you probably have to use different stages of bounce light; one for the foreground, one for the background, etc. Or if the subject is far away from the camera, you can pinpoint the spot with a hard light.

So you augment or supplement it?

Sure you supplement it with individual lights where the bounce doesn't really reach.

When you're bounce-lighting, do you use ratios?

No, I've never been a mechanic. I know that some cinematographers use a calculator to compute light ratios. I do it through the camera and by eye according to what I like. Mechanically speaking, you have to have more intensity with bounce light because it is so soft that it wraps around the subject. You have to increase the intensity to be able to build the modeling. You can also give the light more angle. For example, if you light a subject with a source at a forty-five degree angle and with hard, direct light, the subject will have terrible shadows and appear rather ugly. But if you used bounced light, it would be beautiful. But again, people don't use bounce light in motion pictures because they have a hard time controlling it and therefore it is difficult to produce moody or dramatic effects.

Does the faster film stock help you achieve the type of effect you want with bounce light?

Definitely. Fast film helps because you can light a scene almost as it is in real life. You don't have to use a great amount of light intensity that ends up making the scene look unnatural, takes more power, takes more time and sometimes makes the set too hot for the comfort of everybody, especially the performers.

I understand that you now use more footcandles than you used to. Why is that? Because it seems that most cameramen are cutting back on the footcandles because of the speed of the lenses and film.

I use more because of necessity. I was used to shooting at five to twenty-five footcandles many years ago, so it is not a big discovery for me to be able to expose at this level. But now with bounce light, because of the softness and quality of the source, if I use too little footcandles, it seems there is no shape, modeling or beauty to the subject. So judging by eye, I keep adding intensity until I like it best.

Why don't you think the lenses help you with bounce lighting? Is it that the lenses are too sharp?

They are too sharp. I don't want sharpness because I cannot cope with it. I always use the zoom lens because it's mellow. Then I don't need too much diffusion or fog filters to create the mood I want. High-speed lenses are like razor blades. They're for documentary work or something where you need the sharpness but not for something that is going to have mood. They work against the mood of a feature.

Report to the Commissioner *was a gritty, realistic, urban drama while* Buster and Billie *was very lyrical and nostalgic. How do you adapt your style to such divergent looks?*

You study the story first. Then you meet with the director and he gives you an idea of which way he wants to go with it. But the script itself will tell you. *Report to the Commissioner* was shot in the Bronx so obviously I'm not going to make it look like Caesar's Palace in Las Vegas. I also shoot tests and determine what kind of filters would be suitable for the picture, if any. When I shot *Report to the Commissioner* I used a fog filter. I'm not a heavy user of filters. I establish most of the mood of the scenes through lighting. But since today's film is so sharp and so pictorial, you have to help it sometimes. So I will use a little bit of fog filters; I never use low-contrast filters because they have never convinced me. Lately, on women, I've started using nets, which I think are best for conveying a mood. I started using nets a little bit on Barbra Streisand on *The Main Event*. On *Resurrection*, I sometimes used quite heavy nets because we were shooting in the countryside. On *The Stunt Man*, I used fog filters except in some close-ups of Barbara Hershey, where I used nets. On *Coast to Coast*, with Dyan Cannon, I used lots of nets and she was really happy with the way she looked. So you have to give a visual quality to what the story is telling you. You have to decide on the lighting and the use of filters and nets. The sets and the costumes will also help you in deciding what approach to take. but the main thing is the lighting and the filters that you use.

So you don't use filters that much?

I used to use filters a lot before I started bounce lighting. Now, with bounce light, the light is so good that you really don't need them too much. Production people will tell me that this cameraman is using coral filters or that one is using fast lenses. I always respond that the accessory never makes the quality, it's the lighting that counts. If the lighting has an artistic approach, it's good no matter what. You can use all the accessories around but if you don't have that, you're dead. It's like a painter: if he doesn't have the creativity, he can use the best paint and brushes but it won't help him.

Do you prefer one type of picture over another?

Well, I basically like to do dramatic lighting. I like low-key lighting and I really enjoy shadows and gutsy feelings, etc. So I prefer that if I have a choice. But I also enjoy love stories; they may not be very dramatic in lighting but they can be very moody. Thrillers and love stories are my preference. But lately a lot of directors are asking me to shoot comedies.

With respect to your attention to detail, what is your relationship with the lab?

I always work very closely with the lab people and I have a personal relationship with them. I am always in contact with the lab by telephone while we are shooting to know the situation of my negative and the printing lights. Also I want to give my suggestions on the way I want the film to look. But the most important thing is for the cameraman to be there at the end of the picture when the lab is ready for color correction and timing of the print. You should be there to oversee the work so that all the mood and color you worked for during the filming will not be changed.

For example, in *Carrie*, I lit those scenes in her mother's house specifically like an old painting. I had really deep orange colors, especially when the mother chased the little girl around the house. And when she is crucified, I lit it in an orange, goldish tone like an old painting of St. Sebastian. We took a lot of effort to put deep gels on the lights. Unfortunately, in the timing and color correction, which I did not do, the lab timed it cold and blue and it lost a lot of what I had put into it.

Was that a mistake?

No, it was just the choice of the people doing the timing.

But what you're saying is that it's important to be there for the timing so that you can impose your judgment in that area consistent with the way you shot the film?

Yes, that's one of the most dramatic negative aspects of trying to do quality photography. You work so hard to get some effect that's very touchy when it comes to color exposure and balance. You spend so much time trying to set a mood. But then the film is finished; it takes six months to edit and you are not available for the timing because you are at work on another film. The guy who does the timing has a different point of view on what the picture should look like or maybe doesn't understand what you were trying to do. I mean, you can light a low-key source and they will time it for the fill lights, not the key, and suddenly the scene is not low key anymore. Cinematographers are in a bad spot because very few have the opportunity to time and color correct their own films.

I understand that you favor using a zoom lens and that you also push the film one stop even if you don't need the extra speed. Why?

First of all, I use the zoom lens most of the time because it gives me the continuity of look. It's seldom that you find a set of lenses matched and color corrected. The zoom has the same quality at all focal lengths. But in using the zoom, you must shoot at $f3$; it's not like using a fast lens. So you are up to fifty to sixty footcandles or one hundred footcandles if you don't push. If I push the film, I'm down to fifty footcandles. Then, on printing, I can get another stop so that puts me down to twenty-five footcandles. So if I shoot at thirty-five to fifty footcandles, which is not too much or too little, I'm in a good range for printing and I can still do natural lighting. If I don't push the film, I find myself already up to one hundred footcandles; at that point you must push in a lot of light to bring it up to that level. I wouldn't have to push if I used regular or high-speed lenses but I feel comfortable with a zoom. I think the zoom lenses now have great quality.

When you say "zoom lens," you don't use it as a zoom lens; you use it as a variable focal length lens?

Right. People get confused by the fact that I use a zoom lens. You use it just as you would a straight lens; it just gives you much more freedom to find the frame size that fits perfectly. You can also use it for small framing adjustments on motion during a pan to control the composition better.

What makes getting good skin tones so difficult?

The film stock is very sensitive to red and green. We are also fighting against the usual way of making up performers. The make-up being used today is the same make-up that they were using twenty or thirty years ago. The make-up hasn't kept up to date with the film stocks and the processing. I found out one way to do a face the way I like, especially the face of a woman, is to use make-up that is used for clowns. You know, the white clown make-up, but you mention it and people think you are crazy. However a light coat of clownish make-up comes out just great on film. Regular pancake make-up has a red cast to it and that just compounds the film's sensitivity to that color.

What kind of problems does doing a film with a top Hollywood female star, like Barbra Streisand in The Main Event, *present for a cameraman?*

On that film it was a problem, not only photographically but also to convince

Barbra to do things my way. First of all, I was brought into that film by the director, Howard Zieff, whom I had done *Hearts of the West* with. And although Barbra agreed to use me, she did not know me. Of course, being a lady and big star, she was very concerned with looking her best in the film. She is a beautiful, talented lady and she knows exactly what she wants. But I am hired because they think I can do a good job as a cinematographer; I am supposed to have more expertise in that area than a performer. I'm supposed to do my job. Well, the first week of testing and shooting was a little difficult for me because Barbra was trying to tell me where to put the lights and suggesting that we do things a certain way. So I had to compromise with her but slowly I would sneak in a few more elements of cinematography that I felt were necessary such as filters or a certain way of lighting. Gradually I was able to photograph her in different key; she later told me she had never been photographed that way before. Why? Because she never allowed another cameraman to do it. For example, we were shooting with the key not just on the left side of her face, but we were shooting both sides. Therefore when she saw the dailies, she would say, "Well, that's different but I really like it." So after the first week, she started gaining confidence in me and started to really enjoy my work. The only thing I couldn't do was use all the filters I wanted to use and that was a decision made by Barbra and the director. They wanted the film to look rather clean and stark. I would have liked it with a little more diffusion so it would look a bit softer. They objected to that because the picture was a comedy.

Did you do a lot of bounce lighting on her for the film?

I had to convince her first. Other cameramen had never used bounce lighting on her before. The cameraman whom she respected the most was Harry Stradling, Sr., who is now passed away. Harry was using hard light and enormous scoop lights. Barbra knew she looked good with that kind of lighting and, in the beginning, that was the only type of lighting she wanted. She wanted these big, enormous, old fashioned scoop lights sitting on top of the lens. So we started with that but slowly I started bringing in my white cards and bouncing the light at an angle. She got used to it and, in fact, enjoyed it.

So you did use a lot of bounce light on the film?

Oh yes, absolutely; it's the only way. With a lady especially, you cannot use hard lights. The quality of the bounce light enhances beauty. I am now getting very used to filming ladies. I shot Barbara Hershey in *The Stunt Man*, I shot Barbra Streisand in *The Main Event*, I shot Dyan Cannon in *Coast to Coast* and I shot Ellen Burstyn in *Resurrection*. They are all fantastic talents and fantastic-looking ladies but they are not eighteen years old anymore. You have to take particular care in capturing their beauty. And bounce light is the best answer because it is soft and it enhances their beauty.

You utilized a lot of natural light situations in The Main Event, *especially in the scene where Ryan O'Neal and his manager go to Streisand's apartment. You shot it with a strong back light coming from a bank of windows. It was a great effect to have those windows blooming with light.*

Yes, that was a typical example of a natural lighting situation. It was not shot on a stage but on location in an apartment. We had the windows which were giving us the source and I supplemented that spill light, which wasn't reaching her, with a lot of bounce light from a card as if it were coming from the windows. And it was as simple as that. I had one source and I may have had just a touch of fill light. I thought it looked very good not only for the actors but for the background. To me, the background is very important. Sometimes I spend more time lighting the background than the subjects. When you put your key light on the subject, there isn't much more you can do; but with the background, there is much you can do such as enhancing the furniture or a painting on the wall. That's why cooperation with the art director is very important; it insures that the ingredients will be there on the set to make it look good.

Now the white cards were inside the apartment supplementing the natural light. When you use white cards, you always put them as close to the edge of the frame as possible so you can get the right angle. In that scene, I also poured light in other windows that were hidden so that it would hit the furniture and the walls. I used the white card bounce light for the subjects who were sitting on the couch. All these elements together gave a really natural feeling to the scene.

It's a very balanced and consistent type of lighting. If the performers get up and walk around, it's to going to destroy the mood you've set through your lighting.

I give quite a lot of freedom to the performers. With this kind of lighting, you do not really pinpoint their motions. They don't have marks to hit. They can move any place they want and it will be fine. It's not like hard lights that only cover a certain area and then start to fall off.

What was your artistic and visual approach to The Stunt Man?

The film was very difficult because of the stunts and the enormous amounts of different sequences, one after another. Also we had a great many problems because of the weather. The thing I tried to achieve is the story itself. And the story itself is something in between hard, human reality of life and fantasy and I tried to bring this out visually in the film. I tried to make the fantasy evident but not too obvious. I wanted to do something soft, something that almost blends in with the rest of the film. When Peter O'Toole tells Steve Railsback, "Come into the magic world of the movies; this is the door that opens up and brings you in," I had just a little touch of diffusion on that shot. It was not really that strong but it was something to do that might make people subconsciously feel that there *is* something behind that door.

It's up to the audience and the critics to judge if I succeeded or not, but I tried very hard to make a distinction between reality and fantasy. But there were a lot of problems to cope with. The worst problems were the stunts because they all were so difficult to shoot. We shot half the movie on top of the Hotel Coronado so we had to be extremely careful.

There was a sequence where Railsback was doing a stunt on an old biplane while it was raining. It must have been hell shooting that.

It was raining all the time. That scene was not a fake; the weather was actually like that. You know, to be able to see a rain effect on film, you have to make it phony—you have to light it! So when it's raining naturally, you very seldom see it. But every time you see an overcast scene in the film, it was raining even though you can't really see it. Maybe it made it look more dramatic but what a struggle it was. All the equipment was wet and we were soaking. People got sick. We couldn't stop and wait for better weather either, because we were behind schedule, so we had to keep going.

There was an interesting scene early in the film where the entire cast is gathered around a long dinner table.

There is a lot of composition with foreground and background in that scene; we didn't go for the boring close-ups alone. We tried to do something else with it. We were trying to create a new syntax for motion picture filmmaking. And I think we did create some eccentricities. I mean, it was eccentric but it wasn't bothersome. Sometimes a filmmaker does something so obvious that it bothers the audience. On *The Stunt Man*, I think we approached it in a sophisticated and interesting way and it didn't bother the audience.

For instance, the best technological advance in filmmaking in the last few years has been the Steadicam. It's fantastic but it can be overused or used only to save time. When it's used for those purposes, you lose control of lighting and composition and you end up with a mediocre shot. You have to decide when to use it. We used it in *The Stunt Man* several times but we used it efficiently and for the dynamics of the story. Actually the audience should see the film twice: once for the story and once to study the way we made it.

The director, Richard Rush, had the tendency to rack-focus a lot in his earlier films. He did it again in The Stunt Man. *As a cameraman, do you like that technique?*

I don't like to overuse any technique; there's a right time for everything. But he used the rack-focus effectively because you were not really conscious of the change of focus. Actually, if you think about it, rack-focus approximates what the human eye does. The secret of rack-focusing is to try to do it as naturally as possible so it does look more like it was a human eye rather than a camera lens racking.

What were some of the unique things involved in the shooting of Whose Life Is It Anyway?

One of the major things about the production was that John Badham, the director, had the idea to shoot the film in black-and-white but the studio didn't agree with him totally. So they compromised and agreed to shoot the film in color but to print it in black-and-white. Now this created a big problem for me because the labs don't do that process too much anymore. The lab has to go through many, many involved mechanical steps before they get a good print with this process. It's too lengthy to describe here but it's very long and involved.

So what you're saying is that you shot the film in color . . .

We shot it on color negative and then we were seeing dailies in black-and-white, taken straight from the color negative, which looks very bad. That's why it was difficult to judge what was happening during the shooting from the dailies. I agreed with John that we should shoot it in black-and-white. I thought the story would have been much more dramatic. The other interesting idea that John had was to shoot the film in anamorphic instead of spherical. I was somewhat negative about the idea because I thought anamorphic was good for landscapes and panoramas or when you have some wide scene to frame. But John was pretty set about it. So we agreed to do a good day of testing in both spherical and anamorphic. And after I saw the tests, I found that John was right. In anamorphic, the film looks so much more impressive; it adds a special look to the film itself.

Did going anamorphic present any technical problems?

I generally light between twenty-five and fifty footcandles and I use a zoom lens, which is $f4.5$. I like to use the zoom as a prime lens, not as a zoom. But we decided not to use the zoom lens. Another problem that we came across during the tests was that I found that I couldn't use any filters whatsoever. I couldn't even use a quarter of a fog filter or a soft net because any filtering in front of the camera would break down the negative. Any filtering would make the fine grain black-and-white print (from color negative) so grainy that you wouldn't see anything. So those were the major problems I faced going into the film: shooting on color stock and printing in black-and-white and not being able to use the zoom lens.

But not using the zoom lens just forced us to move the camera constantly on a dolly or to move the people. It was really more of a challenge to make the film look interesting and I think we succeeded. You know, the story concerns a man who is paralyzed from his neck down and who spends seventy-five percent of his time in bed.

Cinematically, that presents quite a problem.

Yes. Going into the film, I was concerned about what I was going to shoot. I mean, I was going to shoot a bed and a little room? But the story was so good that I wanted to do it anyway. We were always thinking of things to do to make the story visually interesting. So we worked out a lot of dolly shots through the hospital corridors. We had different moods of lighting for day, for night, for when it was raining and for when it was snowing. So the mood would change all the time. I also worked out a way to change the key during the shot, which I had done before but not as extensively as in this film. While we dollied around his bed or his wheelchair, I might change the key around three or four times so that the faces always had good modeling.

The movie was taken from the play and, as such, it was a one-set piece basically. So you have the problem of trying to constantly keep the film interesting.

I think I got the most satisfaction visually from shooting in his hospital room. Dollying from one side of the bed to another, going from a tight to a wide shot or moving from a high to a low position made the film interesting. Then we were always enhancing the key from the window. John wanted to do some scenes with rain outside the window; I also suggested that we add some lightning to it. So we were able to dramatically enhance several of the scenes that way. It turned out that, from just a small simple room, you could get a great deal of visual satisfaction.

Directorially and in performance the satisfaction was already there. But the visual satisfaction is the one that would have been minimized due to the confinement of the room. We really gave it a great deal of thought and worked hard to make it interesting.

Did you have to change your lighting style to any degree?

I did continue, most of the time, to shoot with bounce lighting. Since I wasn't using the zoom lens, I had to increase the *f*-stop a little bit. The lab required a good solid negative which I gave them. It would have been a very big problem for me to use the zoom on this film. I couldn't push the film like I usually do. But going with a straight lens, it worked out very well.

How would you advise someone who wanted to pursue a career in cinematography?

It's very difficult to answer that from my background. As I say, photography is very simple, mechanically and technically. You can go to any rental house and learn how to load a camera and use the lenses; in a few days, you know everything if you're smart. The success that comes afterward depends on the skill and creativity of the individual. Also it depends on your own strength and fitness because camerawork is physically demanding. You have to be able to carry on good relationships with various members of the crew and cope with all the problems of the business itself.

So there are many problems involved in being a successful cinematographer; it's not just making a pretty picture. But, in any case, I didn't have much training. If someone wants to go to a university to learn about it and get a general knowledge of editing, writing and directing, like they teach at UCLA, I don't think it can hurt. But the success is all up to the individual—how much skill, taste, desire and artistic feeling he has.

What's your basic attitude about what you are doing? What do you try to achieve?

There are many cinematographers, many styles and many approaches. My point of view is that I see cinematography as the final and last medium left in this society, artistically speaking, that can be enjoyed by many people. Painting, sculpture, etc., have limited audiences. Theatrical cinematography is the only thing left that has a widespread audience who can enjoy it. People should make a big effort to keep it as an art medium. Cinematographers should really make an effort to maintain the best quality level possible. My approach has always been like that, even when I was just starting out in the business. I just like to make it beautiful because when you see it on the screen, it's great. I like to paint on the screen. I like to create a mood and treat it as an art form, the last art form. I hate to hear, "Oh, it's just another film." Or "Look, we only have so much money and so much time and the audience won't know the difference anyway." I try to do the best I can with the time and money available. I still like to consider it not just a job but an artistic effort.

12

Haskell Wexler

"I love shooting film. I get terrific joy holding a camera and seeing things happen in the viewfinder."

Will the real Haskell Wexler please stand up? Haskell Wexler #1 is the imaginative Hollywood cameraman who has won four Academy Awards, a man who routinely talks with celebrities and superstar performers in the natural course of his business. Haskell Wexler #2 is the liberal, concerned documentary cameraman who fights from behind the camera to bring unpopular political realities and human truths to a wide audience. Haskell Wexler #3 is the director/cameraman of television commerical blurbs for Marlboro, Schlitz and STP—because some days you have to go out and make a living just like everybody else. If you wanted to make a feature film on Wexler's life or even, say, a documentary on his social contributions or even a thirty-second spot to time capsulize his career, the overriding theme would have to be that Wexler is all of these things rolled up into one very articulate, intelligent and talented man.

A Midwesterner, Wexler spent four and a half years as a merchant seaman and came home to Chicago after World War II wanting to make films. Without knowing a great deal about it, he and his father bought and refurbished an old armory in Des Plaines and made it into a studio. With this one giant step, Wexler was a filmmaker, so to speak. Unfortunately, the price of humility came high. "The hardest thing," says Wexler, "was to realize how much I didn't know." He soon closed the operation and started working as an assistant cameraman. He shot quite a number of documentaries during that time, finally making the transition to dramatic Hollywood films in the late fifties.

Some thirty years later, he is still as energetic and inquisitive as he was in his youth. Although he's less idealistic now, tempered by the knowledge that change is not quickly effected, his social and political consciousness remains consistent. He still shoots documentaries, seeing them as an instrument for social change. *Introduction to the Enemy, Underground* and *Interviews with Mai Lai Veterans* are classic works in the field and indicate the level of his commitment. His one foray in feature directing, *Medium Cool*, was both an entertainment and a social document of its time: the tumult of the 1968 Democratic Convention in Chicago. For a variety of reasons, including government pressure, the film was never properly released or promoted by the studio. A century from now, people will look back on these films and gain some insight into what the social and political life of our times was like.

Wexler's feature film projects are chosen judiciously; he rarely shoots more than one a year. Lately he's been able to combine his social concerns with Hollywood entertainments, as in *Bound for Glory* and *Coming Home*. And although it might seem risky to have the reputation of a radical documentary filmmaker in the Hollywood community, Wexler has survived just fine. One reason is that there are enough people in the business who believe in the same things he does. But also, when he's behind the camera, he delivers the goods every time with an artistic and visual flair that few people can match.

1958 *Stakeout on Dope Street*
1959 *The Savage Eye*
1960 *Studs Lonigan*
       Angel Baby
1961 *The Hoodlum Priest*
1962 *A Face in the Rain*
1963 *America, America*
1964 *The Best Man*
1965 *The Loved One*
1966 *Who's Afraid of*
       Virginia Woolf? *
1967 *In the Heat of the Night*
1968 *The Thomas Crown Affair*
1969 *Medium Cool*
1973 *American Graffiti*
       (Visual Consultant)
1975 *One Flew Over the Cuckoo's*
       Nest† (Shared Credit)
1976 *Bound for Glory* *
1977 *Coming Home*
1978 *Days of Heaven*
       (Additional Photography)
1979 *Second Hand Hearts*

1980 *Looking to Get Out*
1981 *Richard Pryor Live on the*
       Sunset Strip

As Director:
1969 *Medium Cool*

Documentary (partial listing):

The Living City
Land of My Birth
War Without Winners
The Bus
Introduction to the Enemy
Interview with My Lai Veterans**
A Right to be Merry
Brazil: Report on Torture
Interview with Allende
Underground
The Swine Flu Case
The Case Officer
Paul Jacobs and the Nuclear Gang
No Nukes

*Academy Award for best achievement in cinematography.
**Academy Award for best documentary.
†Academy Award Nomination for best achievement in cinematography.

You started out as a documentary cameraman; why did you jump into features?

I've always been a documentary cameraman and am continuing to be a documentary cameraman. But I believe there is more to moviemaking than documentaries. The first feature I photographed was done more like a documentary than other features at that time.

Speaking as a man who has filmed a lot of documentaries, do you have any special attitude or philosophy when you go in to shoot a documentary, not from the making of the film but just from the camera work?

Well, my attitude is first determined on what documentary I choose to do because there is predisposition toward subject matter, toward the person, toward the idea. And then I try to adopt a viewpoint, an open-mind viewpoint and I do this not just for ethical reasons but for cinematic reasons. If you decide to do a documentary on a certain subject and have preconceived notions about the conclusions of that subject and one tries to impose those views on the subject, then the film will suffer. One part of a documentary is learning. I could expand on that but, in general, making a documentary (the kind I work on) is an adventure and like all adventures if you know everything then you might as well make a scripted film. You have to be able to be loose, otherwise it's no adventure. And that process continues particularly in vérité documentaries in the editing. The vérité documentaries that I like are ones where scenes are allowed to go on a little longer than they might in a theatrical film, when there are little codas, little things that happen so that the viewer discovers on the screen some aspects of human activity or consciousness, whereas in a film which is more controlled, you have to keep grabbing the audience, you have to keep hitting them every moment. Your obligations are different.

When you are doing a documentary, are you the Haskell Wexler who is the Hollywood cameraman and the perfectionist who does everything right: lighting, framing, composition? Do you sort of turn that off in favor of the situation, of the truth? Or are you thinking about that also?

Even with features, although we do have all these controls and like to make it as perfect as possible, I always think of a documentary when I'm making a feature. In fact I learned in shooting documentaries how I can frame in a feature, how I can muss up a frame, how I can have something in the foreground which in a documentary would be in the foreground because you couldn't get it out of the foreground, because you had to stand in the corner of that room. And when I make features, even though I have a set where I have the possibility of moving a wall out or moving furniture, I try to keep those things at least in my mind so that when I frame a shot it will be the way it happens in documentaries. So I look at shooting documentaries as an area of great resource for my feature films.

Is it the other way around too? Do the features bring anything to the documentaries?

I found the more I work on features, the less loose I am on documentaries, and I have to fight that. I have to go in and when I see a room I say, "Gee, if I had two HMIs out the window hitting through a silk I could light this room beautifully." Well, I don't have two HMIs so I have to quickly say, "Erase that from your mind.

How can you do the same thing the way you used to do it in Chicago 25–30 years ago." So I'll take four par lights or three clip lights and put them over the window; not show the window itself because I can't put a neutral on the window the way I would if I were doing a feature, and use the window light. In other words I try to make my framing work for the lighting that I have.

Have you developed any lighting techniques that you use in documentaries that tends to be a work horse for you, that you can do quickly and that you like the way it looks?

A lot depends on how much control you have over where your "actors" go. If you are, in fact, the director of the documentary, you can sort of lead people into areas of a room, let's say, where the light is to your advantage. Of course the easiest way in color is to take some bounce unit or some reflected unit off a white ceiling and get general illumination, then you get exposure and usually that's not too unpleasing to the eye. It can, however, be boring visually. So I would say that if you can control your actors then you use the natural sources of light that are there. If you are at the mercy of a director or a situation where a table or machine or some object is far from good, natural interior light then you would have to enhance that light, generally with some one source soft light whether it's a bounce off a card, off a ceiling, off a piece of aluminum foil. Or in the case of night shooting, of enhancing the light by putting in a PH211 or number 1 photoflood into an existing fixture.

Do you follow source lighting when you are doing documentaries or is that a primary concern?

Well, on a documentary when you walk into a room or into an office, you don't have the time usually to move the lamps around and move the fixtures around. So you may, where there's a venetian blind, decide to open it up or you may decide to close it. You may decide, if there's a lamp there, to enhance the source of the lamp or if you are concerned about fluorescents in a room, you may decide to turn them off or if you have the time, you may purchase fluorescent tubes which are of a better color temperature—like a warm light deluxe instead of a cool light. But in general you are obliged in a documentary to use what's there, build it up. And also where you put the camera is important. I mean, if what's there is built up in back of your actors, to give you an obvious example, you may be stuck with no light on the front of their face—which could be okay for certain types of things, but could be a problem in other types.

What kind of lighting kit do you usually carry when shooting documentaries?

The last documentary I shot I had four clip lights and I think I used them twice, and the lighting was absolutely fantastic. I think that one tip I could give to some people who do that, if they have a chance, is to work with a still camera. I mean just go in different rooms and take stills with negative film and you'll be astounded at how beautiful nature is. But you have to be able to recognize when it's a good nature system and when it's a bad nature system. But in general you see a lot more on film than you think you'll see, and the quality of light, particularly when there are windows, is so marvelous that you often can screw it up by lighting.

Would you basically say to hardly use any light?

No. I mean, well, I have shot in some places like in the Smithsonian Institution and big museums. In Moscow I shot in the Moskvitch automobile plant. Well, I couldn't have lit it even if I wanted to and I was astounded at how beautiful it looked on the screen. I said, "Jeez, good thing I didn't have a full crew and a full set of lights, I might have screwed it up."

What was the film?

It was a film against nuclear proliferation. It was a film trying to show that the dangers of nuclear war are so great that, although we have political differences with other nations, unless we work out something we are likely to kill the whole world.

How do you choose the basic subjects for your films?

I don't really know. It's part of my whole person. Like you ask guys how they choose their girlfriends and they may say "I just like redheads" but it's very likely an oversimplification or rationalization. It may truly be because their voice sounds something like their mother's voice or something more obscure. So I think that I choose what I do because of inner voices, although since one can be asked questions by interviewers, I have a whole rationale to tell you about my conscious beliefs and my obvious political bent and so forth. But I don't really think that that's truly why I choose what I do.

Will they always be politically motivated?

Well, I'd have to address myself to the phrase, "politically motivated." I mean suppose a guy says, "I make films where I make the best bucks, I make films where they pay me the most, I'm interested in entertainment and screw all this ideology stuff." Now you couldn't find a stronger political statement than that, yet no one says that's a political statement. Whereas if I say, "I make films that I feel are positive human statements that enlighten or enlarge man's view of life and of the earth and of one another," well that becomes a political statement. Now that's because our culture has adapted itself to accept consumerism, to accept the profit motive, to accept the personal selfish attitude as "nonpolitical." And to consider the things which are a basic part the Declaration of Independence as political statements. I maintain that every act that a person takes as a social human being is a political act. So that's that speech.

What about Underground?

Underground was sort of an adventure. De Antonio came to me about a year before the film was actually shot and, in sort of abstruse terms, asked if I would be available if such a thing were put together. And then there were various clandestine meetings with different members from time to time to test me out, I think. And that was it. We shot it. We had various James Bond-like meetings where I was told to be at a certain phone booth at a certain time where when someone walked past me I should get out and walk to the corner and there would be a young woman and I should walk with this young woman to a certain place—that type of thing. So that went on for quite a while, and in fact when I was on *Cuckoo's Nest* in Oregon, after some of these preliminary meetings had taken place, the FBI was up there, stirring things up, asking questions about me.

So were you technically in violation of the law?

No.

I mean in shooting Underground?

No. What the subpoena that I received said is they wanted to see our film and hear our tapes, and we refused to do that. The only law potentially that you are liable for if you meet with people who are fugitives from justice is the harboring law—aiding, abetting, and harboring. And that involves more than a one-evening filming of people. You have to keep them in your apartment for some substantial period of time, and they have to show that you fed them, or that you gave them clothes or you aided them in some substantial way.

But you were obviously taking certain risks. This is the kind of question we were talking about before. How do you decide between what you think is right or the art of what you are doing, and what the FBI thinks, or the powers that be?

I think that I was interested in the adventure. I was curious about the people because I knew people like that were in the student movement during that time. Politically I disagreed, and still do, with violence for political ends. Particularly with the way things are in America, I think there are more avenues open for political response before anyone could ever think of dropping a bomb or doing violence. I stated that to the underground people, not in such pompous terms, but when I was with them, so that they knew where I stood. But they also knew that I would never turn them in.

Introduction to the Enemy *was a real unpopular film, as far as the establishment—about Vietnam and all that. There was talk that you people were traitors. Have things like that,* Medium Cool, *and* Underground . . .

You don't even know half the scurrilous documentaries I've made. I've made about four this year. Yeah, go ahead with your question, excuse me.

Well, I'm talking about the ones that really came up in the public light, that came in for some criticism by the establishment during the war, things like that. Do you think that they had a negative effect on your career?

Probably. It could have a negative effect on my career, but the point is you only live one life and you have to decide at what point you want to say, "This is what I believe in, or even just what I am interested in." Because actually I wanted to go to Vietnam with Jane Fonda and Tom Hayden to learn. Sure, I was against the war but I learned a lot of things there that I couldn't have learned otherwise. And that's one advantage of being a documentary filmmaker. It's the most marvelous way to learn, you know.

So then you haven't experienced that much prejudice within the industry?

Well, I'm sure that there are many people in power in the business who would prefer that I were just a good technician and not someone who has opinions about things that technicians are not supposed to have opinions on. But I am who I am and that's part of the package.

What documentaries have you made in the last few years?

I made a film called *The Case Officer* with Saul Landau. There was a CIA man, John Stockwell, who was going to defect. He was Chief Case Officer in Angola and before he told "the company" he was going to leave, he contacted me and my friend Saul Landau and wanted to have his story on film and on tape so that he wouldn't be killed. He was afraid that they would slip him something somewhere and that would be the end. So we did that. The film was put away and then he told "the company" that he was leaving. The film was a very insightful film of the man's life and his work with the CIA, which is what I liked about it. I don't believe or like films that are political diatribes because they don't influence anybody. The people who agree with it, like it and the people who disagree, hate it; it doesn't do any good. I like something that will increase people's perception of other human beings. So *The Case Officer* is a good film in that regard. Then I made a film called *The Swine Flu Case*, which is an exposé on the swine flu thing done with a Dr. Tony Morris, who was in the government, and knew all about the fraud perpetrated on the American people about the swine flu. They just fired him and kicked him around. He's actually been vindicated. And the film is one of the things that has helped vindicate him. Then I made a film in Jamaica for Michael Manley, the Prime Minister, which he credits with getting him reelected. He's a socialist. Jamaica is a semi-socialist country. Well, he calls it "democratic socialism." And the film is used in Jamaica extensively with mobile units to show around to the people to explain Michael's policy and platform. So those are some political things.

You've got your hands in so many different types of filmmaking: feature films, TV commercials, socially conscious documentaries, etc. Do you have any trouble keeping your sensibilities straight through each of those? They all seem to take a little different sensibility—or do they?

Well, in order to live from day to day you have to do a lot of rationalizing. You have to give yourself reasons which really wouldn't stand up under a strict personal self-scrutiny. So what I want to do is I want to express myself in a dramatic feature film, and the other things are things I do because that's what I'm able to. I love to shoot films. I get terrific joy holding a camera and seeing things happen in the viewfinder. And I think that happens in commercials, that happens in documentaries, but I recognize it's a limited joy and I would like to enlarge that.

It's like any artist. I mean artists have to do their thing and you hope that the thing you are doing is seen by other people and you hope that the thing you are doing expresses your person. When society puts limits on what you're doing when you're doing your thing, then you do your thing for them, and at some point you say, "Well, that's enough, I'm not doing my thing for the Ku Klux Klans. But there are a lot of gray areas in between. Should I shoot commercials for Standard Oil? Well, yeah, let's see what the commercial is and how much they pay. So once you establish the fact that you're a whore, the price and the ethics involved always have to be weighed.

As a socially conscious filmmaker, what do you think about using sophisticated film techniques to sell things—not products, I'm talking about political ideas, things like that.

Well, listen, it's a condition of our society, of the world really. We're a media world and so the only salvation really is to try to be conscious of what they are doing and what you are doing—conscious of the fact that when you see O. J. Simpson running through the airport and getting his card right away, flying into his rental car without any interruption, conscious of the fact that that's not the way it really is. If you've ever rented a car you know that you plough through a crowd, you wait for your bag, you wait in line while the girl behind the counter gets off the phone and finishes her cigarette, and can't find your card. Then when she finds your card, you have to walk halfway through the airport and get on a bus to get your car, and you go around 700 cars until you get in your car, and it still has the dirty ashes of the previous driver. In other words, you have to keep saying to yourself that what they're telling me are lies to sell me something, and sometimes the lies are worse and sometimes they are less offensive. You have to listen critically and know those words are carefully calculated to make you feel and think a certain way. I mean it's not like one guy is getting a flash to say this word; it's ten or fifteen guys for months and months sitting around a table in an advertising agency in New York and saying, "This is the approach we have to take, this is a sexy word that will creep in there, which will sell this toothpaste or that deodorant." You have to educate yourself to know that business will do anything to sell. They will kill you to sell. They will build the Pinto gas tank to sell. They will build a Firestone 500 to sell. They will kill you with asbestos to sell, and know that they are doing it and yet the media and the films will never say we have murderers in our midst.

The "murderers" are a guy, a dark guy, an Italian guy, a black guy, a guy with a gun: those are the film-TV murderers. Murderers are never Harvard graduates speaking good English—Ph.D.'s who say, "Well, we might burn 3000 people if we put this gas tank out but it will cost us $4.5 million to recall these things, so let's put it out and we'll correct the gas tank on the next run." Cold, quiet, calm, impersonal murderers—murderers—not even murderers of passion, but murderers of some unknown kid or some unknown woman. And yet our society, our media, our stories, our films don't say that these guys are murderers. That goes for military people, that goes for the whole fabric of our culture.

At the other end of the spectrum, what role do you think film plays or should play as a catalyst for social change?

I think that film, motion picture film, and I'm including television because television is what people see, is the most potent force to influence people's habits. Look at the newscasters and think about 1968 and realize that they wouldn't let some of the members of my crew into a restaurant in Chicago in 1968 because of the length of their hair, because one guy had a beard. Now you look at the newscasters—the most respectable people on television. They have long hair, they have beards. Look at Gene Shallit—they wouldn't let him in the NBC building (or is it CBS) fifteen years ago. So you realize that the media have an opportunity to change people's ideas about what is proper, what is right, what is desirable. The potential for social change is there. But you can't lose sight of the fact that the forces in our society recognize the power of the media and exercise control about where we can go to and where we can't.

I'm just wondering, were you more idealistic about the potential of film to "change the world" back when you were doing your early documentaries, compared to now?

Yes, I see now the world changes slowly and it doesn't get changed by people coming to conclusions about political philosophies. It's when they come to conclusions about the fact that they just bought something for $50 which has a built-in obsolescence of say two years. Or they realize the fact that they pay tax, 80% of which is going towards weapons of destruction which can never be used without ending the world. In other words, it has to come through some personal connection. Americans particularly do not come to political conclusions on the basis of abstract study or thought—which I think is healthy in a lot of ways because you can get screwed by the abstract thought.

How about some of your early features that you did with Irvin Kershner, which were documentary in style and nature. Was that dictated necessarily by the budget, or was it intentional?

Well, I made three films with Kersh. I made *Stakeout on Dope Street*, *The Hoodlum Priest*, and *Face in the Rain*. Kershner came from documentaries; in fact I met him when I was visiting California and I saw his Paul Coates *Confidential File* on TV and I loved the shooting and I thought, "Gee that's what I want to do." So I asked a friend of mine how I could meet this cameraman and so I met him and he's crazy as hell, real crazy, but a marvelous person with a good eye and a good filmic sense. So when we met we said we wanted to make a feature. Both of us came from documentaries and we dealt with a subject which was taboo up to that very moment. You could not make a film about dope. I think *The Man with the Golden Arm* came out about the same time. In those times the only kind of films that ever dealt with dope would be a film showing Chinese guys sitting around in a big opium den. The idea of the documentary style came about because that's what we knew and we wanted to blend the two. On *The Hoodlum Priest*, some of that style was still there. It was losing its edge because we were getting slicker and we had more equipment and we had actors of greater consequence. Then on *The Face in the Rain* which we made in Italy, I remember one scene where I ran with the camera after an actor down a narrow street. At that time, hand-held camera was something which occasionally was done by Jimmy Howe or some far-out guy for one scene. But I used to do a lot of hand-held things. In fact when I used to take my CM3 out on a set, even on *Virginia Woolf*, all the oldtimers would walk away and there would be a lot of snickering. And when you turned the camera on it sounded like a coffee grinder, so they'd say, "What the hell is going on?" So I think that's why the documentary approach for the first features.

That's what you were coming out of?

Sure, you do what you can do, you know. And then when I did *The Best Man*, for example there was a scene that took place in an automobile. They called the process department and they had the mock-up on the set and I said, "Why don't we do it in a real car?" and Henry Fonda encouraged the crew to try it without process. So I got in the car with the hand-held camera and there were only four lines so we figured we could dub it because the camera was too loud. But everyone said, "Why are you doing that?" Of course, we take those things for granted now. So that even the ideas of not shooting on sets was still fairly avant-garde. It astounds me how fast we have come away from that, but the courage to do those things and to tell Hollywood that that's the way you should do it only came from the fact that I knew it could be done because that was the way I used to do it, and I couldn't do it any other way. I didn't even know what the hell a process screen was. As a matter of fact, before sound, the cameras were always used "live" and "real" in cars.

We sort of get the impression from talking to you and several things that we've read that you get more of a kick out of making documentaries?

It's hard to say. I like to be in control of the images that I gather and when you work in a normal feature, as a director of photography, it's a cooperative effort. It's an effort that's spelled out in advance by the script, by the art director, certainly by the director, and ultimately by the cutter. In a documentary I have more control of that. Now I prefer to do that as a director in feature films but I haven't been able to do that except in *Medium Cool*, which is quite a while ago.

You said in an interview that America, America *was the toughest film of your life. Could you explain why?*

Well, *America, America* was sort of my big break because I hadn't done anything but *Stakeout on Dope Street*, and my brother, who was an actor at that time, was in *Tea and Sympathy* and knew Kazan and got *Stakeout on Dope Street* to Kazan to see and my brother sort of introduced me to Kazan. So Kazan was taking a big chance on me, rather than taking a regular Hollywood cameraman. And then the film was very, very personal to him. It was a film that had so much pent-up intensity about the subject matter plus we were working very, very long hours with mixed crews who spoke Italian and Greek along with a few Americans in the crew. Also I think that I wasn't that sure of myself and when you're not that sure of yourself things are tougher because you have all that conflict, all that nervous energy coming out and so that's some of the things that made it tough. And it was physically tough too. It was very hot in Greece. We shot in Turkey for a while and the Turkish government did not like Kazan and they sort of suspected that he gave them a false script, which he did. But then like a lot of things where adversity is associated, in retrospect, I still feel that it was some of the best photography that I've done, well, 50-50 with *Days of Heaven*.

What did you like about America, America *that makes you say that?*

Well, I liked the look. It really looked like an old movie. And I liked the immigration thing which I sort of worked out pretty much on my own. A lot of that I shot while the extras were waiting for Kazan to do the scene. I shot maybe 40 minutes of film just of the extras who were in wardrobe, in their cages and they're moving around and it just seemed like I was right there where the real immigrants were. That was shot in Greece although it was supposed to be on Ellis Island.

You used the same technique later in Bound for Glory. *Just standing around and by happenstance you picked up whatever nuances.*

Yes, exactly. I guess you don't do too many new things. I just had a *déjà vu* a few weeks ago when I shot something and I remember I did that shot when I was 17 with my Bolex—same shot.

Many of your early features were documentary in style. And then Virginia Woolf *was shot almost exclusively in the studio. What were some of the difficulties in moving from the realm of the documentary style to the sound stage?*

I am trying to remember back to those times. Yes, there were a lot of difficulties in that I had this immense control. I had almost every light on the set on a dimmer. Many people made mention of the fact that it was Mike Nichols's first film and that I helped him and sometimes they give me more credit for *Virginia Woolf* than I think I truly deserved. Now that I'm thinking back, I had a gaffer, Flannigan, who helped me. And often in films, always still in films there are people who work in the crew who are really of immense help, immense help. You get stuck—everybody gets stuck—and you say, "How in hell am I going to do this right," and somebody will help, somebody will give you an idea, somebody will touch off something. This gaffer was very, very helpful to me and very supportive so that he helped me make the transition from some of the things I didn't know about working in a confined studio setting.

You hand-held some of the shots. Why and in what kind of situation did you use it?

I remember there was a shot where Richard Burton leaves the living room and goes down the hallway and goes into a closet, takes a gun off the shelf and goes back into the living room. That was a hand-held shot and I don't think, with the tools available at that time, it could have been done well with the dolly. Then there were hand-held shots in the parking lot when they left the roadhouse. Again I remember seeing a Fellini film where there were bright lights in the background and so I decided to light it that way. There were some hand-held shots there although most of that was shot with a long lens outside, and window screen, an idea I got from a book called *Simple Photo Tricks*, which I bought the day before we were to shoot it. My assistant and I went to a hardware store and we spent about half an hour looking through the window screen in the basement of the hardware store, holding it up to the light and looking at it. I remember there was this little guy, I guess it was in Amherst, Massachusetts, looking at us and saying we were really getting crazy looking through this window screen, until we picked out what we wanted.

What place does the hand-held camera have in a dramatic feature, I mean, do you just use it for expediency, when nothing else is going to get it? Or does it have a dramatic use also?

Usually in features I find that I use it when nothing else will work. Now Lelouche for example uses it as a style; he will just decide this whole section of the film I'm going to hand-hold. It gives him an opportunity to make minute adjustments to the left or to the right. It also gives him an opportunity to let the actors be freer because he can literally look through the camera while he's shooting and not worry that the operator's going to say, "Well, he's only supposed to go to the door handle but that time he went to the window, so I lost him."

In In the Heat of the Night *was your first color film. You said you lit it just like a black-and-white film, and we were wondering what you meant by that.*

Well, again, at that time color films had a lot more fill light. In all the books there were big signs everywhere: ratio 2:1 if you want to make good color pictures; maybe, if you're dangerous, 3:1. Well, I didn't know how to light that way. I mean I knew my eye said that a certain kind of lighting looked good and I lit things as I would black-and-white, but keeping color temperature in mind. It looked fine to me and no one said, "Gee, that's terrible or that's too contrasty," so that's how I worked it. It's another example of doing what you're comfortable with or what you're experienced with. And what you're experienced with is not what was being done generally so that what to some people would be avant-garde to yourself would actually be conservative, if you can interpret that statement.

So really you didn't give any special consideration to the color style.

No, except I remember there were a couple of scenes where I just stretched a silk over the top of the set and pounded some 10Ks into the center of the silk and used that as lighting, which of course had been done before in the old movies where they just had open sets and which has subsequently been done all the time because it's basically your built-in bounce light, but at that period in U.S. photography, that was different. Also I used umbrella lights which also used to get a big laugh from the crew.

So essentially you were lighting it as you would black-and-white film only you were leaning a little towards softening it.

But it was basically a key-light picture. You know, except for just the police station. I can't remember any other areas of the interiors. They were lit hard light, key light, fill light, back light, kicker.

Do you still light color films that way?

No.

How has it changed.

It's changed mostly because we use bounce and soft light a lot. And that kind of lighting in black-and-white would be good but it wouldn't have the snap in blacks and the interest that you want in black-and-white.

In The Thomas Crown Affair, *you used hidden cameras. What kind of situations did you use them in and what kind of drawbacks were there?*

Again, I think this comes from my documentary experience. I know that real people in real situations do things which the most brilliant director couldn't tell a person to do. I mean just oddball things. So when Norman Jewison said that the bank robbery was supposed to happen out this doorway, I said, "Look, Norman, let's just conceal 'em." I think we had four cameras, one in the building across the street, two on different places on the road, and one in a van, the back of a truck. "Let's just tell our actors what to do. Just let it go." Well, it was fantastic. Of course, in the ultimate film, they couldn't use it. But people literally walked by our crooks walking out the bank with sacks of money in their hand and the guys just didn't look like Brinks men anyway. And they'd just walk by and turn around and keep walking and it was marvelous. We let the traffic go so the scene was interrupted by traffic and it gave the illusion you were seeing the real thing. We shot it over and over about four times, and by about the fourth time someone reported it to the police. We had already notified the police, but at a different station and so these other police came in and there was a moment where guns were drawn and when the real world started to impinge on our pretend world.

The chess sequence, I suppose you've been asked about that a number of times, but how did you light that? It was really soft and had this euphoric quality to it.

Well, the chess sequence is where Norman gave me the script and literally said, "They play chess with sex" and that was it. So I suggested he let me try some things. Some of my ideas were pretty vulgar and at least adolescent, but apparently that's where the audience's minds were or are—with things like feeling chess men up and down and rubbing your finger on your lips and I think I had her leg move against his under the table. About the lighting, basically there were two 4K soft lights up high at about a 45-degree angle so it was lit as if there were a big round, soft source above the chess table, with a couple points of light hitting the walls so it didn't go utterly black in the background; hitting a picture, hitting a fireplace, that type of thing. When we went down to the close-ups, I enhanced the effect of the fireplace light with low kickers with gels on them.

Why do you think cameramen have such a hard time making that step up to director when it seems such a logical step?

I don't know. If I truly knew the answer of what the problem is for *this* cameraman to make a transition to director, I would immediately do or undo that thing and then direct. I really don't know. There's a lot of suppositions. I know that this business is highly compartmentalized. It's easy to say, "Well, he's a good editor but we don't think of him as a director," just as they type-cast actors. So I think that that element exists. I think that, because the one film I did direct was an overtly political film, people in power assumed that that's an all-consuming viewpoint of mine and that if I did direct a film, I would direct it from some soapbox.

But Medium Cool *was a film that spoke very well in the period of time when it was made.*

Well, I agree with your evaluation. You see, at the time, that film was a severe threat to the establishment, more severe than I even realized at that time. On the basis of Freedom of Information papers I have received, the film was under surveillance by no less than four government agencies. The government—I can give you some of the documents to back this up—put severe pressure on Gulf and Western Corporation not to release the film. The film was given an X-rating which was part of the compromise that was made so it basically kept an audience of any consequence away. Basically the film was directed to a young audience and no audience was allowed in under 18 under any circumstances. It upsets me to go into the details of what happened. But the general public believed when there were antiwar demonstrations that this had no effect on the government in Washington and it was a futile gesture by a ragged few dissidents. Yet now since Watergate, we can hear how every time there was a demonstration it shook up Nixon and Mitchell and the whole sea in Washington—shook them up beyond belief. We realized there was a power afoot in this country, the power of the people which the government did not want to admit, because once people recognized that they did have the power, they might do even more. Whereas if they could say, "Well, what good can I do . . ."

Did you have that feeling, when you were making the film, that it was a very powerful film? I had the feeling that you were making a film that was about this particular subject and that you were approaching it from a fairly objective viewpoint.

Well, I was interested in the overall subject which I still am interested in, and that is the subject of the voyeur and the persons involved. This is the same problem the cameraman is always faced with: whether you are going to photograph and make a fantastic shot of someone who has just been shot and is dying, or whether you put your camera down and help the guy, get an ambulance and call doctors as quickly as possible. I am just sort of giving an extreme example. But I have done *vérité* documentaries where someone is terribly upset and crying, just utterly a helpless, hopeless human being. So you're faced with the idea that you can get this terrific scene, it's going to make your documentary; or again whether you put your camera down, put your arm around that person and say, "Look, please don't cry." And so I wanted to deal with that as it related to the problems of newsreel cameramen and the fact that it was at that time (1968), sort of just gave it more fabric. There were certain specific things in the film that made it very volatile. For example, I had learned that the government was looking at all film shot by news stations and examining it frame by frame to identify people who were in peace marches. That was not known and I had actors say that in the film. I didn't know it for a fact, but this, according to FBI documents which I now have, upset them greatly. Since then it's also come out that about 70 % of the people with news credentials in Chicago at the 1968 Democratic convention were actually people who were doing surveillance work for various agencies of the government.

Also through the Freedom of Information Act, I found that the government makes evaluation of your work. I have a document which says—this was from some time ago—"Haskell is fairly good on documentaries but would never be good on commercials or feature projects because he's too finicky." This is an FBI artistic judgment—government money spent on film criticism! These are not just judgments. They don't just make judgments which they pass among one another as letters; you know that someone in authority in the motion picture business who may think about hiring me for a film wouldn't say, "The guy is a commie." They would say, "Well, he's 'finicky' or he's slow or he's trouble." So that when someone gathers a secret file, the secret file is never *just* for information because the information is too delicious, too tempting not to use.

Did you think it was a commercial project or a project that would do some business as opposed to an art film?

Yes, I thought that it would be very popular and that the people would want to see it. I thought that it would be very exciting. I thought if I just finished this thing and got it out, I'd have it made. And actually the reviews all over the world were fantastic, they were very very positive on the film. It was a full union film and cost $600,000 to make and, according to Paramount's bookkeeping, it has never made its money back.

That was the next question I was going to ask. It was never a success?

It has never made its money back. First, I'll say it in public, I'll say it in the press, and in your book: The major distribution companies, at least from my experience in those days, are crooks. They will steal from you any way they can and they have the most expert nontraceable ways of stealing. Their kind of stealing is an accepted part of the game. If somebody went into your house and stole $1000, there would be cops and special detectives to catch that son of a bitch. And if they catch him he's going to the hoosegow. But when the big companies rob for big money it's hardly worth noting. That's just part of the business. That's the game.

It's corporate crime?

They don't think of it as crime; it's just the way it's done. So what actually happens in feature films is other smaller people figure little ways to steal while they are doing it—get a kick-back from gaffers or a kick-back from the transportation firm. It's all peanuts, but in other words, when you deal in a society of monetary dishonesty, if everyone's doing it, then it takes the onus off you.

So back to Paramount. There were certain pressures on them, as far as the release time of the film and so on and so forth. Now did they just dump it out there without any support?

They had immense pressures from Gulf and Western Corporation. Any big corporation has many dealings with the government—favors from different commissions, rulings in courts, tax situations. Many dealings are dependent on the good wishes or good offices of the government and high sources in the Democratic Party let it be known to Paramount that if this film went out certain things in Gulf and Western's favor would not happen. I'm just speaking in generalities. But now I'm prepared, if ever questioned on these things, to back them up with sources and documents as well, but it's taken quite a while to get it.

Would you like us to print that, or would you . . .

Oh, you can print that. Definitely.

In American Graffiti *you shot a lot of night-for-night over large areas of space, how did you do that?*

Well, the lighting in *American Graffiti* was so simple I'm ashamed to say it in print but it is another example of what I learned from working in documentaries. It's also an example of giving yourself limits and disciplines, but basically I'll tell you exactly what I did. Wherever there was a light pole, I put a couple of mini-moles shooting down. Where there was a lit store, I put a clip light or photo-flood. Where we had to see inside a car I got a 12-volt recreational vehicle light and a gaffer taped that either to the sun visor or to the dash board. Then when we did shots inside cars where we wanted light changes on the people's faces, I would have either another

car with a couple of guys with sun guns in their hands to flash the car, or I would get
high-beam headlights on trucks or cars on cross streets so that when our car would
go through the intersection the lights would change on them. Or if I was fortunate
enough to place a light on the street, I would just take a baby and hit it from the
street into the car so that there would be light changes on the people's faces in the
car. And that's the whole picture. Well inside the drive-in I had strip lights.

How much freedom do you basically have in creating a visual style for a feature?

I've been really fortunate in recent years. I've had a lot of freedom to create a
visual style. I would hasten to add that freedom isn't always the best thing to have. I
mean, I think best when in a bounce-off situation. I like to talk to art directors, I
like to listen to the director, I like to go into a room with my gaffer and not just say,
"Okay, this is the way we do this because it's in the style." I do this just to sort of get
the feel of some inspiration, to feel some cross currents of ideas, and I function
better that way than just saying, "This is my plan, and do it, regardless."

*I'm curious about how some of the styles come about. Obviously the script must
have something to do with the style that you decide to go with. I was wondering
what things other than the script have an effect.*

Well, what you have to photograph. If you have a film where you have an actress
who should look good from the point of view of the part she is playing and from the
point of view of the story and also because she's an actress and people expect her to
look good, then you don't make a naked picture. You don't make a film with no
garbage on the lens and hard light; you just don't do it because then you'd be boxed
in whenever you got around to her close-up, so that type of thing somewhat depends on your style. And then the actual locale depends on your style. If you have a
locale where there are a lot of big windows for daylight scenes, you're going to
want to hit big units into those windows and have general soft floodlights. If you
have scenes in a film which takes place in nightclubs, there will be dark areas and
spots of light. So that on *Second Hand Hearts*, after reading the script and looking
at the locations, I had a feeling that the film should be a wide-angle film and should
be a sharp film. Now that doesn't mean that it's all wide angle, and all sharp but
there's a lot with a 20mm lens shooting at f 8, f11, f12.

*Are there some times when you work better or become more creative under
certain restrictions?*

Well, it's like anybody. I don't think it's right for anyone in any endeavor to be so
cocky, so sure that they can or should close their minds off completely to ideas
which may set their juices flowing. There are a lot of ways of doing a lot of things.

*Along the same lines, we saw this 1968 article you wrote about how studio
cameras were too heavy. We thought that was one of those instances where cameramen really had some influence over the technology, and we were wondering if you
still have things that you would like to see changed?*

The HMI units have been a good breakthrough. Of course the things that Panavision has done, even though it's so very expensive, are advantages. The wedding of
television viewing and the movie camera: this utilization of TV is increasing.

How do you think it will be used in the future?

First it will be used to save the script clerk and the director from matching problems. It's really the proof positive because every film has a time when there's a 10- or 15-minute discussion between script person and cameraman and the director. "Well, did he pick up the notebook when he said, 'rocks' or did he pick it up when he said 'projector'?" Nobody knows. So we shoot it both ways. With video, you just press the three buttons and look at it quickly and say, "This is how he did it," and we have the matching. So for matching it's absolutely invaluable. I think it could be used intelligently with director and actors to look at the day's work afterwards, playing it back and forth and noting certain mannerisms; it depends on the actor and the director as to how analytical they get in their work and whether this analysis depletes their creativity or enhances it. Theoretically.

With your own production company you do commercials and other things like that?

Yeah, Conrad Hall and I are partners in that business and we do commercials.

Does that allow you to keep up on technological advances or just to pay the bills?

We do it to make the money. There are tangential advantages in that we do get to experiment, we do get to keep our hand in.

Do you get a chance to experiment on a commercial as compared to a feature?

Sure, you can experiment. Actually the experimenting on a commercial comes in trying something this way and if it doesn't work, so what, it's only four seconds, you know. Now the commercials we did with John Wayne on the other hand, we just had to dig into our feature experience and background and concentrate on doing it because we didn't have him for a very long time and he tended to be if not critical, a very strict task master.

You started principal photography on a number of films and then you left before completing it. In general, what kind of things cause this type of artistic disagreement? And where do you, as a cameraman or as an artist, take your stand?

There are only two films, and they happened back to back. And neither one of them was artistic disagreement. I did a good part of *The Conversation* and Francis Coppola had some problems with his script and with his approach to the theme. He came into the film unprepared; he was doing an opera. He had about eight irons in the fire when we began *The Conversation* and he needed three to four weeks off of the film. This also can be verified because he has subsequently said this in interviews and said it to me—that he needed someone to be his reason for the hiatus. And I was it on *The Conversation*. So he said everything was looking good, everything was fine. The only basic disagreement I had with Francis was at the beginning of the film. I said, "Francis, we're making an audio blow-up. We have to work out more visual things to make this conversation film, or film it." And, in fact, I shot the whole conversation with nine cameras in that square. I shot that in one day. He had scheduled a week to shoot that. And I think that that took some of his time, that he was hoping to have to write during that week, away from him. In any event, Francis and I had a lot of bad feelings after that film and then we had a number of meetings afterwards and I think we're friends again. I recognized his problem, and he apologized to me. On the other film I'd shot most all of the film, that was *Cuckoo's Nest*, and that film remains a mystery to me. Because there were no disagreements with Milos Forman. We were on schedule so there was no question about being fiscally responsible. In fact, he was relying on me heavily. I wrote some of the scenes that were in the film, I gave him some lines. Milos didn't understand a lot of the colloquialisms. I was told, not even by Milos, but by Saul Zaentz, by Michael Douglas, arbitrarily that I couldn't continue to work on the film.

There was no reason? Just "Your services are no longer needed"?

Never any reason. Well, they used the word "artistic differences." And in fact I went to Milos that night at midnight and I said, "What are the differences, why didn't you say something? What is it that I've done that you don't like?" It was really quite shocking to me because I really worked hard on that film; very, very hard in fact.

From doing all these interviews we've found a recurring theme of the cameraman as scapegoat.

Well, if you think about it, replacing actors is really difficult. You've got them and they're on the screen and what are you going to do? The cameraman runs the crew, so he's like the foreman; so if you want a big head to roll, you just have to turn around and that's the biggest head to roll immediately. The first person who changes the script from an abstraction to acetate is the cameraman. If the dailies do not fulfill expectations, the cameraman can get killed as the messenger who brings bad news, if, in fact, it is bad news. But one thing about my fellow cameramen, and one thing I want to say about replacing and being replaced, is that I would never replace another cameraman without first talking to him and finding out what the situation was. Never. It would just be a courtesy.

And also one of the more insidious areas that come out is that as budgets balloon to 25–30 million, the money to make the film gets less, or stays the same. We've heard people say that you've got a $30 million budget and that two-thirds of it goes above the line and you're still left with $4 million to make a $30 million picture. Again the cameraman comes in. He's the guy who takes the heat. He's the guy who's too slow, so immediately you see the pattern forming that if he has to worry about being too slow, how good a job is he going to do? In your case, Bound for Glory *is a situation where, I guess the film was over budget and I guess the pressures were very intense, but still the film is beautiful. No one could argue with that fact.*

What makes a cameraman slow—and *Bound for Glory* is a perfect example of this—is that if you have to wait for a train to be where it is supposed to be for two or three hours, and then they say to shoot this thing in 15 minutes, and you take a half an hour to shoot it, then you become a slow cameraman. But in general, you wait for what you have to photograph. There are a lot of things you wait for: you wait for an actor to come out of the dressing room, you wait for the director to make up his mind, and then, because the act of commission to film is the cameraman's act, then he is what becomes slow. You see it's hard for people on the outside to realize what is taking time.

On Bound for Glory, *you flashed the whole picture, is that right?*

Practically. Some scenes I didn't but mostly all of it is flashed.

How did that help you contribute to the look that you were going for?

Well, I shot a lot of tests and I found that the flashing helped to soften the shadows. That's about it. Theoretically it pastelled the colors a little bit, although I'm not sure it did. I flashed different percentages for different scenes.

You knew all that from your previous tests.

Yeah, even while you're shooting you're still testing, but I did do quite a few tests.

In the dust storm scene in Bound for Glory, *how did you do that?*

Well, there are a number of dust storm scenes. The big cloud that comes in there, there's only one guy who can take the credit for that, a guy named Albert Whitlock, who is a famous matte man and the only thing I did was climb to the top of a very shaky water tower with a Panavision camera and photograph the town. And then he did the rest. There were a lot of dust scenes on the ground which were horrendous to shoot just because you couldn't see and couldn't breathe but it doesn't look that spectacular.

In establishing the visual look of that film, which had a very distinctive look, did you have any trouble keeping it consistent through the time that it was shot?

I had a lot of help from the art director, Michael Haller, a lot of cooperation. Also I spent a lot of time with wardrobe. The thought was, as Woody went to California, to increase the intensity of the colors. To begin with flat earth colors as much as possible and when he came to California to allow more color to creep in. Most of that was controlled by all of us who had the power over what was in front of the camera, not just filters and such.

So a lot of that was achieved just by keeping what you are photographing constant.

Right. And everybody on the set knew I did not want any strong colors. So, a stand-by painter, if he saw a bright red sign somewhere, he would go there, and without my even telling him after a few weeks, he would tone it down.

How did you retain that kind of style, that look, consistently? Were you shooting at a consistent number of footcandles throughout or a certain f-stop? Do you try to maintain that kind of thing?

Well, the look basically would maintain no matter what *f*-stop you shoot at. We tried not to shoot in front light because front light means more saturation of color. I liked to keep as much garbage in the air as possible—dust, smoke, whatever you can to diffuse.

What kind of things were you using?

Smoke inside. Avoiding harsh sunlight as much as possible. Big silks, little silks, back light. Now when you were forced to shoot in straight sun without silks I'd use big hunks of beadboard so that the shadows were filled and so that there was a certain translucency.

I thought that the scenes in the hospital in Coming Home *were really nicely done. Somehow you managed to make it look like a hospital but not objectionable. How did you do that?*

Well, the fluorescent lights were not fluorescent lights. They were fake fluorescent. I had units built that looked like fluorescents but actually had photofloods in them. Then the lights along the walls were also constructed and the top part were fluorescent. They were warm white deluxe and the underpart were PH211s. These are small darkroom lights. In *Coming Home* I tried a lot of hard sun slashes, using arcs coming in and just to overexpose or hit something harder than it should to get things out of range like you would in documentaries. But in *Coming Home*, there's very little diffusion in it. Just enough to get me by Jane Fonda, but very little.

So basically it was really just the angle that the light was coming in. Were you using any supplemental lights or were you lighting it all with what you had?

Sometimes I had my practicals on, sometimes I had the wall practicals on and sometimes I had lights coming in the windows. And then the times when you could move in closer, we would use lights to enhance the source so that if someone were near one of those wall lights, and we didn't see the wall light and the fixture, we had a bounce card that would be from the same direction of that wall light which would hit the actors.

Talking about diffusion, a lot of the cameramen we have talked to think that the lenses are too sharp and the film is too good. They feel that they have to degrade the film and throw something in front of the lens to cut it down because it's too clear for them. Do you share that view, or is it basically up to the individual project?

It's true that the modern negative film is very sharp, very fine grained. And if shot naked, it will give you a sharp fine-grain picture. And if you want to flatter a woman or make something pictorial in the museum-art sense of the word, you generally have to degrade the image. That all depends on whether you want to do that or not, just as it does with a painter.

What relationship do you have with your crew? Do you have a constant crew that you tend to use?

I have had a constant crew and I love them so much, and I don't work that much myself, that I have recommended them to fellow cameramen. Gordy Willis has had most of my crew for two pictures. Owen Roizman has had part of my crew. I always have mixed feelings about it; I'm pleased to be able to recommend them because I think they're so good but at the same time, I think that they will tell these other guys my tricks. But then I start thinking about my tricks and I know that most of them I got from other cameramen myself.

What did I read in the paper, something about you directing Sheena, Queen of the Jungle?

Oh, was that in the paper, really? Because they asked me to direct that. The script was horrible and I rewrote the script some and they finally decided not to do it. Orion asked me to do that. I get asked to direct things but I don't want to just do shit, that's all.

Now that you've done one, you know what you want to do.

Yeah, so we'll see whether being pure pays off.

Can't hurt.

13

Billy Williams

*"The films I'm happiest with are the films where eve-
rything comes together, starting with a good script,
the right director, a good cast and a good art director.
It's the bringing together of a team of people to bring a
wholeness and a unity to the subject. I think the cinematographer's work is part of the whole."*

A mainstay of British cinematography and former president of the British Society
of Cinematographers (B.S.C.), Billy Williams has only recently become more
widely known in the United States for his American films: *Boardwalk*, *Going in
Style*, and his Oscar-nominated *On Golden Pond*.

The son of a cinematographer who shot everything from silents to newsreel to
features, Williams started working as an assistant to his father after he got out of
school. This paternal apprenticeship provided enough technical knowledge and
discipline that he soon was hired as an assistant cameraman by a documentary
company. All the while, Williams was looking for a way to move into features.
That break finally came with the advent of British commercial television and, consequently, commercials. A new wave of young commercial-directors including
Ken Russell, Richard Lester, and John Schlesinger emerged, searching for fresh
photographic approaches; this opened the door for Williams and a whole new
breed of British cinematographers. The directors soon went on to features and
their cinematographers moved with them. Williams, because of his documentary
work in particular, brought a sense of adventure and openness with him to features.
He didn't feel restricted by the time-honored studio traditions.

His first wide recognition in this country came with the release of Ken Russell's
Women in Love, for which he received his first Oscar nomination. Among his other
notable achievements in the seventies were his tastefully understated *Sunday,
Bloody Sunday* and his expansive and panoramic *The Wind and the Lion*. Show-
ered with critical praise for *On Golden Pond*, he again received an Oscar nomination and, in the following year, he finally won the golden statue for *Gandhi*. As an
elder statesman of British cinematography, Williams still approaches each new
project with a youthful enthusiasm. The constant challenge of new sights and
sounds renews his creative vigor and, as a result, he continues to be an influential
force in contemporary cinematography.

1965	*San Ferry Ann*	1973	*The Glass Menagerie*
1966	*Just Like a Woman*		*A Likely Story*
	Thirty is a Dangerous Age, Cynthia	1974	*The Wind and the Lion*
	Red and Blue	1975	*Voyage of the Damned*
1967	*Billion Dollar Brain*	1976	*The Devil's Advocate*
	The Magus	1977	*The Silent Partner*
1968	*Two Gentlemen Sharing*	1978	*Eagle's Wing*
	Woman in Love†		*Boardwalk*
1969	*The Mind of Mr. Soames*	1979	*Saturn 3*
	Tam-Lin		*Going in Style*
1970	*X, Y, and Zee*	1980	*Gandhi**
	Sunday, Bloody Sunday		*On Golden Pond†*
1971	*Pope Joan*	1981	*Monsignore*
	Kid Blue	1983	*The Survivors*
1972	*Night Watch*	1984	*Ordeal by Innocence*

* Academy Award for best achievement in cinematography.
† Academy Award Nomination for best achievement in cinematography.

How did you come to be interested in the cinema and cinematography in particular?

Well, I was really born into it. My father was a cinematographer. He started in the silent days: 1910. He was a cinematographer in the British Navy during World War I. He became an expedition cameraman in 1928 traveling across Africa. He worked in everything from newsreels to documentaries to features in the thirties. So I'd always been associated with cameras and the cinema; when I left school it seemed to me to be a natural and obvious thing to do. So I started off as his assistant for three or four years. I learned a great deal because he was a very hard taskmaster. I think father-and-son relationships can sometimes be more severe than others. But I felt that he taught me a discipline which I valued later on.

I decided though that I should become more independent and, after I did my National Service, I joined a documentary company called British Transport Films. They made documentary films about the railways, docks and harbors. I was there for about five years as an assistant cameraman. At that time, there were two other assistant cameramen with the company and over the years, they became really quite well known. David Watkin was one and Robert Paynter was the other. So the three of us were buddies for a long time before we actually got our break to become cameramen.

By the time I was twenty-three or twenty-four, I felt that I was ready to become a cameraman in my own right on documentary films. But I had to leave British Transport Films in order to fulfill that. There wasn't the opportunity there. So I left and became a freelance documentary cameraman. I should say here that I'd always had a great ambition to become a feature cinematographer. At that time in England, although we were all in the same union, the camera department was really divided into two camps: either you were a documentary filmmaker or you were a feature filmmaker. And it was almost impossible to go from being a documentary man to doing features because the feeling was that you didn't understand studio procedure and how to use lights. The documentary craft was very much a sort of second-rate affair. Well, all that changed when commercial television came along and with it, commercials. Because that brought in a whole new wave of directors. And when these directors started to make commercials, which was a lucrative thing for everybody concerned, they were searching for a new kind of look. And it meant that a lot of documentary cameramen, like myself, got an opportunity to photograph commercials and use lights creatively for the first time. This was a very valuable experience for me both in terms of experimenting and developing techniques for working on interiors and working with the new, young directors, people like Ken Russell, John Schlesinger and Ted Kotcheff. I worked with them on commercials before I did features with them. So commercials became a stepping stone for several British cinematographers. After a few years in commercials, I was in a much better position to move into features. I shot my first feature in 1965; it was a little black-and-white picture called *San Ferry Ann*, a low-budget comedy. It's the only feature I've done in black-and-white. Although all my other pictures have been in color, when I'm lighting I think in tones of black-and-white and gray rather than in color. When I'm lighting I always try to get a separation, a light subject against the dark or a dark against a light. I like to rely on tonal separation rather than just relying on the color to separate it. I mean, color can say a great deal but if you can incorporate the right use of color with tonal separation, you get a greater perspective in composition, a greater depth. If you look at the great paintings, you'll find that although they're in color, they have tonal separation which gives them greater perspective and makes them almost three-dimensional. I dislike flat compositions and flat photography. I hate seeing faces against the wall of the same tone so that they end up blending into the wall. I like to achieve a separation; by doing that, you can emphasize what you want the audience to view. I mean, there's a lot of things going on in a film and some things are more important than others.

You can make it selective?

There are a number of things that combine to make the selection important: the set-up, the lens, the placement of the light and the placement of the actors. It can make a world of difference as to what the audience is going to perceive by the way you do that. If you do that well, you direct the audience to what the scene is really about. Whereas if you do it badly then you give an audience a picture that has no focal point. It's like a bad painting. You've got to have a focal point. You've got to direct your audience towards what is dramatically important. And you do this, as I've said, by a combination of lenses, movement and tracking. I love to move the camera; I do not like being too fixed for a long time. I know that there are some scenes where you have to shoot people sitting around the table and talking. In that kind of situation you don't get too many opportunities to move the camera without becoming self-conscious. But when there are opportunities to move the camera and track across a room, I think that all helps to establish the location, the type of place that these people live in. The set dressings and the backgrounds are essential parts of the story. I mean, a cinematographer's job is to give a visual enhancement to the screenplay, which is going to make it dramatic and visually more exciting. He's going to give an added emotion to a scene which can give a little more emphasis to the performance. The actors and actresses are out there giving their best, the director is helping them. Now the cinematographer's job, I feel, is to get close to those people, to get to know them and to photograph them in a way that will enhance the character that they're playing. You can do this by different styles of lighting. You can make a person quite different by the way you place the lights.

How did your documentary work and your work in commercials prepare you for the time when you became the director of photography on your first feature? What kind of training was that?

I think that I had a certain sense of adventure about my work. I didn't feel restricted about the way things had been done by my predecessors, who were studio cinematographers with many years of experience working on sets. I regret to say that a lot of the earlier cinematographers used to work to a rather uniform style. I'm not going to generalize because they did some very fine work too. But I think a lot of people turned out pictures that always looked the same. A cinematographer would shoot a film where one scene looked just like another; every scene was photographed the same way. Now today, particularly with the younger cameramen, there's much more adventure in approach. I didn't feel myself restricted by too many conventions. I was prepared to have a go. And that's where commercials were invaluable because I had done a lot of fooling around and practicing, if you like, there. So when I came on to features I was quite well prepared technically but not in a conventional sense. It was particularly helpful when I photographed *Women in Love*, the screenplay that had the most opportunities, I think, in terms of expressing myself with color. I deliberately used very warm firelight and candlelight effects, day-for-night that was very blue-green, very often mixing the two so that you cut from an interior that was absolutely golden to a blue-green exterior in the forest. I think to use color like that makes it much more exciting for an audience.

It's much more involving.

Yes, it holds the interest. And it presents another view, another way of looking at things. It's realistic too, when you think about it, because firelight is very warm and when you go out at night in the moonlight, it's blue-green. Not everyone was doing that. Very often you would find that scenes were matched up so closely that there was hardly any difference. And I like the difference. I like the feeling that at dawn there is a very cold blue look. If the scene calls for that look then I will go for it and enhance it. Then when you cut to the next scene and it's later in the day, it has an entirely different look. The color and the quality of the light is different. I try to do that whenever possible. If you go from a lounge that's lit with very soft light to a bathroom that's lit by a harsh neon strip light, you should make it look like that. Get the feeling of the strip light compared to the soft, romantic feel of the lounge. Then out in the street, there is strong sunlight; go for strong sunlight and don't try to flatten it out so it's all even.

You're talking about enhancing the reality of the situation?

Yes, the enhancement of the reality is what I'm talking about. But of course it doesn't mean that you always have to stay with what's presented to you. You can change things as well. I think you should give yourself the freedom to do that. One of the most exciting parts of our job is working with a director who is aware of the visual potential and is able to discuss how a particular scene should be developed. I feel the director and the cinematographer are sounding boards for one another. They have a very close, almost man-and-wife relationship for several months.

Over the years, what directors have you had the best relationships with and why?

I've done two pictures with Ken Russell, *Women in Love* and before that, *Billion Dollar Brain*. But *Women in Love* was probably one of the best visual opportunities because it was such a marvelous subject with a variety of locations and moods. It had almost every lighting style, from candlelight to firelight to night interiors, day interiors and day exteriors. It had dusk and dawn scenes, snow scenes, day-for-night, night-for-night. It had everything going for it, all the opportunities.

Now Ken is a very demanding director. He's emotionally exhausting to work with. He has great vision. But at times he's very headstrong so that I found myself struggling sometimes to get what I wanted and what I felt Ken really wanted. But there was sometimes a conflict. I can give an example. Ken in the past, when he had worked with the BBC, had perhaps worked with cinematographers that overlit, particularly on location. He has an intense dislike of cinematographers using lights on day exteriors. As soon as a lamp comes out on a day exterior, he says, "What do you want that for? Why do you want to use lights?" Well this particular scene, which was with Alan Bates and the principals of the cast, was under a huge tree. There was a long table set out and all the principals were present. It was the scene with the fig. It's a very long scene with Alan Bates peeling the fig; it's a very erotic scene. But it also introduces you to Oliver Reed and Glenda Jackson. We shot this on location in England under a huge beech tree. Now when you looked out favoring Alan Bates, you looked onto brilliant sunlight and Alan Bates was in silhouette. When you looked back the other way, to Oliver Reed and Glenda Jackson, the light was totally different. You were looking further into the forest; the whole background was much darker. Ken didn't want me to light it because he was afraid it would look overlit. So I had a terrible argument with him. If I didn't light Alan Bates and all the people on his side of the table, who were backlit by this very strong sun, you would be crosscutting from someone who is in virtual silhouette to somebody who is lit by soft light coming in from the side. I told him, "I'll balance it up so it doesn't look lit." So I was able to reassure him. I did it by pushing brutes through a silk so that I had a very soft shadowless light; it looked as if there were no lights used. But I balanced it sufficiently that Alan still looked shaded. He was about a stop and a half underexposed, I guess. The background was still a stop and a half or two stops overexposed. But it brought it sufficiently into line so that when you crosscut the two, it wasn't a terrible shock every time. I think it worked and that, in the end, Ken was happy with it. I often had to struggle with Ken about using lights. But if you go out into a forest and you've got changing light—and in England the light changes a great deal more than on the West Coast—then you do need lights to keep the continuity of the scene. Otherwise your exposures and your contrast levels are going to be bouncing around. You'll have a lot of trouble when you try to match things together later on.

Day exteriors are almost a given—I mean, you look up and there's the light. How do you impose your will on it to make a day exterior look the way you want it to look?

First of all, when one goes to a new location, one has to try and get the feel of the values of that location in terms of geography, the mountains, the trees, the streets and also the type of weather you're likely to encounter. In some places you get fairly constant weather and you can rely on it from day to day. In other places, it's changing all the time. So you have to bear that in mind when you're making your first assessment. But if you go to a place where the sun is shining for most hours of the day, you realize, first of all that the sun is going through an arc of one hundred and eighty degrees. So I try and plot with the director what time of the day we'll do certain scenes. I like to get away from a very flat look; I don't like working with the sun very flat. Of course, in some places where it gets straight up overhead, you are stuck with that toplight. But if there's any chance to work with more of a crosslight or backlight, then I'll choose to do that. You work around the sun so you avoid getting into a situation where everything gets very flat. Most directors understand this and it can be done without losing too much time. That's one way of doing things. The other is the degree of filler that you choose to put in. I don't use a lot of lights on the streets; I prefer to use soft or white boards so that the fill light you're putting in isn't noticeable. It looks completely real. In overcast situations, you go for a completely different effect. Sometimes you can create your own shadows by bringing in trees, branches and large gobos. Generally speaking, on exteriors, you're adding to what's there. So the most creative part of it is the angle that you choose to shoot, the lens you select and the time of day that you do it.

Do you prefer location work or studio work? Or is it that they're just both different?

There are some subjects that just have to be done in the studio but there are many things that can be done either in the studio or on location. If I'm given the choice, I prefer to work on location. Somehow a real location seems to present more opportunities, particularly in terms of working from exterior to interior and tracking with your characters through the door of an exterior. That's something to link up the interior to the exterior. I think you get more of a sense of place. In the studio, you're so restricted to what you can see outside of a window; there's a lack of movement, a lack of people on the streets. So you get a bonus when you do location work although you are fighting the weather. But having difficulties imposed on you like that sometimes leads you to find another way of doing things. It forces you to be more creative. By being in the studio you're more inclined to do things in a set pattern. It's easy to fall into that trap.

It's easy to take a wall out or just drop a bank of lights down.

That's right. I think location work gives you that added opportunity to capture something unusual.

There's something I wanted to go back to; you were asking about directors. The picture I did after *Women in Love* was *Sunday, Bloody Sunday* which John Schlesinger directed. One of the first things John said to me was that he liked very much what I'd done on *Women in Love*, which was a very powerful visual subject. It was a very romantic approach; the photography had a scale to it. I hope it wasn't overpowering. It had breadth to it that he didn't want for *Sunday, Bloody Sunday*. He wanted the film to be underphotographed. He felt it was a very intimate story; he wanted to know those three characters and he wanted attention paid to every detail. He didn't want the photography to be, in any way, a distraction to the performances. He wanted it underplayed and not overly dramatic. And I accepted that as a challenge; there have been films since then when I've adopted the same approach. *On Golden Pond* has certain similarities to *Sunday, Bloody Sunday* in its close personal story without great dramatic visuals. I hope that I kept it interesting but not overpowering. Now those are two pictures where perhaps you can say that the photography didn't have to say too much. But with a picture like *The Wind and the Lion*, I had to use broader strokes because it was a bigger palette, a broader canvas. It called for spectacular scenes and visuals to get the maximum of excitement out of it. Those are the type of things where you have to have a different approach. But that's dictated by the story and discussion with the director. It's very important to have this understanding with the director before you go in, as to how the picture is going to look and where the emphasis is going to be and the way the light is going to be used.

Interesting that your work has wide diversity. You're able to do a small intimate picture as well as something with a much greater scope. You're able to stretch yourself to either extreme and everything in between.

Gandhi really has a combination of those two things. It's the story of the man and fifty years of his life so that we have to know that man and be a part of his environment. There are scenes of great intimacy intercut with scenes of vast expanse showing the millions that inhabit India and how their way of life is so different from ours. That film has both the intimate scenes and the broad action scenes.

What of your work are you most happy with?

The films that I'm happiest with are the films where the whole thing has come together.

Not just your own work.

Yes, because I think the cinematographer's work is part of the whole. If it's divorced from the whole, then it doesn't work. It's when everything comes together, starting with a good script, the right director, a good cast, a good art director. It's the bringing together of a team of people to bring a wholeness and a unity to the subject. Those seem to be the occasions when the result is the most satisfying. Maybe that's because you're all working together and not just trying to get your little bit right. I think *On Golden Pond* is a good example of this. Things came together very well on that film. *Women in Love* and *Sunday, Bloody Sunday* were also films where I felt there was a complete unity of purpose. There are three films that I'm satisfied with. But looking back sometimes, there are things that I might have done a little better.

When you're doing a picture, how closely do you monitor the lab? What kind of control do you try to exercise in that area?

Well, I don't fool around with the development too much. I have, in the past, used forced development and would still use it if the subject called for it. But generally speaking, I think that forced development just degrades the negative and lifts the fog level.

Which some people want.

Yes, which some people want. I don't particularly like it. I don't like forced development and flashing. Because I do like a fairly rich negative with good blacks. I'm not keen on the strong use of fog filters, although on occasion I use them. I don't like the effect they produce; I think you lose a lot of control because when you find yourself in a changing light situation, the fact that you've got that extra piece of glass on the front of the lens can produce unwanted flares according to the strength of the light. So I prefer not to have too much in front of the lens.

What you're saying is that these things are just another tool that you have the opportunity to use if you want. If something calls for it, then you will use that tool.

Yes. I would even consider using a certain filter or certain variations in development just perhaps for one scene rather than the whole film, if I wanted that scene to look different. I don't think you have to commit yourself to using a certain technique for a whole picture. But as a generalization, I don't like a degraded negative. I think one of the things you have to consider is that when a cinematographer and a director go to a lab and take their first answer print from the original negative, there it that way. You've got to think about the fact that you're going to have to make a dupe negative. So you're into a degradation of the negative with the dupe. Then any opticals that are in the picture give you a further degradation. Then you're going to go out to a theater where the projector is not so good; it hasn't got a very sharp lens or there's not enough light. At every stage along the line, the picture's going to deteriorate. You're never going to see it as good again as you see it in that screening room at the lab. So I'm very reluctant to have a degraded negative in the first instance. I think you're cheating your audience. They've got a right to see what's on the screen. And if you've produced a negative that's underexposed or degraded, they're not going to see it.

I know you came back to the States to time On Golden Pond. *How important is it to you to be able to time your pictures?*

It's extremely important. I now have it in my contract that I will be contacted and transported to wherever the lab work is being done. A few years ago I had an experience where the producer promised me that I would be brought over to do the timing. It wasn't in writing. Consequently I wasn't brought over and when I saw the finished print, I was very unhappy with it. I felt that a great deal of the visual quality had been lost because I hadn't been around to do the timing. Now on the occasion of *On Golden Pond*, the lab had done a print before I got here. So they'd done a lot of the groundwork. But I was still able to bring to the picture those little added things that I'd had in mind when I photographed it. I knew what the quality of light was. I knew the color I was going for and the density I had to achieve. I knew what was on the negative and whether it would stand being printed light or dark. Therefore you're able to get back what you originally intended to do, although you shot it a year ago.

It's like following through?

Yes. If you leave it to someone else, even someone who is close to the picture, like the director or editor, they don't always have the same things in mind. Not many directors understand light, you see, really understand light. They don't understand how much is going to pick up relating highlight to shadow. There are a few but the majority of directors, looking at the set or looking through the camera, are not able to judge what the contrast level is going to be like when it comes up on the screen. Of course, that contrast level can be altered by printing and the shadow detail can be affected considerably if it's printed too dark. If you've got a low-key scene and the print is too dark and you're not seeing in the shadows, you can sometimes lift it up that little bit just to get what you wanted in the shadows by hitting the right light. The director doesn't always know that.

Do you ever think photography can overpower the subject or theme of a film? How do you keep things in control so that doesn't happen?

Well, if the screenplay doesn't hold up in its own right, then you're starting off with a certain weakness. Sometimes photography can overcome that weakness by making the visuals interesting and exciting enough to give it a little bit more support. You can give visual interpretation where the words are weak or where there are no words at all. I did a picture a few years ago which unfortunately hasn't been shown in the United States because the distributor went bankrupt. It was a western called *Eagle's Wing*, starring Martin Sheen and Sam Waterston, and it was virtually a silent movie: there was practically no dialogue. It was the story of a white man and an Indian who were both obsessed with the possession of a beautiful white stallion. They pursue one another and they duel over the horse. But neither speaks the other's language. So the conflict of that film had to be conveyed visually. It had to be done with the camera and with the musical score. I knew from the beginning that it was a story with very little dialogue and that it could be told visually. Now I don't like to think that the visuals overpowered the story. But there are occasions where the visuals become unnecessarily dominant and it's up to the cinematographer to know when to restrain things.

But how do you know that? Is that taste?

I think it's taste and instinct and experience.

On Sunday, Bloody Sunday, *you could have done a lot of things with it but I have the feeling that you held back for the sake of the intimacy of the story. So that you were perfectly in synch with Schlesinger and the material.*

I can only describe it as an instinct and an understanding that you have to have with the director about what you're doing. That's where the cooperation is terribly important; I'm talking about the understanding and the confidence that the director and cinematographer have in each other. They can be confident in one another to be able to discuss everything and to know what emphasis a scene calls for. Pace is terribly important too. A certain indulgence creeps into shots sometimes where the camera just seems to go on endlessly panning or tracking; it's something that's visually exquisite but hasn't got anything to do with carrying the story along. You develop a feeling of pace so you can help a director when something seems to be playing too long. You can shorten it then and get to the essence of it. Training in commercials is very useful in this respect. With commercials, you've got to have the ability to tell a story in thirty seconds and it's got to be precise and to the point. So therefore, you've got to put over the message in a much shorter space of time. Now with a movie, you don't have that constraint. Sometimes you are inclined to let things run much longer than they will sustain. So commercials training gives you an added understanding of how to inject a little more life into a scene or how to shorten it by using certain techniques.

How important do you think the photographic style is to the success of a film?

With some films it's more important than others. I think there are very few occasions where it should be the dominant element. The performance of the actors is the most important thing of all. If you can therefore enhance what they're feeling and what they're thinking, then you must be making a contribution to the picture. I think the best films are when all the creative elements come together on a high plane. And if the film has a weakness in the script, or in the direction, or in the visuals, that's all going to pull the film down. And although the audience doesn't always analyze things, it does affect their participation and enjoyment of the film. For instance, if the framing is bad and the performances are good, you're not quite sure what to look at. Or perhaps it's not lit very well and you can't see expression in the faces.

To your eye, what determines a good frame, a good composition?

I don't think there's any single element. It's something that you're born with or you can acquire. There are people who can never compose properly. It's not something you can describe in words; you can only describe it with the pictures that you take. For instance, you go see somebody's holiday snaps; some take good holiday snaps and some people take atrocious ones. Well, that's an instinct. I think the best cinematographers have an understanding of composition. They have a vision.

When I go to see other people's work, I know whether it's giving me satisfaction. It's the same way when I see my own work; I can tell if I got it right. Other people may not notice that but I know when it hasn't worked as well as I'd liked it to.

How do you achieve consistency from set-up to set-up? How do you maintain that?

Let me tell you about *On Golden Pond* again. There's a sequence toward the end of the film where Henry Fonda and the boy go out in a boat and it's getting dark. The sequence lasts for ten or fifteen minutes and it has to gradually get darker until it's almost dark but you've still got to be able to see their boat hitting a rock and their falling out of the boat. Now in that kind of sequence, I know exactly how much I've got to underexpose it to give it that certain degree of darkness. But you're also relying on your eye and remembering what you did three or four days ago. You've got to have a picture of it in your mind because when you come back to shoot it, you've got to try to reproduce that. When you're shooting at that time which we call "the golden hour," that is, the last minutes of the day, you have very little latitude. You're really just relying on your experience and that picture in your mind of what you've got to achieve and what you've got to match to. It's all got to be in your head. You have an exposure meter to help you but you just seem to know when it looks right. Now I think that comes partly with experience.

When you start a picture, do you tend to want to maintain the same level of footcandles throughout the picture?

No. On interiors, as a general rule, I try to work at an f-stop of about four. I find that a comfortable stop; it doesn't require too much light but it does give sufficient depth of field to keep enough of the frame in focus. I don't like to be put into the position of doing a two shot where one person is always wildly soft, which is the sort of thing you get if you're working at $f2$. I don't particularly like working at that level; I much prefer to work at about $f4$. If necessary for a particular scene, I'll go to $f5.6$. I don't like going much over that with the present stock. I only work at very low light levels if there are certain things within the scene like practicals or candles or firelight which provide a good reason for not using too much light. In other words, don't overpower what's already there. I'll work at $f1.4$ or $f2$ or whatever I feel looks right, if necessary. But I don't, as a general rule, like very shallow focus. I don't like rack focus very much although you have to do it sometimes. Things like that make the audience aware of technique.

In Women in Love, *how did you enhance the firelight in the wrestling scene? What level were you working at?*

That was real fire, which is much better than having a studio fire with gas. You would never get the same effect. I framed it so that I could have the firelight on one side of the frame or the other rather than in the middle. By having it on one side I could then get my lights down low at floor level just out of the frame. I used an orange filter to match the firelight and I got my electricians to produce a flickering effect from the firelight. The wrestlers were sweated up which gave more highlight and reflection to them. So there was a constant movement of light with the movement of the wrestlers. I was working at about $f3.5$. There were two cameras working hand-held because the actors only stripped off naked for one day. And the rest of it had to be done in close up because they wouldn't do it again. One camera had a

28mm lens and the other had a 50mm or 75mm. We went back about three months later and shot the slow motion because Ken felt he needed a bit more building up.

Is source lighting a sacred commandment to you?

You phrase it in a difficult way. When I sit here and look at you, the window is on the left and therefore one side of your face is lit from the window and the other side is in shadow. Now if I establish you sitting there, that's where the light's got to come from. That's the source light. If I did it the other way, it would look wrong; so in this instance, it is sacred.

But do you have any compunction about changing that? Taking artistic license, so to speak?

For a start, you don't always see where the source is. However, if you see somebody sitting close to a table lamp, then you want the lamp to be the source. But there are other times when you get into a situation, particularly with a woman, where you want to cheat the source light a little bit. For example, where a woman would logically be sitting in cross light, you may have to cheat more to the front because she doesn't look very good in cross light. If you put a lady in a bad light, you're doing her a disservice and you might be in trouble yourself. So occasionally you have to do things like that and it's a liberty that I think is acceptable.

How do you choose your projects now? Is it the script, the director . . .

It's a combination of things. It does start with the script. If I really don't like the subject matter of a script, then that's it and I don't do it. But if I like the script and I like the idea of working with a particular director, then I start considering what the visual potential of it is. So it's a combination of three things. It has to be a story that I want to do; a director whose work I like or who I would like to work with for the first time; and the visual potential of the picture. Also it has to do with whether I feel I can get some satisfaction out of doing that particular film. I don't and I can't do pictures that I really don't care about. I can't do a picture unless I really care about what that picture is really trying to say. One of the most satisfying films I've ever done may be *Gandhi*, because I think what Gandhi stood for and what he tried to teach should be known by millions of people. So therefore I was absolutely thrilled when Richard Attenborough asked me to photograph it. Here was a story about a man of peace who was in love with humanity and who tried to find a way to bring a greater love and understanding to the world. The film doesn't preach that but it does put it across. And I'm sure it can stand as a great piece of entertainment as well. Now that was something that I was very proud to be associated with.

What are the films that you've shot here in the United States?

On Golden Pond, Going in Style and *Boardwalk.*

Do production companies and crews operate any differently in the United States than elsewhere?

The main difference is the breakdown in the responsibilities of the electricians and the grips compared to working in England. In England, the electricians set all the flags and the cutters whereas here the electricians only set the lamps. And any kind of shading is done buy the grip. Also I find that the grips here, generally speaking, do carry a lot more equipment. They carry a lot more bits and pieces which help in setting up. There is one other difference: some British cameramen have their operator do the set-up and then they just light the picture. Quite a few work that way, where the operator works closely with the director in setting up a scene and breaking it down into shots and angles. And the cinematographer is concerned solely with the lighting. I don't work that way because I can't divorce myself from the frame. The frame, the positioning of everything and the lens you're going to use is the first stage in recording the visual. Unless I can get that done to my satisfaction, I would feel a bit cheated. If I had to hand over that responsibility to someone else, I would feel that I was missing something. I want to contribute from the beginning and I want to be able to carry through in terms of the frame, the lens, the camera movement and the lighting. There has to be unity. Once I decide with the director how we are going to do a certain scene, then I hand it over to the operator and let him put in some fine brush work and make improvements. But the original concept of how you're going to approach something is terribly important and I wouldn't want to hand it over to someone else. Of course, it is good to have an operator who has worked with you before and understands what you're trying to do. Then you can quickly hand over the responsibility without having to be too precise about everything. If your operator knows how you work, he'll develop improvements along the same lines.

What is your relationship with your crew? Are you a hard taskmaster? Are you open to suggestions?

The operator is free to give input. You know, sometimes I'll be stuck on a particular point and the operator comes up with something. I always like to feel that if the operator wants to make a point, he'll make it rather than say nothing. I do like input from the operator. The assistant's task doesn't really call for that. The sort of question an assistant will ask is, "Where do you want me to hold the focus here?" If I've got to have a certain stop, I expect the assistant to tell me. But I would call that more of a technical relationship.

Generally speaking, how much creative freedom do you have in determining the visual look and style of a particular film?

I think it depends a great deal on the director; he's in charge. If the director doesn't like the way the cinematographer is lighting, and supposing there is a conflict, then probably the director's will would prevail. The cinematographer would either have to change his style or he'd be replaced. The important thing here is to have a good understanding with the director so you can work as a team. Once you have that, and have a confidence in one another, then you can build on that. The best directors I have worked with always want to get the best out of their crew. They pick a certain cinematographer because they want his contribution.

There's an implicit trust there.

Yes, you want to give input so you can constantly be improving on what's written down on the page. That doesn't happen in isolation. If it does, you're in danger of things not holding together properly. Obviously some directors are more understanding about visuals than others. I like the directors who have a full range of ability, who have a concept of what they want and who put their ideas forward. Then you have something to start with and build on.

What makes a cinematographer worth what he's paid?

Well, he has a big responsibility. After the director, the cinematographer is most responsible for whether the picture is going to be shot on schedule. He has a big responsibility to the budget of the film in terms of the amount of time he takes to do something and the amount of time that he's prepared to wait or convince the director that it's worth waiting for to get the right weather. For *On Golden Pond* we had the most changeable weather; it would change from a brilliant, clear sky to totally overcast. Immediately you're in trouble photographically. You have to try to predict what the weather's going to do. If you start to shoot a scene under overcast skies, then you're stuck with trying to match it. By guessing the weather, choosing the set-up and having enough equipment to effect changes, you can maintain the style of photography that the sequence started with. At times, that calls for a lot of invention and ingenuity to make it look as if the weather hasn't changed. You do that by placement of the camera, choice of the lens and choice of background. You have to cheat a little sometimes—like picking up a shot later somewhere else but making it look as if it was at the original location.

You also have to have the flexibility to say, "Look, I know we're not going to get this shot here tonight but I can do it later on in another place and it'll match." You have to recall what you've shot, what you have left to shoot and how to put it all together so it looks complete and unified. You're also responsible for a great deal of equipment. You're responsible for how much you carry in the way of lenses, cameras and lights which are very large factors in the budget. I don't like to carry more than I need. That's why I think good preparation is terribly important. It's very bad news if a cinematographer has to go into a picture without sufficient preparation time. Also he needs sufficient opportunity to go around with the director to see what the locales and the climates are likely to be. Then you can do a breakdown of what you need. There's a great tendency for the cinematographer to take more gear than he needs just in case the director changes his mind. Of course, you don't want to restrict the director but if you can get a feeling of what the requirements are going to be, then you order what you need and maybe give yourself just a little bit extra. But don't take twice as much as you think you're going to need and then leave it sitting on the truck. That will never show up on the screen. I don't order equipment unless I'm going to use it and the result is going to be on the screen. We all want to make pictures that are successful but also within a reasonable sum of money without going sky high on the budget because that sort of thing is destroying the industry. Massive spending means that pictures, that at one time might have been made, are not going to get made now.

Can we discuss a bit about the problem you face, as a British cameraman, coming to the United States to work?

Well, I would like to see the cinematographer treated as more of an above-the-line cost. He should be hired because of his artistic contribution, because the director or producer want him and because he's the best man for the job. I don't think one should be restricted by artificial barriers. I've worked in many, many countries in Europe and Africa and Asia without any union restriction. But I do understand why there are restrictions here; the restrictions are partly due to the fact that there isn't a reciprocal agreement with Britain or Europe for American cameramen to work there. I would like to see the whole thing open up much more so that we can work in each other's countries without restrictions. I think that would be to the benefit of the industry and to the benefit of individuals. I've appreciated working in America; it's broadened my experience. You find different ways of doing things; you come across different items of equipment. And when American cameramen go to Europe, they probably gain something too. It's by experience that you gain. You're able to put something different, better or more exciting up on the screen. It's great for a cinematographer to come to a new country. He's going to see it quite differently from the guy who's lived there all his life. He's going to find and emphasize certain things. That's what makes the opportunity to do that so exciting.

I'd like to get a general overview of your artistic and visual approach to several films. For instance, how did you feel The Wind and the Lion *should be done?*

I felt it had to be richly colored and have strong movement and excitement. It had striking scenery and great action scenes where the camera actually got in the middle of the fighting. The picture had to be boldly composed. I welcomed the fact that it was a film of contrast in terms of light. There was an opportunity to do scenes where there were very brightly lit areas and very strong shadows. I think the characters called for that too. Sean Connery played a legendary bandit; he was always in black, a dark figure. Candy Bergen, who was kidnapped by him, was all in white. It was a picture of lightness and darkness.

Your approach to Sunday, Bloody Sunday?

That was much more an enclosed, softly lit, intimate film. You had to be close in with those people; you had to know what their environment was. The camera didn't stand back too often to take in the view like we did in *The Wind and the Lion*. It was a story of three people's relationship with one another. I used a much softer lighting technique and I shot it in 1.85 to 1 format. I think the Panavision ratio was ideal for *The Wind and the Lion* but it would have been quite wrong for *Sunday, Bloody Sunday*.

What about Women in Love?

Women in Love was a mixture really. As I said, it was an opportunity to do many different things. Anyone who's read the novel knows that Lawrence is very descriptive and visual.

But you invested the material with such an emotionality, a sensuousness. What about your approach to On Golden Pond?

It has some of the elements of *Sunday, Bloody Sunday* in that the three characters and their relationship is of prime importance. You have to feel close to them; you have to know them. So they all have to be seen close although I don't think there's an overuse of close-ups. It was very interesting how often we stayed with the master shot and didn't use very much of the coverage. With the interiors I had a certain intimacy that had to be sustained. I played all the night interiors in a very warm light to enhance the tones of the wooden walls. Outside was the dark blue lake. For the day interiors, I concentrated on source lighting from the windows. Then, on the lake exteriors, brilliant hard sunlight with lots of blues and greens for the day scenes moving to overcast for the dusk to night sequences with very strong blue. So that the film has quite a range in color and style.

Now *Gandhi* was back to the big canvas again. I had huge action scenes with thousands and thousands of extras. I had strong Indian sunlight which I favored; I used the contrast of that sunlight and made it look hot and bright. Of course, there were interiors where it was darker and the light had to be softer. *Gandhi* has a tremendous range of visual styles. But again, I didn't use any filtration, fogging or flashing techniques. It's a very clean negative. It's very realistic. We want people to feel that this is a story that's as relevant today as it was then.

How would you advise a student whose ultimate career goal was to be a cinematographer? How does one go about achieving a certain stature in that field?

One of the things I've always done through the years is to go to art exhibitions and galleries and study the works of great painters. I think that builds up your knowledge of composition and your understanding of how to use color and light. That's something that everybody can do and can learn a great deal from. You've then got to study the work of the great directors and any particular cinematographer whose work you like and see how they do things. That's really the easy part because it's very different when you have to get out there and make the decisions for yourself. The hardest part very often is making the decision to do things in a certain way or to do things in a certain light. You might have wanted to shoot a scene in sunlight and now it's overcast. So you've got to make a decision. And you've got to convince the director that this is the best way to go in that set of circumstances. You constantly have to be prepared to adapt your ideas to changing conditions.

Regarding training, I think it's a good thing to spend some time as an assistant. You'll learn the rudiments of the camera, lenses, film stock and depth of field. You'll get to know the equipment. I mean, you don't *have* to spend a large proportion of your life doing that if you want to be a cinematographer. But I think if you try to become a cinematographer without having been an assistant, then there's going to be a gap in your experience. It helps to have been an operator but I don't think it's essential. But certainly you've got to build up a knowledge of how cutting works because the director and the cinematographer are going to decide on the angles. It's from that that the editor has to build the scene. Unless you have a good understanding of editing and angles, you're not going to be able to put things together properly. It's very easy to make a mistake on the set and then find out later it doesn't cut well. You should also think of giving the editor a choice; you should have an instinct as to when a close-up might be needed or when a bit more coverage would be good. This is something that develops from experience and watching the scene play.

But going back to your original question about students, I think you've got to have a lot of determination if this is what you want to do. Take every opportunity you can to watch people working and talk to film crews and cinematographers if you can. Try to learn from their experience. If this is your ambition, don't give up on it. It's never easy. There are so many people who want to be cinematographers, who want to be part of a film crew. It's a great job and you travel the world. There's always a lot more people wanting to work in the industry than there is space for. But I think that real talent and real enthusiasm will always get its just reward. You're going to need a bit of luck too. Because it's so often a matter of meeting the right person at the right time.

14

Gordon Willis

"Movies are craft, they're not art. The art comes out of the craft. For example, you may have a great idea for a painting, but can you paint? If you say 'no' then your idea is worthless because there's no way for you to project that idea. It's being able to execute the idea that sets you free."

Gordon Willis is the best cinematographer working in America today. Without a doubt. Period. End of discussion. And when he gets through rewriting the history of the American cameraman, he will no doubt be considered the most consistently brilliant cameraman this country has ever produced. Even in the present day, his influence in the industry is pervasive. But oddly, Willis's name is not well known to the filmgoing public, nor is even the Hollywood community that familiar with him. Certainly the majority of the members of the Motion Picture Academy of Arts and Sciences—the people who vote on the annual Oscars—barely even know he's alive; they have consistently ignored his Oscar-caliber efforts. But the producers and directors who hire him know he's exactly the man for the job they have in mind. Just ask Francis Coppola, Alan Pakula, James Bridges, Woody Allen and Herb Ross. Better yet, ask his peers, fellow cinematographers who know how hard it is to maintain consistency on the screen and who therefore can sit in better judgment of his work.

When the cinematographers who were interviewed for this book were asked who of their contemporaries they admired most, overwhelmingly the name they mentioned was Gordon Willis. Haskell Wexler, a seasoned veteran, says, "What nobody realizes is that Gordon is about the most thorough door-to-door cameraman that there is." Even a young cinematographer like John Bailey recognizes Willis's contributions. "I don't speak for everybody my age, but for me Gordon Willis is the preeminent American cinematographer," says Bailey. "I think he's single-handedly responsible for the support and acknowledgement that cinematographers now have."

Part of the reason Hollywood people have been lax in responding to Willis's talent is that he is not one of them in a geographical sense. He lives an hour or so outside of Manhattan, with his wife and children, free from all the attendant pressures of Hollywood. Moreover, he has never courted the attention of the press and thus his personal profile is fairly low. Prior to *Pennies from Heaven*, the last film he actually shot in a Hollywood studio was *All the President's Men* in 1976. He's not much of a socializer either; he likes to work and then go home. That's not to say he's just punching a time clock; he'll give eighteen hours a day if that's what is necessary. He's there weeks before the picture starts, testing lenses, equipment and film stock. He's there weeks after the shooting is completed, too, making sure the film is timed and printed correctly in the lab. In short, he is obsessed with perfection.

Willis's contemporaries are most envious of his relative power to control almost every aspect of how the final image will appear on screen. He realized very early in his career the difference a cinematographer's work means to a production and he was one of the first to fight for that difference whether it was in terms of more production money, better equipment or greater location time. "Everything happens on the set the way Willis wants it to happen," confides one cinematographer. "That's power." And the reason for his power stems from his ability to deliver what he promises: a unique vision. That's the bottom line: when a producer or director hires Willis, they know they're going to get something special.

Willis has consistently shown courage, imagination and creativity in his work, from the requirements of a light comedy like *Annie Hall* to the heavy drama of *The Godfather*. In just over ten years he established his reputation and is now the most respected and influential cinematographer of his generation. Michael Chapman, a brilliant cinematographer in his own right, was Willis's camera operator for several films. He explains it this way: "Gordon is the most wonderful example of the American autodidact that I've ever met." And, it might be added, very simply, a genius.

1970	*End of the Road*	1977	*Annie Hall*
	Loving	1978	*9-30-55*
	The Landlord		*Interiors*
1971	*Little Murders*		*Comes a Horseman*
	Klute	1979	*Manhattan*
1972	*Up the Sandbox*	1980	*Stardust Memories*
	Bad Company	1981	*Pennies from Heaven*
	The Godfather	1982	*A Midsummer Night's Sex Comedy*
1973	*The Paper Chase*		*Zelig†*
1974	*The Drowning Pool*	1983	*Broadway Danny Rose*
	Parallax View	1984	*Perfect!*
1975	*The Godfather II*	As Director:	
1976	*All the President's Men*	1979	*Windows*

†Academy Award Nomination for best achievement in cinematography.

How did you first become interested in filmmaking?
Actually, I was born in the business. It wasn't related to camerawork but my

father was a make-up artist at Warner Brothers (East Coast) during the depression. So I was always around it. I was an actor for a while when I was a kid; I wasn't a very good actor. As time went on, I got interested in stills and stagecraft and I fooled around with that for a while. I did a lot of still work but it was not commercially profitable. Then the Korean War came along and I enlisted in the Air Force. I was fortunate enough to get involved in a motion picture unit. For four years I made documentaries. I came out and started as an assistant cameraman on the East Coast. Commercials were going very strong then.

What year was that?

That was 1955 or 1956. I worked as an assistant for a long time and then I finally got an opportunity to work as a first cameraman. One thing led to another and I was just fortunate in getting opportunities and taking advantage of them. The business has been very good to me.

Under what circumstances did you make that transition to first cameraman?

In those days, there was a very big commercial business in New York. I shot commercials for a long time. I shot documentaries. I was freelance; it was difficult but I was fortunate. My first feature was a picture called *End of the Road*, the John Barth novel. And the rest sort of took care of itself after that. I just went from one feature to another. I've been selective about what I shoot.

Can you tell how End of the Road *came up for you?*

It was one of those things. This man was looking for a cameraman to shoot this material and he was looking at all kinds of people's reels, which you really can't tell too much from. I think the bottom line on it was that I just talked to him and it was dumb luck finally. So there wasn't a specific involved; there's not a "how-to" involved in this particular case.

Were you in any hurry to make that jump to your first feature?

No, strangely enough, I wasn't. While I was delighted that it finally happened, I'm always one to focus on what I'm doing at the moment. And, at that time, it happened to be commercial work. So I didn't really place that much importance on getting the job.

What was it like on the first day of your first feature when you walked on the set? What were your feelings?

Strangely enough, I was confident about the picture because it was a very interpretive movie. The things that we were doing on it were off center, so to speak. No, I didn't feel at all apprehensive; I jumped right in and started doing it. Maybe that's because you're too stupid to know any different, you know? And maybe it's better that way sometimes; maybe it's better just to jump in and do it. Of course, the demands on that film weren't as high as things I've done that were more commercially oriented or on bigger movies. There was a very contained group of people involved and so it made it easier to do. Also the thought pattern was simpler.

What about the "therapy room," where you had lights and images blinking on and off both on the walls and ceiling. There was all the craziness with the chair not to mention the antics of Stacy Keach and James Earl Jones. How did you rig that up?

Well, that room was interesting, actually, because it was built out of muslin. If you remember, there were projections on the wall that kept changing. What we had were a series of silent slide projectors behind the set. Now muslin is very translucent when you shine light through it from the back. So in fact, the walls became rear-projection screens. Only we used projections all over the walls that were changing all the time, going on and off within the scene. And that was quite a lot of fun. I mean, we had to come up with all of this for very little money. I sometimes wonder if I could do some of the same things I did then. I have a theory that what you're capable of doing at one point in your career, you're no longer capable of doing at another point. You may be further ahead in a lot of ways, but sometimes you drop behind. You know, you're not capable of dealing with it in the same way. Your point of view changes. You can't go home, you can't go back. You might get better but you will not always be as inventive.

Loving was an urban comedy/drama; what kind of general approach did you take there?

I liked *Loving* a lot; I thought it was an interesting movie and probably, in many ways, ahead of its time. I guess philosophically I call that kind of work "romantic reality." I mean, I've applied that kind of approach in a lot of movies that I've photographed. I guess a lot of it is just me and that kind of movie. It's a feeling and movies essentially are feelings. I guess "romantic reality" is the closest I could come to how we did it. I did a lot of things badly in that film also, but then I did a lot of things well. I was still at a stage where I would tend to use the minimum amount of equipment—I still do—but, in those days, I used very little.

One of the secrets about doing anything is to see what you're looking at. And when you go to a location or when you work on a property like *Loving*, what you want to do is to retain the essence of the area you're working in. You can't always be literal; you have to rebuild what you're looking at sometimes in order to retain what you're looking at.

You were shooting the interiors at 200 ASA?

Yes, I was force-developing a lot.

You liked the look?

I liked the look. Essentially you don't gain much speed when you push motion picture film. You raise the fog level of it, which has a tendency to make it look like you gained because the fog level fills in the highlights and you get more density. But you really haven't gained much speed. If you've got a good negative that's properly exposed—"properly" meaning what you want it to look like—you're not going to change it much by overdeveloping except the look of it. You'll raise the fog level. I was pushing on that film. And you could push more successfully in those days because, in general, lab chemistry was better.

The Godfather and The Godfather II were, to the best of my knowledge, among the first films to utilize relatively low light levels. How did you evolve that kind of lighting philosophy and how did you come to give it a full application on The Godfather *and an even greater application on* The Godfather II?

That technique or that approach to the movie visually just came out of a thought process. And the process, in my mind, was based on evil; it was based on the soul of the picture. I guess the best example of it, based on relativity, was the wedding where outside in the garden there was a very sunny, almost Kodachromey, 1942 kind of feel to it. Then when we cut inside the house with Brando, it was very down and very ominous. So while one thing was happening out here, another thing, in fact, was happening inside. And so it was a very simple philosophy. However, the overall look of *The Godfather* was a kind of forties New York grit, with the exception of the scenes in Sicily. *The Godfather II* is basically the same approach only more romantic. We had period work to deal with. My thought was that I wanted to keep all of the work tied together in a linear fashion. The thing that ultimately kept it together was the same color structure throughout. Even though I changed the lighting and the shot structure a lot between the periods, I felt it was best to just hold this yellow tone through all of it. And that way, there would be one thread that united all of it. I wanted to hang onto the essence of *The Godfather I.* In *Godfather II*, it was the same thing; I used yellow. In fact, yellow broke out like the plague after I did it on that picture. And today, people still apply it. It's applied indiscriminately, I might add. Because doing that does not automatically make it a period movie. The photographic structure, the lighting structure and the set structure have to come together in the same fashion, otherwise it's meaningless.

I understand what you're saying in that context, but you don't generally like the color of yellow, do you?

I used the term yellow; it's really kind of an amber.

More of a golden tone?

Right, a golden amber kind of feeling. But in laboratory terms, it's adding yellow. It gives a golden amber tone to the movie. Now I don't like pure yellow or pure blue in movies, that is, on people and furniture and so on. I think it's disruptive.

A lot of people thought it was really incredible that you shot at such low light levels because it wasn't really accepted at that time. Do you have any rules of thumb for shooting at low light levels?

The rule of thumb is you have to know what rule you're breaking. Because you can't arbitrarily say, "This is going to be this, and this is going to be that," unless you understand what it is you're manipulating. Once you learn what's normal then, from that point, you have to learn what's not normal and what can be applied properly against the norm. So you have to understand basic exposure principles and also you have to understand the tool you're working with, the film itself. I mean, you may have an incredible amount of light on a set. But it's not the amount that you're using; it's based on how you're exposing the material, whether it's half a stop under, normal or whatever. In your mind, as a photographer, there's always a norm. You're always working against a norm. You must know what the norm is. You must know what a stop under-exposed looks like on the screen or what a half stop under looks like. You must understand all that. Exposure is a tool; how you expose film is a tool. You have to understand what happens when you under-expose or over-expose because that's another way to paint, another way of making emotional statements on the screen. Choice of lenses is another way; where you put the camera is another way.

But exposure is one of the most critical choices.

It's very important. You've got to know what you're doing at that level. In simplest form, before you try to photograph anything, you should learn that. Then you know how to use it. Then you understand what it is you're doing. I mean, if someone is standing by a window in a room, they're not going to be functioning at the same light intensity at the window as they would be if they walked across the room and stood by the door. It's going to be different. Now unless you know how to do that, you're not going to know how much tolerance the film has related to the exposure. And the bottom line of all that is: how do I make it look real on the screen? Or how do I make it look like what I want it to look like? Listen, there are hundreds of people running around photographing pictures who don't grasp that principle. They don't understand that. They do not know where film bottoms out or where it tops off.

So it's an experiential thing? I mean, you just have to go do it? If I was a student, I would just go out and shoot and shoot and shoot with some understanding of the limitations of what I was doing.

I rarely see anybody do it or understand it at the student level because no one bothers to teach it to them. But what every student who's interested in photography should do is he should take the film that he's going to use and simply put a person in a room. Now he should light that person very simply from the front and make a normal exposure—whatever a normal exposure is for him. Then he should make an exposure which is a half stop under normal, a stop under normal, a stop and a half under normal, two stops under normal. He should also do the same thing above the normal end. Expose a half stop over, a full stop over, etc. Then he should simply look at that on the screen and he will understand where he maintains detail and where it begins to fall off. So that the next time he has a person standing next to a window, who has to go from the window to the door and the window is normal or half a stop over, then he knows that by the time the person gets to the door that the light will look fine if it's a stop or a stop and a half under. So that on the screen, it looks like he's got good lighting relativity. He doesn't want the same light at the door as he had at the window. But not knowing how much light he's supposed to have at the door, he lights up the door.

So what you're saying is you need a visual understanding, a visual readout?

Right. You have to know what it's going to look like on the screen, not what it's looking like in front of you at that moment.

Do you have any techniques that allow you to maintain depth of field at low light levels? Because there is a lot of depth in many of the scenes in The Godfather I and II. *It may be dark, but there's detail in the foreground and also detail back on the wall too. How do you do that?*

Lighting detail, you're talking about?

Right.

Well, again it goes back to the principle we were just discussing. It's knowing what's black and what's not really black. Do you know what I mean? What gives the impression of being dark but is not really dark? It's knowing the relativity of light-ing ratios and what you're finally going to end up with on the screen. The applica-tion of that is taste. How you apply that is taste.

Some people have bad taste; some people have good taste.

Right. Selznick once said, "There are two kinds of class: first class and no class." And it's the same thing with visual taste. You can teach certain principles to people but the application of those principles may not function for them.

How do you maintain consistency from set-up to set-up, from scene to scene? Do you try to shoot at a certain number of footcandles, a certain f-stop?

You decide to shoot a picture at a given f-stop and you want to maintain that f-stop throughout the picture. There will be variations for minor demands here and there. But in order to make the picture cut together from shot to shot, there has to be a mechanical consistency which is based on your philosophical approach to the movie. Let's just take a simple f-stop, say f 4. You decide you want to use f 4 be-cause it's right for the picture and it's the most practical stop lighting wise. You want to maintain that from cut to cut because if you just start arbitrarily dialing stops to compensate for lighting that you haven't properly set, the movie is going to start jumping around. You're going to have depth-of-field problems cutting from one person to another, one scene to another. So what will happen on the screen is that you'll inadvertently put a lot of images together that really don't flow. They'll move from soft to contrasty and back to soft. There will be no consistency in mechanical imagery. How you choose the stop to use in the first place is dependent on what it is that pleases you aesthetically. And sometimes it's a matter of what's practical too. You try and marry the two.

Doesn't one of your assistants make copious notes about exposure and other details of each shot?

Yes, he does. I make notes also. And those notes are kept for every shot in the movie. If somebody picked it up and read it, they wouldn't learn anything. It's just a lot of f-stops, numbers and things. But if I have to go back and shoot something in a month or two, which happens in movies, then I want that information because by then I may have forgotten what I did. So I have to rebuild it again and the quickest way to do it is to have that information.

That consistency is one of the most important considerations.

That's very important. And it's not easy because you constantly have to keep reminding yourself and others that you have to maintain the same point of view through the movie in order to make it work as a total piece of material. I'm talking about maintaining it structurally, mechanically, photographically and everything.

How do you do that? Especially if you have a director who is going off course?

There are directors who go off course; there are cameramen who go off course too. But it's your job. If you're working with the right kind of people, they would expect that you would help maintain a state of order and not have everybody drift-

ing off in different directions. Once you're committed to an idea, you should perform at that level. You must maintain that integrity.

*And so far, from the people you've worked with, that hasn't presented any
problem?*

No. I've been fortunate from that standpoint. But they've all been intelligent
people. It's very easy to be creative in ten different directions at once but generally
only one idea applies at that moment and it should be the one you've been working
with all along.

But how do you do it? How do you keep it straight?

Well, you have to keep the whole movie in your head all the time. I mean, there
is a style to it. And most of the time it's easy to see when you're stepping out of line.
You can see stylistically if you're not dealing with it appropriately. Directors can't
always see that because sometimes they become overburdened with the major
problem of dealing with actors and telling the story. So it's easy to understand how
they can get confused sometimes about how a film should be mounted and how it
should be maintained at a certain level. And listen, a lot of them don't think that
way. I mean, most movies today are recorded; they're not photographed. They're
not mounted; they're just recorded.

Could you elaborate on that?

They make the amount of cuts required and they move on.

As opposed to . . .

As opposed to thinking out exactly what the film is supposed to accomplish and
what the scene is supposed to accomplish; and then thinking about how we put that
up on the screen appropriately. I mean, you can photograph two cars running into
each other and you can do it twenty different ways. Or two people talking to each
other. Which is the right way? It's very easy to just record it. You just get the scene
in the camera. You shoot a close-up and then another close-up in a two-shot and the
scene will be done. But maybe there was another way of doing it so that the content
was strengthened. And maybe that other way was better filmmaking.

Better in the context of the whole film?

Right. Also you have to consider cutting. The decision on how you make a cut is
based on what comes before and what comes after. And that's not always a consideration in a lot of films being done today.

The opening scene of The Godfather *was impressive. The scene was in the house
where the immigrant is pleading with Don Corleone. How did you light that? Is that
an obscure question?*

That's obscure.

*But, you know, when you saw that first scene come on the screen, you just knew
that whole film had the potential of being really incredible—just from that first
scene!*

It's important that you kind of set everybody appropriately, at least in that picture. Mechanically, all of the lighting in that picture as well as *The Godfather II* is
all overhead, soft light. It's also light that's below Kelvin, meaning that the temper-

ature of the light was below 3200 degrees Kelvin; it was more in the 2900-degree range. That was part of the color structure as well for the period. It's all overhead, soft light with the addition of whatever was necessary on the floor to accentuate someone's face or eyes. I had a philosophy, which I used more in *The Godfather II* than in the first one, that I didn't give a shit whether I saw their eyes or not. My thought was that it was better not to see their eyes in some scenes. It seemed more appropriate not to see their eyes because of what was going on in their heads at certain moments. I had a lot of trouble with that from traditionalists. Because Hollywood is full of rhetoric—there's a standard rhetoric everybody uses when they watch dailies. They never really see what they're looking at. It's only if they don't see what they think they're supposed to see that they begin to say things. I got a lot of comments about not being able to see anybody's eyes. And I said, "That's the way it is because I think it's appropriate at this moment. In another scene, you will see their eyes because it's appropriate at that moment."

All of the sets were lit with very large bounce lighting that was hung over the sets.

Do you use white cards?

I do use white cards but these units were built.

These were the units you invented, right?

Yes. I started by inverting lights and bouncing them into muslin frames of various sizes. So those lights and a bar and a frame were all one unit. And they would be hung over the set. Then I'd use skirts around those in order to shave the light off the walls or wherever. After a while, I changed the system. I made it more contained. Now it's a four-by-four frame which is a basic diffuser and within that diffuser I add whatever lights are necessary to do it.

I started using them on *The Godfather II*. Soon after that, they broke out like the plague. They were being used all over the place. I don't think too many people understand them but they figured if they use the units, the movie is going to look like *Godfather II*. It's that mentality. But it doesn't work that way. Like anything else, it's not an indiscriminate tool.

We were talking about how some of the actors looked in The Godfather II. *Sometimes they were mere silhouettes. One scene I remember is where Michael and Fredo are talking in front of the sliding glass doors at the place in Lake Tahoe. The audience doesn't really see what's happening there. And I guess you've already answered the question by saying that it's not always necessary to show the actors' face or eyes, according to the dramatics of the film.*

Well, you want to think in terms of how the scene plays best, not how do we shoot so we see the actors' faces. But sometimes it's the total confrontation of what's happening on the screen, the whole of what you've mounted totally that makes the scene work. It's the emotional content of the way the scene is structured. You certainly don't want to go through a whole movie at that level but it's effective once in a while. Many times, what you don't see is much more effective than what you do see. But not too many people understand it. And not too many people understand relativity as far as going from light to dark to light, big to small and small to big. It's important.

One very interesting scene was the interior of a diner where they take Tom Hagen and tell him that the Don has been assassinated. There are a couple of small pools of light there but it's just incredibly dark. However, it was all there; you didn't need any more light and you didn't need any less.

Now that scene was done with a light bulb which was mounted behind the practical. You know, one light put in the right spot essentially does the job.

Did that scare you?

No.

I mean, compared to the norm, that's quite a risk.

That's only a risk if you don't know what's going to happen. Again, it's based on the principle of understanding what it is that you're working with. If there's no light in a given area or even if there is some light in a given area, you have to know what's going to happen. The whole movie was structurally in that category.

The other scene is the exterior night scene in front of the hospital where Michael comes out after guarding the Don. The police are there and there's a lot of commotion. It's really dark but you can still see movements and expressions on people's faces. What kind of approach do you take on a night exterior like that?

Generally night lighting is cross lighting, particularly so in that scene.

I mean, you couldn't have been using much lighting or does it just seem that way?

It just seems that way. I wasn't using an excessive amount of units but they were all where they were supposed to be related to lighting the scene. That scene just felt okay to me at the time; it wasn't something that I really pondered. Again, I probably wouldn't do it the same way today; I'd do something else. But, at that moment, it felt okay.

In The Godfather *and* The Godfather II *you took different visual approaches to the different geographic locations, in New York, Los Angeles, Sicily, etc. I'm sure that was intentional.*

Yes. In New York, we did a lot of period work. As I said before, you want to separate the places in time and still hold a thread throughout the whole picture. So the color of the picture was what held it all together. The photographic structure was different in the period work in that all of the period was shot practically wide open, including the exteriors. It was all shot at $f2.8$, inside and outside. All of the period work was filtered down to a degree. Simply using some wider f-stops, with some minor diffusion plus the lighting technique, separated the period work. But it still functions as the same movie. Period work, for the most part, is all flat light and I felt that was needed and appropriate. Whereas, in other parts of the picture where we moved into other time periods, that was not a consideration. We would shoot in the sun or wherever. As for the Sicily segment, I felt the same way about it as I did in the first picture, only this was period Sicily. I felt that it theoretically had to be just the opposite; there should be a lot of sun. So between New York and Sicily, there were two different things going on. You had the same photographic structure and the same feel but Sicily was all sunny and New York was all flat. Emotionally they were two different places. The physicality was different even though the approach to the period look was the same. Then when we moved into the Tahoe sequence, the photographic structure changed somewhat. The trick, of course, is to keep it reminiscent all the time. But we would shoot in the sun there; we would shoot in rooms that were different. A lot of that is emotional, you know.

Doing these films over a period of years, keeping all of this straight in your head must have been quite a task.

Right, keeping it straight in your head is hard. But if you have one idea that you hang your hat on, it's easy. You just have to remember what you're doing and when you're doing it for what reason.

Pretty photography is easy; it really is the easiest thing in the world. But photography that rounds a picture off, top to bottom, and holds the content together, is really the most beautiful. That means it can be visually very beautiful; it can also be very pedestrian in certain ways if it happens to be appropriate to the story. You try not to put the photography in front of the story; you try and make it part of the story.

But don't you think that happens sometimes? That the visual aspects really overpower the script?

Sure, it happens all the time. What you try to do is good work that in itself will be quite wonderful with the picture. You don't try to do a tour de force photographically. *End of the Road* permitted more tour-de-forcing than a lot of pictures that I've worked on because that was just the nature of it. You should do what's appropriate for the story. It's when you step outside of the picture that you've made a mistake.

From what I understand The Godfather *was tightly budgeted as opposed to* The Godfather II. *Now in that kind of situation where you're trying to preserve the look and thread of the original, how did the bigger budget affect your photographic style if at all? And were there things that you did in* Godfather II *that you couldn't have done in the original because of the money?*

The sheer magnitude of *Godfather II* required that money. Some of the things done in the film were expensive by nature of staging. Conceptually, photographically and mechanically I didn't do any more and didn't have much more than I did on the original. It's just that you had more sometimes because the requirements in the scene were larger so you needed more. In fact, I took the same camera, the same lenses and the same everything onto *Godfather II* that I had on *The Godfather*. It was somewhat dated equipment but I wanted the same thing to maintain that consistency.

Bad Company *was your first western. How did you approach it?*

That was a new experience for me. But philosophically the experience was people in space. I mean when you're alone out there in that country, you're really alone, especially in that time period. A lot of the shot structure was based on that kind of feeling—the feeling of being out on the flats in Kansas. It was simple and stylistic. Again, it was a period picture. I've always felt the period work should be mounted simply, in a tableau fashion, which is a painting kind of fashion as opposed to more contemporary films. So that approach was essentially used on *Bad Company* as well as *The Godfather* and *The Godfather II*.

I was just about to say that the tableau approach was used for The Godfather.

Yes, exactly. But it's tricky unless you understand it. It's based on tableau and cutting, that's what it amounts to. It's how you cut. So you have to have a thorough understanding with the director so that he's comfortable and projecting his ideas at that level.

You know, a great many of your films are urban drama pieces. Do you have any special overriding feelings about "the city" that attracts you to that kind of film?

No, it's just where I came from, I guess. But it's also how I look at things, and that I can't explain to anybody. Because it's just the way I look at things. But there's no way to say, "You've got to look at it this way and then you'll see it all," or "You'll see it that way if you do this." I don't know how to do that because that's not how *you* look at it. I have no explanation; I have no way of bottling it. There again, it's taste.

In Comes a Horseman, *you were dealing with a contemporary western. You were dealing with a lot of wide open spaces to the point where the sky and the land became a character in the film.*

That was essentially the approach.

What were the differences as opposed to Bad Company? *Did you have any philosophical viewpoint changes?*

Well, again, it was people in space. More so than in *Bad Company* because it was land and people's relationship to land. So the land in itself was a character. That's an easy approach to have when you're doing that kind of movie. I'm not so sure it's successful. I've always said that you can never make movies about a thing because nobody cares about a thing. You always have to make movies about people because that's where everybody gets screwed in. So that can all work successfully together as long as you don't forget about people. And I'm not really so sure that *Comes a Horseman* really worked at certain levels because I think it's hard to intellectualize that kind of subject. You can be intelligent about it and tell a good story but I think you have to be very careful about intellectualizing in westerns.

You don't like the color of blue but there isn't much you can do about the sky. But the sky and the clouds were beautiful in Comes a Horseman.

Right. If something is there already, you have to use it appropriately. There's nothing you can do about the sky. But also, that was a place where the weather was quite extraordinary—there were a lot of physical changes in the weather there. So it was a little more interesting, in many ways, than just simple dirt and sky. In fact, there was a place called Wet Mountain Valley where it was shot and it had horrendous lightning and thunderstorms around one or two o'clock in the afternoon. We shot in a couple of them so it made it a little more interesting. Obviously blue skies are not as dramatic. I don't like blue related to costuming of people. It's kind of vulgar and it's also distracting.

In the deep-focus scenes in the newsroom of All the President's Men, *you were using split diopters. First of all, let's define what a split diopter is, then how did you use them and why?*

A diopter is just another element; you think in terms of half a lens element placed on one side of the lens or the other. You're altering the focal length of the lens somewhat. It's like these bifocals I have here; with these glasses you have one strength to read with and another strength to see out in the distance. That's basically a split diopter. It changes the focal plane on subjects. If you have someone very close to the camera and somebody who is way upstage of the camera, by using a diopter it enables you to carry the focus from this very close subject to a subject that is further upstage. That's when you can't get a split—a split is enough focus to carry one person to another without using a split diopter.

Now the requirements of *All the President's Men* were that it be a deep-focus movie because of everything that was going on. There were times, in order to make that idea work, we applied diopters to hold people in the foreground as well as in the background. There's one shot of Redford on the telephone, a zoom shot actually, that took place over a two- or three-minute period. There was a lot going on upstage. The shot was actually a combination of making a zoom move and floating a diopter in at the same time. The diopter is mounted on a calibrated bar so that when we were at given focal lengths, the bar was where it should be. It was a tricky shot but it worked. We used them at other times too. But I had to be able to float them in and out; we had this system built so I could do that.

You described the look of All the President's Men *as having "a graphic, poster-like quality." Could you elaborate on that a bit?*

Well, I was referring to all the colors in it that were keyed off of the newsroom. It was filled with that kind of graphic, poster-like feeling. So I felt that was a way of dealing with it. I don't think that was totally a successful overall approach to it because there were other times that we couldn't do it. But it kind of had that feeling.

You said that All the President's Men *was one of the hardest films that you ever shot. Why is that?*

It was awful from the standpoint that you were constantly in the state of delivering information. You had to mount it well and you had to use a lot of discipline in how you dealt with it because you were, after all, delivering this relentless story. I mean, if you went out to the restroom during the movie and came back, you would have missed something important. It was a constant thing of people's reactions and the spoken word all the time. So, from that standpoint, it was tedious. But there's no waste in the movie. It's right there all the time. So you have to know how to do that as well as be a romantic on the screen. You have to be able to deliver hard edges when it's necessary. It's hard sometimes but it's important that you know how to do it. There's an outbreak of fog filters in this business; I'd like to take a hammer and start breaking up everybody's filters because it's a bad interpretive sense to feel that you have to put something in front of the lens to make some sort of arbitrary statement. I don't even know what the hell the statement is that they're making.

You know what people say to me? They say, "The film is too good, the lenses are too sharp. I have to degrade the image to get something that doesn't look like an industrial film for Caterpillar Tractor. I have to throw something in front of the lens, do something with the exposure and do something with the lighting to cut that sharpness down."

It's an oversimplification on their part. And also the means by which they do it is not wonderful because it becomes an imposition on the film.

So you don't find that reasoning valid?

I find it valid but simplistic. I mean, they cut off their nose to spite their face. I think they have to get more control of their craft at certain levels because by dropping fog filters in or low-contrast filters in, you're only adding one more element and then you're moving outside of the movie. I just think that approach is arbitrary. It has nothing to do with what's going on in the film.

For the newsroom in All the President's Men, *you went with the fluorescent lighting because that's the basic reality of that environment. It looked very good, all things considered. How did you get that without going to all that much trouble—or maybe you did go to a lot of trouble?*

There was a certain amount of trouble. First of all, it *was* all fluorescent. In making that decision—funny how you come to decisions—I knew we were going to spend ten weeks in that room with the ceilings down on everybody's head. Plus there's a look about fluorescent that's hard and unpleasant. That was part of the decision: that it should be a representation of the *Washington Post* office. So we selected fluorescents which means that all the ballasts for those fluorescents had to be moved outside of the stage because of their noise. Now I could have done it some other way. But there's no heat coming out of fluorescents, and when you have that many people in one room with ceilings down on your head for ten weeks, you want to try to make it easy to function. So you have two things that merge into one decision: what's practical and what's going to look good.

I made no provisions for correcting the fluorescents in the camera because you can't do it. They have a variable wave length and you'll never correct them that way. I just photographed them flat out and the corrections were done in the laboratory, which is the easiest way to photograph it if you're not mixing light. The interesting part of that is there was a daylight backing that was all lit with tungsten. So the next problem was how do you correct the fluorescents without interfering with the tungsten. Because if you correct the fluorescents, what happens is that you end up with pink backgrounds. So we used cyan filtering on the tungsten lamps to bring them in line for correction with the fluorescents. It was a pain for a minute because I knew I had to find the color to do it. And then I had to find that much cyan filter because the backing was sixty feet long. But you solve those problems and it worked pretty well in that case.

What about the famous Library of Congress shot? While I understand the idea behind it, it seemed to me like a needless trick. It was overkill.

That was tour de force. The basis of it was the needle-in-the-haystack theme.

It also seemed out of character for you to do that.

Well, it was out of character for me. I would have just as soon done it another way. But it was also an interesting challenge. It was something that Pakula wanted and something that I found interesting although it was a little tough to do. I think, in retrospect, that it was out of character for the movie; it bordered on that at least but it ended up in there anyway.

It seems like you would need a half dozen engineers and whatever else to really pull it off. It's an incredible shot; it must have been difficult.

It was. What we did was put a winch up in the ceiling of the Library of Congress. And then the camera was on a special rig with some gyros on it. The camera and the focus was by remote control. And, on a given cue, we just took the camera up with the winch. But the trajectory of it had to be changed because it was over the desk where Redford and Hoffman were sitting, which was not in the center of the room. So we had to change the trajectory as it went up. At one time, it was actually all one shot but it took too long so they did it in two dissolves.

What determines a good composition to your taste? Is it symmetry, lighting, color, focus? What are the elements that are most important when you compose?

Symmetry, first of all, because that's how you pick it. After that, the rest of those elements finish it off and make it right. But the initial thrust of it is always on symmetry and how it's going to cut against something else.

But if you get five different people behind the camera, you'll get five different compositions. There's a differential here somewhere that we can't put our finger on.

There again, it's how I see it. It's taste. Also the decisions are emotional; it's what's being said on the screen. You do what you physically can to help promote what's going on. You decide that way.

Generally how much freedom do you have in determining the visual look and visual style of a film?

Generally a lot. You're working as an extension of the director all the time. And to make a film successful obviously you have to work together; you can't be making two different movies. So yes, I have had a lot of freedom at that level and it's been very good for me. But it's always based on an idea that a director has or an idea that we come up with together. It's not singular; it's watering down or extending his thought process.

In the last three or four years, if somebody wants you to shoot a film for them, they generally know beforehand, I assume, what they're going to get—at least in the sense of the kind of things you do, what your past work is and what kind of input you can bring to the project?

Yes, they feel essentially that they're going to get something different. Sometimes it's hard for me to tell them what they're going to get, that is verbally tell them what they're going to get based on an idea or something.

Do you use a lot of visual references then?

Directors tend to use them. And I understand that because there are a lot of directors who find it hard to work without a reference of some kind. So you take those references so you can understand what it is they've got in their mind. You don't have to reproduce that reference but it makes it easier for them.

Do you think you work better under restrictions and limitations than with carte blanche?

I think probably everybody does. But carte blanche to me is only having the requirements necessary to do it; that doesn't mean you do it. You don't have to use everything you own or carry in order to function. So selectivity comes into play there. Movies are about limitations and you have to understand that. It's like a prizefighter; he's in a square ring and he learns how to use that ring. It's the same with movies. There are those in the business who have not learned how to do that. They don't understand what the limitation is. But once you understand the limitation, you have a lot of freedom.

I think we're talking about people who are primarily undisciplined in the first place; they don't have that discipline or that single unified vision.

Right. It also requires a lot of patience so that the totality of everything cut together is the point where the vision is finally focused. Many of them can't function on a totality level; they try to make it all happen within one given moment on the screen. It doesn't work that way in most cases.

It seems like some cinematographers work well with certain people but when they get into a project with other people, because of whatever, their work just goes to hell.

Sure it does. It's like good actors. An actor can be very good with one director and just dreadful with another because he mishandles the actor. It's the same thing with cinematographers. A director can mishandle a cinematographer and he's not going to get the kind of work that he hired the guy to do to begin with. He's better off with another kind of guy. It's chemistry too. Bad chemistry happens in this business a lot. You try to make it good chemistry and you try to make an honest effort to do a good job.

You've been pretty successful at that.

I have—knock on wood.

Why?

Part of it is the choice of the people you work with. And the other part is what it is they're doing. I mean, is it something which has the potential of being wonderful? So it's a combination of both of them.

It all keeps coming back to taste.

It does, right.

Up the Sandbox *was another of your urban dramas; it was gritty and realistic. How concerned is someone like Streisand going to be about how she looks?*

Actually I had a very good experience with Barbra on that movie. As a matter of fact, in my opinion, she looked better in that movie than she's ever looked in any movie. She looked good and she was inside the picture; she wasn't in front of the picture, if you know what I'm saying. I had a very good relationship with her and I liked her a lot. But, as you say, she has those concerns and she voices them.

Rightly or wrongly? Or is that for you to say?

Well, it doesn't matter. The bottom line of that is, if you have something in your head and it's really bothering you, it doesn't really matter whether someone else thinks it's right or wrong. If that other person is unable to function with that, then you have to bow to their feelings. If it blows them away every time their right side is facing the camera rather than the left side, you have to say, "Well, okay, we'll work with it."

But, in a sense, that contradicts that unified overview that you talk about.

Well, it didn't. I managed to do it anyway. Again, you're sort of pressed into service at levels that you wouldn't have come to otherwise.

Jane Fonda looked very good in Comes a Horseman. *And she's not eighteen anymore.*

No. In fact, I think she's more beautiful now than she ever was. She's really a terrific, good-looking woman.

Do you take any kind of special care or do anything out of the ordinary to make her close-ups look good?

I take special care by the way I choose to execute something. Many times it's not what you do, it's what you don't do that makes it better. The better the choices, the less you're going to have to do. In that case, it was easy for me. First of all, she did look terrific. Secondly, it wasn't a matter of maintaining glamorous overtones. You know, I shot Jane in *Klute* too and that all worked out for everybody, in my opinion. But that was a different problem. So we took more care in selection in dealing with her. They also have to have faith that you're going to do the right thing for them too. Then it makes it easier for everybody.

I'm beginning to see that while the details count, it's not just the details. It's the way the details fit into the overall program. Each is going to contribute something but it has to be with that perspective.

It has to be the round ball theory, as I call it. If you have a chip in the ball, it doesn't roll. It just plunks along. So if every element is totally unified, you've got a round ball.

Is source lighting a sacred commandment to you?

No, because the commandment is that you give the impression of that on the screen. How you do it can sometimes be pure; it can be very simple because that's how it is at that moment, for example, you sitting next to a lamp. Walking around a room and trying to maintain the feeling that the only light on is the lamp, now that isn't so easy. Theoretically you want to maintain that on the screen; how you create that illusion is up to you. The approach varies, depending on what the problem is. The bottom line is that's what I like to have happen. But if you're such a purist about it, you'll just mess it up. So the illusion has to be there but not totally pure, not always on the nose.

When you come on to a set or a location for the first time, what are the first things that you do? What's going to attract your attention immediately?

The first thing that's going to attract my attention is whether it's any good or not—whether it's a good set or a good location. And that doesn't mean that the room you're in is a great room; it means whether or not the room is going to shoot well on the screen. Many people hunt for locations with a 360-degree swivel on their head. They never see what they're finally going to see on screen. If they'd just look through a viewfinder once in a while, they'd see what they're going to see. And standing in the middle of Death Valley wouldn't look so great when they're only going to see a small part of it. So I look for what's going to happen on the screen when I look at a location. If I don't think it's going to be anything, then I'll say something.

Some filmmakers that I worked with in the early stages thought that if you play a scene in an airplane, the plane should be in the air because the essence of the scene will be different. That's nonsense. The essence of the scene is not going to be any different; the adversity will certainly be different. I mean, it is make believe. It is a business about re-creating reality.

But if you don't do it well, it looks terrible. Maybe that was what these filmmakers were thinking about?

No, it's a copout based on the feeling that it's going to be better if I go with the reality. And the truth of the matter is, you never get reality that way. The bottom line is that you get reality the other way, which is to reconstruct it. But you have to do it well, as you point out.

How important do you think a photographic style is in contributing to the success of a film?

I think it's very important in contributing to the success of a movie if the basis of the movie is good. In other words, if the totality of the project has something to offer, then the appropriate photographic style for the picture will help the movie and will help mount it properly. But I have a theory that you can take a terrible movie and photograph it very, very well and it won't help the movie at all. And you can take a very, very good story and photograph it badly and it won't matter. But the ideal thing is to take them both, put them together and come out with something special. A good story will survive bad photography; a bad story will not survive with good photography. There's not much you can do with a bad story. You can romance scenes and make scenes work if you do them well photographically. You can make scenes work that might have never worked at all if they are well shot. That has to do with shot structure and the choices. You can sell the emotional content of a scene but you can't fix a bad movie overall.

In an October 1978 interview, you said that you weren't really interested in directing and "that you are better as an improver, better at working out concepts with directors." You then went on to direct your first film, Windows. *What happened to change your mind?*

If I'm anything at all, I'm what I said I was there. I'm not a good director for the same reason that some directors are not very good photographers. I'm very weak at certain things. I'm very weak at dealing with the whole thing. I don't have the patience to be a director. I have the patience to help guide projects into the right slot and make sure they go up on the screen that way. I'm very perceptive about that. But it's only that four feet of distance between me and the director that makes me capable of doing it. Because I know what goes on in directors' minds and I know what kind of load they're carrying. But I'm really just good at that. I got talked into directing one and I did it.

Talked into it?

Yes, I got talked into it.

Somebody twisted your arm?

They really did, in all honesty.

C'mon!

No, really. I didn't want to do it but I thought it would be a change of pace. No, seriously, you don't believe this but it's true. I thought I'd try it and see if I'm wrong about myself. And I found out I'm not wrong about myself. I find that the reality of it is that I am a better executor, a better improver. I'm much, much better at that than I am at any other thing.

I guess I shouldn't be surprised to hear you say that.

It's a reality. You have to be honest with yourself. It's not life or death for me to direct.

I'm thinking, and maybe unrealistically so, that if Gordon Willis is going to direct a film—with his integrity and background—he is going to wait until he finds a film where he really has something to say: a film that he feels a strong commitment to, strong enough to move out of the cinematography category and into the directing category. Is that thinking unrealistic?

Yes. I want to tell you something about the "I've got something to say" mentality in directors. It's okay if a good director says, "I've found a great project and I'm very interested in doing it." But I'm always worried about the director who says, "I have something to say." Maybe that is going on at some subterranean level in his mind. But I've found that kind of dangerous for people because I'm not even sure they believe it anyway. I mean, a director's job is to mount a story on the screen well so that an audience can go in and get excited and feel like they've seen something, not necessarily intellectually but on an entertainment level.

So you are saying that directors are not artists?

No, there's a fine line there. Art comes out of the craft. That's where the art comes from. Movies are craft, they're not art. Art comes out of the craft. For example, you may have a great idea for a painting. But can you paint? If you say "No," then your idea isn't worth a shit. Because there's no way for you to project that idea. But basically, movies are a craft. Yes, there have been many fine movies made that have something to say; they're damn good stories. But the reality of it is you hire a director who knows how to put that story up on the screen and who is interested in doing that story. I like to stay a little bit away from that whole "meaningful" mentality. I mean, I see people I like a lot getting into that. And I understand it. If you do believe that whole thing and you're doing it, I think it's hard for you to see what you're doing.

Are you saying that you're better at dealing with the mechanical aspects of motion pictures rather than the directing and people-oriented aspects of it?

Yes, sure. But I can overlap on that a lot. I can make it better for a director. I can fix a lot of things, structurally and emotionally in a movie, when he's having trouble. Or if I'm having trouble, he can do the same thing. There are a lot of bad directors; there are a lot of good directors too.

There are a lot of traffic directors in the business and who needs to be another traffic director? If you feel you're not good at it, then it's not going to break your heart.

It's not a disaster. If you can do what you do, and do it well, that's the thing you have to keep in mind. If I do this well or continue to do it well, I'm in a better position to make movies than if I go out and direct badly. I'm not unhappy about all that. It's hard to find good people to work with, I'll admit that. That's tough. There aren't that many around.

Can we explore how you actually became involved in Windows?

Well, somebody came to me with this project and I said, "This is awful. It's got a lot of problems and I don't feel like fooling with this anyway." And yet there were things about it that interested me cinematically. They were pounding me over the head with it, so I thought, "Well, why not? Let me try it and then I can feel whether I'm really suited for this or not." And that was really the only motivation behind it. There were things in it cinematically that I enjoyed; there were things in it that were good. But on another level, it was pure theatrical nonsense. It was also a movie that made people uncomfortable on a lot of levels so that they became outraged. But it was pure theatrical nonsense and kind of fun, I thought, on certain levels. And that's all I thought of it.

What about your split responsibilities on that film because you were directing it and also photographing it? Does that do justice to either aspect?

It's not something that I approve of. It's not something that I think should be done. I got caught in a situation there where I had a whole group of people who were afraid to shoot it, right? Then there was another group of cameramen who were so bad that I wouldn't have them shoot it. And by the time I got that all sorted out, it was too late and I sort of had to do it. Also I had a lot of things that were built into the picture based on economics that I knew not too many people would know how to do. So I thought, "Now that I'm at this point, I might as well shoot the thing. It might be easier." But it's not. I don't recommend it. It's exhausting.

But you tend to use the same people, the same crew from film to film?

Whenever possible. It's always my tendency to do so.

And therefore, if you were using the same crew, they generally know how you like to function. So they are thinking in the same vein as you are and consequently it's going to make it easier.

Oh, sure, that's helpful by any standard, whether you're doing that or just shooting.

What's generally your relationship with your crew? Are you dictatorial? Democratic?

My general relationship with people that I've worked with for many years is that I try to be as civil as I can possibly be. I'm not one of the guys because that's counter-productive and that can tend to hurt you. There has to be some structure in the way you function otherwise you'll go nuts. But I'm not a dictator. I don't have a whip and spurs. You can't get anything done that way either. I'm generally focused and know what I want to do.

You said that in all your films, you tended to have the same approach philosophically; yet they don't look the same even though the attack is the same. That's a rough paraphrase of what you said.

Yes, the basis of that is correct. The bottom line is that I use the same tools but I use them differently; I apply them differently to each movie. And sometimes I'll apply them the same way but, just based on the way the movie is structured, it'll look different. Those are selections you make at the time before you start to shoot the movie.

In that same context, everybody uses the same cameras, the same lenses and the same film stocks. Doesn't that contribute to a homogenized look, a sort of sameness? And doesn't that make it more difficult to make something look different?

I don't think so. It gets down to the nitty gritty again. It would get down to how you drive your car. What I'm saying is it would really come down to how is it you think. It's really coming out of your head. If you give everybody the same paint brush, you're not going to get the same paintings.

That's sort of a nebulous aspect that you really can't pin down. It's taste or it's in your head.

Right. I always can't believe it when network or movie spying takes place. It's so simplistic to think that because this cameraman has this light or that filter, that it's the thing to jump on and use.

Like the Steadicam, for example.

Right, they say, "Look at the problems it will answer," not "Look at the problems it will create." This kind of jump-on-the-bandwagon attitude is laughable and it's a sickness in the business that I've never been able to understand.

Over the past few years, you've had the tendency to work with the same directors—in fact, three or four directors make up 60–70% of your credits. Why do you tend to work with the same directors?

I think there are two reasons. First of all, they want you back, which is kind of nice because that's a hard relationship to build. And then the bottom line is if you can do better movies with certain people than you can with other people, then why not do it? It's getting along with that particular person at a level which is suitable for both of you.

Do you ever pay any attention to lighting ratios and color temperatures or do you just do it by eye?

No, I pay attention to lighting ratios. That goes back to the idea of how do you know what it's going to look like on the screen. And the way I function is that I project my aesthetics mechanically so I have to know what it is that I've done.

That's what Michael Chapman said about you. He said that you feel that if there's any aesthetics in filmmaking, it comes through the mechanics.

Yes, it's true. It's not the ideas. You can have a great idea for a painting but what I want to know is, "Can you paint?" It's being able to execute the idea that makes you free.

But you're not just a mechanic?

No, I'm not. But I'm very free with my ideas because of that. I'm not afraid of an idea because I know how to do it. If I don't know how to do it, I'll work to find out how. Nothing is more frustrating than guessing your way through it.

Or to have a concept and not be able to achieve it.

If you can't do it, it's frustrating.

Do you ever have any of those type of problems?

Yes, sure, but you solve them eventually. There are times when you can't do it by yourself; you have to take in other people to help you solve the problem. Of course, once you've solved it once, when any other similar problem comes up, you've got it. But all of us are prone to reduce or expand things to a level that we understand; everyone does that. So I think the danger is in not accepting the fact and sort of stepping in over your head and bullshitting your way through it. That's dangerous.

Maybe I'm projecting again, but I feel that you're thought of as a serious, artistic cinematographer who brings a certain vision to serious dramatic films. But in 1977, you did Annie Hall *for Woody Allen and, since that time, you've done several comedies. Why? Maybe I'm just trying to pigeonhole you.*

Yes, you are, because it's the movie that counts. It just so happens that some of the first films I shot were dealt with at that level because that was the nature of the movie. It's just an opportunity to deal with material at a different level. I was delighted because it's a very pleasant working relationship.

You don't see any contradictions in going from heavy drama to light comedy?

No, and I'll tell you why. I modify my thinking depending on what's going on and what the movie is going to be. But there has always been this kind of Hollywood rhetoric thought pattern—not totally unfounded—that dictates that a comedy has to be lit one way and a melodrama has to be lit another way. Not true. Obviously you have to take the material into consideration and decide how to deal with it. But it's not that cut and dried. I mean, it is in many minds but it's not in mine.

Cinematographer Winton Hoch, now passed away, once told me, more or less, that cinematography doesn't matter in a comedy. And that you'll never see an Academy Award for cinematography go to a comedy. To him, it was because a comedy doesn't demand that kind of dramatic lighting and dramatic overview.

At the Hollywood level, the basis of what he's saying is absolutely correct. They have a way of subdividing their culture in the film business so that what he's saying has a lot of validity in this time and place. Because they've decided that's the way it is.

That's the reality of it in Hollywood but it's not necessarily right?

Exactly. Now I was very proud that *Annie Hall* did nail all the awards that it did. It just proves that most of it is bullshit. The extension of that Hollywood thinking is that it went for comedies as well, not just the Academy Award for cinematography: you know, comedies shouldn't win the awards.

Comedies weren't "meaningful."

Right. So I was happy that *Annie Hall* did very well.

You were recently quoted as saying, "I like to shoot color as if it were black-and-white."

I've always shot it like it was black-and-white. In other words, there are differences obviously from the standpoint of what you have to pay attention to, but as far as lighting ratios and the feel of color on the screen, I feel the same emotionally with that as I do with black-and-white. I handle it basically in the same way on a narrative level; if something special is taking place, obviously you step out of line to do it. Lighting ratios and feelings are the same in my mind. I transpose the same way. Mechanically you have to execute two different ways but I transpose them the same way in my mind.

The old adage I always hear is that while color separates itself by virtue of the color, with black-and-white you're going to have to help it separate.

Because you're dealing in values. When you're shooting in black-and-white, all you're dealing with is values so, yes, you do have to separate an actor from a wall. Whereas if you're in color and you have an actor and a colored wall, then you get automatic separation. But even then, philosophically, I will tend to finally deal with him visually the same way. But not mechanically the same way.

What effect do you think the quality of photography of a film has on an average audience?

I think it has a very good effect on an audience if it's done well within the structure of the movie. I also feel that it can get in the way and disturb an audience. They won't know why they're being disturbed but they will be.

It's something on a subconscious or emotional level that they are reacting to?

You can be pulling them two different ways. The cameraman can be doing one thing and the story is doing something else. But done properly, the photography is a very large contribution. It just can't look like a large contribution.

The impression that I gathered from other cameramen is that you were one of the first cinematographers to say, "I know that this or that is going to make a difference on the screen and I'm going to stand up and fight for it." Whereas maybe some other cameramen just went along with the program and didn't say anything.

I'll fight to get it right. If you have any integrity, you want to do it right. But also, within that context, you have to know what you're asking for. You can't be a bimbo and say, "I'm going to sit out here for seven days and wait for the right conditions."

Or "I want forty arcs."

Right. You can't be crazy. What you have to be asking for is something that makes relative sense and is in the right proportion to what's going on. Generally, people aren't asking for the right things on movies. It gets very diffuse; they forget what they're doing.

I would think that by now you don't have to fight for those things anymore?

The percentage of fighting is not very high anymore.

It seems that you were a catalyst in fighting for that kind of thing. And that allowed other cameramen to say, "I'm going to fight for this too." Are you aware of that?

In all honesty, I'm not aware of that. But now that you mention it, it's kind of scary because it depends on who's asking for those things. There aren't too many people walking around in this business with a good overall perspective about what's going on in the movies. I would hate to think that there was any footstomping going on, in general, that really didn't mean anything. So I worry about that a little because that will ultimately destroy everybody. That's multiple *Heaven's Gate* in a lot of ways. I don't like to see that either. You know, I don't get involved in any of those things at an ego level or at least I try not to. I try to keep it at the level of what has to be done, not an "I want" attitude. When I say, "I want . . .," it's based on being able to execute what's going on in the material.

A lot of cameramen I've talked to have great admiration and respect for your work, yet you and the Academy Awards have never gotten along.

No, it goes back to the structure of the film business. Look, my philosophy is simply this: I like to shoot and go home, you know what I mean?

You don't court the attention of the press or your peers?

Right. If you want to spend enough time, politically and socially, you can win anything. But then you really haven't won anything. All you've done is you've greased everybody and they, in turn, say, "Well, he's a nice guy and he also shot a couple of nice pictures. Give it to him."

Now I'm not socially or politically oriented and it's hard for people to understand. I also have never gone out of my way to make any of that possible. I mean, if they moved the Academy Awards to Switzerland or somewhere and they had a board there that did nothing but look at movies, and had nothing to do with Hollywood, that might be better. You can't go nuts over those things. You just have to do your work. The other thing is that I don't make movies for other cameramen; I make movies for directors and producers. So I don't care whether other cameramen like it or not. I have other friends who are cameramen but I would never make a decision based on what they think.

Also you're an outsider because you live in New York. You're not here with everybody else in Hollywood.

I don't know why that makes everybody so nervous. I think people should be able to live and work where they want to.

In The Godfather, *you weren't shooting for a heavy, thick negative. You were, effectively, under-exposing a half a stop and you were getting a more translucent effect. At the time, you said you disliked a full negative on aesthetic grounds. But you also said that you shoot in such a narrow range so that the lab can't mess up your negative.*

Right, I'm in such a narrow band that they can't fool with it. They have to print it the way it was intended.

Which, in essence, gives you more control.

Right. Now when Technicolor was still functioning in Hollywood, we were still in the position of making dye transfer prints. But today that's no longer in existence. So everyone's stuck with the IP and CRI. So I have to lower the ASA rating a little bit so I get a fuller negative as opposed to what I was doing when I had control with three-strip printing. I don't like it; it's not a great situation. You have to work your way around the mechanics.

How closely do you monitor the lab when you're shooting?

Very closely!

How closely do you monitor the timing?

I set one light for the picture and they print everything I shoot on that one light. I don't time. Then for twenty or thirty weeks, they keep printing on that one light. And ideally, they're on the same positive stock. You see, Technicolor will take enough positive and put it aside for a movie I'm shooting; so at least we have that control factor. And you have the same emulsion number on the negative. You want to eliminate as many variables as you can.

Somebody said that you were "the best door-to-door cinematographer in the business." Meaning that you were there weeks before the film rolls and that you were there at the end of it all to time the release print. How closely do you monitor that final process of going to the release print?

I use the same technique in release printing as I do in setting up the movie in the front end. What I'll ask them to do is one-light the cut negative and develop it all at the same time. You can't time from dailies because, even as closely monitored as they might be, there are still going to be variations. So what you want to do is neutralize the cut negative on a one-light and develop it. Then you look at that. And generally it's very simple because I'll just make corrections based on a mistake I might have made or a variable in the lab chemistry. But there are not many corrections; the movie will print out just about like I shot it.

A number of cameramen do the timing themselves, whether it's in their contract or not, whether they get paid for it or not. They'll do it on their own; it's a matter of pride.

But they have to let you do the timing. You can't have twelve people timing the movie; you can't have even two people timing the movie. Photography is not play-dough; there's a terrible habit of trying to change the look of the movie after it's been photographed through all of this horrendous printing that goes on in laboratories. Well, it's bullshit because you're not going to change anything that way. If it's junk, it's going to look like junk. If it's good, leave it alone and print it the way it was designed to be printed.

A lot of directors of photography would still operate the camera, if the union would let them (and some do anyhow). But I have the feeling that you wouldn't necessarily care to operate.

No, I don't care about that. I know directors who want to operate too. As a director of photography, if you're doing what you're supposed to be doing, you don't have time for that. It would be exhausting, for one thing. Hopefully, you get a good operator and he understands what you give him. I don't want to do twenty takes of somebody running up a flight of stairs. I'm looking at the scene and trying to make improvements. There's no way you can see that through the camera because you're too busy with the framing. I'm a good operator but it's a pointless use of your own energy during the day. But a lot of guys like to do it.

I get the feeling that you take your job very seriously.

Yes, I do take it seriously because I want to do a good job. My average is about two movies per year but I would prefer to do one, frankly, because I put a lot into it. So it's hard for me to shoot back-to-back films. A lot of guys shoot back-to-back because they function at a different level—not a lesser level, just a different one.

Are you afraid of burning yourself out? Is that a distinct possibility?

Well, I don't think you burn yourself out the way a director can burn himself out. But, if you're not careful, you can end up making decisions which are not appropriate for the movie. What you'll do is that you'll drag in stuff that you did on another movie because it's easier right then than to think it out and do it another way. So that's the danger there.

Some people say that you take your job too seriously, to the point of obsession. For example, in a particular scene, there is really only one place for the camera to be. And you can make a case for that.

I want the camera right where I put it. I want it right on the mark.

Should we call that obsession?

No, it's not an obsession because I do it very quickly. I put the camera where it belongs. I mean, you can shift it six inches and you're not going to have the same shot. What someone watching you doesn't understand is that they're only watching one shot, while you have already cut six shots together in your head. You know what comes before and what goes after. So it makes a difference on an overall scale.

One of your assistants says that when you put the tape down and measure it, that's where the camera goes. You don't change it from there; that's it.

I'll make minor adjustments because of optics but basically that's where the camera goes. And it's a quick way to work. I hate fishing around all over the place with a camera; it's nonsense. I'm not saying you don't evaluate where you put it. My general overall trend is that if the director knows what the scene is about and where everybody's going to be, he can set shots quickly and get on with it. Because I don't like to spend anymore time fooling with that than anybody else. I'm not an equipment freak; it's only a tool as far as I'm concerned. So the quicker we can get all that out of the way, the better.

I'm sure there must be times when the director asks, "Why are we setting up here?"

Yes, but those discussions, hopefully and generally, go on before you set it. It's not always a visual decision. It's a decision based on whether the shot is best for the scene.

But people tend to take that attitude of setting the camera in a very simplistic way. It sounds very autocratic. But it's not really that way at all.

The director and I have already had many discussions and the basis of it is that you want to get on with it. The ideal way to work is that you decide with the director whether a scene plays in one cut or three or four. If you lay all that out before you even set a camera, then everybody knows what they're doing and where they're going next. And that includes the performers because they're more comfortable with that too. There's no confusion that way. The worst way to work is one shot at a time; it's a hopeless technique because you just paint yourself into the corner.

What was the difference between Manhattan *and* Stardust Memories? *The photography in* Manhattan *was great but I thought it was even better in* Stardust Memories. *What did you learn or accomplish in between?*

Manhattan was, by its sheer nature, romantic reality again. And *Stardust Memories* was a more theatrical and more poetic approach to shooting a piece of material. So it's different from that standpoint. Whether you like one or the other, the difference was laid out at that level.

I know this is very simplistic, but is there anything you improved on from one film to the other?

I don't think so. Not at the level you're asking. At a craft level, no. On an interpretive level, they were two different things.

Were there things that you improved on from The Godfather *to* The Godfather II?

Definitely. *The Godfather II* was a much classier movie than *The Godfather.* It was shot and structured better. What it amounted to was that we had the opportunity to do it again. Also the opportunities to do things were there at a much greater level. So there were improvements. I felt I did a much better job on *The Godfather II* than I did on *The Godfather.* Even though they were different, they were the same in many ways.

What would you personally advise a film student, interested in cinematography, who's looking for a way to break in?

It's one of the biggest problems and I get letters about this. I guess the bottom line of advice is that you just have to shoot film. You've got to go out and shoot film. And you get any job you can that will deliver that for you. You don't necessarily have to try and get in the IA right away; there are other unions and there are other people making movies. The important thing is to get out there and do it. There are some very fine people around who are doing some very interesting stuff. Probably some of the most interesting stuff is happening outside what's going on in my part of the business. So I don't think a student should set his sights for Hollywood or bust. If they work at it, eventually they'll surface.

But is talent going to necessarily win out?

Talent won't necessarily win out because you have to be lucky and aggressive. And when your opportunity arrives, you should have the ability to take advantage of it, whatever and how small it may be. Also you never know what an opportunity is in this business. It's such a small business that you can do one thing and it can bloom into something that's all out of proportion. But the point is that it does catapult you through the business at a very fast rate, maybe sometimes too fast. So do as much as you can whenever you can.

15

Vilmos Zsigmond

"I know pretty much what the difference is that really shows up on the screen and I fight for those things. I'm not going to get another picture if I shoot like every other cameraman. I go for excellence."

Vilmos Zsigmond is not a man to be trifled with when it comes to making movies. He makes it perfectly clear that he has no patience for idle talk and half-hearted excuses in place of excellence. After all, along with his countryman Laszlo Kovacs, he dodged Russian tanks in order to get documentary footage of the Hungarian Revolution in 1956. Understandably, working on a nice quiet Hollywood sound stage or in a distant location in Montana doesn't present much of a problem to him.

A native of Szeged, Hungary, and son of a celebrated soccer player and coach, Zsigmond developed an interest in photography while still in high school. He became involved in portrait photography and was soon accepted as a full-time student at the State Academy of Motion Picture and Theater Arts in Budapest where he received an M.A. in cinematography. After his formal training, he got five years of hands-on experience at a Budapest feature film studio, handling a variety of duties, culminating in a director of photography title. But the Hungarian Revolution changed the course of his life and put him on the road to Hollywood. After chronicling the revolution on thirty thousand feet of film, he escaped to Austria and then immigrated to the United States. In a modest biographical sketch, he admits that it was difficult to break into the film business. "My first occupations in Hollywood were hardly connected to filmmaking: an insurance company (microfilming), a custom photo lab and a home portrait studio," writes Zsigmond. But by 1963, he had made a number of contacts with independent filmmakers who were working with low budgets and non-union crews. In the short span of four years, Zsigmond shot fourteen low-budget features for little or no compensation, but at least he was getting the experience and learning the ropes of the Hollywood system.

His European training and long apprenticeship on low-budget productions made him a natural when the fast, lightweight style of filmmaking came into vogue in the late sixties. However, it soon became apparent that he could do much more than just shoot a picture quickly on a tight schedule. He could also give a director a specific look and visual style. It was his superb work with Robert Altman on *McCabe and Mrs. Miller, Images* and *The Long Goodbye* that drew public and critical acclaim for his enormous talents. In film after film, Zsigmond's creative

311

cinematography has shown him to be a master at evoking the intended visual mood and ambience of a given project. His innovation in the use of filters and lab processes have expanded the limits of creative cinematography.

Recently, his effort to wed special effects with rich, full-scale cinematography culminated in an Oscar for *Close Encounters of the Third Kind,* an honor that was long overdue. Unfortunately, one of his premier efforts has gone largely unseen; the unjustly maligned *Heaven's Gate* features his full and consistent application of natural photography that weaves an emotional texture into this period piece. Brash and outspoken, Zsigmond continues to pursue his kind of excellence without regard to his more conservative contemporaries.

1963 *The Sadist*
      Living Between Two Worlds
1964 *The Incredibly Strange Creatures*
         Who Stopped Living and
         Became Crazy Mixed-up
         Zombies (with Joseph
         Mascelli)
      What's Up Front
      The Time Travelers
1965 *The Nasty Rabbit*
      Deadwood '76
      Tales of a Salesman
      A Hot Summer Game
      Psycho A Go-Go!
      Rat Fink
1967 *Mondo Mod* (with Laszlo Kovacs)
1968 *The Name of the Game Is Kill!*
      Jennie, Wife/Child (with Robert
         Cohen)
      Picasso Summer
1969 *Hot Rod Action* (with Vilis
         Lapenieks, Mario Tosi)
      The Monitors
      Five Bloody Graves
      Futz
1970 *Horror of the Blood Monsters*
         (with William Troiano)

1971 *Red Sky at Morning*
      McCabe and Mrs. Miller
      The Hired Hand
      The Ski Bum
1972 *Deliverance*
      Images
1973 *The Long Goodbye*
      Scarecrow
      Cinderella Liberty
1974 *The Sugarland Express*
      The Girl from Petrovka
1976 *Sweet Revenge*
      Obsession
      Winter Kills
1977 *Close Encounters of the*
         *Third Kind**
1978 *The Last Waltz* (camera
         operator only)
      The Deer Hunter†
1979 *The Rose*
1980 *Heaven's Gate*
      Blow Out
1981 *Jinxed*
1982 *Table for Five*
1983 *The River*
1984 *No Small Affair*

*Academy Award for best achievement in cinematography.
†Academy Award Nomination for best achievement in cinematography.

Most of the time you operate your own camera, don't you?

That's not true anymore. I used to because Hollywood didn't have good enough operators. Coming out of non-union films, I knew how to operate the camera. I knew how to handle hand-held shots and how to make nice zooms and pans at the same time. Consequently, when Laszlo [Kovacs] and I went into features, we found that Hollywood operators were not able to do that and we ended up with lousy shots. So you had to do your own operating in those days to get a good shot.

That's essentially why you were doing it?

Yes. Later on they developed electric zooms. Also some of the younger operators, who have grown up since, started to handle the camera much better than the older operators. But still, it was very hard to find good operators; even today it's hard. Many people think that we have to show off and do the camerawork. It's not that; it's just that you have something that you want to do and you don't want the operator to goof it up. If you have a good operator behind the camera, it's fine.

That frees you for other things?

Yes. There are so many other things to do. It's a pain in the ass to have to jump back and forth behind the camera. On the other hand, I still love to look through the camera. Shooting on a small set, for example, there's maybe no other way to see the scene. Even the director cannot see the scene because there's a flag over here and a reflector over there. Now in those cases I would love to be behind the camera but the union doesn't let you do that.

*In a number of films that you've worked on (*McCabe and Mrs. Miller *and* Images *come to mind), you've had to deal with inclement weather and the natural elements. What sort of problem does that present to you as a cameraman?*

Well, it's always a problem when you are not shooting under a totally controlled situation. In the days of old Hollywood, they worked on stages where they could control everything, the rain, the snow.

But they couldn't get it to look like McCabe and Mrs. Miller.

Well, when Altman decided to do those kind of pictures and some of the younger directors decided to go that way, basically it was against the establishment, against the old Hollywood style. I mean, we tried to photograph rain the way it was naturally and it didn't show up on the film; we had to create our own rain. Funny thing, we go up to Vancouver and it's raining all the time but it doesn't show up on the film. So we had to do what old Hollywood used to do. We had to get our rain birds out and control our own rain.

Many people think that in the new Hollywood you just go out into the street and shoot it the way it is. That's not really true because we had to adopt many, many of the old techniques in order to make it work. Like lightning—many people think that the new Hollywood cameramen like locations because they look more real. But the lighting is much more difficult on location than on a stage. So we have to work much harder to give the feeling that you are seeing the real thing. Of course, in most of these films with Altman, we shot lots of exteriors. That's the beautiful thing about realistic pictures versus old Hollywood: we utilize locations. Since we are there, we might as well use the location. For some reason, film always looks better when you shoot outside. I don't know why, there's just a feeling of reality.

Over the years, you have developed a lightweight method of shooting, that is, minimizing the amount of equipment that you carry with you. Do you still do that?

I like to use the minimum amount of equipment all the time. I like the new lights because a smaller unit will give you as much light as an older unit used to give you. We are also using less light because film is better. Our film today is much more sensitive than even ten years ago.

What about the new cameras, the small Panaflex and the little Arri? How does that help you?

It's basically helping us to get better shots by allowing us to move into corners the older, bigger cameras couldn't get into. It gives you mobility. The smaller the camera, the easier you can get the shots. It saves set-up time. If you have a heavy camera, it takes three guys to lift it and put it on the tripod. Now, you can just grab a hand-held camera, like the Panaflex, put it on your shoulder, find your shot using it as a viewfinder, get the tripod there and then you have your shot. It helps in speeding up production.

What about the Kodak 5247 stock?

I shot *Close Encounters of the Third Kind* on 5247 because of the really finer grain. I found that it's a very good film and I had no problems with it at all. In fact, I understand you can push it two stops without any problem, which is amazing. 5254 you could only push one stop.

You've done a lot of forced development?

Yes, I like to push film. I don't like to use lights; I use the minimum amount of lighting and it helps if I can use the smaller lighting units. If I can use a baby spot instead of a junior, it saves electricity and I can use a smaller generator. For some reason, even the smaller lights work better for me. The small baby has a much cleaner look; you can cut it better, you can shadow it better. It's faster and it looks better. By pushing the film a stop I get a little bit of grain but considering the subject matter that I usually was shooting, like *Cinderella Liberty* or *McCabe and Mrs. Miller*, it really didn't need that perfect look. *Close Encounters of the Third Kind* was a different story. We didn't push the film there because we needed a very clinical, realistic look.

You talk about "cutting the light" and "shadowing the light." Could you elaborate a bit on that?

If you used a larger light unit and diffused it to bring it down to the same level of footcandles as a smaller unit, it would still not look like a smaller unit. You will get two different kinds of looks. The smaller lighting unit is much sharper. You can cut it easier because the smaller the unit, the more it becomes a point-source unit, like the sun. The sun gives you a very sharp shadow because it's a point source; it's a big source but it's so far away that it becomes a small source. So with a small unit, you can create a harsh shadow, you can control it better. A big unit, on the other hand, is not really a point source. It's a bigger source so the shadow is not going to be that controllable. So you are losing control with a bigger source. But again, everything is relative. With today's soft-lighting technique where you use bounce lighting, you are tending to use the bigger units. But that's the style now where you use lots of soft, diffused lighting. But for night interior shooting where you really need control and sharpness, you would choose as small a unit as possible.

How closely do you monitor the lab work when you're involved in pushing the film?

Very closely. Usually I make my tests and normally I don't even push one full stop because I found out that by just cutting down a little bit, like to two-thirds of a stop, it already gave me a gain in the grain structure. I found that by pushing two-thirds of a stop that it didn't increase the grain at all but it gave me the speed. Whatever was left over of that one-third of a stop, I could print it up. I found it was better to do it that way. I usually find out from each lab how far I can go without getting bad results. I never push more than is necessary.

Do you watch the lab closely once you start sending the dailies in?

It depends on which lab you are going to. I usually like to work with Technicolor because there you have one guy, Skip Nicholson, whom you can call day or night. He sees all the dailies. I can ask artistic questions and I can rely on his judgment. When you are on location so many thousands of miles away, for example, you need someone who saw your footage and who can give reliable information. He can criticize your work and tell you that maybe you ought to bring up your exposure a little bit; maybe your light meter is not working exactly right. He can catch things like that which other labs would never catch because they are not interested. The lab should be on your side, it should be helping you, it should be personal.

The fights we had over Altman's *McCabe and Mrs. Miller!* No Hollywood lab would flash the film for us. The labs said, "Why do that? You're crazy; you're ruining the film." So we found a very small lab in Vancouver that didn't even have 35mm printing machines. But Altman told them that we were going to develop the whole film there, 300,000 feet of film, so they invested the money in the developing machines and they did a brilliant job of flashing the film.

It took Hollywood another two years to accept the flashing technique. They wouldn't touch it.

Sometimes I vacation in Europe and, when I do, I usually take a few days off and go to Technicolor Rome to see what they are doing. And I get information there that I cannot believe! They showed me a film, Visconti's *L'Innocente*, and it looked fantastic. It looked like old Technicolor used to, with very dark and very great contrast. And I've always had this dream—if I could have a nice soft negative and underdevelop it to get the full scale negative and then get something like #4 paper and really get some contrast into the thing, like a photographer does. But in motion pictures there is one kind of negative and one kind of positive, so all films look the same. So I came back to Hollywood and I fought with the lab here for weeks to try to get them to get the information from Rome on how they do it. But the lab says, "Why do you want to do something different? It's good enough for Laszlo and for Gordon [Willis], why do something different?"

When we spoke to one of your peers, he fondly recalled some of his early "no-budget" features. He pointed out that even though he's working with much larger budgets now, it's still the same hassles. One would think that it would be easier now but it's worse.

Exactly. You know, when we did our low-budget features in the early days, we did it for very little money. So no one could tell us, "We are going to shoot this scene in five minutes." I would tell them, "We will shoot this scene when my lighting is ready." The producer wasn't paying us so we didn't have to prostitute ourselves. So we did our own thing. Even though it was low-budget, we still did what we wanted to do with the equipment we had and we did it right. They were not the greatest pictures but photographically they had some nice things in them. You can't do that today with big budgets.

The money situation in the industry is getting worse. They are cutting down the budgets and the shooting schedules. Everything is push-push. The "good" cameraman here is the guy who doesn't care about his artistry and just does it on time. In the meantime, they are hiring me because I have a different "look," right? And I have to give them the different "look" on the same time as the guy who cannot give them the "look." So this is a big problem.

It's getting worse, from what you've seen?

It's definitely getting worse when you shoot a picture in Hollywood. Money is very tight; everybody knows that to make a movie today costs twice as much as it did last year and three times as much as four years ago. So they don't want to spend the money on it. That's why I still have the idea I told you about years ago. I would like to get a tight group together, get a few crew members, work for scale and go for a percentage of the film. Everybody would work overtime and Saturdays and Sundays deferred if they could earn a percentage of the movie. Maybe this way we can keep the costs down.

You've said that, outside of having a good relationship with the director, the most important thing in a project is having a script that excites you and fills you with enthusiasm. Could you give some examples of scripts you have been enthusiastic about?

All the films I have photographed I was pretty much excited about. There are a couple of exceptions: I did a couple pictures where I was excited about the script but when I started to work on it I was not excited about the director. I want to have fun when I'm shooting a movie. It's hard enough work to begin with so if you don't enjoy it, why are you shooting it? You want to have fun with it; you want to be able to talk to the director, to do things together. I found Altman to be tremendously creative because he likes good photography on his films. He liked to experiment each time so it was really exciting to work with him. It was the same way with John Boorman, who is a very great director. He knows exactly what he wants but he gives you lots of leeway. He starts out with a fabulous idea but if you come up with an even better one, he's going to buy it. If Boorman didn't like my idea, I knew my idea didn't come up to his idea, that's all. I can adapt myself very easily to the director's point of view because I like good, exciting things and I keep trying to improve on everything. If he accepts one of my twenty ideas, that's great. I feel like I contributed something to the film. But if the director doesn't accept one of fifty of my suggestions and I know my idea is better, then I know I'm dealing with a guy who has an ego problem. Actors, art directors, composers—they all want to contribute something.

Most likely Altman knows how to convey what he wants and that goes hand in hand with trusting you. Why would he get Vilmos Zsigmond in the first place if not for his exceptional camerawork?

It's funny you mentioned this. Altman was in London and *2001* was playing in a twin theater on one side, and *McCabe and Mrs. Miller* was playing on the other side. Somehow it happened that Altman was watching *2001* and Kubrick was watching *McCabe and Mrs. Miller* at the same time. On the way out, they bumped into each other. And Kubrick started to ask Altman questions. He said, "Robert, how do you do those beautiful zoom shots, when the camera starts zooming in and it pans and ends up on that beautiful composition? Do you do that yourself?" And Robert said, "No, I'm not doing that myself; it's my cameraman doing it." And Kubrick said, "Do you trust him?" To which Robert replied, "Of course I trust him; he's doing it exactly the way I would do it if I was behind the camera, that's his job."

With Altman, how difficult is it when you have to deal with a lot of actor improvisation.

It's very exciting actually. It's exciting because it's basically a fluid camera. All those pictures that he did in that style, I was actually operating my own camera, which helps a lot. The operator becomes the director of photography in those situations because you really have to decide yourself what you are going to do in improvised situations—whether you move the camera or not, whether you zoom in a little bit more. You have to grab a lot of things. We did a lot of grabbing in *The Long Goodbye*. Even in *McCabe and Mrs. Miller*, we did lots of things like that. I love it and it's really a nice kind of moviemaking.

The actors feel free to do anything they want to do. In *The Long Goodbye*, we practically never knew what Sterling Hayden was going to do. We made marks on the floor so just in case he hit that mark we knew where the focus would be. Sterling would say to me, "Is that my mark?" I told him to forget about it, like it wasn't even there—that he should step anywhere he wanted. At the end of the show it was really nice when Sterling came to me and said, "Vilmos, you know what? I was never so happy in any other picture before. I didn't know why but now I understand. It was because, in every other picture, half my performance went down the drain because I had to step into marks. And if I didn't hit the marks, they would stop the camera and tell me I couldn't do this and I couldn't do that." He was happy in *The Long Goodbye* because he did not have to concentrate on the mechanics of his performance. And that's very important to actors. That's why they love the stage; it's much freer, they can do improvisations.

With Easy Rider, *Peter Fonda emerged as the young director as cult hero. How much did he have straight in his mind about what he wanted in his next film,* The Hired Hand?

He knew pretty much the kind of film he wanted to make. He showed me a film that his dad did, *My Darling Clementine*. It was a black-and-white film. He said to me, "Vilmos, if you could make a color film that looks like this I would be very happy. This is the kind of movie I want to make; it's an old-fashioned movie. I don't mind if the actors sit down and say dialogue. I don't want to make an *Easy Rider* out of this. I want to have a straight dramatic picture with good characters." That's exactly what we did. We tried to get it as realistic as possible—maybe a little bit better than real.

It was interesting because, for the first couple of weeks, I had to help Peter because he didn't know much about screen direction. He'd ask me, "Why can't the actor walk on from this direction?" He knew about it but he kept forgetting. I'd say, "Well, he can walk on that way but then you have to shoot the whole film that way." But he was an amazingly fast study. After two weeks he picked up everything and I hardly had to talk to him anymore. He had a good idea of the film. I tried to visualize what he wanted to have and let him do what he wanted to do.

Many people we talked to about the film raved about the cinematography but faulted the content. Which leads to the next question: do you think the cinematography on a film can overpower the story and the script?

There was not much to overpower actually. I think that was one of the problems with *The Hired Hand*, that it was really an anti-dramatic film. Now if you don't have a really dramatic film, what do you do? Do you underplay the photography? Then you have nothing, you don't even have style. Why are people going to see a film which has no photography and no story? So what do you do? With films that are over-photographed, the screenplay is not dramatic. Everybody said the same thing about *McCabe and Mrs. Miller*. They said the film didn't have a strong and valid story and I disagreed with that because I think it had a lot of things to say. Many times they say the photography is too good. The photography can never be too good.

What sort of preparation do you do for a film before you begin shooting?

Basically, I would say that I spend most of my time getting into the head of the director—you know, having discussions, seeing locations, finding out about the style of the film. I want to find out what he wants to do. Many times it's difficult to find out because maybe the director himself doesn't know exactly what he wants. But at least you get as close to it as you can. You want to get as much information as the director has in his mind at that time. If you do that in the preparation stage, you have won half the game because at least you are going to be in synch with him. I don't want to direct the picture, that's his job. I want to photograph it the way he wants it to be photographed. If he doesn't have an idea about that, I'll give suggestions and sit down with him and show him some color still photographs of certain kinds of lighting or mood that will suit a particular scene. I watch his reaction. Then I can begin to find out what he wants.

You would assume that those couple weeks of preparation would be very important in establishing the overriding mood and style . . .

It's like a rehearsal for an orchestra when you have a new conductor. He has to get into all the instruments, he has to shape the instruments to his liking so the music that has been selected can be performed. So that's what it is here. Usually you need lots of time for that and usually we don't have that. Many cameramen are allowed only one or two weeks of preparation. So what happens? If you want to do a good picture, you give your own time and find your own way to communicate with the director beforehand. You do it for free on your own time. Or you don't and it shows up in the picture.

Deliverance *had a very naturalistic look as opposed to the dream-like quality and style of some of your other films . . .*

Well, the film called for a very stark look so we didn't flash the film, we didn't push it. We went for that stark look. In selecting the locations, we didn't go in for colorful locales at all. Most of the forest and the water were selected to be shot on an overcast day which eliminates the blue sky and all the reflections in the water which usually makes water very cheerful. On an overcast day the water really has blacks and whites. The foliage or whatever is reflected in the water became black. So we only had to deal with greens, blacks, whites and greys. Now, in the opening scene when we find the little banjo player, unfortunately it was the beginning of spring and it looked very cheerful with yellows and reds. So we decided, at that time, that we were going to desaturate the film; so that's what happened later on at the lab. Technically we printed black-and-white into the color. So in the beginning we desaturated it and later on when they get to the village, we had to desaturate that also because it was just too colorful. It's very hard to find locations that are dramatic and desaturated in America today. There are too many reds and yellows; it's too colorful. John Boorman has a real good sense of style. He knew what it meant to wait for the clouds; he never pushed me to shoot a scene when the sun was out, unlike many American directors who would. He knows that the quality of the photography has a great impact. Sometimes we waited two hours for a single cloud so that a particular scene would match the rest of the sequence.

What kind of problems did shooting on the rapids present?

Just physical problems. To get down there we had to use boats or jeeps to carry all the necessary equipment. We could hardly get four set-ups a day. It was very physical and we had a dedicated crew that we hand-picked. The actors were dedicated too. Burt Reynolds and Jon Voight were not like stars. They were hardworking guys and they helped by doing every single stunt. Originally we had planned to do three weeks of stunt work at the end of shooting but it was not needed because they did it themselves. This way we never had to go to a wide angle or phoney it and hide their faces. When Jon Voight was in trouble in the water, that was Jon Voight. He was in the rapids, he was trying to swim. We had four guys on the shore ready to jump in the water if he got into trouble. We had equipment standing by to save his life if anything happened. They were doing it themselves and that's the great reality of the film.

I imagine that sometimes you have to compromise your photography to please a director or a studio? Or just to get the shot?

It always happens on every single picture. I don't think you can always give it your best shot. It's just impossible because you would run into budget problems. You always have to find out how far the director or producer is willing to go. You have to play that limit because otherwise you have an unhappy producer and many times an unhappy crew. So you cannot really be too artistic and get away with it. Not too many cameramen can do that; I think Gordon Willis is the only one who could get away with it.

I pretty much know what the difference is that really shows up on the screen and I fight for those things. I am a very hard fighter when it comes to important things. Most of the time I have to compromise which means I have to alter my mind and make it work. Say I have to shoot a scene on an overcast day. How long will the producer wait for that overcast day? You would be foolish to try to fight for something when you know you are losing. So you do the best you can; you talk the director into shooting backlight or shooting it in a way that will still give the scene some kind of dramatic quality. I would really refuse to shoot something that is bad. And I would get to the breaking point where maybe they would fire me. It's not worth it. If I know something is bad, I'm not going to do it. If somebody hires me, they know that about me.

There comes a certain point where your reputation is on the line too.

I'm not going to get another picture if I shoot like other cameramen. I go for a sort of excellence. So I like to find directors who play with you, who really want you and hire you because they think you can contribute to the film. If it's worth the pain in the ass that I'm causing to the production, then they will hire me next time. If it's not worth it, then they won't rehire me.

The Sugarland Express *was Steven Spielberg's first theatrical feature. Were there any problems in his making the transition from TV to the big screen?*

No, he is very talented and very open. He really wanted to make a good picture and we really worked together as a good team. It was marvelous; it was one of the best experiences I've had. We felt that we were doing an important picture. Commercially it wasn't too successful but I think the studio didn't exploit the film properly. I think it's a terrific film and Spielberg is a joy to work with.

I had read an early script version of Close Encounters of the Third Kind *and it was interesting but it had some problems. And the finished film had more gaps and less character than this early working script.*

Part of it is really that Steven set out to make a commercial film. And he knew exactly how to make a commercially successful film; that's exactly what he did. He did not set out to make an artistic film; he did that on *Sugarland Express.*

There were an incredible amount of special effects in Close Encounters. *How closely did you have to work with Doug Trumbull to integrate all those special effects with your photography?*

Very closely. Actually I had to expose the negative the way he wanted it. I had to change my style in order to accommodate his needs. Usually my pictures don't have that much sharpness. I don't like to shoot sharp pictures; I like the negative sharp to the eye but I build in softness. I couldn't do that on *Close Encounters* because Trumbull could only do his matte work if he had a sharp negative to begin with. Also it had to be a fully exposed negative, which I don't usually go for because I don't like the colors when the negative is fully exposed. It's too bright, too contrasty. But obviously if you make a special effects picture, you have to satisfy the man who is going to do the matte work and special effects. I think that, technically, part of the success of the film is that we were not fighting each other but helping each other. Many times I had problems in giving him a certain exposure and I would call him over and say, "Doug, this is a problem here. What are we going to do because I cannot give you the exposure that you want?" He would say, "Okay, fine, I will find a way around it." So we were working together all the time. Of course what made it easy for us is that we had storyboarded the whole last part of the movie. We had one storyboard for each sequence and listed under that was the description of how we were going to do it. One sequence might involve four or five different things. For example, we had to do light effects right there on the stage because Doug could not superimpose light effects on people. And we had to know what he was going to add to the picture later on. So we would have to ask him, "What kind of light is this UFO going to emit? How bright and what kind of color?" So we had to work together on that too because otherwise the final effect would not work.

So, in a way, that sort of restricted your normal style? You had to light for a scene you could not see?

Right. Special effects are always tricky. You cannot really do a one hundred per cent good job on it. That's why I'm very proud about the way *Close Encounters* looks. It could have looked like *The Towering Inferno* and *Airport '77* and all those special effects pictures, which are pretty bad-looking pictures to me. You always see the special effects and you know when they come on the screen. But in *Close Encounters* you are really seduced, in many cases, into thinking that it's real. You think what's happening is really real because the special effects are very well coordinated with the lighting and the photography.

The special effects don't call attention to themselves.

Right. It's not grainy. In many special effects pictures of the past, you knew what parts were special effect because suddenly the film became grainier. We shot all the special effects on 65mm so that by the time Trumbull put in his effects, it matched the 35mm footage. There were many, many sequences where we didn't have any special effects and we shot it on 35mm and forced the film one stop deliberately to match the grain structure of the 65mm, when it was duped several times.

How does that work? You shot all the special effects on 65mm?

We shot all the special effects on 65mm—anything that Trumbull had to superimpose some effect on or add something to. We had shots where he didn't have to superimpose anything, so we knew that the original photography would be on 35mm. I mean, we could have done it all on 65mm and gone to second and third generation printing. We didn't want to do that and I think it was easier and less expensive to do it the way we did.

What I'm getting at is what is the basic reason for shooting special effects on 65mm as opposed to 35mm?

It's a bigger negative. The registration on the 65mm optical printer is much better.

This is the first picture you've done where you've really been involved with a lot of special effects. What kind of things did you get out of it that increased your knowledge of what film can do? What kind of things did you learn?

A special effects film is one type of film. If you are a cameraman, you have to be able to handle all kinds of films. I was never boxed into a kind of situation where someone would say, "Well, he's a good exterior cameraman" or "He's a good interior cameraman." I hate to be categorized anyhow. My films all look different. I shot *Deliverance* which was an exterior film and then I shot *Images* which was almost totally an interior film. For a cameraman, it's a challenge to do all kinds of things.

I understand that on Close Encounters *Spielberg wanted a look to the film that had a complete range of colors, from blacks all the way through the color spectrum to white.*

Right. That was partially the reason why we didn't want to desaturate the colors. We didn't want to flash the film. So I had to move away from my original style which is usually the opposite. I usually don't like a wide range of colors. I like to control the colors like a painter does. Painters don't have that wide range of colors and contrasts. You look at a painting and it's either on the warm side or the full side. Selection of colors makes art. Just having a wide range of colors and contrasts from white to black doesn't necessarily mean it's artistic. It's more technical. And since Spielberg wanted to make his picture look very technical in that sense—he wanted it to look very perfect technically—he didn't want to really make it look artistic. He didn't want you to believe that you were seeing a fantasy or a made-up story. He wanted you to believe that it was the real thing.

Very clean, realistic and sharp.

It's like industrial photography. When you see industrial photography, the colors go from white to black and they are perfect. The reds are red. He wanted to have that look in the movie. That doesn't necessarily mean that I like that kind of approach for moviemaking but I did it anyhow. That shows that cinematographers have to work with directors: we photograph their movies.

Do you enjoy using the 5247 film stock?

I think it's a fabulous film. Kodak improved that film so much. It's fine-grained and you can do anything you want to do with it. I like to fool around with film a lot and I find that 5247 has a great latitude. If I want to, I can degrade it for my taste. I don't mind doing that. I'd rather start out with a good film and degrade it to the point where I like it. Sometimes you want a good film and many times I don't diffuse and I use a sharp lens to get that effect. So you think of it as a tool that you can do almost anything you want with.

Would you say that 5247 lends itself to lighting situations that are more heavily lighted?

No. I always push only one stop on 5247. Some people push two stops and it still takes it. You can go that route but I don't like to push two stops because it becomes more difficult to balance the lighting. Because if I push one stop I can just about get what my eye sees on the set. When you start pushing two stops, some unpredictable things start happening. For instance, you may not get the shadow details that you want to get. I don't want to make it that difficult for me. When you are pushing the film one stop you are rating it about 250 ASA for night interior shooting and that's just about the right ASA number for the lenses and lighting available to us now. You know you cannot get smaller lights than inky-dinkies but when you push one stop, you can use an inky-dinky for key lighting.

At one time, In *The Long Goodbye* I was using very, very low lighting levels, between four to twelve footcandles. I was using all the existing light available of lit windows on streets. I had a real hard time balancing the light of the people in the room. Just imagine that I had to use four footcandles. Now an inky-dinky ten feet away will give you twenty footcandles or so. And you start to diffuse that light with scrims or any diffusion materials and you end up having a lamp which doesn't act like a lamp anymore. All those scrims and diffusions together add up to a "dirty" light source and it's a terrible lighting situation. So you get to the point where using too little light is very impractical unless you do what Kubrick does by lighting with candles in *Barry Lyndon*. Then you really can make use of the low footcandle level.

Do you always push one stop or do you shoot it at its rated ASA?

Generally speaking, I like the look of the film when it's forced one stop. It's more pleasing to my eye, the colors are not as saturated as shooting at normal ASA. And since I'm really not doing industrial photography in my movies, I like to control the colors a little bit that way.

In Close Encounters, *that dolly shot through the helicopter was one of the most difficult shots you' ve ever done. Could you explain the problems involved?*

It was very tricky because of the way Steven created the scene. He wanted to start from one side of the helicopter, pull through the inside of the helicopter as the people are being seated and then come out on the other side of the helicopter and have the doors closed. The only way to get that shot was that we had to get a long board and set the camera up on the end of the board attached to our Chapman crane arm. It was a 2 x 12. It had to be wide enough that the operator could lie on it. In fact, I operated the shot because I was the lightest person in the crew. So this 2 x 12 was sticking through the helicopter. There was just enough room between the seated people.

The board was going through the middle of the helicopter where the people were seated.

Yes, the people were seated on both sides. There was not much room—maybe fourteen inches between their legs. Actually the shooting of it was amazingly easy. Designing the shot was the difficult part.

The lighting must have been difficult also.

The lighting was complicated because there was no way to hide the lights any place. That was the only scene in the whole film that I had to flash. I convinced Steven that in order to get a good balance between the people on the outside and the inside, we had to flash the film. And he didn't mind because he was interested in the result. It was a daylight scene and there were no special effects involved there anyhow. So we could accept a certain grayness or less contrast.

Although it's been forgotten now due to its enormous success, there were a num-

ber of production hassles and over-budget problems with Columbia Pictures.

Near the end of the picture there were lots of problems with Columbia. They were mad because they really wanted to make money. Their idea was to shoot the film on schedule and on the original budget. There was no way to do it on schedule and on budget. The film was way under-budgeted and we couldn't do it; we were struggling all the time to maintain a certain quality. We were going to do certain things in certain ways. We were going for the utmost in quality. But then when it started to cost too much money, the studio got excited and said we were taking too much time. We had to take the time. We had to use all those brutes, we had to do all those lighting effects and there was no way to do it faster.

This kind of thing happens many times and most cameramen are faced with the same problem. In order to do a quality job, we have to spend time. We have to spend more time, in many cases, than the budget allows. Now our job is really to put the quality on the screen. If somebody doesn't have the money for that, they should tell us right away. They should come to us up front and say, "Listen, we have to do these scenes in three days. Can you do it or not?" Then we can say, "I can do it but only if I have this and this and that." We understand budget problems. We know exactly what things cost. But we have to be involved in it; they have to tell us what the problems are.

In our conversations with other cameramen, we've found that the cameraman sometimes becomes the sacrificial lamb for the supposed good of the production.

Most of us, like Conrad Hall, Haskell Wexler, Laszlo Kovacs, Owen Roizman and myself decided that the only time we will take over a picture from another cameraman is if the cameraman himself asks us to do it. It would be a situation where one of us might call and say, "I've had it with these people and I can't finish this picture. Would you do me a favor and take this picture over for me?" Then I would do it. Recently I was asked to take over a picture and I told them the same thing: I would take it over if the cameraman involved asked me to. So my agent called the cameraman involved and it was a big shock to the cameraman. That was the first time he had heard that someone was unhappy with his work and that he might be replaced. So this cameraman immediately got together with the creative people on this film and they talked things over, worked things out and he finished the picture. And, by the way, he did a great job.

So that's the whole thing. If I had been anxious to take over the film, this camera-man would have been hurt.

You've had the reputation for the lightweight method of shooting, not using a lot of light, flashing the film, and so on. Close Encounters was all the way to the opposite extreme. You used dozens of brutes and arcs; you had huge sets. What were some of the major problems involved in doing it "the old way" and using all the heavy equipment?

One problem was a matter of getting enough electric power. We had to get all the power we could from Mobile, Alabama. Unfortunately we needed a lot of D.C. power for our brutes, so we had to take all the available generators from Hollywood and bring all the available arc lights from Hollywood to Alabama.

We had a huge set there. The catwalk was one hundred feet high. If you turned off one brute on the set, nothing happened; you didn't even notice it because its effect was negligible. If you wanted to make a change in any portion of the set, you had to bank lights together to make a change. And remember we had to use colored gelatin filters on those lights and a gel usually cuts the light down by fifty percent or more. So that means we had to use even more lights.

We even had to invent something which I don't think anybody ever used before. By accident, we found that the center of the gel burned out first because of the heat. We found that it created a very interesting effect. In the center was a hot spot and around it was a nice orange light that gave you a lot of exposure in the center. We decided to use this technique in order to get the overexposure on the people, as Steve wanted. So we either burned the center of the gels out purposely or just cut a little hole in the center.

Speaking of using enough light, Steven's idea was to use so much light that it flares the vision out of the eyes. We were using Panavision high-speed lenses and we were overexposing four or five stops in order to get that kind of effect. We just had to use a tremendous amount of light all the time. All those lights have to be set, have to be banked together and connected together on the same switch and the same console. Just logistically it was a difficult thing to do.

Does using all the heavy equipment and a vast array of lights change the way you approach a project or the style in which you shoot?

It just takes more time. Many, many times you are confronted with problems on big sets. On *Winter Kills* and *The Deer Hunter* we had some big sets. On *The Girl from Petrovka* we had to light two or three city blocks at night. So when you need to light a big set, you use many more lights and it takes more time. But you try to prepare it as much as you can by walking the set beforehand and discussing the problems with your gaffer on how to prepare and rig, so you can save time when you actually light. But again, it takes time and you really have to find the time to do it. In the case of *Close Encounters*, it was a nightmare, how stupid and ridiculous the attitude of the studio really was towards lighting. One day we were shooting scenes at the railroad station and we were scheduled the next day to move into the huge almost finished set in Alabama and shoot there. And I said, "We can't shoot there. We have to light it first." It's unbelievable. They imagined that I could walk in there the next morning and start shooting at eleven o'clock. So I asked for a lighting day. They said, "You can't have it; we have to shoot." So finally we decided that I had to leave the set (we were shooting exteriors fortunately) and leave it to my gaffer and operator. I could not be with the first unit which made me very unhappy because if I am the director of photography I want to be there on that set where I can influence the look of the picture. We did not start shooting on the big set until five in the afternoon the next day. We needed time. It was a big lighting job; it was not like walking into a little room and shooting a few hours later.

I think all departments, from set decorator to costumer, feel the time and money squeeze to a certain extent. And it really kills you because, here you are working on a thirty million dollar picture and you can't get what you need and you don't have time to do what you want.

The problem, I think, is that we don't have any more producers left in Hollywood who know what the business is about. Most of the producers today start out in different areas; they used to be agents or whatever. What they understand are figures and they don't understand how motion pictures are made. They don't understand what difference it will make if I get two more hours to light. They cannot see that. That's why you need strong directors who know what they want and know what the cameraman wants. Many directors will go over budget by millions of dollars but it doesn't show up in the film. You can only go over budget or over schedule if that difference shows up on the screen. If it doesn't, I don't think you have any legitimate reason for doing that. I am always very conscious of that. So I make sure that when I take the time, it shows.

Is there a look that you've wanted to obtain on film, that you've seen in your mind, that you've never been able to capture?

I think every picture has its own world and I want to create a look for that particular picture each time I'm doing one. My mind only starts working when I read the script and see the sets. Then you start creating that world. I don't think there's such a thing as having the look first and then striving to find a vehicle to make that look work. I don't think that that's necessarily important.

You always have to try to capture the look of that particular picture. *Obsession* needed a certain different kind of look. And we tried for it. Each time you have a new picture, you try a different look. If you see *Deliverance* it looks completely different from *McCabe and Mrs. Miller* or *Obsession*. That's the job of a cameraman actually. We should not try to force a look on a particular picture.

I've heard that sometimes you'll refer to a particular painter's work to express to the other people you're working with what kind of a look is good for a certain picture. Is that true?

I do that a lot when we start a picture and I don't really know how to explain to the director the look we are trying to create. I have lots of picture books at home— photography books and art books. When we did *McCabe and Mrs. Miller*, I had an Andrew Wyeth book I had bought in Vancouver. I brought over to Bob Altman and said, "What do you think of these kind of faded, soft, pastel images?" And he liked it. Then I took the same book to the lab and explained to them that this was what we were aiming for. They understood right away why we were flashing the film. So it helps; a picture is worth ten thousand words. A picture can immediately tell you your feelings about something. For *Images* there was a picture I selected out of a picture book; the picture was very much like a black-and-white picture with color in it. It really looked like what *Images* should look like. I showed it to Altman and he said, "Perfect, go for it." In fact, the sets had already been painted when I showed him that picture. But we liked the look so much that we had the sets repainted. So a picture can be a great help. If you consider motion pictures as a visual art, it has a lot in common with painting and photography.

Do you think cameramen should have a background in the visual arts?

Definitely. I think it helped me a great deal that in Hungarian film school our studies were concentrated on the arts. We studied the history of painting; we went to museums at least once a week. It helps to learn feelings for compositions, lights, colors and all that. If you start living in an artistic world, you start thinking like an artist. It's not bad for a cameraman to be a sort of painter. Composition is in my blood. I walk into a room and I set the camera and it's there; I cannot explain why. Many directors start trying to get another composition but often end up back where I set the camera. Why? I don't know. It's a feeling. But that shot expressed what the whole scene is about. It just seems like it's right. Cameramen should have something to say, something to tell and if you don't have that, you should be working somewhere else.

Very few American cameramen have that background in visual arts.

Conrad Hall does. Haskell Wexler . . .

All the good ones?

Yes, right. In fact, I go to see some of their movies and say, "Jeez, I wish I would have done that." With Lazslo Kovacs, I could get him to do my last week of shooting on a picture and probably no one would notice that someone else shot the picture. Because he has the same background, the same feeling for composition. When Bill Fraker shot some scenes of *Close Encounters* he shot it exactly as I would have tried to do. I couldn't tell the difference. I thought those scenes that Fraker did in the desert were perfect and just gorgeous. He's the kind of cameraman who can do that. He worked very hard to maintain the quality we started in the filming. I thank him for that.

What are the key things to remember when you're lighting something and you don't want it to look like you're lighting it?

In a lighting class in Hungary, when I was a student, we had a professor who said, "First, establish the light source." We did a lot of studies in class where we shot by candlelight. What we did was put the candle on the table and turn off all the lights and we watched how the candle lit the room. So you start out basically from nature. If you want to make it look like it's real, you basically have to duplicate how it looks in real life. When people go to see a movie, they recognize what is real and what is not. So if there is a lamp in this corner here, you would want to light from that corner. Or if daylight is coming through here and you have a warm light over there, you would mix that light. So I think you have to imitate real life. But when you study paintings, you will see many, many times that nature is altered. That's when the artist decides that something can be done better. The best lighting is when the audience feels it's real. When you compare it to nature, sometimes it's better than nature. There are many times when a performer's face can be kept dark and the audience wouldn't really mind. But some other times it would be boring. So you make it a half silhouette. These are decisions only the cinematographer can make. The other people on the set might not even see! Not even the average director. That's why it's so important to work together with your director.

So it starts as source lighting but you have to be ready to deviate from that or to create your own source.

Exactly, you create you own sources. When I walk onto any set, the main thing I discuss with the art director is where are the light sources. When an art director works with me, they know this so they do it without being asked. Without light sources, of course, there is no lighting. And that's boring. There is nothing more boring to me than fluorescent overhead lighting in a supermarket, for example. So many times I alter that reality. I'm usually using that overhead lighting but I will introduce some soft, side light which does not exist in a market. But nobody will question that because it's soft. It will look real but interesting. It gives you more modeling, it gives you a little better look.

When a director comes to you with a story or an idea, what are the elements that will excite you or that will challenge you?

Well, something that's visually difficult and that's going to challenge me. In *The Rose* re-creating the feeling of a rock concert in the sixties was exciting because, first of all, I had to study some of the old rock concerts that were shot as documentaries. I tried to find out what gave you the sense and feeling of a rock concert. I decided the difference is what they have never really done before in a feature film: they never really let the audience participate in a rock concert. They always kept the audience dark. And I discussed that with Mark Rydell. I felt we really should make the audience visible this time because part of the excitement of the whole thing is how the audience reacts to the music. Just to re-create that was exciting to me. You had to do theatrical stage lighting but, at the same time, you had to make it work for the motion picture. That means that you have to use more lighting than they actually did. You not only have to light the stage, you have to light the audience. It had to look real so you lit the audience like the light was coming from the stage, like it's bounce light. In a real situation, you see the audience lit but when you photograph them, it doesn't look like it because there's really so little light. So you really have to balance the light for the eye to where it will look real.

On Deliverance, *what were the elements that attracted you to the film?*

That was such a crazy idea to make a movie anyhow: to shoot a major portion of the movie on a river. Just the difficulty of getting cameras down to the river, shooting from a boat, and so on was enough. That whole story was visual and moving. Some stories are more exciting visually than others. A dialogue picture is not exciting to me. I don't like to shoot people sitting in a room and making conversation. The best I can do in that kind of situation is create the mood and light the room so the look is real and it fits the story. But that's not as exciting as doing a movie like *Deliverance* where you are constantly on the move with the actors and doing dangerous things. Obviously that's a better visual concept.

What determines a good composition to your eye? Is it symmetry, light, color, focus? What elements are involved when you set up a composition?

The most important thing is that it should be clear. In talking about composition, basically you're talking about long shots, I think. Of course, you have to compose close-ups also but that's more like framing. Composition is very important when you have a big shot. Film is a moving image and it has a certain time element to it. If the editor is cutting a long shot so that it lasts five seconds on the screen, that audience must clearly see, in that five seconds, what that picture is about. It's very important where you place the main actors within the composition so that the eye will be attracted to them right away. But at the same time, you have to light the background on a level where the audience will be aware of the mood. So composition is really important in creating a mood; it also helps sort out what things the eye wants to see and in what order it wants them. Basically it's like a painting except that with a painting you can stand in front of it for hours and see every detail of it. In a motion picture composition, you don't have that much time so it has to be very clear. It actually has to be better than a painting and that's very difficult to do. The painter can sit in front of his canvas for months. As cinematographers, we are thrown onto the set and the production manager says you have thirty minutes to light it. In that time, you have to create a composition that will not necessarily be as remarkable as a painting but the composition will have to be clear and show the major elements of the shot.

I know it depends on the circumstances, but how do you go about doing that?

You get together with the director on it. First, the director would stage the scene and if you are watching him, you might have some suggestions for him. Most directors are very good about composition because they are experienced with what is in front of the camera.

As the director is staging the scene, you get an idea of camera placement and composition?

Many times when the actors are rehearsing a scene, you will see the director standing on one side of the room and watching the action while the cinematographer is standing somewhere else. After a while, they both will change to different positions. They are searching for an angle where the shot would work best. Usually in the end, you may end up standing in the same position. Or you will have a discussion on what viewpoint is best. Sometimes, you decide that it would be good to cover it from both viewpoints. Composition really helps the director in staging the action.

What's the first thing you do when you come on a set or a location? What's the first thing that attracts your attention?

Obviously you are telling a story and you are trying to find an angle where the camera includes something interesting in the background, which has something to say about the action. The second thing that gets my attention is the lighting conditions. I would think about what time I will be shooting and I would try to visualize where the sun would be and what kind of lighting I would get. I very seldom like to shoot in flat light so I would try for side light or back light. I try to think how that location will look when we will be shooting there. Or how the location will look when we shoot the master shot, which is the most important thing. If you have a big scene to shoot with lots of extras, you know you are not going to roll until ten or eleven o'clock in the morning. It would be foolish to think that you could shoot it at six o'clock in the morning when the light is perfect. You know you are not going to be able to shoot then so you have to think about what the conditions will be like at ten o'clock. You have to be aware of these things so that the angle which you have selected will look good under those conditions.

What special considerations do you have with interiors on a sound stage?

On interiors, I am always looking for light sources; that includes windows, doors and other practical lights. I want to know if there are enough of those. If not, I would ask the art director for some more sources. When you first read a scene, you feel it requires a certain mood and obviously you are creating a mood with the lighting.

Is creating that mood on the sound stage more fun or more exciting? Because on the stage, you start with total darkness and you essentially create everything.

Right. The lighting is really fun for the cameraman because that's one area where you really see a cameraman doing his job. Very few directors can interfere with you in that realm or even help you much. You are pretty much on your own when it comes to lighting. The director can tell you whether he likes it or not but most of them don't even know how it's going to show up on the screen. Through experience, the cameraman knows that what shows up on the screen is different from what the eye sees.

But is that more challenging necessarily?

It's challenging but that's your job. In my opinion, it's the lighting that makes one cameraman different than another one. Very few cameramen can really light; they can light for exposure but very few can light for mood.

Why is that?

Well, why, out of hundreds of painters, are there only a handful of good ones? It's the same thing with cameramen. Some are better than others.

So it's that knowledge, experience and the application of your own personal taste . . .

It's also feeling and talent. That's where talent really comes to the fore. It's how you see things. The lighting is really the creative aspect of the cameraman's work. That's why directors like certain cameramen. The director falls in love with the kind of lighting and mood you create through it. The director feels that the cameraman is really doing what is right for the film. Many directors like to use more light and see the face of the actors all the time. Others don't care; they enjoy seeing a good composition when the composition is more dominant than the actor's face.

But as you said before, you can't prove that good lighting or taking a little more time on a scene will sell more tickets.

Nobody could ever prove that. The only way to do that is to shoot the same picture twice using two different cameramen. You might be able to draw some conclusions from that but it would still be very hard.

The problem with exteriors is that you basically have to take what's given by the sun or other weather conditions. How do you deal with those conditions and impose your will on them to make it conform to your artistic vision?

You can alter that by altering the shooting schedule. You can tell the director, "This particular scene would be great if we could shoot it in the afternoon. Is there anything else we can shoot in the morning?" Certain scenes would obviously be totally different if you shot them at sunset. You are creating lots of problems if you want to shoot a scene at sunset because you may not be able to finish that scene at one sunset. So you have to go back and complete it the next day. Maybe you need another day following that. So the director and the producer will decide whether the request of the cameraman is valid. They have to consider whether shooting that scene at sunset is really going to be so much better—whether it is worth it for the pictorial effect and whether it will enhance the overall quality of the picture. In the decision-making process, the cameraman loses many times. Then you have to decide whether you want to create a sunset-looking scene during the day or do you totally change the idea and try to make it moody-looking in the early afternoon.

Let me give you an example from *Jinxed* with Bette Midler. Don Siegel was directing. There was a scene that was written for night time in the desert. At one time, we considered shooting day-for-night. But when I realized that the scene was playing in front of car headlights with Bette walking away in the distance at very early sunrise, I decided it could not be done at night or even day for night. That was a situation that absolutely had to be shot at a certain time of the day. We knew that the studio was not going to let us go out two or three days and shoot in the late night and very early morning. So I proposed that we shoot everything that we could at one sunset and sunrise and what we didn't get shot, we could make plates. Now I'm a cameraman who hasn't worked too much with plates in the past; I like to shoot everything for real. But I realized that doing it the old studio way would give me a better result on the screen. It would be more economical but it would look better too. So I took a Vistavision camera and shot some plates at sunrise and sunset. Later on we went onto a sound stage and we dressed it with a couple of cactuses and Joshua trees and I don't think anybody will be able to tell that we didn't shoot it on location. It was much better because it was more controlled. The dialogue was more controlled because the actors were not rushed. No one was shouting, "C'mon, the sun is coming up—let's get one more take." We didn't shoot it only once or twice; we did it as many times as we wanted to do it. That's where a cameraman's technical expertise can really help a production. He realizes what you can and can't do within time limitations and he uses the best technique to make it look right.

In this case, you shot plates?

Vistavision plates. The Vistavision camera shoots a negative twice the size of a motion picture frame; it's just a bigger negative camera. So that when you project it as background projection on the sound stage, you have a bright, fine-grain image that you can shoot the actors against. If you maintain a good balance between the background projection and the live action, you can get away with anything. In our case, we could actually shoot against the setting sun all day.

Many of your films have excellent photography and excellent production values, but some of them haven't been critical or box-office successes or both. How does it make you feel when you've done the best possible job under the circumstances and the film dies?

Obviously you are unhappy. When I first accepted the film assignment, I liked it and I thought the audience would like it also. I liked it when I read the script and I worked hard with the director to make it accepted by the audience. But if it doesn't happen, it doesn't happen. What can you do? I come back to the analogy of the painter again. When he begins a new canvas, the painter doesn't set out to make a bad painting. If an audience doesn't respond, he can't sell his painting. He'll hang it on his own wall at home and admire his own work but he still didn't get the response from the audience. That doesn't mean that the painting is not good. Maybe it was ahead of its time. I've made many pictures that were not accepted by the public but I think most of them were ahead of their time.

Like Scarecrow*?*

Scarecrow probably was one of those. *Futz* was definitely one; it was way ahead of its time. *Heaven's Gate* is a classic example of this. Everyone was trying to judge that picture in relation to present-day pictures. And on that basis they find fault with the film. But I'm pretty sure that as the years go by, somebody will dig up the picture and say, "What a genius this Cimino was! He realized he didn't need a strong story to make a motion picture." Right now maybe you'll laugh at that. But I think the time will come when a plot is not going to be that important for a picture.

What will be important then?

The visual quality of a picture. Movies should be a visual experience. Unfortunately when sound came in, movies became photographed theater, where the play was the thing. We are still at that stage.

We've been there for the last fifty years.

We are still there. Some directors, like Kubrick, are trying to continue the era of silent films. But there is a big resistance because people got used to photographed theater. You have to have a good plot, a good story; if you don't have that, forget it. The picture is not going to be successful commercially. *Heaven's Gate* had other problems so maybe it is a bad example. We spent so much money on making that picture that everybody was angry with Cimino and why he spent thirty-six million dollars.

For openers, they started reviewing the budget, not the film.

Exactly. If that picture had been made on a ten-million-dollar budget, everyone would have hailed it as one of the greatest pictures of the year.

But could it have been made for ten million dollars?

I think it could have been made for fifteen million dollars. Maybe. But Cimino wanted to go first class; he thought the picture was going to work and he didn't realize that there was so much anger against the picture.

He tends to be a perfectionist and you are too, to a great extent.

All good cameramen are perfectionists. But we don't have the kind of luxury in spending the money that directors have. Very few cameramen can ever ask for an extra day of shooting. You can't do that. You really have to obey the budget and the schedule. If a production goes over schedule, they can never say that it was the cameraman's fault because the director is the one who makes those kind of decisions.

There have been a few million words written about Heaven's Gate. *What were the problems and the opportunities in doing the film, from your perspective?*

I had the opportunity to create a total mood in a picture in a way that I never had a chance to do before. It was a big-canvas picture. We had lots of extras and many beautiful sets. I had the opportunity to photograph something I could never have done before. The closest thing I came to it was *McCabe and Mrs. Miller,* which was a very small-scale picture in comparison. It was done for two and a half million dollars ten years ago. *Heaven's Gate* had a much bigger scale. I got to do things I always wanted to do, like creating old images by using smoke in the interiors. The stoves really smoked in those days. If you were living in 1900, that's the kind of image you would see. It was a very pictorial picture. I think that I was lucky to be able to do the film. When the critics began criticizing even the visual effects, I couldn't understand it. I can understand their criticism of some of the other aspects, but I couldn't really see why they would hate the look of the picture. I still like it very much.

A lot of diffusion in the picture.

Yes. I didn't use as much diffusion as I did in *McCabe and Mrs. Miller.* Here I actually diffused images with the smoke and the dust. I flashed the print which softened the image and gave it some faded pastels, making it look more like old photographs.

Did you flash to a greater degree than you had before?

Well, I flashed both the negative and the print. We tried to get more details into the shadows and more details into the highlights that way. It's the same type of technique that I used before but this time it fit the picture so well.

Blow Out was a picture where seventy percent of the action took place at night. How do you get those blacks that are always right on the money?

By not diffusing and not flashing as much. It was a totally different look than *Heaven's Gate.* Basically, I just shot *Blow Out* straight. That doesn't mean I necessarily like that look but I think it was good for the picture. You see, I like a softer look, a more diffused look.

Do you think the lenses are too sharp? Do you think the Eastman stock is too good?

I think the lenses are too sharp. I think the Eastman film is too saturated. When you stick your neck out and photograph a film straight, you really have to have a good art director, interior decorator and costume designer. Because any mistake that you make will jump right out at you and look ten times as bad. Most of the time when I employ my flashing technique, I can photograph faster and I don't have to worry as much because it's going to create the style on its own. But there are certain stories that are not compatible with that style, like *Blow Out,* so you have to work harder.

What films are you the happiest with and why?

I'm mostly happy with all my work actually. There are certain pictures that didn't succeed as well as they should have. I make an effort to do my best work on every picture. For example, *Winter Kills* is a film that didn't succeed either critically or commercially. When we were shooting the picture, we really loved it. But it just didn't work; it was a failure that you can't really explain. But that doesn't mean that I don't like my photography in it. Of course, you tend to like your pictures that succeed critically as well as commercially. I haven't made too many pictures like that. *Close Encounters of the Third Kind* is the only picture of mine that enjoyed huge commercial success. And I like the picture very much but I like *The Deer Hunter* much better. I think *The Deer Hunter* was a much better work for the subject matter involved. It was much more difficult to do. It was a fairly successful picture. I like *The Rose* very much; it was well received. Another fine picture which I like very much that was not even an artistic success is *Images*. It was wonderful—I still enjoy seeing it and I think it is one of the best movies I photographed. Of course, *McCabe and Mrs. Miller* is an all-time favorite for everybody. It's become a cult film now. Obviously that's one of my favorites also because many, many film buffs and students like to see that movie. *Deliverance* is a favorite too; *Cinderella Liberty* also. I was very lucky. I know that every film that I did was hard work and that we did the best that we could.

How do you maintain consistency from set-up to set-up and from scene to scene?

That's where your technical knowledge comes into play. I happened to be lucky enough to spend four years in a very good school in Hungary. I learned how important consistency and matching was in a cameraman's work. You have to think about what your long shot was and how you have to match that in a close-up. You have to match shot by shot. Even when the sun leaves you, you have to create the sun. It's a technical thing and something that you have to learn.

Some films are more consistent than others.

That's what separates a good cameraman from a bad cameraman. They know how to keep it consistent.

What experiences, unrelated to filmmaking, have helped make you a better film-maker or have helped to increase your visual awareness?

Painting is a great influence on me. Whenever I can I go to museums and look at the classics, the Dutch masters, Rembrandt and Georges de la Tour. These are the classics. These are the basics for cameramen because we can learn lighting from them. We can study every single painting and try to use that technique of lighting in our photography.

Traveling has also been a great influence. I love to travel. It's in my blood; my father took me on a long trip when I was just three weeks old. I was traveling with him in the early years of my life. I remember my father telling me that when I was three years old I would stand at the window of the train and watch the scenery go by for hours and hours. I was fascinated with moving scenery. Today I also like to travel. You take your experiences of life into the studio with you and you try to re-create them.

Do you think you work better with restrictions and limitations rather than more freedom?

I think it has to be in balance. You have some limitations no matter what. Money is a limitation. I don't necessarily think it's right to have those limitations but we all have to live under those conditions. Both time and money are important. Maybe you only have two hours to light a set; if you've done your homework and have planned it out, then you can do it in two hours. You have to work very hard on your own time also. Sometimes you spend your weekends or nights thinking about upcoming scenes. You cannot create a perfect piece of work based on just the time the studio gives you to shoot the film.

Generally, how much creative freedom do you have in determining the look and style of a picture?

It depends on the director. Some directors give you a tremendous amount of freedom while other directors try to take over your job. Usually a director hires a cameraman because he trusts his vision and creative ability. But then some directors don't give you the chance or the time to do it your way. So why bother with me? In a case like that, why didn't they just hire somebody else?

How important do you think the photographic look and style is in determining the success of a picture?

The problem is you can never predict that. There are pictures which obviously could live without good photography. Then there are pictures that would have never been noticed without good photography. *Tess,* for example, needed good photography. *Cabaret* needed good photography. I think *Close Encounters* needed good photography. There are certain pictures where the photography is very, very important—maybe more important than anybody thinks. But again, it's hard to say. If you had a picture with bad photography playing in one theater and the same picture with good photography playing in another theater, then maybe you would have a basis for comparison. You might possibly find out what good photography does for a picture, commercially speaking.

Could you give me a thumbnail sketch of your artistic and aesthetic approach to a couple of your films. For example, what were you trying to do visually in McCabe and Mrs. Miller?

We wanted to make it look like the Northwest if you turned the clock back sixty or eighty years. We wanted to give the audience a window to look into the life of those people. But since it was sixty or eighty years ago, we had to add a romantic element to it. It had to be faded. You would be looking through lots of haze to give you the feeling that the things you were seeing were really old and that they did not exist anymore. It's like looking at old photographs, except that these are moving pictures, not photographs. They are faded, old, hazy and not too clear but you have the feeling that you are seeing the real thing.

How about Images, *which was a totally different kind of picture?*

Images was a very clinical look at people who really only existed in the mind. It was clinical, sharp and desaturated. We didn't use much color; the palette was more blacks, whites and greys, which the art director provided. I lit and photographed the film in such a way as to give the feeling that all this is not really real—that what was happening was not true but only existed in the mind.

The Long Goodbye?

It was a visual experiment. We decided that we were going to move the camera every single frame of the picture to create the nonexistent third dimension. Just as in painting, the third dimension in photography is created by lighting. But if you watch dolly or crane shots, that image becomes so three-dimensional because suddenly you see the foreground, background and middleground moving against each other. So we decided that every single shot had to be a moving shot even if it was a close-up. We just kept the camera moving right or left or we zoomed in and out. Also I didn't want to do too much lighting because it was basically a low-budget picture. We decided that we would flash the film tremendously to degrade the contrast. It had an interesting look. I don't say that it's my favorite look of all my pictures but, as an experiment, it was interesting to follow through on it.

The Deer Hunter?

The Deer Hunter is probably one of my most realistic pictures. I wanted everything to look very real. When you think of a steel mill town, it's smoky, hazy with bluish tones outside. Inside the mill, you have the warm tones of the furnaces and the lighting in contrast to the outside. The Vietnam footage was very sharp and had a newsreel quality to it. Up in the mountains, I wanted to create the feeling of freedom and freshness. There was no flashing or diffusion there; I wanted it very clear and crisp.

Heaven's Gate?

Heaven's Gate is going back to the *McCabe and Mrs. Miller* concept, except we wanted to execute it much better. We didn't want it to be as hazy and look as old as *McCabe and Mrs. Miller* did. We wanted to create the haze within the picture. And to justify it we used stoves that created smoke; we had dust being kicked up by horses and wagons.

It's been twenty five years since the Hungarian Revolution and since you escaped to this country. How would you summarize those years? Did you ever think that you would be where you are today?

I was lucky to be able to come to the United States. I feel that I found a creative atmosphere for cameramen. It's a free atmosphere where if you obey certain time and budget limitations, you can express yourself pretty well. There is really no comparison between working here and working in Hungary. You have more money to make pictures here and a tremendous audience that wants to see better and better quality pictures. That pushes the producers to also accept the cameraman's art. These twenty-five years here have been a very rewarding experience for me. I had to start from scratch. I had to learn the language first. I had to get into the movie industry. But my technical background that I developed in Hungary helped me a lot because I didn't have to go to school again. I could rely on my basic technical knowledge here; I just had to put it to work.

Even in Hungary, your ideal was to be a filmmaker. You had a lot more obstacles but you pursued that career.

I couldn't have developed to such a degree that I have here if I were still in Hungary.

Has it been a short or a long period?

It went by very fast. Actually the first ten years were a bit slow because it took me that long to break through and do some pictures. So I feel myself to be a working cameraman only in the last fifteen years. The first ten years I was trying to establish myself, trying to relate to people here and trying to get to the point where they would hire me as a cameraman.

It's kind of ironic for you to hear students complain about how hard it is to break into the industry when you overcame ten times the obstacles that they will ever face.

I always tell them that it will take ten years. Very few people find themselves becoming a cameraman after finishing USC or UCLA. Very seldom will you become a cameraman in less than ten years. You have to put in a lot of work in those years. You have to sacrifice a lot. You cannot lead a terrific life, play around and then occasionally think about becoming a great cameraman. You have to work hard at it everyday.

A lot of people aren't willing to make that commitment, to make those sacrifices.

I believe that if someone has a little talent but is willing to sacrifice a lot, he can be a cameraman, or a director or anything. If you work very hard, you can be almost anything in ten years. Cinematography may look easy to an outsider: you use your meter and get a good exposure but it's not that simple.

Do you have any aspirations to direct in the future?

Probably, eventually. You know, I've been saying for the last five years that I don't want to be a director. But I'm getting to the point where if I cannot shoot a picture, as a cameraman, the way I want to shoot that picture because of economic or other reasons, then maybe I should become a director and make it possible for me to photograph the picture the way I want to photograph it. Then I can call the shots. And within the limitations of budget and schedule, maybe I can still get what I want. You know, when you see Claude Lelouch's pictures, you have the feeling that he really makes pictures the way he wants to make them. That really would be a great satisfaction, for a moviemaker to really do a film the way he sees it. Whether it's right or wrong, it's his movie and nobody can take that away from him.

The European attitude toward film is different.

It's more like art.

Glossary

ASA	Refers to the exposure index or speed rating denoting the sensitivity of a film stock.
Action	The movement that takes place in front of the camera; also a director's command for action to begin.
Ambient lighting	The light level around and beyond the main area of interest.
Anamorphic	Optical system having different magnifications in the horizontal and vertical dimensions of the image.
Angle shot	Any shot in which the camera lens is not aligned straight-on to the subject.
Animation camera	A camera used for single-frame stop-motion filming, usually mounted on a vertical animation stand.
Answer print	The first complete print delivered by the lab.
Aperture	The diaphragm opening of a lens controlling the amount of light transmitted; usually expressed in terms of f-stops.
Arc light	High-intensity light created by the discharge of electricity between two electrodes.
Art director	Person responsible for supervising the design and construction of the set.
Aspect ratio	The ratio between the width and height of a motion picture frame. Standard ratio is four units wide and three high, expressed as 1.33 to 1.
Back lighting	The lighting of a subject from behind.
Barn doors	Adjustable flaps mounted on the rim of a lighting unit to control the shape of the light or to shade off spill light.
Blimp	Soundproof cover fitted over a camera to prevent camera noise from being recorded.
Broad	A large floodlight used for general illumination.
Brute	A high-intensity spot lamp.
Camera crane	A large power-operated camera platform that permits the camera to be moved smoothly into any position on the set.
Camera crew	The work group responsible for the filming of the picture, usually headed by the director of photography.

339

Cameraman,

First
Director of Photography. Directs the movement and setting of the cameras and lighting of the set; manages the camera crew.

Second
Camera operator. Acts on instructions from the director of photography and physically operates the camera.

First Assistant
Focus puller. Keeps camera in focus during shooting and generally assists the second cameraman.

Second Assistant
May load the camera, operate the clapper or perform any number of tasks in assisting other members of the crew.

Camera operator
The technician who physically operates the camera during shooting, usually the second cameraman.

Camera set-up
The location of the camera in relation to the set.

Cherry picker
Truck-mounted crane that can raise camera operator to a great height.

Color temperature
A measure of the color quality of a light source on the Kelvin scale.

Contrast
The difference in intensity between the brightest highlight and the darkest shadow.

Cookie
A patterned flag placed in front of a light source to throw a light pattern on a scene.

CRI
Acronym for color reversal internegative; the negative from which the lab makes the release prints.

Cross lighting
Lighting which comes from the side of the set or scene.

Cut
Command given by director for action to cease.

Dailies
The first prints produced from the negative. Dailies are processed by the lab as quickly as possible with limited corrections so that the footage can be examined on a timely basis by the director and members of the crew.

Definition
The fidelity with which the detail of a scene can be reproduced by the camera on film.

Degradation
The degree to which the quality of the film image is inferior (or degraded) compared to the original scene or the film image at some earlier point.

Density
The opacity of a film image.

Depth of field
The distance within which the subject may move and remain in focus through the camera lens; the area on which a lens is focused within which the subject may move in depth and remain in focus.

Diffusion
A technique where a filtering material is placed between the light source and the subject; usually characterized by a relative lack of shadow on the subject.

Diorama
A small set used in place of a much larger one.

Dolly
An easily moved wheeled vehicle used to support the camera and operator during shooting.

Dollying
Also tracking or traveling. The moving of a camera on a dolly during shooting.

Dolly tracks
Metal tracks on which a camera dolly is positioned and moved in order to facilitate the smooth and fluid movement of the camera while shooting.

Emulsion
The light-sensitive coating on photographic film.

Exposure	The process of subjecting film to a particular intensity of light so that it produces a latent image on the emulsion.
Fill light	Secondary lighting used to raise illumination in the shadow areas; helps to reduce the overall contrast of a scene.
Filter	A transparent material (glass or gelatin) that fits over the camera lens to absorb or reduce certain colors and transmit others.
Flag	Small rectangular piece of wood or cardboard mounted on a stand and adjusted to prevent stray light from reaching the camera lens, or, when placed in front of a light source, to shade off part of the scene.
Flashing	A laboratory process that exposes a negative to a certain intensity of light in order to achieve certain visual effects.
Flat lighting	Lighting that provides even illumination; thus lighting that is lacking in contrast.
Focal length	The distance from the optical center of a lens to the point where it brings into sharp focus an object placed at an infinite distance.
Focus	The point at which the image attains maximum definition.
Focus puller	The technician who maintains focus throughout the shot, usually the first assistant cameraman.
Fog level	The photographic density of unexposed film after development.
Fogging	Photographic density appearing on film due to the effects of extraneous light or unwanted chemical reaction prior to the completion of processing.
Follow focus	A technique of altering a lens setting to ensure that the image is in sharp focus when the relative position of the camera and subject change during shooting.
Footcandle	A unit of illumination. Technically, the light intensity produced at a surface all points of which are at a distance of one foot from a uniform point source of one candle.
F-**stop**	A unit of measurement indicating the relative diaphragm opening of a lens.
Gaffer	Chief electrician of a film crew; makes the proper amount of light available and moves and controls lighting units as required by the cameraman.
Gel	A transparent filter or sheet placed in front of a lighting unit.
Gobo	A large black screen or flag used to shield the lens from unwanted light or to shade off part of a scene.
Gofer	Literally, a member of the production crew who "goes for" whatever is needed at the moment; sometimes formally referred to as "production assistant."
Grain	Small particles of metallic silver remaining in a photographic emulsion after development, forming the dark areas of a photographic image.
Grip	Crew member who physically moves the dolly or camera crane on the set; also carries equipment and sometimes repairs it.
Grey scale	A graduated range of tones extending from white to black, with intermediate greys in between.
Headroom	Space allowed in frame above a performer's head.
High key	Lighting style where the majority of tones reproduced are at the light end of the grey scale.

Highlighting	The emphasis on a particular area of the scene by means of a tone variation or extra illumination.
HMI lights	A brand of lighting equipment that provides a perfect color temperature match for daylight.
Inkie or Inky Dink	A small incandescent lighting unit used for local lighting.
IP	Acronym for interpositive; a lab process no longer used with the advent of CRI.
Junior	A 2,000-watt spotlight.
Key light	The dominant light used for illuminating a scene.
Laboratory	Business which specializes in film processing, from negative development to release printing.
Lens	An optical device made of glass which focuses light by refraction.
Lightflex	A process of flashing a preselected amount of light on the film stock by means of a mechanical unit placed on the camera matte box; used to introduce color and/or contrast variations.
Lighting	The illumination of a camera subject so that it becomes visible.
Location	Any place used for filming other than the studio lot.
Low key	Lighting style where the majority of the tones reproduced are at the dark end of the grey scale.
Marks	Guides, usually of tape on the floor out of camera view, to show performers the exact positions they should take.
Matte	Any material placed in front of the lens to obscure or block out part of a scene.
Matte box	A box on the front of the camera to hold mattes.
Mini mole	A small 500-watt spotlight made by the Mole-Richardson Company.
Modeling light	The accent light that defines the structure and texture of the subject.
Negative	Raw stock that has been exposed but not processed.
Net	A hair net placed over the lens in order to diffuse and soften the image; often used for close-ups.
Ninelight	Nine small, individually controllable lights fitted into one square lighting unit.
Pan	To move the camera on a horizontal plane.
Photoflood	An incandescent lamp with a high-voltage filament; results in high intensity light but short life of the lamp.
Point source of light	A device in which all the light emitted emanates from a single point.
Printer	A machine used for reproducing the images of one film onto another.
Printer light	The variable light setting on a film printer used to compensate for density differences in the film to be printed.
Raw stock	Film which has not been exposed.
Rear projection	The projection of a film or slide on the rear of a translucent screen to provide a background for a set.
Reflector	A light-toned or polished surface used to reflect light. It transfers light falling upon it to illuminate an area indirectly.
Rim light	A light placed behind a performer so that the rays catch his or her edges and are directed toward the camera. Provides a halo effect around the subject distinguishing the figure from the background.

Saturation	The condition achieved when a color is pure and vivid in hue.
Scrim	A transparent material used to diffuse a light source.
Senior	A 5,000-watt spotlight.
Set-up	The arrangement of the camera and what is seen through it (i.e., scenery, props, performers and light) for a particular shot.
Silver halides	Generic name for the three light-sensitive salts used in photographic emulsions.
Soft focus	A diffused image effect obtained by use of an appropriate diffusing material.
Sound stage	A shooting stage that has been soundproofed.
Sputnik	A device placed on a camera dolly that allows the camera and the operator to rotate a full 360 degrees.
Stock	Motion picture film, usually before exposure.
Stopping down	The process of reducing the aperture of a lens.
Story board	A collection of drawings of the shots planned to cover the main incidents or action of the script.
Teaser	A large flag.
Tilt	To move the camera in a vertical plane.
Timing	Adjustment of printer light intensity to modify final print quality.
Tripod	A three-legged device used to support the camera.
Walk through	Rehearsal of the action of a scene.
White card	Large piece of white cardboard appropriately positioned to reflect light onto a scene.
Wide-angle lens	Any lens of shorter focal length than normal that gives a wide angle of view.
Wide screen	A motion picture format that has an aspect ratio greater than the standard ratio of 1.33 to 1. Often 1.85 to 1. CinemaScope is 2.55 to 1.
Wild walls	Walls of a set, generally built on a sound stage, that can be removed to facilitate lighting effects or camera movements.
Zoom lens	A lens of variable focal lengths; allows a continuous magnification effect to be obtained in one controlled smooth movement.

Index

Absence of Malice, 195
action, 339
Adam's Woman, 75
Adventures of Enea, 220
Adventure of Orlando, 220
Agatha, 117, 220
Agfa film, 12
Airport '77, 321
Aldo, G. R., 6–7
Alex and the Gypsy, 75
Alex in Wonderland, 176
All the President's Men, 58, 165, 284, 285,
  296–298
Allen, Woody, 284, 305
Almendros, Nestor, 5–22, 51, 52, 125, 126
Aloha Bobby and Rose, 128, 134, 141
Alonzo, John, 20, 23–46, 51, 180
Altman, Robert, 311, 313, 316, 317, 326
Amarcord, 171
ambient lighting, 339
America, America, 248, 256
American Gigolo, 47, 48, 51, 52, 53, 55,
  56, 62, 65, 66, 70, 71
American Graffiti, 248, 261–262
American Hot Wax, 128
American International Pictures, 39, 121
American Society of Cinematographers
  (A.S.C.), 127, 231
anamorphic ratio, 31, 32, 41, 160–161, 197,
  245, 339
Angel Baby, 248
angle shot, 339
animation camera, 339
Annie Hall, 147, 217, 285, 305
answer printing, 61, 210, 339
aperture, 339

Apocalypse Now, 157, 219, 220, 224, 225
Apted, Michael, 72
arc lights, 7, 14, 21, 40, 67, 90–91, 148,
  205, 206, 266, 324, 339
Arriflex camera, 26, 28, 96, 103, 120,
  179, 314
art director, 30, 45, 168, 180, 215, 237,
  243, 262, 265, 327, 339
Arthur, Karen, 54
ASA, 339
Ashby, Hal, 24–25, 118
aspect ratio, 339
At Long Last Love, 176, 183
Attenborough, Richard, 278
auteur theory, 3–4, 64
available light, 28–29

Baby Blue Marine, 176
back lighting, 339
Back Roads, 24, 42
Bad Company, 99, 100, 285, 294
Bad Day for Aries, 220
Bad News Bears, The, 24
Badham, John, 74, 81, 244–245
Bailey, John, 47–73, 284
barn doors, 339
Barry Lyndon, 323
Barth, John, 286
Barwood, Hal, 49
Beach Blanket Bingo, 121
Beauborg, 6
Beauty and the Beast, 70
Becker, Harold, 194, 217
Bed and Board, 6, 19
Before the Revolution, 53, 222

Belle Starr, 24
Benton, Robert, 19
Bergman, Ingmar, 49, 111
Bertolucci, Bernardo, 53, 219, 222, 225, 226
Best Little Whorehouse in Texas, The, 128
Best Man, The, 248, 255
Betsy, The, 234, 237
Big Chill, The, 48, 58, 59
Big Trouble, 75
Billion Dollar Brain, 268, 271
Bingo Long Traveling All-Stars and Motor Kings, The, 75, 81, 89
Bird with the Crystal Plumage, The, 220
Bitzer, G. W. "Billy," 2
black and white cinematography, 122, 156, 192, 244, 258, 305–306
Black Marble, The, 195, 217
black performers (lighting), 27–28, 30, 62, 89
Black Sunday, 24, 34, 37, 40, 41
Bleu Gang, 220
blimp, 339
Blinded by the Light, 24
Blood of Dracula's Castle, 176, 179
Bloody Mama, 24, 25, 37, 39
Blow Out, 312, 333
Blue Lagoon, The, 5, 6
Blue Thunder, 24, 43, 44
Boardwalk, 267, 268, 278
Body and Soul, 123
Body of Love, 220
Boffety, Jean, 41
Bogdanovich, Peter, 180, 189
Boorman, John, 74, 316, 319
Born to Kill, 6
bounce lighting, 201, 207, 209, 237–239, 242–243, 250, 258, 292, 314, 328
Bound for Glory, 83, 248, 257, 264–265
Boulevard Nights, 48, 62, 63, 71
Brazil: Report on Torture, 248
Bresson, Robert, 33, 70
Bridges, James, 284
British Society of Cinematographers (B.S.C.), 267
broad, 339
Broadway Danny Rose, 285
Brooks, Richard, 130, 133, 138, 139, 140, 142, 143, 144, 146–147, 160, 162–163
Brown, Garrett, 43, 60, 213
brute, 339
budgets, 39–40, 141–143, 178–179,

195–196, 217, 264, 280, 316, 324, 326, 332
Bullitt, 127, 128, 129, 131, 133
Bus, The, 248
Buster and Billie, 233, 234, 239
Butch and Sundance: The Early Days, 176
Butch Cassidy and the Sundance Kid, 152, 153, 157, 159
Butler, Bill, 20, 74–97, 102, 141
Butler, Michael, 173
Byrne, Bobby, 130

Cabaret, 335
cameraman, 340
camera crane, 339
camera operating, 59, 69, 101–102, 230, 308, 313, 317
camera operator, 340
camera set-up, 340
Can't Stop the Music, 75
Capricorn One, 75, 79
Capra, Frank, 9
Carrie, 234, 236, 240
Cartier-Bresson, Henri, 63
Casablanca, 177
Case Officer, The, 248, 253
Casey's Shadow, 24, 35
Cassavetes, John, 65
Cat People, 48, 51, 52, 62, 63, 70, 72
Catch-22, 143
Chabrol, Claude, 49
Champion, 123
Champions: A Love Story, 24
Chapman, Michael, 20, 38, 99–126, 285, 304
Cheap Detective, The, 24, 33, 36, 41, 42
cherry picker, 340
chicken coop, 33–34
Chinatown, 23, 24, 26, 30–33, 41
Chloe in the Afternoon, 6, 19
Cimino, Michael, 332
Cinderella Liberty, 312, 314, 334
Cinemobile, 233
Citizen Kane, 3, 159, 177
City for Conquest, 123
Clear and Present Danger, A, 75
Claire's Knee, 6, 19
Clan of the Cave Bear, The, 100
Close Encounters of the Third Kind, 128, 149, 312, 314, 320–325, 327, 333
Coast to Coast, 234, 240, 242

Coates, Paul, 255
Coblenz, Walter, 54
Cockfighter, 6, 10
Cocteau, Jean, 52
coffin boxes, 145
color reversal internegative (CRI), 35, 307, 340
color temperature, 58, 258, 291–292, 304, 340
Comes a Horseman, 106, 285, 295, 300
Coming Home, 248, 265–266
commercials, 3, 172, 195–196, 201, 247, 252–253, 263, 267, 269, 270, 276, 286
composition, 33, 49–50, 56, 93, 169–170, 185, 276, 298, 327, 328–329
Confidential File, 255
Conformist, The, 53, 54–55, 219, 220, 224, 226, 228
Conrack, 24
Conrad, Joseph, 224
consistency, 63, 127, 141, 168–169, 277, 290–291, 334
Continental Divide, 48, 57, 58, 65, 72
contrast, 340
Cooke lenses, 197
cookie, 340
Cool Hand Luke, 153
Coppola, Francis, 2, 40, 41, 45, 74, 81, 82, 84, 85, 88, 89–90, 157, 178, 219, 225, 263, 284
Corman, Roger, 10, 25, 39, 179
Cortez, Stanley, 31
Coutard, Raoul, 6, 51, 100
Crackers, 176
crews, 40, 46, 64–65, 87–88, 107, 114, 191–192, 201–202, 229, 235, 266, 279, 303, 339
Crime at the Tennis Club, 220
Crosby, Floyd, 23
cross lighting, 340
Crosscreek, 24, 41, 42
Curtis, Edward, 55
cut, 340

dailies, 60–61, 67, 69, 202, 340
Darling Lili, 143
day exteriors, 56, 59, 106, 271–272, 282, 330–331
day for night, 28, 78, 331
Day of the Dolphin, 128
Day of the Locust, 134, 143, 152, 153, 156,
159, 166–169, 170
Days of Heaven, 5, 6, 11, 12, 15–18, 19, 20, 47, 248, 256
De Antonio, Emile, 251
de la Tour, Georges, 334
Dead Men Don't Wear Plaid, 99, 100
Deadly Affair, The, 59
Deadwood '76, 312
Decae, Henri, 51
Deer Hunter, The, 312, 325, 334, 336
definition, 340
Degas, 312
degradation, 340
Deliver Us from Evil, 75
Deliverance, 76, 312, 319, 322, 326, 328, 334
Deluxe lab, 41, 211
Demon Seed, 75
density, 340
depth of field, 41, 44, 196, 289–290, 340
Deren, Maya, 5
Devil's Advocate, The, 268
diffusion, 31, 32, 62, 167, 193, 243, 265–266, 323, 333, 340
diorama, 340
direction, by cinematographers, 36, 46, 70, 97, 126, 149–150, 153, 171, 193, 259, 266, 301–303, 337
Divine Madness, 128
Divorce American Style, 153
Dixon, Maynard, 19
documentary film, 5, 10, 12, 25, 26, 38, 76, 160–161, 249–253, 255–256, 260, 267, 268–269, 286
dolly, 340
dolly shots, 107–108
dolly tracks, 340
dollying, 340
Dovzhenko, 177
Drive, He Said, 74, 75, 79, 81
Drowning Pool, The, 285
Duellist, The, 117
Dusty and Sweets McGee, 128

Eagle's Wing, 268, 275
Eastman Kodak film, 12, 41–42, 44, 58, 134, 213
Easy Rider, 175, 176, 179, 181–183, 317–318
Eclair camera, 96
Edison, Thomas Alva, 2

Eisenstein, Sergei, 177
Electra Glide in Blue, 153, 172
Electric Horseman, The, 195, 214–215
emulsion, 340
End of the Road, 100, 285, 286–287, 294
ENR, 214
Enrico, Robert, 51
Evans, Robert, 31
Execution of Private Slovik, The, 75, 79, 80
Exorcist, The, 149, 194, 195, 200, 202, 204, 206, 207–209, 217
Exorcist II: The Heretic, 128, 148–149
exposure, 17

Face in the Rain, A, 248, 255
Fade In, 128, 131
Fakers, The, 179
Farewell, My Lovely, 24, 30, 33
Fat City, 153, 156, 158, 163–166, 174
Fear on Trial, 75
Fearless Frank, 75
Fellini, Federico, 171, 257
fill light, 341
film noir, 105
filters, 14, 15, 16, 30, 37, 61, 192, 239–240, 245, 274, 296–297, 325, 341
Fingers, 100
firelight, 17, 168, 277
first-time directors, 38, 81, 132
F.I.S.T., 176, 187
flag, 341
flashing, 42, 59, 212, 214, 264–265, 274, 315, 319, 323, 326, 333, 336, 341
flat lighting, 341
Flicker, Theodore, 131
fluorescent lights, 58, 120–121, 204–205, 266, 297, 328
FM, 23, 24
focal length, 341
focus, 341
focus puller, 341
fog level, 341
fogging, 341
follow focus, 341
footcandle, 341
Footprints, 220
Fonda, Peter, 181, 317
For Pete's Sake, 176
forced developing, 16, 18, 41, 44, 95, 111–112, 134, 164, 197–198, 241, 274, 287, 314–315, 322–323
Ford, John, 20
Forman, Milos, 74, 82, 264

Fortune, The, 24, 34
Fox, The, 128, 131, 142
Fraker, Bill, 40, 83, 94, 127–151, 162, 191, 327
Frances, 179
Francesca, Piero della, 19, 227
Franju, Georges, 52–53, 70
Frankenheimer, John, 23
Freebie and the Bean, 176
French Connection, The, 194, 195, 198, 202, 204, 205, 209, 211, 217
French New Wave, 3, 5, 7, 8, 49
Friedkin, William, 74, 81, 194, 209
Friendly Persuasion, 234
Frogs, 234
Front, The, 100
f-stop, 341
Fuji film, 12, 30, 134
Fujimoto, Tak, 38
Futz, 312, 332

gaffer, 341
Games, 127, 128, 131, 132
Gandhi, 267, 268, 273, 278, 282
Gang That Couldn't Shoot Straight, The, 195
Gator, 128
Gauguin, 19
gel, 341
Gentleman Jim, 123
Gentleman Tramp, 6
Get to Know Your Rabbit, 24, 37
Getting Straight, 176, 184
ghost glass, 148–149
Ghostbusters, 176
gimbal, 91
Giordano Bruno, 220
Girl from Petrovka, The, 312, 325
Girl in Daddy's Bikini, A, 179
Glass Menagerie, The, 268
gobo, 341
Godard, Jean-Luc, 49, 51, 124
Godfather, The, 29, 30, 99, 100, 285, 287–288, 289, 291–295, 307, 310
Godfather II, The, 285, 287–288, 289, 291–295, 310
gofer, 341
Goin' South, 5, 6, 7, 11, 13–15, 18, 19, 20
Going in Style, 267, 268, 278
Gone with the Wind, 132
grain, 341
Grease, 75, 76, 93, 143
Great Santini, The, 65

Green Room, The, 6, 9
grey scale, 341
Griffith, D. W., 2, 19, 33
Grimes, Steven, 211, 215
grip, 341
Grosbard, Ulu, 194, 212
Guercio, Jim, 172
Guffey, Burnett, 152
Gunrunners, The, 6

Hall, Conrad, 20, 54, 94, 127, 130, 131,
    134, 147, 152–174, 222, 263, 324, 327
Haller, Daniel, 10
Haller, Ernest, 152
Haller, Michael, 265
hand-held camera, 28, 35, 39, 40, 41, 91,
    102, 138, 255–256, 257–258, 297, 313
Happy Ending, The, 153, 163
Hardcore, 100, 118–120
Harold and Maude, 24–25, 30, 33
Harper, 153, 155
Harry and Walter Go to New York, 176
Head, Edith, 45
head room, 341
Heart of Darkness, 224, 225
Heartbeat, 176, 185
Heartbreak Kid, The, 194, 195
Hearts of the West, 234, 241
Heaven Can Wait, 127, 128, 135, 143,
    145, 147
Heaven's Gate, 307, 312, 332–333, 336
Hell in the Pacific, 153, 157
Hellman, Monte, 10, 20
Hell's Angels on Wheels, 176, 181, 182
Hernandez, 75
Hickey and Boggs, 75
high key, 341
highlighting, 342
Hired Hand, The, 312, 317–318
HMI lights, 204–205, 249, 262, 342
Hoch, Winton, 23, 305
Hockney, David, 19
Hollender, Adam, 20
Hollywood Knights, The, 128
Honky Tonk Freeway, 48, 54, 57, 63, 65,
    66, 67, 70, 71, 72
Hoodlum Priest, The, 248, 255
Hopper, Dennis, 181
Horner, Harry, 30
Horror of the Blood Monsters, 312
Hot Rod Action, 312
Hot Summer Game, A, 312
How to Stuff a Wild Bikini, 121

Howe, James Wong, 23, 24, 28, 34,
    142, 255
Huckleberry Finn, 176
Hustling, 75, 79, 86
Huston, John, 163, 165
Hutton, Brian, 154
Huyck, Willard, 49

I Heard the Owl Call My Name, 75, 99
I Will, I Will . . . for Now, 24
Ice Castles, 75, 87
Identikit, 220
Idi Amin Dada, 6, 12–13
Images, 311, 312, 313, 322, 326, 334, 335
improvisation, 86–87, 317
In Cold Blood, 153, 156, 160–162,
    168, 173
In the Heat of the Night, 248, 258
*Incredibly Strange Creatures Who Stopped
    Living and Became Crazy Mixed-up
    Zombies, The,* 312
Incubus, 153
Indict and Convict, 75
inky dinks, 84, 104, 145, 202–203, 208,
    323, 342
Inside Moves, 176, 191
Interiors, 285
Interview with Allende, 248
Interviews with Mai Lai Veterans, 247, 248
Introduction to the Enemy, 247, 248, 252
Invasion of the Body Snatchers, 100, 106,
    109–113, 119
Invitation to a Gunfighter, 24
IP, 342
Island of Lost Souls, 110
Islands in the Stream, 149
It's My Turn, 75

Jaws, 75, 76, 78, 81, 90–93, 96, 102
Jennie, Wife/Child, 312
Jesus Christ, Superstar, 76, 93
Jewison, Norman, 258–259
Jinxed, 312, 331
Judge Horton and the Scottsboro Boys, 234
Julia, 134
junior, 342
Just Like a Woman, 268

Kaufman, Phil, 74, 99, 102, 109, 118, 121
Kazan, Elia, 256
Keaton, Buster, 124
Keller, Frank, 133

Kershner, Irvin, 74, 88, 255
Kertesz, André, 63
key light, 342
Kid Blue, 268
Kid from Nowhere, The, 24
Killer Inside Me, The, 128
Killing Kind, The, 234
King, 100
King of Marvin Gardens, The, 176
Kleiser, Randall, 47, 49, 74
Klute, 99, 100, 285, 300
Koko, The Talking Gorilla, 6
Korty, John, 74
Kotcheff, Ted, 269
Kovacs, Laszlo, 20, 38, 45, 51, 126, 150,
     175–193, 311, 313, 315, 324, 327
Kramer vs. Kramer, 5, 6, 11, 19
Kubrick, Stanley, 118, 317, 323, 332
Kuweiller, Luigi, 51

La Collectionneuse, 6, 7, 8, 10, 11, 12, 22
La Terra Trema, 7
laboratories, 12, 35, 39, 41, 60–61,
     112–113, 122, 136, 210–211, 214,
     230–231, 240–241, 274–275, 307–308,
     315, 342
Lady Sings the Blues, 24, 27–30, 34, 37
Ladyhawke, 220
Land of My Birth, 248
Landlord, The, 25, 285
Last Detail, The, 100, 103, 108, 113
Last Metro, The, 6
Last Movie, The, 176
Last Tango in Paris, 219, 220, 224, 226,
     228, 230–231
Last Waltz, The, 100, 114–116, 123, 124,
     176, 312
Late Show, The, 47
Legacy, 54
Legend of the Lone Ranger, 128, 176, 191
Lelouche, Claude, 257, 337
lenses, 15, 31–32, 41, 62, 69, 120,
     136–137, 183, 196–197, 239, 245, 342
Lester, Richard, 267
Leven, Boris, 116
Lhome, Pierre, 51
lightflex, 42, 59, 213, 342
lighting, 342
lighting ratios, 58, 206, 239, 290, 304, 306
Likely Story, A, 268
liner, 156
L'Innocente, 315
Lipstick, 75, 141

Little Murders, 285
Living Between Two Worlds, 312
Living City, The, 248
Lloyd, John, 168
locations, 11, 27, 35, 57, 63, 103, 122,
     160–161, 182, 194, 199–200, 205,
     206–207, 209, 236–237, 243, 272–273,
     300–301, 313, 329, 342
Lone Ranger, The, 127, 130
Long Goodbye, The, 311, 312, 317,
     323, 325
Looking for Mr. Goodbar, 127, 128,
     143–147, 149, 162
Looking to Get Out, 248
Love on the Run, 6
Loved One, The, 248
Loving, 285, 287
low key, 342
Lucas, George, 47, 49
Lumet, Sidney, 203, 216
Lumière, 2

MacArthur, 234
MacDonald, Richard, 167, 168
Madame Rosa, 6, 11
magic hour, 15–16, 56
Magnificent Ambersons, The, 31
Magnificent Seven, The, 24
Magus, The, 268
Main Event, The, 234, 240, 241, 242
Maîtresse, 6
Malice, 220
Malick, Terrence, 15, 18
Man Called Dagger, A, 176, 179
Man Escaped, A, 70
Man Who Loved Woman, The, 6, 19
Man with the Golden Arm, The, 255
Man with Two Brains, The, 100
Manchu Eagle, 75
Manhattan, 122, 285, 309–310
Marathon Man, 153
Marcus Nelson Murders, The, 234
Mark of the Gun, 176
marks, 342
Marquis of O, The, 6, 9, 18, 19
Marriage of a Young Stockbroker, The, 176
Mary White, 75
Mask, 176
Masterpiece Theatre, 43
matching, 10, 15, 143, 184, 263, 280,
     319, 334
matte, 342
matte box, 42, 342

McCabe and Mrs. Miller, 311, 312, 313, 314, 315, 317, 318, 326, 333, 334, 335, 336
McCarey, Leo, 9
McCord, Ted, 131, 152, 154, 163, 222
McCoy, 75
Medium Cool, 247–248, 252, 256, 259–261
Mekas brothers, 5
Méliès, Georges, 2
Melinda, 75
MGM lab, 35–36
Midsummer Night's Sex Comedy, A, 285
Milius, John, 47, 49
Miller, Arthur, 233
Mind of Mr. Soames, The, 268
mini mole, 342
Mishima, 48
Mitchell camera, 41
modeling light, 342
Mohr, Hal, 152, 233
Mondo Mod, 312
Monitors, The, 312
Monsignore, 268
Monte Walsh, 128, 129, 131, 149–150
More, 6
Morituri, 127, 130–131
Morris, Oswald, 42
MTV, 43
Murch, Walter, 49
Muscle Beach Party, 121
Mutiny on the Bounty, 152
Mutrux, Floyd, 134, 143
My Darling Clementine, 317
My Night at Maude's, 6, 12
My Soul Runs Naked, 179

Naked City, 135
Name of the Game Is Kill!, The, 312
Nasty Rabbit, The, 179, 312
natural light, 12, 18, 57, 163–165
negative, 342
nets, 30, 59, 62, 167, 214, 240, 342
Network, 195, 198–199, 203, 204, 215, 216
neutral density, 35
New York, New York, 176, 183, 193
Next Man, The, 100
Next Sting, The, 75
Nichols, Mike, 45, 257
Nicholson, Jack, 13–15, 20, 33, 74, 81, 82, 88, 113, 181
Nicholson, Skip, 315
Nickelodeon, 176

night exteriors, 59, 62, 85–86, 134, 212
Night the Lights Went Out in Georgia, The, 75
Night Watch, 268
ninelights, 87, 89, 90, 342
1941, 127, 128, 137
1900, 220, 224
9-30-55, 285
No Nukes, 248
No Small Affair, 312
Norma Rae, 24, 35, 40, 41
Nouvelle Vague, 49, 51
Nykvist, Sven, 125

Obsession, 312, 326
Old Boyfriends, 128, 151
Oliver Twist, 42
Omen II, The, 75, 94
On Golden Pond, 267, 268, 273, 274, 275, 276, 278, 280, 281–282
Once Is Not Enough, 24
One Flew Over the Cuckoo's Nest, 75, 82–84, 128, 141, 248, 251, 264
One from the Heart, 63, 219, 220, 225, 228, 230–231
Ondricek, Miroslav, 125
Onion Field, The, 218
Open City, 6–7
Ordeal by Innocence, 268
Ordinary People, 47, 48, 52, 54, 57, 62, 66, 71
Outer Limits, 127
overexposing, 157–158, 288–289, 324
overlighting, 160, 202, 271
Ozzie and Harriet, 127, 130

Paint Your Wagon, 128, 131, 142
Pakula, Alan, 284
pan, 342
Panacam, 42, 60, 213
Panaflex, 41, 60, 91, 136, 314
Panaglide, 43, 91, 137
Panavision, 31, 41, 43, 60, 62, 64, 91, 96, 103, 161, 197, 262, 165, 281, 325
Paoloni, Otto, 211
Paper Chase, The, 285
Paper Moon, 176, 182, 183, 192
Paradise Alley, 176
Parallax View, 285
Paris Vu Par, 6, 7
Paul Jacobs and the Nuclear Gang, 248
Paynter, Robert, 218

Pennies from Heaven, 63, 284, 285
Perceval, 6, 21–22
Perfect!, 285
Perry, Frank, 140
Personal Best, 100
Pete 'n' Tillie, 24
Peterson, Gene, 49
Petri, Elio, 51
photoflood, 342
Picasso, Pablo, 34
Picasso Summer, 312
Platt, Polly, 180
Play It Again, Sam, 194, 195, 217
Pocket Money, 176
point source, 342
Polanski, Roman, 31–32, 45, 137–139
Pollack, Sydney, 194, 197, 214, 215, 217
Pope Joan, 268
Pope of Greenwich Village, The, 48, 59
Porter, Edwin S., 2
Portrait of a Stripper, 24
President's Analyst, The, 128, 131
Pressman, Michael, 48
printer, 342
printer light, 342
Private Secretary, 130
production designer, 31, 51, 211
Professionals, The, 127, 130–131, 153, 156, 163
Protocol, 128
Psych-Out, 176, 181
Psycho A Go-Go, 312
Pudovkin, V., 177
pushing, 16, 18, 41, 44, 95, 111–112, 134, 164, 197–198, 241, 274, 287, 314–315, 322–323

quartz lights, 84–85, 179

Racing with the Moon, 48, 58
rack focus, 184, 244, 277
Rafelson, Bob, 190
Raging Bull, 99, 100, 117, 122–124
Raid on Entebbe, 75, 79, 80, 87
Rain People, The, 74, 75, 79, 81, 84–85
Rancho Deluxe, 128, 140
Rat Fink, 312
raw stock, 342
rear projection, 34, 342
Rebel Rousers, 176, 181
Red and Blue, 268
Red Sky at Morning, 312

Redford, Robert, 52, 54–55, 56, 66
Reds, 219, 220, 231–232
Reflection of Fear, A, 128, 150, 176
Reflection of Murder, 234
reflector, 342
Rembrandt, 334
Renoir, Jean, 9, 70, 124
Report to the Commissioner, 234, 239
Repulsion, 32
Resurrection, 234, 240, 242
Return of a Man Called Horse, The, 194, 195
Return of Count Yorga, 75
Richard Pryor Live on the Sunset Strip, 248
Richter, Hans, 5
Right to be Merry, A, 248
rim light, 342
Ritt, Martin, 25, 28, 36, 40, 41, 45, 46, 117
River, The, 312
Robbins, Matthew, 49
Rocky II, 75
Rocky III, 75
Rohmer, Eric, 5, 7, 8, 9, 18, 20, 21
Roizman, Owen, 29, 54, 134, 180, 194–218, 266, 324
Ronconi, Luca, 221
Rose, The, 312, 328, 334
Rosemary's Baby, 127, 128, 131, 137–139
Rosher, Chuck, 130
Ross, Herbert, 284
Rotunno, Giuseppe, 214
Ruddy, Al, 154
Rules of the Game, 124
Runaway, 24
Runner Stumbles, The, 176, 185
Running Wild, 75
Rush, Richard, 179, 184, 236, 244
Russell, Ken, 267, 269, 271–272
Rydell, Mark, 131, 328

Saboteur: Code Name Morituri, 153
Sadist, The, 312
Said, Fouad, 233
San Ferry Ann, 268, 269
Sargent, Alvin, 52
Sargent, Joe, 236
Saturn 3, 268
saturation, 343,
Sautet, Claude, 51
Savage Eye, The, 248
Savage Seven, The, 176, 181

Scandal, 220

Scarecrow, 312, 332

Scarface, 24, 41, 42

Scarfiotti, Nando, 51, 55, 64, 65, 72

Schlesinger, John, 53, 54, 66–67, 71, 72, 163, 167, 267, 269, 273, 276

Schrader, Paul, 52, 53, 55, 56, 70, 71, 118

Schroeder, Barbet, 5, 7, 8, 12, 13

Schuller, Fred, 108

Scorsese, Martin, 2, 99, 105, 107, 114–115, 117–118, 122, 124, 125

Second Hand Hearts, 248, 262

second-unit work, 67

Seconds, 23

Selznick, David O., 290

senior, 343

Senso, 7

set, 11–12, 21, 29, 51, 58, 63, 137, 148, 199, 236–237, 257, 270, 273, 300–301, 329–330

set designer, 30, 168, 215

set-up, 343

Seurat, 117

Sgt. Pepper's Lonely Hearts Club Band, 195

Shampoo, 176, 185

Shamroy, Leon, 44–45, 142

Shane, 149

Sharkey's Machine, 128

Sheena, Queen of the Jungle, 266

Shining, The, 44

Shoeshine, 6

Siegel, Don, 331

Silent Partner, The, 268

silver halides, 343

Sing Sing, 6

Single Room Furnished, 176

Six Pack, 234

sixteen millimeter, 7, 8, 11, 13, 54, 114

sixty-five millimeter, 321

Ski Bum, The, 312

skin tones, 18, 135–136, 209–210, 241

Skycam, 43–44, 60, 213–214

Slither, 176

Slocombe, Douglas, 134

slow motion, 44, 123–124

Smile, 153

soft focus, 343

Some Call It Loving, 234

Something Evil, 75

Sophie's Choice, 6

sound stage, 343

Sounder, 24, 25, 27–29, 37

source lighting, 34, 57, 95, 161, 200, 278, 300, 327–328

South Pacific, 142

Southern, Terry, 181

special effects, 207–209

Spider's Stratagem, The, 220, 224, 226–227

Spielberg, Steven, 2, 74, 81, 91, 96, 102, 320, 322, 323, 325

split diopter, 296

sputnick, 108, 343

Stakeout on Dope Street, 248, 255, 256

Stardust Memories, 285, 309–310

Steadicam, 43, 44, 60, 102, 137, 244, 304

Steelyard Blues, 176

Stepford Wives, The, 195

Stevens, Leslie, 154

Still of the Night, 5, 6

still photography, 55, 112, 201

stock, 343

Stoney Burke, 154

Stop, 195

stopping down, 343

Storaro, Vittorio, 53, 117, 214, 219–232

Story of Adele H., The, 6, 9, 19

storyboarding, 187–188, 321, 343

Stradling, Harry, 242

Straight Time, 195, 199, 211–212

Stranger Who Looked Like Me, The, 234

Strenge, Walter, 23

Stripes, 75

strobe light, 146–147

Struss, Karl, 110

Studs Lonigan, 248

Stunt Man, The, 234, 242, 243

Sugarland Express, The, 312, 320

Summer Without Boys, 234

Sunday, Bloody Sunday, 267, 268, 273, 274, 275, 281

Sunshine, 75, 79

Surtees, Robert, 152

Sweet Revenge, 312

Sweet Smell of Success, 105

Swine Flu Case, The, 248, 253

Sybil, 234

Sylbert, Richard, 30, 31, 32, 138, 165

Table for Five, 312

Taking of Pelham One, Two, Three, The, 194, 195, 198

Tales of a Salesman, 312

Tam-Lin, 268

Taps, 195

Target Risk, 75
Targets, 176, 180
Tavalouris, Dean, 30
Taxi Driver, 100, 105–109, 111, 119
Tears on Johannesburg, 233
teaser, 343
Technicolor lab, 41, 60, 112, 113, 122, 136, 211, 214, 307–308, 315
television, 24, 46, 74, 79–80, 130, 233, 254, 267, 269
Tell Them Willie Boy is Here, 153, 157
Tess, 335
Texas Project, The, 6
That Championship Season, 48
That Cold Day in the Park, 176
Thirty is a Dangerous Age, Cynthia, 268
Thomas Crown Affair, The, 248, 258
Three Days of the Condor, 134, 195, 197–198, 215
Three Women, 47
tilt, 343
Time Travelers, The, 312
timing (laboratory), 14, 240–241, 274–275, 308, 343
'Tis Pity She's a Whore, 220
Toland, Gregg, 3, 202
Tom Horn, 24
Tommy, 76, 93
Tootsie, 195, 213, 214
Tosi, Mario, 1, 233–246
Touch of Evil, 16, 53
Towering Inferno, The, 321
Toy, The, 176
T. R. Sloan, 75
Traveling Salesman, The, 179
Trial, The, 53
tripod, 91, 165, 314, 343
True Confessions, 195, 212–213, 214
Truffaut, François, 5, 9, 11, 20, 21, 49, 51
Trumbull, Douglas, 320–321
TV Newscaster, 75
TVC lab, 41
Two English Girls, 6
Two Gentlemen Sharing, 268
Two Lane Blacktop, 54
2001: A Space Odyssey, 317

Umberto D, 7
Uncle Joe Shannon, 75
Underground, 247, 248, 251–252

union (cameramen), 37–38, 49, 129–130, 178, 180, 231, 281, 310
University of California at Los Angeles (UCLA), 38, 128, 178, 246, 337
University of Southern California (USC), 38, 47, 49, 127, 128, 132, 152, 153, 158, 163, 337
Unsworth, Goeffrey, 51
Up the Sandbox, 285, 299

Valley, The, 6
Vampire Blood, 75
Vanishing Point, 24, 26–27, 37, 40
Vermeer, 117
video, 43, 60, 80, 213, 262–263
Visconti, Luchino, 6, 315
Visionquest, 195, 213
Vistavision, 331
Vorkapich, Slavko, 153
Voyage of the Damned, 268

Wagner, 220
walkthrough, 343
Walsh, David, 150
Wambaugh, Joseph, 218
Wanderers, The, 99, 100, 109, 121, 124
War Games, 127, 128
War Without Winners, 248
wardrobe designer, 30, 31, 45, 215
Warriors, The, 48
water box, 91–92
Watkin, David, 268
Wattstax, 24
Welcome to L.A., 47
Welles, Orson, 3, 16, 53
West Side Story, 233
Western Marshall, The, 130
Wexler, Haskell, 20, 25, 75, 83, 130, 141, 247–266, 284, 324, 327
What's Up Doc?, 176
What's Up Front, 312
Which Way Is Up?, 24
white cards, 35, 343
White Dawn, The, 100, 102–104
Whitlock, Albert, 265
Who's Afraid of Virginia Woolf?, 248, 255, 257
Whose Life Is It Anyway?, 234, 244–246
wide-angle lens, 343
wide screen, 343

Wild Child, The, 6, 11, 19
Wild Racers, The, 6, 10
Wild Seed, The, 127, 130, 152, 153, 154, 156, 170, 173
wild walls, 343
Williams, Billy, 267–283
Willis Gordon, 20, 29, 34, 38, 50, 53, 54, 57, 58, 61, 96, 99, 101–102, 105, 112, 122, 125, 126, 180, 266, 284–310, 315, 320
Wind and the Lion, The, 267, 268, 273, 281
Windows, 285, 301, 303
Winogrand, Gary, 63
Winter Kills, 312, 325, 333
Wise, Robert, 233
Without A Trace, 48, 58
Wolper, David L., 23
Women in Love, 267, 268, 270, 271, 273, 274, 277, 281

Woodstock, 114
Wyeth, Andrew, 326

X, Y and Zee, 268

Yates, Peter, 133
Young, Freddie, 59
Young Winston, 59
Youthful, Youthful, 220

Zelig, 285
Zieff, Howard, 242
zoom lens, 31, 69–70, 241, 245, 323
Zorro, The Gay Blade, 24
Zsigmond, Vilmos, 20, 38, 45, 51, 126, 175, 176–178, 180, 182, 311–337